E. S. Shuckburgh

Herodotus V, Terpsichore

E. S. Shuckburgh

Herodotus V, Terpsichore

ISBN/EAN: 9783337194628

Printed in Europe, USA, Canada, Australia, Japan

Cover: Foto ©ninafisch / pixelio.de

More available books at **www.hansebooks.com**

Pitt Press Series

HERODOTOS

V

TERPSICHORE

WITH INTRODUCTION NOTES AND MAP

BY

E. S. SHUCKBURGH, M.A.

LATE FELLOW OF EMMANUEL COLLEGE CAMBRIDGE
FORMERLY MASTER AT ETON

EDITED FOR THE SYNDICS OF THE UNIVERSITY PRESS

CAMBRIDGE
AT THE UNIVERSITY PRESS
1890

[*All Rights reserved.*]

PREFACE.

IN revising the text of this book I have constantly consulted the older editors, Schweighaeuser, with the variations of Wesseling and Schäfer given in his edition, and Gaisford. I have also used Stein's critical edition, and the larger edition of A. Holder (Leipsic, 1886). The notes and indices have been composed on the same principles of arrangement as those of Books 6, 8 and 9. Most information as to persons and places has been reserved for the Historical and Geographical Index; while the notes are principally directed to difficulties of grammar and interpretation, or to points of archaeological interest arising from the text. The annotated editions of Baehr, Stein, Abicht and the Translation of Rawlinson, as well as many other books, have also been constantly in use. I owe thanks to Mr E. S. Roberts, of Caius, for leave to use certain illustrations from his *Introduction to Greek*

Epigraphy, and for his kindly revising my notes which referred to the question of the Greek alphabet. Also I have to thank Professor Middleton for prompt and kind answers to some questions connected with Archaeology which I addressed to him. Last, but not least, I owe more than I can say to the never-failing skill and patience of the officials of the Press.

CAMBRIDGE,
March, 1890.

TABLE OF CONTENTS.

	PAGE
PREFACE	v
INTRODUCTION	ix
TEXT	1
NOTES	79
HISTORICAL AND GEOGRAPHICAL INDEX	185
INDEX TO THE NOTES	247
MAP	*facing title page*

INTRODUCTION.

THE Fifth Book of the history of Herodotos takes up the story of the extension of the Persian interference in Europe from c. 144 of the Fourth Book. There we learn that at the end of the Skythian expedition of Dareios the king returned to Asia, leaving an army in Europe under Megabazos to secure the Persian supremacy in Thrakia and Makedonia [4, 143—4].

But as the writer's object is not only to tell the history of the collision between the Persians and Hellenes, but to give a comprehensive picture of the growth of both these powers previous to this collision, he here interrupts his narrative to give an account of a Persian expedition in North Africa under Aryandes[2], undertaken from Egypt (in which Kambyses

War in Libya under Aryandes, ? B.C. 510—9[1].

---

[1] This date is very difficult to fix. The Athenian envoys [c. 73] found Artaphernes governor of Sardis, to which he was appointed after the Skythian expedition, which must therefore have been at least as early as 510 B.C., and the expedition of Aryandes is said to have been just about the same time, 4, 145. Then again the peace which followed the campaigns of Megabazos, and was interrupted by the Naxian war [B.C. 501], is said to have lasted 'no long time'. See Grote, note to c. xxxv. I do not accept his view of this expression.

[2] Left in Egypt as governor by Kambyses, 4, 166.

had established Persian supremacy in B.C. 525) with the avowed object of punishing the people of Barca for the murder of Arkesilaos, king of Kyrene[1], but really, Herodotos thinks, with the view of subjugating Libya: 'For Libya is inhabited by many various races, of whom only a few were subject to the Persian king, far the greater number holding Dareios in no kind of respect[2].' This leads to a long and interesting account of the geography of North Africa, and the tribes inhabiting it, derived to a great extent from the writer's own travels, and connected with the general drift of his story by the fact, among others, that this expedition, which extended as far as Euesperides [4, 204] on the E. coast of the Syrtis Major, must have done much to raise the prestige of the Persian power in the eyes of the Karthaginians, who in the subsequent war of B.C. 480 were to make a great and unsuccessful attack on the Sicilian Hellenes on the very same day as the similarly unsuccessful attack of Xerxes at Salamis[3].

Thrakia. The country of Thrakia, which Megabazos was left to subdue to the authority of the great king, had once been called Πέρκη or 'Αρία[4], and was held to include all Europe north of Greece: that is, the Greeks knew nothing beyond it. But in the time of Herodotos it was looked upon as bordered towards the North by the

---

[1] At the instigation of Pheretima, mother of Arkesilaos and after his death queen of Kyrene, who had a claim on Persian gratitude for having caused the submission of Kyrene to Kambyses, 4, 165.

[2] Herod., 4, 167.   [3] 7, 166.

[4] Steph. Byz. s. v. Θράκη. This is an interesting statement in view of the recent theories as to the earliest home of the Aryans: which is now held to be 'the great Plain of Northern Europe, stretching from the Ural Mountains over Northern Germany and the north of France as far as the Atlantic'. Taylor, *Origin of the Aryans*, p. 30. Rendall, *Cradle of the Aryans*, p. 63.

Danube (Ister) and by the Strymon on the West. It is a mountainous country intersected by three offshoots of the lofty range of Haemos, (1) Pangaeos and Rhodope towards the West, (2) a central range from the source of the Hebrus to its junction with the Tonzos (Hadrianople), (3) the Easterly range now called *Stravadja-Dagh*, running parallel to the Western shore of the Euxine.

The people inhabiting the mountains, valleys and plains of this country were divided into very numerous tribes, of which Herodotos mentions the names of eighteen[1], and of which about 50 altogether are known to us from various other sources. They were then, as they still to a great extent are, fierce and barbarous; and the Persian conquest does not seem to have penetrated into the interior[2]. It was the cities and tribes on the coasts of the Aegean, the Hellespont, and the Euxine that were the object of attack, and which submitted more or less completely to Megabazos. These coasts were studded with Greek colonies; and thus the spread of the Persian power was once more placed in antagonism to Hellenic civilization, however distant from the centre of Hellenic life. But this extension of the Persian conquest was not confined to Thrakia.

The Thrakians.

The Paeonians on the Strymon were conquered and transferred to Asia [cc. 12—17], and the next step was to demand tokens of submission from the king of Makedonia. The Makedonian dynasty claimed

Paeonians and Makedonians.

---

[1] Bessi (7, 111), Bisaltae (8, 116), Bistones (7, 110), Brygi (6, 45), Kikones (7, 110), Krobyzi (4, 49), Dersaei (7, 110), Dolonki (6, 34), Edoni (7, 110), Getae (4, 93), Nipsaei (4, 93), Odomanti (7, 110), Odrysae (4, 93), Paeti (4, 93), Sapaei (7, 110), Satrae (7, 110), Skyrmiadae (4, 93), Trausi (5, 3). Rawl.

[2] 5, 16.

a Greek origin; the Makedonians themselves, though not Hellenes, were a mixed people with probably some Hellenic elements; and at any rate their country barred the way to Thessaly and Greece: and if the Persians once secured complete supremacy in Makedonia, an invasion from the North would always be a possible danger. This Makedonian incident therefore [cc. 18—22] is of importance as helping to account for the growing feeling of alarm in Greece, which may have influenced the Athenians subsequently, both in their determination to be always hostile to the Persians [cc. 73, 96], and in their readiness to assist the revolted Ionians.

When Megabazos had done his work in Makedonia, *Reduction of Hellenic cities.* he was, for some reason of which we are not informed, superseded in his command by Otanes; who proceeded to reduce to submission the Greek colonies of Byzantium, Chalkedon, and, crossing over to Asia, those of Antandros and Lamponium, as well as the islands of Lemnos and Imbros [c. 27]. Histiaios, who had excited the royal jealousy by what looked like an attempt to secure independence for himself at Myrkinos, had been summoned to Sardis, and thence forced to accompany the *Period of quiet, B.C. 507—502.* court to Susa: and the Persian power seemed secure. Accordingly there followed a brief period of repose. Such remnants of Greek independence as existed in the islands of the Aegean was not interfered with; and the Greek towns under the Persian suzerainty, though compelled to submit to the government of tyranni, were not further molested [c. 28].

This season of comparative happiness proved short-*Origin of the fresh troubles and the Ionian revolt.* lived. The circumstances which brought it to an end did not occur in the district lately subdued by Megabazos and Otanes, but in

Ionia. Of the twelve cities which formed the Ionian Union[1], the richest and most powerful were Ephesos and Miletos. Ephesos, however, being at the starting place of the great road up the country was apparently restrained, either by the watchfulness of the Governor of Sardis, or by its own sense of self-interest, from taking part in the subsequent movement. The town of Miletos was at this time at the very height of its prosperity and was regarded as the 'glory of Ionia' [c. 28]. Like the other Ionian towns it had fallen under the supremacy of the Lydian monarchs [Alyattes, B.C. 625—560, Kroesos, B.C. 560—546], and afterwards under that of Kyros [after B.C. 546]. Like the other Ionian towns also the chief effect of this subjection to Persia, over and above its liability to tribute, was chiefly that it had to admit a tyrannus acceptable to the Persian government, instead of a qualified oligarchy which had been the result of internal differences settled by the arbitration of the Parians [cc. 28—9]. At the time of the Skythian expedition the Milesian tyrannus was Histiaios, who during his absence on that occasion, and subsequently while he was engaged at Myrkinos, had entrusted the government of Miletos to his son-in-law Aristagoras. This man, like his father-in-law, was ostensibly submissive and friendly to the Persian satrap at Sardis, the king's brother Artaphernes; and there seemed to be no reason to expect any outbreak. The one Ionian State which had appeared likely to gain such strength as to throw off the Persian yoke had been Samos, which Polykrates had raised to a high state of wealth and political importance. But on the death of that king by

[1] Myus, Pirene, Miletos in Karia; Ephesos, Kolophon, Lebedos, Teos, Klazomenae, Phokaea, Erythrae in Lydia; the islands of Samos and Chios [1, 142].

the machinations of the satrap Oroetes [B.C. 522] the island had been once more made secure by being put in the hands of the brother of Polykrates, Syloson, who was content to hold it in subservience to Persia. Ionia, therefore, was quiet. But this seeming security was overset by one of those revolutionary movements so characteristic of Greek states, and which so often brought unforeseen events in their train, affecting neighbouring states apparently unconnected with them.

The island of Naxos was the largest and most powerful of the Cyclades. It had not long before this been under the tyrant Lygdamis, the friend of Peisistratos [1, 64]: its government had afterwards become oligarchical [c. 30]; and about B.C. 503—2 some popular movement, the particulars of which we do not know, had resulted in the banishment of certain of the richer class of citizens. These men being connected with Histiaios by the tie which the Greeks called ξενία, naturally came to Miletos and appealed for help to Aristagoras. Partly, perhaps, from respect for the obligation implied by this connexion, and partly from a natural antipathy to the action of a democracy, and partly again, perhaps, because he saw his way to curry favour with his Persian masters, by promoting their interference in one of those islands which were still outside the Persian supremacy[1], Aristagoras expressed his willingness to undertake their cause. He could not however, he said, furnish them with a force from Miletos sufficient to overpower their countrymen; but he would apply to Artaphernes, the governor of Sardis, and felt sure that he both could and would supply the necessary means [c. 30].

Movement in Naxos, B.C. 502.

Artaphernes readily listened to the proposal which

---

[1] τῶν γὰρ νήσων τῶν Κυκλάδων οὐδεμία κω ἦν ὑπὸ Δαρείῳ, 5, 30.

Aristagoras thereupon laid before him. It was an opportunity of securing a hold on the Cyclades which he would not be likely to omit; and having obtained the king's sanction by a message to and from Susa, he ordered a fleet of 200 triremes and a large army, under the command of Megabates, to be ready for work in the spring of B.C. 501. The expedition started; took on board Aristagoras with some Ionian troops, and the Naxian exiles; and then proceeded towards Naxos. By some means, which are hard to understand, the people of Naxos had apparently been quite unaware of what was going on, were not prepared for an attack, and supposed (as Megabates gave out) that the expedition was destined for the Hellespont. But Megabates and Aristagoras soon quarrelled on the question of which was to be in supreme command; and in his anger Megabates frustrated the object of the expedition by secretly giving the Naxians warning of what was coming. When the fleet, therefore, arrived at Naxos, the town was found in a state of defence, and in fact was able to stand a long siege. There was neither money nor any other provision for this; and after spending a great deal of his private fortune Aristagoras not only found that there was no prospect of success, but that he would also be unable to fulfil his promise to Artaphernes of paying the expenses of the expedition. There was no help for it: the fleet and troops had to be withdrawn from the island, having accomplished nothing but the building of certain forts from which the Naxian exiles might annoy their countrymen [c. 34].

Artaphernes consents to aid in restoring the exiles from Naxos.

Failure of the Naxian expedition.

Aristagoras could hardly pay his own troops, much less those of the king. He had failed to secure even the political advantages which he had promised the Persian Court. He felt that he would have to pay the usual penalty of ill-success either with his life, or at least with the loss of his office as governor (ὕπαρχος) of Miletos. His thoughts turned therefore to the idea of anticipating his danger by a revolt from Persia. In the midst of this perplexity the message came from Histiaios, tattooed on a slave's head, urging him to 'raise Ionia' [Ἰωνίαν ἀναστῆσον]. Aristagoras caught at the suggestion which thus came at the moment of his own difficulties, and which was the result of the weariness of Histiaios at his prolonged detention at Susa [c. 35]. To carry out the plan it was necessary to secure the cooperation of the Ionian states; and this could only be done by deposing the various tyrants of the cities, all of whom were in the interests of the Persian government, to whose support they owed the maintenance of their own power. After consultation with friends, therefore, in which the historian Hekataios urged counsels of prudence,—advising first that they should not provoke a war with the Persians; or secondly, if they did so, to secure the means of fighting by seizing the treasures at Branchidae,—it was resolved, to the neglect of this advice, at once to take the necessary step of seizing the tyrants. This was done. Aristagoras himself made a show of laying down his own power at Miletos, though he seems to have retained it under another name; and the other tyrants, with the exception of Koes of Mytilene and a few others, were allowed peaceably to quit their states after a forcible abdication of their powers. The fleet that had been collected to attack Naxos was next secured; and having thus shewed unmistakeably what the object of the movement was, Aristagoras next

Perplexity of Aristagoras.

Message from Histiaios.

The revolt concerted; and help asked from Sparta and Athens.

sailed to Greece to secure the help of Sparta and Athens [cc. 36—8].

The first application was to Sparta, where the king of the Senior house at this time was Kleomenes, son of Anaxandridas [B.C. 520—491].

Here Herodotos interrupts his narrative to tell us of the curious circumstance which attended the birth and succession of Kleomenes [cc. 39—41]; and the very interesting notice of the consequent departure of Dorieus, the eldest son of the first, and, as he held, the only lawful wife of Anaxandridas, upon a roving expedition to find a new settlement for himself and all who would join him. He first attempted a settlement on the coast of Africa; but when, after three years' trial of that, he was obliged to return to Peloponnese, he was induced to turn his face westward, to the country which was always a favourite home of Greek colonisation, and lead out his friends to found Herakleia in Sicily. He was diverted however from his direct object by an invitation from the people of Kroton to assist them in their war against Sybaris. Here he fell. This episode [cc. 42—48], which is not connected with the general history in any marked degree, we owe to Herodotos' interest in that remarkable event in the history of Magna Graecia, the fall of Sybaris; and to the personal inquiries which he had been able, during his residence at Thurii, to make among the descendants of the surviving Sybarites. *Birth and succession of Kleomenes; and the Italian expedition of Dorieus.*

The application to Sparta was ineffectual, in spite of the persuasive eloquence of Aristagoras, and the rich bribes which he was prepared to offer to the king. The Spartans were not likely to wish to undertake any dangers or responsibilities for the sake of the Ionians. They had indeed made a vain attempt to protect them against the encroachments of Kyros [1, *The king of Sparta refuses the request of Aristagoras.*

152—3]; and about B.C. 525 they had interfered in the politics of Samos, sending an expedition to force the restoration of certain Samians exiled by Polykrates: but the ill-success of that attempt was not likely to tempt them to take further interest in the Ionian Greeks [3, 39, 46, 54—6]. Moreover the Spartans were constitutionally cautious and disinclined to distant expeditions; and they had close on their own borders an enemy in the Argives, whom they were much more concerned to suppress than they were to assert the freedom of the Ionians. Aristagoras therefore, after more than one interview, had to leave Sparta without obtaining the desired promise [cc. 49—54].

If Sparta was by this time acknowledged to be the lead-ing city in Greece, the second place was unanimously given to Athens. Moreover there were special reasons for hoping that the Athenians would be ready to help. In the first place they were looked upon not only as Ionians, but in a sense the metropolis of the Ionians; and Miletos itself was said to have been founded by a son of the Athenian Kodros. Moreover the Athenians were particularly hostile in feeling to Persia. They had indeed offered some sort of alliance to the Persians in B.C. 509—8, when expecting an attack from Sparta in favour of the Peisistratids: but when they found that Artaphernes would only consent to the proposal on the terms of submission to the Persian king by sending earth and water, the people indignantly declined, and severely censured the envoys who had consented [c. 73]. This had shewn the Athenians what the view of the Persians was in regard to Greek freedom. But they soon had still greater reason for indignation. After his last unsuccessful attempt to regain his power (probably about B.C. 503) Hippias had retired to

Application to Athens.

Reasons for hoping better success in the application to Athens.

Sigeium, and from thence visited Artaphernes at Sardis and
did all he could to raise the wrath of that Satrap against the
Athenians, and to induce him to persuade the king to force
his restoration and thus secure a hold upon a principal city
in Greece. The Athenians tried to counteract these intrigues by sending envoys to expostulate at Sardis. But
finding Artaphernes decidedly hostile, they resolved to
anticipate active injury on the part of Persia by any means
in their power [c. 96]. This temper of the Athenian people
therefore promised better for the success of Aristagoras,
when he came to ask help for Hellenes against Persians.
But Herodotos is not content with noting these facts. The
purpose of his history is to shew the state of preparation
on both sides for the great contests which were to come
in B.C. 490 and B.C. 480—479. He therefore takes this
opportunity of accounting for the present state of Athens:
the revolution which had resulted in its democratical form
of government, and the consequences of that revolution on
its external policy.

From chapter 55 to chapter 96, therefore, we are
stopped in the course of the history of the *Digression on the revolution at Athens*, cc. 55—96.
Ionian revolt to learn the story of the
revolution which overthrew the Peisistratids, and the attempts made by Sparta to force their
restoration, after having, owing to an intrigue at Delphi,
assisted in obedience to the Oracle in driving them out.
But this digression has other digressions within it.
First, after the murder of Hipparchos [cc. 55—6], we
are told of the Phoenikian origin of Harmodios and
Aristogeiton, the assassins of Hipparchos [c. 57]: this
leads to a digression on the Phoenikian settlement in
Boeotia and on the Phoenikian origin of the Greek
alphabet [cc. 56—61]. We then go on to the result
of the murder in the increased severity of Hippias, the
multiplication of disaffected exiles, and the influence
brought by the Alkmaeonidae to bear on the Oracle of

Delphi to induce the Pythia to urge on the Spartans the duty of 'freeing Athens'; and the two expeditions consequently dispatched to Attica to carry out this order; and finally the chance capture of the women and children of the Peisistratidae, which enabled the invaders to insist on the withdrawal of Hippias [cc. 62—66].

Fall of Hippias, B.C. 510. Reforms of Kleisthenes, and ineffectual efforts to restore the Peisistratids.

After a brief reference to the consequent political controversies between Kleisthenes and Isagoras, and the constitutional reforms of Kleisthenes [cc. 66, 69, 70], he is led into another digression on the doings of Kleisthenes of Sikyon, maternal grandfather of the Athenian Kleisthenes, who had initiated and carried out an anti-Dorian movement in that town [cc. 66—7]. Another interference of the Spartans invited by Isagoras brings in another digression on the origin of the curse under which the Alkmaeonid laboured, τὸ Κυλώνειον ἄγος [c. 71]. The Spartan interference failed, though the Akropolis for a time was in the hands of Kleomenes. Isagoras himself managed to escape; but his fellow conspirators were put to death and Kleisthenes recalled [cc. 72—3]. Then followed a second invasion of Kleomenes at the head of a combined army of Peloponnesians, which was frustrated partly by the opposition of the other Spartan king Demaratos, and partly by the defection of the Korinthians [cc. 74—5].

To avenge this invasion the Athenians proceeded to attack the Chalkidians of Euboea who had aided it; and gained a brilliant victory over a Boeotian army which had come as far as the Euripus to the aid of the Chalkidians [cc. 76—77]. After commenting on the increased power thus shewn by Athens [c. 78], Herodotos proceeds to relate how the Boeotians sought to be revenged for their defeat by renewing the war, and by engaging the Aeginetans to assist them by plundering the seaboard of Attica [cc. 79—82]. This leads to another digression on the origin of the feud between Aegina and Athens: which is chiefly of interest for certain indications of ancient customs

Athens, Thebes and Eretria.

Feud between Athens and Aegina.

contained in it; and for the fact that this feud eventually resulted in the formation of the Athenian navy, which conquered at Salamis [7, 144] and thus saved Greece [cc. 82—89]. The Athenians were preparing to retaliate on the Aeginetans when they were threatened with a fresh invasion *Last attempt to restore Hippias.* from Sparta, instigated partly by jealousy of the growing strength of Athens, and partly by the discovery that the Oracle had been tampered with when it ordered them to 'free Athens'; a discovery said to have been made from documents in the Akropolis, which came into the hands of Kleomenes during his occupation of it. This invasion was again frustrated by the remonstrances of the Korinthian leader Sosikles, into whose mouth a speech is put containing an account of the rule of the Kypselidae in their town [cc. 90—93]. Hippias, who had accompanied this futile Spartan invasion [apparently about B.C. 504 or 503], now withdrew to Sigeium: which leads Herodotos to another short digression on the origin of the Athenian hold upon that *Contests of Athens and Mytilene.* place, and their contests with Mytilene for the possession of the neighbouring Achilleium [cc. 94—5]. Then followed the intrigues of Hippias at Sardis, mentioned above, the rebuff administered to the Athenian legates by Artaphernes, and the consequent feeling of irritation at Athens [c. 96].

The temper of the Athenians, therefore, when Aristagoras arrived was such as to promise an easy task. Herodotos looks upon his success as a *Aristagoras at Athens.* misfortune, and as an instance of the ease with which a democracy may be misled; and, strong as his Hellenic and democratic sympathies evidently were, he seems to regard Aristagoras as a charlatan, who was plunging Greece into danger and suffering for the sake of his private ends, and the security of his own position. Perhaps the Athenians felt that they would have in any case to fight the Persians sooner or later; and that it would be wiser to take the first step and strike a blow at their growing power at a distance, rather than to wait tamely at home while it advanced step by step, from island to island, within a measurable distance of the shore of Attica. Whatever the motive which influenced them, the Athenians promptly responded to the appeal; voted a squadron of twenty ships; nominated a commander; and prepared to render active help [c. 97].

Encouraged by the promised aid Aristagoras returned to Miletos; and there took a step which Herodotos regards as useless, and as merely meant to annoy the Persian court. He sent a message to the Paeonians, who had been removed to a district in Phrygia by the command of Xerxes, encouraging them to assert their freedom and return home; which they accordingly did. This reversal of a measure which the king had probably taken from the idea of at once making Thrace more secure, and of introducing a useful element into Asia, seems to have been the first step which really roused the alarm of the Persian garrison, and a vigorous but unsuccessful attempt was made to stop the Paeonians [c. 98].

Aristagoras returns to Asia to push on the revolt.

Soon after this the 20 Athenian ships, accompanied by five triremes from Eretria, arrived at Ephesos. Landing there and joined by an Ionian force under the command of a brother of Aristagoras, the combined army marched at once to Sardis: which they took and burnt, although they did not venture to attack the citadel, in which Artaphernes was securely situated[1]. The fire, which seems to have been accidental, prevented any collection of booty, and forced the inhabitants to make a

The burning of Sardis, B.C. 500.

---

[1] Plutarch, de Mal. c. 24, seems to wish to shew that the attack on Sardis was much more successful and prolonged than we should gather from Herodotos.

desperate stand; the Ionians in alarm withdrew, and, ascending the ridge of Tmolos, commenced their march back to Miletos. Probably the resistance encountered in Sardis was not the only reason of their hasty retreat. All the principal towns in Asia were strongly garrisoned with Persian troops, and a system of posts (ἄγγαροι) secured swift communication between them. The advance of the Ionian army had been a signal for the concentration of a large body of these troops, which was on the march to Sardis. It arrived there in fact very soon after the Ionians had evacuated the town; and was able by a swift pursuit to catch them just as they arrived near Ephesos, where the road to Sardis commenced. In the battle that ensued the Ionians were decisively defeated, the Eretrian commander killed, and the whole force dispersed [cc. 99—102].

But though the Athenian squadron now deserted the allies and returned home, Aristagoras and the other leaders were too deeply committed to desist. They could hope for no more resistance at present on land, though Miletos was apparently relieved by the movement on Sardis from a siege which the Persians had begun; but they still had the fleet of ships which had been collected for the attack on Naxos; and several months must elapse before the Persians could collect one from Phoenikia capable of attacking it. This fleet had begun operations, first sailing to the Hellespont and winning over Byzantium and the neighbouring cities to join in the revolt, and then returning to Karia and inducing the Karians to throw in their lot with them [cc. 102—3]. *The Athenians return home, but the revolt goes on.*

But though there was afterwards some fighting in Karia, which on the whole was disastrous to the Persians [cc. 118—121], the fate of the revolt, which seems to have been going on with inter- *Kypros joins the revolt* B.C. 500/499, *and is subdued* B.C. 498/7.

mitted skirmishing, presently centred round the island of Kypros, most of the towns in which had been encouraged by the raid upon Sardis to join the movement and assert their freedom [cc. 104, 105]. To that island the Persian fleet, which had been meanwhile collected from Kilikia, Egypt, and Phoenikia [6, 6], now directed its course; the Persian troops were landed from the coast of Kilikia, while the Phoenikian ships sailed round the eastern extremity of the island, and encountered the Ionian fleet and were beaten by it. But on land the Persians were successful, and soon reduced the whole island to submission, little more than a year from the time of its joining the revolt [cc. 108—115].

Rapid reduction of revolted towns and flight of Aristagoras. The Ionian fleet now scattered, each ship to its own city: and the Persian generals seem to have left the Ionian League cities alone, and to have directed their efforts entirely to the detailed subjection of all the other towns which had joined in the revolt. Thus the towns on the Hellespont fell one after the other [c. 117]; the same fate befell those on the European coast of the Propontis [c. 122]; and with the single exception of some successes in Karia [cc. 118—121] the rebels were everywhere losing [c. 123]. Aristagoras' heart failed him. He determined on flight; and for a time hesitated between Myrkinos, the city of his father-in-law Histiaios, and that dream of Greek explorers—Sardinia. Finally, in spite of the advice of Hekataios, he decided on Myrkinos; and arriving there safely seems to have been unmolested by the Persians, and to have met his death shortly afterwards [B.C. 497] in a war with the natives [cc. 124—126].

Such was the state of affairs when Histiaios arrived at *Histiaios sent down to Sardis from Susa.* Sardis, having induced Dareios to send him down to suppress the revolt [c. 106]. To a great degree it had been stamped out; but the Ionian league [τὸ κοινὸν τῶν Ἰώνων] was still holding out: it still had a fleet ready; and Miletos was still untaken, and indeed seems hardly to have been pressed as yet with anything like vigour or regularity. Its fall, following on the defeat of the Ionian League fleet off Lade [B.C. 495], is narrated in the early chapters of the Sixth Book. The story in the Fifth Book breaks off here; but one other important fact, as bearing on the future, is told us. In relating the effect of the news of the burning of Sardis on the Persian court, we are told that Dareios was so much enraged by it that he vowed to have vengeance on the Athenians for their part in it [c. 105]. Thus the way is prepared for the two attempts related in the next book, the expedition of Mardonios, which was wrecked at Athos [6, 44—5], and that of Datis and Artaphernes, which was repulsed at Marathon [6, 112—116].

It may be instructive to consider here the ancient criticism of this book contained in the treatise of Plutarch known as *de malignitate Herodoti* [περὶ τῆς Ἡροδότου κακοηθείας] c. 23—24. The writer first objects to our author's statement that Kleisthenes bribed the Pythia to deliver false oracles urging the Lakedaemonians to free the Athenians[1]. He does not exactly say that the story is false; but he regards it as a wanton depreciation of a glorious deed, and a derogation of the honour of the god.

Plutarch's criticisms on Herodotos.

He next denounces the slander on the honour of Isagoras involved in the story of his wife's intrigue with Kleomenes; and in the assertion of the Karian origin of his family [εἰς Κᾶρας ὥσπερ εἰς κόρακας ἀποδιοπομπουμένου τὸν Ἰσαγόραν].

---

[1] Herodotos (5, 63) says nothing of Kleisthenes personally in this matter. It is the Alkmaeonidae generally who were believed, he says, to have bribed the Pythia.

Similarly he thinks it a piece of malice to assign a Phoenikian origin to the Gephyraei, the clan of Aristogeiton, asserting that Herodotos in this statement had absolutely no authority to go upon [αὐτὸς οὕτω πεπεισμένος].

Again to represent the Lakedaemonians as quickly repenting of their noble deed in freeing Athens was only meant as another slur upon their glory, and on that of the deed itself, and a slight upon the Athenian people as ungrateful [δήμῳ ἀχαρίστῳ παρέδωκεν τὴν πόλιν]. Here again Plutarch does not deny the fact: he seems to think it malicious to mention it.

The story, again, put into the mouth of Sosikles contains an unwarrantable slander on Periander, of whom no deed of cruelty is reported, except that of the attempted exportation of the 300 youths, which was frustrated by the Samians.

His account, again, of the expedition of the 20 Athenian ships in aid of Ionia is malicious. In calling these ships 'a beginning of mischief' (ἀρχεκάκους) he has managed to cast a slur on a patriotic action, directed to the enfranchisement of a large number of Hellenic cities. He has also made very light of the part taken by the Eretrians, who gained a victory over the royal fleet of Kyprians before the men landed at Ephesos and advanced upon Sardis.

This last statement Plutarch makes on the authority of Lysanias of Mallos [see Grote, 4, p. 217], and moreover declares that the story of the Eretrians having been defeated in battle on their way back to Ephesos and driven on board their ships is not supported by the historian of Eretria, Charon of Lampsakos; who is supposed to have been contemporary with these events. [Suidas, Pausan. 10, 38, 6 Plut. Themist. 27.]

We may observe that the story of an Eretrian victory over the Persian fleet *before* the attack upon Sardis is quite

INTRODUCTION.   xxvii

inconsistent with the order of events as given by Herodotos. For it was not till some time after this that the Phoenikian and Egyptian fleet was collected; and nothing is said of any ships from Kypros. One other sentence however is instructive. Plutarch says that the object of the attack on Sardis was effected, namely, to raise the siege of Miletos. And certainly Miletos appears to have been free from attack during the two or three years following the burning of Sardis, and not to have been effectively invested until after the battle of Lade [B.C. 495]. The account of the five years B.C. 500—495 in Herodotos is in fact very meagre and fragmentary. Perhaps it could not be otherwise. No great event took place; the reduction of the Greek towns was accomplished in detail, and without any striking incidents; and the Ionian cities of the League were left alone until the conflagration which they had caused was patiently stamped out. In the course of these years some small successes may have been occasionally gained by their ships, which still seem to have kept the sea; and perhaps the Eretrian vessels may have been hovering about the coasts for some time. But though Herodotos does not give us details of all that happened, he sufficiently indicates the kind of desultory skirmishing that was going on, until at last the Ionian community made a feeble and fruitless attempt to combine and hold out against the common enemy [6, 7—14]. And on the whole his conception of the function of an historian compares favourably with that indicated by Plutarch in this treatise.

NOTES ON THE TEXT.

[The MSS. of Herodotos of most importance for the formation of the text are
1. A, the Medicean in the Laurentian Library, of the 10th Century.
   B, Angelicanus, in the Library of the Augustinians at Rome, of the 11th Century.
   These two are from the same Archetype.
2. R, in the Vatican Library. This MS. (of the 14th Century) Cobet calls *codex optimus*. But it does not contain the fifth book.
   V, Vindobonensis. In the Imperial Library of Vienna (10th Century).
   S, The Sancroft MS. in the Library of Emmanuel College, Cambridge (14th Century).
   These three are again apparently from one Archetype.
3. Among other MSS. corrected from various sources are C (Florentine, 11th Century): P (Parisian, 13th Century).]

p. 2, l. 26. γενόμενον. So the best MSS. followed by Cobet and Stein, as also ἀπογενόμενον in p. 3, l. 2. But it does not follow that we need correct (with Cobet) γινόμενον and ἀπογινόμενον in l. 25. In this latter the present participle indicates what is of constant occurrence, viz. birth and death.

p. 5, l. 19. κατά. P and one other MS. have κατὰ τά as in 6, 89. But cp. 2, 99; and 5, 22, 89.

p. 6, l. 1—2. Cobet (with Valckenaer) would omit ἦν as 'ex 'AσίHN natum', and οἱ as having been added after the false ἦν had been put in. But Herodotos generally begins a story thus, cp. 1, 6, 60; cp. Polybios 8, 17. And when the predicate precedes a double subject the singular is often used. Madv. *Gr. Synt.* § 26.

p. 6, l. 12. ἐκ τῆς Ἀσίης. Stein proposes τῆς ἄλλης Ἀσίης, but this seems scarcely necessary with οὐδαμῶν.

p. 7, l. 1. αὐτά ABC. Others have ταῦτα which Stein adopts.

p. 7, l. 27. **Σιριοπαίονες.** So Holsten from Steph. Byz. The MSS. vary between Σειρο- and Σιρο-, but they are not trustworthy guides in proper names.

p. 8, l. 15. **καταπακτῆς.** Reiske suggested καταρρακτῆς, Wesseling καταπηκτῆς, Stein κατεπακτῆς. But the MSS. shew no variation, and it seems unnecessary to change an intelligible word.

p. 12, l. 11. **ὥς εἰσι Ἕλληνες.** Cobet would omit these words.

p. 12, l. 13. **Ἑλληνοδίκαι.** Some few MSS. [among them S] have Ἑλλήνων, and Valckenaer and Wesseling regard Ἑλληνοδίκαι as a gloss. But it was the natural word since the 25th Olympiad. See Pausan. 5, 9, 5.

p. 12, l. 14. **ἑλομένου.** MSS. ABC have βουλομένου, which of the two seems the more likely to have been the explanatory gloss. The majority of edd. retain ἑλομένου. Abicht adopts the emendation of Dietsch, στελλομένου.

p. 12, l. 25. **δωρεὴν μισθόν.** The MSS. have μισθὸν δωρεήν. Schaefer would omit μισθόν, Dobree δωρεήν. Holder brackets δωρεήν. For the accusative Stein quotes 1, 31 τὸ ἀνθρώπῳ τυχεῖν ἄριστόν ἐστι.

p. 13, l. 24. **ἀπίκεο** Baehr, Stein ἀπικνέο. Abicht ἀπικνέεο. But the MS. reading appears to me to be better. The aorist suits a peremptory command, admitting of no delay. Cp. Theocr. 11, 42 ἀλλ' ἀφίκευ τὺ ποτ' ἄμμε, καὶ ἑξεῖς οὐδὲν ἔλασσον.

p. 15, l. 23. **ἐκ.** Bekker omitted ἐκ, and Abicht follows without remark, though all MSS. give it.

p. 21, l. 24. **ναυκρατέες.** The MSS. have ναυκράτεες, and Cobet thinks that the false accent indicates that the true word was ναυκράτορες, cp. 6, 9. Thucyd. 5, 97, 109; 6, 18. But after all, the two cases in Herodotos are different. In 6, 9 μὴ οὐκ ἐόντες ναυκράτορες 'unless they were masters at sea', the word is a substantive, as in Soph. Philoct. 1072 ναυκράτωρ 'a captain'. But here with τῆς θαλάσσης an adjective is required, ναυκρατέες τῆς θαλάσσης 'having naval-mastership of the sea'.

p. 22, l. 1. **εἶχε.** Cobet would write ἔχειν. But the sudden recurrence to the indicative in the middle of an oratio obliqua is not uncommon.

p. 23, l. 17. **ἕξεο** is Schäfer's emendation for ἐκ σέο of the MSS. Cp. p. 24, l. 2.

NOTES ON THE TEXT.

p. 26, l. 8. ὧν. This is de la Barre's emendation of the MSS οὐκ or οὐχ. So Schweighaeuser, Gaisford, Schäfer. Others have proposed ὡς, αὖ (Bekker and Dietsch), κοῦ (Reiske). Stein and Abicht omit it. Bothe reads οἰκότα. Wesseling retained οὐκ.

p. 27, l. 25. ἐβασίλευε. Krüger changed this to ἐβασίλευσε. But the imperfect seems preferable in speaking of a *period*, such as a reign; and the same tense should be retained when the sentence becomes conditional. 'Dorieus would have reigned', not only 'would have become king'.

p. 31, l. 27. ἐκ δὲ ταύτης...ἑκατόν. The transposition of this sentence from following τριηκοσίας p. 32, l. 10, is due to Stein. It certainly does a great deal to remove the difficulty of the passage. The clause καὶ τριήκοντα...ἑκατόν, l. 1—2, was first inserted by de la Barre.

p. 32, l. 5. τρίτος ὠυτὸς ὀνομαζόμενος. J. C. Weissenborn proposed Ζάβατος ὀνομαζόμενος which Holder adopts.

p. 33, l. 10. τῷ ἑωυτοῦ πάθεϊ. Stein brackets these words. Certainly the dative is peculiar, and for that reason seems less likely to have been foisted into the text from a gloss. It appears in all MSS.

p. 34, l. 7. πολλῶν τέων. Cobet proposes ὀλίγων, Madvig and Meier οὐ πολλῶν τέων. But see Pausan. 1, 9, 3 Ἀθηναῖοι δ' ὑπ' αὐτοῦ παθόντες εὖ πολλά τε καὶ οὐκ ἄξια ἀπηγήσεως. It seems more likely that καί is adversative here, 'several *but* unimportant things'.

p. 34, l. 22. βίβλους. Stein βύβλους, and so the majority of the MSS. But P and a few others give βίβλους, and the evidence of inscriptions up to the 1st century B.C. is in favour of this form. See Meisterhans *Grammatik der attischen Inschriften*, p. 22. In the absence of other evidence for βύβλους from Ionic inscriptions, I would therefore write βίβλους, and βιβλία in 9, 4, where I formerly gave βυβλία.

p. 35, l. 1. τισι. Dobree, Bekker, Dindorf, Dietsch give τρισί. I agree with Baehr in thinking the change unnecessary.

p. 35, l. 4. ἀνέθηκεν ἐών is the reading of all MSS., and none of the changes proposed are satisfactory.

p. 36, l. 17. συγκειμένου. Cobet would write συγκείμενον.

p. 36, l. 27. ξείνους. MSS. generally ξεινίους, one has ξενίους. Schäfer is the author of what seems a certain emendation.

p. 36, l. 28. ἀνδρῶν. Cobet proposes ἀνθρώπων, but see p. 48, l. 4.

p. 37, l. 22. **ἰθύς**, always elsewhere in Herodotos ἰθύ. Cobet accordingly conjectures εὐθύς.

p. 39, l. 18. **ἐκβάλλῃ**. Dobree's emendation of ἐκβάλον, cp. 1, 75, 82, 124; 6, 35, 135. See Cobet *Nov. Lect.* p. 363. Cp. also Aeschines in Ctes. § 202, and infr. p. 48, l. 20.

p. 40, l. 20. **ὄνου**. Sauppe adds καὶ χοίρου to correspond to the names given below. But this is not necessary, as both ὕαται and χοιρεᾶται are connected with a word for 'swine'.

p. 41, l. 7. **πάντα**. This is the reading of S adopted by Gaisford. Al. πάντων (Stein), Abicht ἐπανιών. If πάντων is right then τότε is inexplicable after πρότερον, unless something is, as Stein suggests, lost from the text. The reading of S gives good sense; only it is difficult to see why so plain a word should have been altered. Taking πάντων and Stein's suggestion of a loss I would suggest ἐπήβολον as supported by a gloss in A πάντων κύριον.

p. 41, l. 10. **δέκα δέ**. Madv. would omit. Bake gives καὶ δή.

p. 43, l. 18. **σφι** must refer to the Persians [App. C. II. (d)]. To change to σφίσι with Stein makes all things easy, cp. p. 51, l. 10; p. 53, l. 22 where there is the same doubt. Schweighaeuser and Gaisford wrote σφι but cut out πρός, cp. 3, 66; 4, 120. Wesseling ad 3, 66. S has ἐκπολεμῶσθαι.

p. 43, l. 22. **κῇ**. Stein κοῦ. MSS. πῇ and ποῖ. Cp. p. 51, l. 28.

p. 46, l. 8. **ἐν πέδαις**, so three MSS., cp. 1, 67. Stein and Holder write [ἐς πέδας]. Krüger would omit it altogether.

p. 49, l. 5. **ἔφερε καρπόν**. The oldest MSS. A and B omit καρπόν, and it may well be understood from the beginning of the chapter. Still as the other group of MSS. have it, it seems perhaps safer to retain it.

p. 49, l. 7. **καὶ πρὸ τοῦ**. Stein proposes ὡς καὶ πρὸ τοῦ.

p. 49, l. 10. **οἱ Αἰγινῆται**. Cobet would omit. τὸ δέ, Cobet τότε δέ.

p. 49, l. 12. **ἅτε δέ**. Cobet ἄλλα τε δή, omitting τῆς τε Δαμίης καὶ τῆς Αὐξησίης.

p. 49, l. 24. **εἰσὶ δέ...ἱρουργίαι**. Omitted in one MS. Van Herwerden would omit ἱρουργίαι.

p. 49, l. 27. **οὐκ ἐπετέλεον**. Palmer proposes οὐκέτι ἐπετέλεον. Schweighaeuser οὐκέτι ἐτέλεον.

p. 50, l. 1. πρήσσεσθαι ἐκέλευον, del. Cobet.

p. 50, l. 7. τούτους. Krüger and Holder bracket the word. Some MSS. have τουτέων, there was anciently therefore some doubt as to this usage of τούτους where a simple relative would seem sufficient, but in 3, 155 there is a similar use of οὗτος. Madvig [*Adv.* 307] thus reconstructs the passage: τῶν ἀστῶν, τούτους οἷα ἀποπεμφθέντας ἀπὸ τοῦ κοινοῦ καὶ ἀπικομένους ἐς Αἴγιναν τὰ ἀγάλματα ταῦτα ὡς σφετέρων ξύλων ἐόντα πειρᾶν [? πειρᾶσθαι] ἐκ τῶν βάθρων ἀνασπᾶν.

Abicht reads τριηκοσίους as though τούτους had arisen from τ' ους.

p. 51, l. 4. ἄλλῳ δέ τεῳ. Van Herwerden would omit the words.

p. 51, l. 6—7. Αἰγινῆται λέγουσι. Cobet omits.

p. 51, l. 10. βοηθέοντάς σφι should be βοηθέοντας σφίσι.

p. 51, l. 14. γενέσθαι. Naber ἐπιγενέσθαι.

p. 51, l. 22. ἄρα MSS. A and B, others have γάρ (*narrativum*).

p. 51, l. 28. ὅκῃ. Stein ὅκου, cp. p. 43, l. 22.

p. 52, l. 4. μετέβαλον. Some MSS. have μετέβαλλον, van Herwerden proposes μεταβαλεῖν.

p. 52, l. 20. ἐκ τότε S, adopted both by Stein and Abicht; the other MSS. have ἐκ τε τόσου. Holder follows Eltz in bracketing τε.

p. 53, l. 8. ἐπιστρατεύωνται. Naber proposes ἐπιστρατεύσωνται.

p. 53, l. 18—19. τὰ ἐκ τῶν Ἀλκμαιωνιδέων. Holder τά <τε> ἐκ.

p. 53, l. 22. For σφι read σφίσι.

p. 53, l. 24. ἔτι τε. Krüger ἔτι δέ.

p. 54, l. 16. ἐς τὸ...Πεισιστρατίδαι. This clause was condemned by Wesseling as a gloss, but defended by Schweighaeuser and retained by Gaisford. Schäfer, Stein, Abicht, Holder bracket it. Herodotos often gives such apparently unnecessary reminders. See p. 68, l. 14.

p. 54, l. 30. ἁμαρτών. Van Herwerden omits.

p. 55, l. 1. σφεας, Eltz σφεα. ἀκεόμενοι, the reading of V and S, approved by Cobet, and I think evidently right. τίσασθαι is a gloss, and ἀπικόμενοι a consequent emendation.

p. 55, l. 18. ὥστε τυραννεύεσθαι τὰς πόλις. Van Herwerden would omit.

p. 58, l. 1. ἀπικοίατο. The MSS. AB have ἀπικνέοιντο, others ἀπικνέοιτο or ἀπικέοιτο or ἀπίκοιντο. From these Stein elicits ἀπικνεοίατο, and Holder follows him. Gaisford, Schweighaeuser, Abicht retain ἀπικοίατο from the Aldine Edition and one Paris MS. The aorist seems the right tense.

p. 59, l. 19. σχών, al. ἴσχων.

p. 60, l. 22. οὐκ ὦν παύσεσθε V and S. AB ἢν μὴ παύσεσθε, al. οὐκῶν ἢν μὴ παύσησθε.

p. 63, l. 17. ἀρχὴ κακῶν. Cobet proposes ἀρχέκακοι from Plutarch de Malign. 24 ἃς μὲν 'Αθηναῖοι ναῦς ἐξέπεμψαν Ἴωσι τιμωροὺς ἀποστᾶσι βασιλέως ἀρχεκάκους τολμήσας προσειπεῖν, cp. Hom. Il. 5, 63. But Plutarch varies the words of Herodotos too often to be a sure guide in defiance of all the MSS.

p. 64, l. 16. ἐκόμισαν. Van Herwerden omits.

p. 65, l. 3. τῶν ἄλλων ἀστῶν. A and B have τῶν ἀστῶν ἄλλον. But all editions seem agreed in following the other MSS. in the reading of the text. Charopinos was an ἀστός as well as his colleague.

p. 65, l. 31. τὸν Τμῶλον καλεόμενον. Van Herwerden would omit. The Aldine had τό against all the MSS., yet Abicht retains and tries to explain it.

p. 66, l. 22. σφι. Stein's correction for σφίσι. The confusion is frequent, see p. 53, l. 22. Holder gives <ἔτι> τιμωρήσειν.

p. 67, l. 18. στασιώτῃσι. Some MSS. have στρατιώτῃσι, and van Herwerden suggests συστασιώτῃσι.

p. 68, l. 14. τὸν...ἤδη πολλόν. Holder says that Stein rejects the whole clause, though he does not do so in either of his two editions. Van Herwerden rejects ὁ Δαρεῖος. See on p. 54, 16.

p. 69, l. 4. πεπρηχέναι VS: but A and B have πεποιηκέναι. It is a question which of the two is the more likely to have been the gloss. Van Herwerden of course solves the difficulty by cutting out the word. Stein selects πεποιηκέναι, Gaisford, Abicht, Holder πεπρηχέναι.

βαλλόμενον best supported by the MSS.; Gaisford, Stein βαλόμενον.

p. 69, l. 18. ἐκδύσεσθαι Naber and Cobet for the barbarous ἐκδύσασθαι.

p. 72, l. 23. ἐποίεον. One class of MSS. have ἐποίεε which both Stein and Abicht adopt. But perhaps ἐποίεε is the more likely to be a correction; and the ἅρματα means practically 'the charioteers'. See l. 8.

NOTES ON THE TEXT.

p. 74, l. 10. **ἐπ' ἡμέρης ἑκάστην.** Stein reads ἐπ' ἡμέρῃ ἑκάστῃ with A and B. V and S ἐπ' ἡμέρης ἑκάστης. Nitzsch ἐπ' ἡμέρῃ ἑκάστην.

p. 75, l. 17. **ἤ.** Cobet would omit.

p. 76, l. 4. **τὴν ἐν Πηδάσῳ.** This appears in many variations in the MSS.: πιδάσῳ, ἐμπιδάσῳ, ἐπὶ δάσῳ, ἐπὶ δαύσῳ, ἐπὶ λασοῖσι. Wesseling gives ἐπὶ Μυλάσοισι from Valla's *in via quae in Mylasa fert.* Stein suspects that the Archetypal MS. had ΕΠΙΙΗΔΑΣΩΙ corrupted from ΕΠΙ ΠΗΔΑΣΩΝ.

p. 76, l. 13—14. **τὴν Μυσίην.** Kallenberg suggests τῆς Μυσίης which I now think ought to be accepted.

p. 77, l. 8. **ὅς.** Krüger would omit the word, which would certainly make the sentence less awkward. But such broken constructions are not unparalleled in Herodotos, cp. 9, 84.

p. 77, l. 12. **σφίσι.** There is the same variation in the MSS. between this and σφι as before. See p. 53, l. 22; p. 66, l. 22.

p. 78, l. 8. **βουλομένων.** Van Herwerden proposes συνθεμένων. But this is putting the negotiation too forward. The Thrakians offered a submission, apparently, which Aristagoras refused. The reading συνθεμένων would suggest some treachery on their part.

ERRATA.

p. 51, l. 10. *For* βοηθέοντάς σφι *read* βοηθέοντας σφίσι.

p. 53, l. 22. *For* σφι *read* σφίσι.

ΗΡΟΔΟΤΟΥ ΤΕΡΨΙΧΟΡΗ.

BOOK V.

Megabazus takes Perinthus on the Hellespont, a town which had long before suffered severely at the hands of the Paeonians. Megabazus then proceeded with his invasion of Thrace [B.C. 506—504].

I. Οἱ δὲ ἐν τῇ Εὐρώπῃ τῶν Περσέων καταλειφθέντες ὑπὸ Δαρείου, τῶν ὁ Μεγάβαζος ἦρχε, πρώτους μὲν Περινθίους Ἑλλησποντίων οὐ βουλομένους ὑπηκόους εἶναι Δαρείου κατεστρέψαντο, περιεφθέντας πρότερον καὶ ὑπὸ Παιόνων τρηχέως. οἱ γὰρ ὦν ἀπὸ Στρυμόνος Παίονες χρήσαντος τοῦ θεοῦ στρατεύεσθαι ἐπὶ Περινθίους, καὶ ἢν μὲν ἀντικατιζόμενοι ἐπικαλέσωνταί σφεας οἱ Περίνθιοι οὐνομαστὶ βώσαντες, τοὺς δὲ ἐπιχειρέειν, ἢν δὲ μὴ ἐπιβώσωνται, μὴ ἐπιχειρέειν, ἐποίευν οἱ Παίονες ταῦτα. ἀντικατιζομένων δὲ τῶν Περινθίων ἐν τῷ προαστείῳ ἐνθαῦτα μουνομαχίη τριφασίη ἐκ προκλήσιός σφι ἐγένετο· καὶ γὰρ ἄνδρα ἀνδρὶ καὶ ἵππον ἵππῳ συνέβαλον καὶ κύνα κυνί. νικώντων δὲ τὰ δύο τῶν Περινθίων, ὡς ἐπαιώνιζον κεχαρηκότες, συνεβάλοντο οἱ Παίονες τὸ χρηστήριον αὐτὸ τοῦτο εἶναι καὶ εἶπάν κου παρὰ σφίσι αὐτοῖσι·

"νῦν ἂν εἴη ὁ χρησμὸς ἐπιτελεόμενος ἡμῖν, νῦν ἡμέτε-
"ρον τὸ ἔργον." οὕτω τοῖσι Περινθίοισι παιωνίσασι
ἐπιχειρέουσι οἱ Παίονες, καὶ πολλόν τε ἐκράτησαν καὶ
ἔλιπόν σφεων ὀλίγους. II. Τὰ μὲν δὴ ἀπὸ Παιόνων
πρότερον γενόμενα ὧδε ἐγένετο, τότε δὲ ἀνδρῶν ἀγαθῶν
περὶ τῆς ἐλευθερίης γινομένων τῶν Περινθίων οἱ Πέρσαι τε καὶ ὁ Μεγάβαζος ἐπεκράτησαν πλήθεϊ. ὡς δὲ
ἐχειρώθη ἡ Πέρινθος, ἤλαυνε τὸν στρατὸν ὁ Μεγάβαζος διὰ τῆς Θρηίκης, πᾶσαν πόλιν καὶ πᾶν ἔθνος
τῶν ταύτῃ οἰκημένων ἡμερούμενος βασιλέϊ· ταῦτα
γάρ οἱ ἐνετέταλτο ἐκ Δαρείου, Θρηίκην καταστρέ-
φεσθαι.

*Thrace. The three tribes distinguished from the others by
their customs are the* Getae, *the* Trausi, *and the*
Krestonaei.

III. ΘΡΗΙΚΩΝ δὲ ἔθνος μέγιστόν ἐστι μετά γε
Ἰνδοὺς πάντων ἀνθρώπων. εἰ δὲ ὑπ' ἑνὸς ἄρχοιτο ἢ
φρονέοι κατὰ τὠυτό, ἄμαχόν τ' ἂν εἴη καὶ πολλῷ
κράτιστον πάντων ἐθνέων κατὰ γνώμην τὴν ἐμήν.
ἀλλὰ γὰρ τοῦτο ἄπορόν σφι καὶ ἀμήχανον μή κοτε
ἐγγένηται, εἰσὶ δὴ κατὰ τοῦτο ἀσθενέες. οὐνόματα δὲ
πολλὰ ἔχουσι κατὰ χώρας ἕκαστοι, νόμοισι δὲ οὗτοι
παραπλησίοισι πάντες χρέονται κατὰ πάντα, πλὴν
Γετέων καὶ Τραυσῶν καὶ τῶν κατύπερθε Κρηστωναίων
οἰκεόντων. IV. Τούτων δὲ τὰ μὲν Γέται οἱ ἀθανατίζοντες ποιεῦσι εἴρηταί μοι, Τραυσοὶ δὲ τὰ μὲν ἄλλα
πάντα κατὰ ταὐτὰ τοῖσι ἄλλοισι Θρήϊξι ἐπιτελέουσι,
κατὰ δὲ τὸν γινόμενόν σφι καὶ ἀπογινόμενον ποιεῦσι
τοιάδε· τὸν μὲν γενόμενον περιιζόμενοι οἱ προσήκοντες
ὀλοφύρονται, ὅσα μιν δέει ἐπείτε ἐγένετο ἀναπλῆσαι

κακά, ἀνηγεόμενοι τὰ ἀνθρωπήϊα πάντα πάθεα, τὸν δ᾽ ἀπογενόμενον παίζοντές τε καὶ ἡδόμενοι γῇ κρύπτουσι, ἐπιλέγοντες ὅσων κακῶν ἐξαπαλλαχθείς ἐστι ἐν πάσῃ εὐδαιμονίῃ. V. Οἱ δὲ κατύπερθε Κρηστωναίων ποιεῦσι τοιάδε· ἔχει γυναῖκας ἕκαστος πολλάς· ἐπεὰν ὦν τις αὐτῶν ἀποθάνῃ, κρίσις γίνεται μεγάλη τῶν γυναικῶν καὶ φίλων σπουδαὶ ἰσχυραὶ περὶ τοῦδε, ἥτις αὐτέων ἐφιλέετο μάλιστα ὑπὸ τοῦ ἀνδρός· ἣ δ᾽ ἂν κριθῇ καὶ τιμηθῇ, ἐγκωμιασθεῖσα ὑπό τε ἀνδρῶν καὶ γυναικῶν σφάζεται ἐς τὸν τάφον ὑπὸ τοῦ οἰκηϊωτάτου ἑωυτῆς, σφαχθεῖσα δὲ συνθάπτεται τῷ ἀνδρί· αἱ δὲ ἄλλαι συμφορὴν μεγάλην ποιεῦνται· ὄνειδος γάρ σφι τοῦτο μέγιστον γίνεται.

Thracian customs: (1) *their treatment of their children,*
(2) *the tattooing of their bodies,*

VI. Τῶν δὲ δὴ ἄλλων Θρηίκων ἐστὶ ὅδε ὁ νόμος· πωλεῦσι τὰ τέκνα ἐπ᾽ ἐξαγωγῇ. τὰς δὲ παρθένους οὐ φυλάσσουσι, ἀλλ᾽ ἐῶσι τοῖσι αὐταὶ βούλονται ἀνδράσι μίσγεσθαι. τὰς δὲ γυναῖκας ἰσχυρῶς φυλάσσουσι, καὶ ὠνέονται τὰς γυναῖκας παρὰ τῶν γονέων χρημάτων μεγάλων. καὶ τὸ μὲν ἐστίχθαι εὐγενὲς κέκριται, τὸ δ᾽ ἄστικτον ἀγενές. ἀργὸν εἶναι κάλλιστον, γῆς δὲ ἐργάτην ἀτιμότατον. τὸ ζῆν ἀπὸ πολέμου καὶ ληϊστύος κάλλιστον. οὗτοι μέν σφεων οἱ ἐπιφανέστατοι νόμοι εἰσί.

(3) *their religion,* (4) *their funeral rites.*

VII. Θεοὺς δὲ σέβονται μούνους τούσδε, Ἄρεα καὶ Διόνυσον καὶ Ἄρτεμιν· οἱ δὲ βασιλέες αὐτῶν, πάρεξ τῶν ἄλλων πολιητέων, σέβονται Ἑρμῆν μάλιστα θεῶν, καὶ ὀμνύουσι μοῦνον τοῦτον, καὶ λέγουσι γεγονέναι ἀπὸ Ἑρμέω ἑωυτούς. VIII. Ταφαὶ δὲ τοῖσι εὐδαίμοσι αὐτῶν εἰσὶ αἵδε· τρεῖς μὲν ἡμέρας προτιθέασι τὸν νεκρὸν, καὶ παντοῖα σφάξαντες ἰρήια εὐωχέονται, προκλαύσαντες πρῶτον· ἔπειτεν δὲ θάπτουσι κατακαύσαντες ἢ ἄλλως γῇ κρύψαντες, χῶμα δὲ χέαντες ἀγῶνα τιθεῖσι παντοῖον, ἐν τῷ τὰ μέγιστα ἄεθλα τίθεται κατὰ λόγον μουνομαχίης. ταφαὶ μὲν δὴ Θρηίκων εἰσὶ αἵδε.

Beyond the Ister all is unknown. The only tribe with whose name we are acquainted is that of the Sigynnae.

IX. Τὸ δὲ πρὸς βορέω ἔτι τῆς χώρης ταύτης οὐδεὶς ἔχει φράσαι τὸ ἀτρεκές, οἵτινές εἰσι ἀνθρώπων οἰκέοντες αὐτήν, ἀλλὰ τὰ πέρην ἤδη τοῦ Ἴστρου ἐρῆμος χώρη φαίνεται ἐοῦσα καὶ ἄπειρος. μούνους δὲ δύναμαι πυθέσθαι οἰκέοντας πέρην τοῦ Ἴστρου ἀνθρώπους, τοῖσι οὔνομα εἶναι Σιγύννας, ἐσθῆτι δὲ χρεομένους Μηδικῇ. τοὺς δὲ ἵππους αὐτῶν εἶναι λασίους ἅπαν τὸ σῶμα, ἐπὶ πέντε δακτύλους τὸ βάθος τῶν τριχῶν, σμικροὺς δὲ καὶ σιμοὺς καὶ ἀδυνάτους ἄνδρας φέρειν, ζευγνυμένους δὲ ὑπ' ἅρματα εἶναι ὀξυτάτους· ἁρματηλατέειν δὲ πρὸς ταῦτα τοὺς ἐπιχωρίους. κατήκειν δὲ τούτων τοὺς οὔρους ἀγχοῦ Ἐνετῶν τῶν ἐν τῷ Ἀδρίῃ. εἶναι δὲ Μήδων σφέας ἀποίκους λέγουσι· ὅκως δὲ οὗτοι Μήδων ἄποικοι γεγόνασι, ἐγὼ μὲν οὐκ ἔχω ἐπιφράσασθαι, γένοιτο δ' ἂν πᾶν ἐν τῷ μακρῷ χρόνῳ. σιγύννας δ' ὦν καλέουσι Λίγυες οἱ ἄνω ὑπὲρ Μασσαλίης οἰκέοντες τοὺς καπήλους, Κύπριοι δὲ τὰ δόρατα. X.

Ὡς δὲ Θρήϊκες λέγουσι, μέλισσαι κατέχουσι τὰ πέρην τοῦ Ἴστρου, καὶ ὑπὸ τούτων οὐκ εἶναι διελθεῖν τὸ προσωτέρω. ἐμοὶ μέν νυν ταῦτα λέγοντες δοκέουσι λέγειν οὐκ οἰκότα· τὰ γὰρ ζῷα ταῦτα φαίνεται εἶναι δύσριγα· ἀλλά μοι τὰ ὑπὸ τὴν ἄρκτον ἀδίκητα δοκέει εἶναι διὰ τὰ ψύχεα. ταῦτα μέν νυν τῆς χώρης ταύτης πέρι λέγεται· τὰ παραθαλάσσια δ' ὧν αὐτῆς Μεγάβαζος Περσέων κατήκοα ἐποίεε.

Return of Darius to Sardis from Skythia. He rewards Histiaios and Koës for saving the bridge over the Danube.

XI. Δαρεῖος δὲ ὡς διαβὰς τάχιστα τὸν Ἑλλήσποντον ἀπίκετο ἐς Σάρδις, ἐμνήσθη τῆς ἐξ Ἱστιαίου τε τοῦ Μιλησίου εὐεργεσίης καὶ τῆς παραινέσιος τοῦ Μυτιληναίου Κώεω, μεταπεμψάμενος δέ σφεας ἐς Σάρδις ἐδίδου αὐτοῖσι αἵρεσιν. ὁ μὲν δὴ Ἱστιαῖος, ἅτε τυραννεύων τῆς Μιλήτου, τυραννίδος μὲν οὐδεμιῆς προσεχρήϊζε, αἰτέει δὲ Μύρκινον τὴν Ἠδωνῶν βουλόμενος ἐν αὐτῇ πόλιν κτίσαι. οὗτος μὲν δὴ ταύτην αἱρέεται, ὁ δὲ Κώης, οἷά τε οὐ τύραννος δημότης τε ἐών, αἰτέει Μυτιλήνης τυραννεῦσαι. τελεωθέντων δὲ ἀμφοτέροισι, οὗτοι μὲν κατὰ εἵλοντο ἐτράποντο.

Darius, struck with admiration of a tall and handsome Paeonian woman, sends orders to Megabazus to transfer the whole Paeonian tribe to Asia.

XII. Δαρεῖον δὲ συνήνεικε πρῆγμα τοιόνδε ἰδόμενον ἐπιθυμῆσαι ἐντείλασθαι Μεγαβάζῳ Παίονας ἑλόντα ἀνασπάστους ποιῆσαι ἐκ τῆς Εὐρώπης ἐς

τὴν Ἀσίην· ἦν Πίγρης καὶ Μαντύης, ἄνδρες Παίονες,
οἳ, ἐπείτε Δαρεῖος διέβη ἐς τὴν Ἀσίην, αὐτοὶ ἐθέλοντες Παιόνων τυραννεύειν ἀπικνέονται ἐς Σάρδις ἅμα
ἀγόμενοι ἀδελφεὴν μεγάλην τε καὶ εὐειδέα. φυλά-
5 ξαντες δὲ Δαρεῖον προκατιζόμενον ἐς τὸ προάστειον
τὸ τῶν Λυδῶν ἐποίησαν τοιόνδε· σκευάσαντες τὴν
ἀδελφεὴν ὡς εἶχον ἄριστα ἐπ' ὕδωρ ἔπεμπον ἄγγος
ἐπὶ τῇ κεφαλῇ ἔχουσαν καὶ ἐκ τοῦ βραχίονος ἵππον
ἐπέλκουσαν καὶ κλώθουσαν λίνον. ὡς δὲ παρεξήϊε
10 ἡ γυνή, ἐπιμελὲς τῷ Δαρείῳ ἐγένετο· οὔτε γὰρ Περσικὰ ἦν οὔτε Λύδια τὰ ποιεύμενα ἐκ τῆς γυναικός,
οὔτε πρὸς τῶν ἐκ τῆς Ἀσίης οὐδαμῶν. ἐπιμελὲς δὲ
ὥς οἱ ἐγένετο, τῶν δορυφόρων τινὰς πέμπει κελεύων
φυλάξαι, ὅ τι χρήσεται τῷ ἵππῳ ἡ γυνή. οἱ μὲν δὴ
15 ὄπισθε εἵποντο, ἡ δὲ ἐπείτε ἀπίκετο ἐπὶ τὸν ποταμόν, ἦρσε τὸν ἵππον, ἄρσασα δὲ καὶ τὸ ἄγγος τοῦ
ὕδατος ἐμπλησαμένη τὴν αὐτὴν ὁδὸν παρεξήϊε, φέρουσα τὸ ὕδωρ ἐπὶ τῆς κεφαλῆς καὶ ἐπέλκουσα ἐκ
τοῦ βραχίονος τὸν ἵππον καὶ στρέφουσα τὸν ἄτρακ-
20 τον. XIII. Θωυμάζων δὲ ὁ Δαρεῖος τά τε ἤκουσε
ἐκ τῶν κατασκόπων καὶ τὰ αὐτὸς ὥρα ἄγειν αὐτὴν
ἐκέλευε ἑωυτῷ ἐς ὄψιν. ὡς δὲ ἄχθη, παρῆσαν καὶ
οἱ ἀδελφεοὶ αὐτῆς οὔ κῃ πρόσω σκοπιὴν ἔχοντες
τούτων. εἰρωτέοντος δὲ τοῦ Δαρείου, ὁποδαπὴ εἴη,
25 ἔφασαν οἱ νεηνίσκοι εἶναι Παίονες καὶ ἐκείνην εἶναι
σφέων ἀδελφεήν. ὁ δ' ἀμείβετο, "τίνες δὲ οἱ Παίονες
"ἄνθρωποί εἰσι καὶ κοῦ γῆς οἰκημένοι, καὶ τί ἐκεῖνοι
"ἐθέλοντες ἔλθοιεν ἐς Σάρδις." οἱ δέ οἱ ἔφραζον, ὡς
ἔλθοιεν μὲν ἐκείνῳ δώσοντες σφέας αὐτούς, εἴη δὲ ἡ
30 Παιονίη ἐπὶ τῷ Στρυμόνι ποταμῷ πεπολισμένη, ὁ δὲ
Στρυμὼν οὐ πρόσω τοῦ Ἑλλησπόντου, εἴησαν δὲ

Τευκρῶν τῶν ἐκ Τροίης ἄποικοι. οἱ μὲν δὴ αὐτὰ ἕκαστα ἔλεγον, ὁ δὲ εἰρώτα, εἰ καὶ πᾶσαι εἴησαν αὐτόθι αἱ γυναῖκες οὕτω ἐργάτιδες. οἱ δὲ καὶ τοῦτο ἔφασαν προθύμως οὕτω ἔχειν· αὐτοῦ γὰρ ὦν τούτου εἵνεκεν καὶ ἐποιέετο. XIV. Ἐνθαῦτα Δαρεῖος γρά- 5
φει γράμματα πρὸς Μεγάβαζον, τὸν ἔλιπε ἐν τῇ Θρηίκῃ στρατηγόν, ἐντελλόμενος ἐξαναστῆσαι ἐξ ἠθέων Παίονας καὶ παρ' ἑωυτὸν ἀγαγεῖν καὶ αὐτοὺς καὶ τὰ τέκνα τε καὶ τὰς γυναῖκας αὐτῶν. αὐτίκα δὲ ἱππεὺς ἔθεε φέρων τὴν ἀγγελίην ἐπὶ τὸν Ἑλλήσπον- 10
τον, περαιωθεὶς δὲ διδοῖ τὸ βυβλίον τῷ Μεγαβάζῳ. ὁ δὲ ἐπιλεξάμενος καὶ λαβὼν ἡγεμόνας ἐκ τῆς Θρηίκης ἐστρατεύετο ἐπὶ τὴν Παιονίην. XV. Πυθόμενοι δὲ οἱ Παίονες τοὺς Πέρσας ἐπὶ σφέας ἰέναι, ἁλισθέντες ἐξεστρατεύσαντο πρὸς θαλάσσης, δοκέοντες ταύτῃ 15
ἐπιχειρήσειν τοὺς Πέρσας ἐμβάλλοντας. οἱ μὲν δὴ Παίονες ἦσαν ἕτοιμοι τὸν Μεγαβάζου στρατὸν ἐπιόντα ἐρύκειν, οἱ δὲ Πέρσαι πυθόμενοι συναλίσθαι τοὺς Παίονας καὶ τὴν πρὸς θαλάσσης ἐσβολὴν φυλάσσοντας, ἔχοντες ἡγεμόνας τὴν ἄνω ὁδὸν τρά- 20
πονται, λαθόντες δὲ τοὺς Παίονας ἐσπίπτουσι ἐς τὰς πόλιας αὐτῶν, ἐούσας ἀνδρῶν ἐρήμους· οἷα δὲ κεινῇσι ἐπιπεσόντες εὐπετέως κατέσχον. οἱ δὲ Παίονες ὡς ἐπύθοντο ἐχομένας τὰς πόλιας, αὐτίκα διασκεδασθέντες κατ' ἑωυτοὺς ἕκαστοι ἐτράποντο καὶ παρεδί- 25
δοσαν σφέας αὐτοὺς τοῖσι Πέρσῃσι. οὕτω δὴ Παιόνων Σιριοπαίονές τε καὶ Παιόπλαι καὶ οἱ μέχρι τῆς Πρασιάδος λίμνης ἐξ ἠθέων ἐξαναστάντες ἤγοντο ἐς τὴν Ἀσίην.

The lake-dwellings in the Lake Prasias.

XVI. Οἱ δὲ περὶ τὸ Πάγγαιον οὖρος καὶ Δόβηρας καὶ Ἀγριᾶνας καὶ Ὀδομάντους καὶ αὐτὴν τὴν λίμνην τὴν Πρασιάδα οὐκ ἐχειρώθησαν ἀρχὴν ὑπὸ Μεγαβάζου. ἐπειρήθη δὲ καὶ τοὺς ἐν τῇ λίμνῃ
5 κατοικημένους ἐξαιρέειν ὧδε· ἰκρία ἐπὶ σταυρῶν ὑψηλῶν ἐζευγμένα ἐν μέσῃ ἕστηκε τῇ λίμνῃ, ἔσοδον ἐκ τῆς ἠπείρου στεινὴν ἔχοντα μιῇ γεφύρῃ. τοὺς δὲ σταυροὺς τοὺς ὑπεστεῶτας τοῖσι ἰκρίοισι τὸ μέν κου ἀρχαῖον ἔστησαν κοινῇ πάντες οἱ πολιῆται, μετὰ δὲ
10 νόμῳ χρεόμενοι ἱστᾶσι τοιῷδε· κομίζοντες ἐξ οὔρεος, τῷ οὔνομά ἐστι Ὄρβηλος, κατὰ γυναῖκα ἑκάστην ὁ γαμέων τρεῖς σταυροὺς ὑπίστησι· ἄγεται δὲ ἕκαστος συχνὰς γυναῖκας. οἰκεῦσι δὲ τοιοῦτον τρόπον, κρατέων ἕκαστος ἐπὶ τῶν ἰκρίων καλύβης τε, ἐν τῇ
15 διαιτᾶται, καὶ θύρης καταπακτῆς διὰ τῶν ἰκρίων κάτω φερούσης ἐς τὴν λίμνην. τὰ δὲ νήπια παιδία δέουσι τοῦ ποδὸς σπάρτῳ, μὴ κατακυλισθῇ δειμαίνοντες. τοῖσι δὲ ἵπποισι καὶ τοῖσι ὑποζυγίοισι παρέχουσι χόρτον ἰχθῦς. τῶν δὲ πλῆθός ἐστι
20 τοσοῦτο, ὥστε ὅταν τὴν θύρην τὴν καταπακτὴν ἀνακλίνῃ, κατίει σχοίνῳ σπυρίδα κεινὴν ἐς τὴν λίμνην, καὶ οὐ πολλόν τινα χρόνον ἐπισχὼν ἀνασπᾷ πλήρεα ἰχθύων. τῶν δὲ ἰχθύων ἐστὶ γένεα δύο, τοὺς καλέουσι πάπρακάς τε καὶ τίλωνας.

Megabazus then sends to demand earth and water from the king of the Makedonians.

25 XVII. Παιόνων μὲν δὴ οἱ χειρωθέντες ἤγοντο ἐς τὴν Ἀσίην, Μεγάβαζος δὲ ὡς ἐχειρώσατο τοὺς

Παίονας, πέμπει ἀγγέλους ἐς Μακεδονίην ἄνδρας
ἑπτὰ Πέρσας, οἳ μετ' αὐτὸν ἐκεῖνον ἦσαν δοκιμώ-
τατοι ἐν τῷ στρατοπέδῳ. ἐπέμποντο δὲ οὗτοι παρὰ
Ἀμύντην αἰτήσοντες γῆν τε καὶ ὕδωρ Δαρείῳ
βασιλέϊ. ἔστι δὲ ἐκ τῆς Πρασιάδος λίμνης σύντομος
κάρτα ἐς τὴν Μακεδονίην. πρῶτα μὲν γὰρ ἔχεται
τῆς λίμνης τὸ μέταλλον, ἐξ οὗ ὕστερον τούτων
τάλαντον ἀργυρίου Ἀλεξάνδρῳ ἡμέρης ἑκάστης
ἐφοίτα, μετὰ δὲ τὸ μέταλλον Δύσωρον καλεόμενον
οὖρος ὑπερβάντα εἶναι ἐν Μακεδονίῃ.

Misconduct of the Persian envoys at the table of king Amyntas.

XVIII. Οἱ ὦν Πέρσαι οἱ πεμφθέντες οὗτοι
παρὰ τὸν Ἀμύντην ὡς ἀπίκοντο, αἴτεον ἐλθόντες ἐς
ὄψιν τὴν Ἀμύντεω Δαρείῳ βασιλέϊ γῆν τε καὶ ὕδωρ.
ὁ δὲ ταῦτά τε ἐδίδου καὶ σφεας ἐπὶ ξείνια καλέει,
παρασκευασάμενος δὲ δεῖπνον μεγαλοπρεπὲς ἐδέκετο
τοὺς Πέρσας φιλοφρόνως. ὡς δὲ ἀπὸ δείπνου ἐγένοντο, διαπίνοντες εἶπαν οἱ Πέρσαι τάδε· "Ξεῖνε
"Μακεδὼν, ἡμῖν νόμος ἐστὶ τοῖσι Πέρσῃσι, ἐπεὰν
"δεῖπνον προτιθώμεθα μέγα, τότε καὶ τὰς παλλακὰς
"καὶ τὰς κουριδίας γυναῖκας ἐσάγεσθαι παρέδρους·
"σύ νυν, ἐπεί περ προθύμως μὲν ἐδέξαο, μεγάλως δὲ
"ξεινίζεις, διδοῖς τε βασιλέϊ Δαρείῳ γῆν τε καὶ ὕδωρ,
"ἕπεο νόμῳ τῷ ἡμετέρῳ." Εἶπε πρὸς ταῦτα Ἀμύν-
της· "Ὦ Πέρσαι, νόμος μὲν ἡμῖν γέ ἐστι οὐκ οὗτος,
"ἀλλὰ κεχωρίσθαι ἄνδρας γυναικῶν· ἐπείτε δὲ
"ὑμεῖς ἐόντες δεσπόται προσχρηΐζετε τούτων, παρέσ-
"ται ὑμῖν καὶ ταῦτα." εἴπας τοσαῦτα ὁ Ἀμύντης
μετεπέμψατο τὰς γυναῖκας. αἱ δ' ἐπείτε καλεόμεναι

ἦλθον, ἐπεξῆς ἀντίαι ἵζοντο τοῖσι Πέρσῃσι. ἐνθαῦτα οἱ Πέρσαι ἰδόμενοι γυναῖκας εὐμόρφους ἔλεγον
πρὸς Ἀμύντην φάμενοι "τὸ ποιηθὲν τοῦτο οὐδὲν εἶναι
"σοφόν· κρέσσον γὰρ εἶναι ἀρχῆθεν μὴ ἐλθεῖν τὰς
5 "γυναῖκας ἢ ἐλθούσας καὶ μὴ παριζομένας ἀντίας
"ἵζεσθαι ἀλγηδόνας σφι ὀφθαλμῶν." ἀναγκαζόμενος
δὲ ὁ Ἀμύντης ἐκέλευε παρίζειν· πειθομένων δὲ τῶν
γυναικῶν αὐτίκα οἱ Πέρσαι μαστῶν τε ἅπτοντο, οἷα
πλεόνως οἰνωμένοι, καί κού τις καὶ φιλέειν ἐπειρᾶτο.

*The revenge of Alexander, son of Amyntas. The Persians
are killed.*

10   XIX. Ἀμύντης μὲν δὴ ταῦτα ὁρέων ἀτρέμας
εἶχε, καίπερ δυσφορέων, οἷα ὑπερδειμαίνων τοὺς
Πέρσας, Ἀλέξανδρος δὲ ὁ Ἀμύντεω παρεών τε καὶ
ὁρέων ταῦτα, ἅτε νέος τε ἐὼν καὶ κακῶν ἀπαθὴς,
οὐδαμῶς ἔτι κατέχειν οἷός τε ἦν, ὥστε δὲ βαρέως
15 φέρων εἶπε πρὸς Ἀμύντην τάδε· "Σὺ μὲν, ὦ πάτερ,
"εἶκε τῇ ἡλικίῃ, ἀπιών τε ἀναπαύεο, μηδὲ λιπάρεε
"τῇ πόσι, ἐγὼ δὲ προσμένων αὐτοῦ τῇδε πάντα τὰ
"ἐπιτήδεα παρέξω τοῖσι ξείνοισι." Πρὸς ταῦτα
συνεὶς ὁ Ἀμύντης, ὅτι νεώτερα πρήγματα πρήξειν
20 μέλλοι Ἀλέξανδρος, λέγει· "Ὦ παῖ, σχεδὸν γάρ σευ
"ἀνακαιομένου συνίημι τοὺς λόγους, ὅτι ἐθέλεις ἐμὲ
"ἐκπέμψας ποιέειν τι νεώτερον· ἐγὼ ὦν σευ χρηΐζω
"μηδὲν νεοχμῶσαι κατ' ἄνδρας τούτους, ἵνα μὴ
"ἐξεργάσῃ ἡμέας, ἀλλὰ ἀνέχεο ὁρέων τὰ ποιεύμενα·
25 "ἀμφὶ δὲ ἀπόδῳ τῇ ἐμῇ πείσομαί τοι." XX. Ὡς
δὲ ὁ Ἀμύντης χρηΐσας τούτων οἰχώκεε, λέγει ὁ
Ἀλέξανδρος πρὸς τοὺς Πέρσας· "Γυναικῶν τούτων,
"ὦ ξεῖνοι, πολλή ἐστι ὑμῖν εὐπέτεια, καὶ εἰ πάσῃσι

"βούλεσθε μίσγεσθαι καὶ ὁκοσῃσιῶν αὐτέων. τού-
"του μὲν πέρι αὐτοὶ ἀποσημανέετε· νῦν δὲ, σχεδὸν
"γὰρ ἤδη τῆς κοίτης ὥρη προσέρχεται ὑμῖν καὶ
"καλῶς ἔχοντας ὑμέας ὁρέω μέθης, γυναῖκας ταύτας,
"εἰ ὑμῖν φίλον ἐστὶ, ἄπετε λούσασθαι, λουσαμένας 5
"δὲ ὀπίσω προσδέκεσθε." εἴπας ταῦτα, συνέπαινοι
γὰρ ἦσαν οἱ Πέρσαι, γυναῖκας μὲν ἐξελθούσας ἀπέπεμπε ἐς τὴν γυναικηΐην, αὐτὸς δὲ ὁ Ἀλέξανδρος
ἴσους τῇσι γυναιξὶ ἀριθμὸν ἄνδρας λειογενείους τῇ
τῶν γυναικῶν ἐσθῆτι σκευάσας καὶ ἐγχειρίδια δοὺς 10
παρῆγε ἔσω, παράγων δὲ τούτους ἔλεγε τοῖσι Πέρσῃσι τάδε· "Ὦ Πέρσαι, οἴκατε πανδαισίῃ τελέῃ
"ἱστιῆσθαι· τά τε γὰρ ἄλλα, ὅσα εἴχομεν, καὶ πρὸς
"τὰ οἷά τε ἦν ἐξευρόντας παρέχειν, πάντα ὑμῖν
"πάρεστι, καὶ δὴ καὶ τόδε τὸ πάντων μέγιστον, τάς 15
"τε ἑωυτῶν μητέρας καὶ τὰς ἀδελφεὰς ἐπιδαψιλευό-
"μεθα ὑμῖν, ὡς παντελέως μάθητε τιμεόμενοι πρὸς
"ἡμέων τῶν πέρ ἐστε ἄξιοι, πρὸς δὲ καὶ βασιλέϊ τῷ
"πέμψαντι ἀπαγγείλητε, ὡς ἀνὴρ Ἕλλην Μακεδόνων
"ὕπαρχος εὖ ὑμέας ἐδέξατο καὶ τραπέζῃ καὶ κοίτῃ." 20
ταῦτα εἴπας Ἀλέξανδρος παρίζει Πέρσῃ ἀνδρὶ ἄνδρα
Μακεδόνα ὡς γυναῖκα τῷ λόγῳ· οἱ δὲ, ἐπεί τέ σφεων
οἱ Πέρσαι ψαύειν ἐπειρῶντο, διεργάζοντο αὐτούς.

The matter is hushed up.

XXI. Καὶ οὗτοι μὲν τούτῳ τῷ μόρῳ διεφθάρησαν,
καὶ αὐτοὶ καὶ ἡ θεραπηΐη αὐτῶν· εἵπετο γὰρ δή σφι 25
καὶ ὀχήματα καὶ θεράποντες καὶ ἡ πᾶσα πολλὴ
παρασκευή· πάντα δὴ ταῦτα ἅμα πᾶσι ἐκείνοισι
ἠφάνιστο. μετὰ δὲ, χρόνῳ οὐ πολλῷ ὕστερον,
ζήτησις τῶν ἀνδρῶν τούτων μεγάλη ἐκ τῶν Περσέων

ἐγίνετο, καί σφεας Ἀλέξανδρος κατέλαβε σοφίῃ,
χρήματά τε δοὺς πολλὰ καὶ τὴν ἑωυτοῦ ἀδελφεήν,
τῇ οὔνομα ἦν Γυγαίη· δοὺς δὲ ταῦτα κατέλαβε ὁ
Ἀλέξανδρος Βουβάρῃ ἀνδρὶ Πέρσῃ, τῶν διζημένων
5 τοὺς ἀπολομένους τῷ στρατηγῷ. ὁ μέν νυν τῶν
Περσέων τούτων θάνατος οὕτω καταλαμφθεὶς ἐσιγήθη.

The Hellenic descent of the house of Perdiccas.

XXII. Ἕλληνας δὲ εἶναι τούτους τοὺς ἀπὸ
Περδίκκεω γεγονότας, κατά περ αὐτοὶ λέγουσι,
10 αὐτός τε οὕτω τυγχάνω ἐπιστάμενος, καὶ δὴ καὶ ἐν
τοῖσι ὄπισθε λόγοισι ἀποδέξω, ὥς εἰσι Ἕλληνες,
πρὸς δὲ καὶ οἱ τὸν ἐν Ὀλυμπίῃ διέποντες ἀγῶνα
Ἑλληνοδίκαι οὕτω ἔγνωσαν εἶναι. Ἀλεξάνδρου γὰρ
ἀεθλεύειν ἑλομένου καὶ καταβάντος ἐπ' αὐτὸ τοῦτο
15 οἱ ἀντιθευσόμενοι Ἑλλήνων ἔξεργόν μιν, φάμενοι οὐ
βαρβάρων ἀγωνιστέων εἶναι τὸν ἀγῶνα, ἀλλὰ Ἑλλήνων. Ἀλέξανδρος δὲ ἐπειδὴ ἀπέδεξε, ὡς εἴη Ἀργεῖος,
ἐκρίθη τε εἶναι Ἕλλην, καὶ ἀγωνιζόμενος στάδιον
συνεξέπιπτε τῷ πρώτῳ. ταῦτα μέν νυν οὕτω κῃ
20 ἐγένετο.

Megabazus warns Darius of the dangerous designs of
Histiaios at Myrkinos.

XXIII. Μεγάβαζος δὲ ἄγων τοὺς Παίονας
ἀπίκετο ἐπὶ τὸν Ἑλλήσποντον, ἐνθεῦτεν δὲ διαπε-
ραιωθεὶς ἀπίκετο ἐς Σάρδις. ἄτε δὲ τειχέοντος ἤδη
Ἱστιαίου τοῦ Μιλησίου τὴν παρὰ Δαρείου αἰτήσας
25 ἔτυχε δωρεὴν μισθὸν φυλακῆς τῆς σχεδίης, ἐόντος
δὲ τοῦ χώρου τούτου παρὰ Στρυμόνα ποταμόν, τῷ

οὔνομά ἐστι Μύρκινος, μαθὼν ὁ Μεγάβαζος τὸ
ποιεύμενον ἐκ τοῦ Ἱστιαίου, ὡς ἦλθε τάχιστα ἐς
τὰς Σάρδις ἄγων τοὺς Παίονας, ἔλεγε Δαρείῳ τάδε·
"Ὦ βασιλεῦ, κοῖόν τι χρῆμα ἐποίησας, ἀνδρὶ Ἕλ-
"ληνι δεινῷ τε καὶ σοφῷ δοὺς ἐγκτήσασθαι πόλιν 5
"ἐν Θρηίκῃ, ἵνα ἴδη τε ναυπηγήσιμός ἐστι ἄφθονος
"καὶ πολλοὶ κωπέες καὶ μέταλλα ἀργύρεα, ὅμιλός
"τε πολλὸς μὲν Ἕλλην περιοικέει, πολλὸς δὲ
"βάρβαρος, οἳ προστάτεω ἐπιλαβόμενοι ποιήσουσι
"τοῦτο, τὸ ἂν ἐκεῖνος ἐξηγέηται καὶ ἡμέρης καὶ 10
"νυκτός; σύ νυν τοῦτον τὸν ἄνδρα παῦσον ταῦτα
"ποιεῦντα, ἵνα μὴ οἰκηΐῳ πολέμῳ συνέχῃ· τρόπῳ δὲ
"ἠπίῳ μεταπεμψάμενος παῦσον· ἐπεὰν δὲ αὐτὸν
"περιλάβῃς, ποιέειν, ὅκως μηκέτι ἐκεῖνος ἐς Ἕλληνας
"ἀπίξεται." 15

Histiaios is sent for to Sardis, and taken to Susa.

XXIV. Ταῦτα λέγων ὁ Μεγάβαζος εὐπετέως
ἔπειθε Δαρεῖον, ὡς εὖ προορέων τὸ μέλλον γίνεσθαι.
μετὰ δὲ ἄγγελον πέμψας ὁ Δαρεῖος ἐς τὴν Μύρκινον
ἔλεγε τάδε· "Ἱστιαῖε, βασιλεὺς Δαρεῖος τάδε λέγει·
"ἐγὼ φροντίζων εὑρίσκω ἐμοί τε καὶ τοῖσι ἐμοῖσι 20
"πρήγμασι οὐδένα εἶναι σεῦ ἄνδρα εὐνοέστερον,
"τοῦτο δὲ οὐ λόγοισι, ἀλλ' ἔργοισι οἶδα μαθών.
"νῦν ὦν, ἐπινοέω γὰρ πρήγματα μεγάλα κατεργά-
"σασθαι, ἀπίκεό μοι πάντως, ἵνα τοι αὐτὰ ὑπερ-
"θέωμαι." τούτοισι τοῖσι ἔπεσι πιστεύσας ὁ Ἱσ- 25
τιαῖος, καὶ ἅμα μέγα ποιεύμενος βασιλέος σύμβουλος
γενέσθαι, ἀπίκετο ἐς τὰς Σάρδις. ἀπικομένῳ δέ οἱ
ἔλεγε Δαρεῖος τάδε· "Ἱστιαῖε, ἐγώ σε μετεπεμ-
"ψάμην τῶνδε εἵνεκεν· ἐπεί τε τάχιστα ἐνόστησα

"ἀπὸ Σκυθέων καὶ σύ μοι ἐγένεο ἐξ ὀφθαλμῶν, οὐδέν
"κω ἄλλο χρῆμα οὕτω ἐν βραχέϊ ἐπεζήτησα, ὡς σὲ
"ἰδεῖν τε καὶ ἐς λόγους μοι ἀπικέσθαι, ἐγνωκὼς ὅτι
"κτημάτων πάντων ἐστὶ τιμιώτατον ἀνὴρ φίλος συνε-
5 "τός τε καὶ εὔνοος, τά τοι ἐγὼ καὶ ἀμφότερα συνειδὼς
"ἔχω μαρτυρέειν ἐς πρήγματα τὰ ἐμά. νῦν ὦν, εὖ
"γὰρ ἐποίησας ἀπικόμενος, τάδε τοι ἐγὼ προτείνομαι·
"Μίλητον μὲν ἔα καὶ τὴν νεόκτιστον ἐν Θρηίκῃ
"πόλιν, σὺ δέ μοι ἑπόμενος ἐς Σοῦσα ἔχε τά περ ἂν
10 "ἐγὼ ἔχω, ἐμός τε σύσσιτος ἐὼν καὶ σύμβουλος."

*Artaphernes is left at Sardis, and Otanes son of Sisannes
in command of the sea coast. The throne of justice.*

XXV. Ταῦτα Δαρεῖος εἴπας, καὶ καταστήσας
Ἀρταφέρνεα ἀδελφεὸν ἑωυτοῦ ὁμοπάτριον ὕπαρχον
εἶναι Σαρδίων, ἀπήλαυνε ἐς Σοῦσα ἅμα ἀγόμενος
Ἱστιαῖον, Ὀτάνεα δὲ ἀποδέξας στρατηγὸν εἶναι τῶν
15 παραθαλασσίων ἀνδρῶν, τοῦ τὸν πατέρα Σισάμνην
βασιλεὺς Καμβύσης γενόμενον τῶν βασιληίων δικα-
στέων, ὅτι ἐπὶ χρήμασι δίκην ἄδικον ἐδίκασε, σφάξας
ἀπέδειρε πᾶσαν τὴν ἀνθρωπηίην, σπαδίξας δὲ αὐτοῦ
τὸ δέρμα ἱμάντας ἐξ αὐτοῦ ἔταμε καὶ ἐνέτεινε τὸν
20 θρόνον, ἐς τὸν ἵζων ἐδίκαζε· ἐντανύσας δὲ ὁ Καμβύσης
ἀπέδεξε δικαστὴν εἶναι ἀντὶ τοῦ Σισάμνεω, τὸν ἀπο-
κτείνας ἀπέδειρε, τὸν παῖδα τοῦ Σισάμνεω, ἐντειλά-
μενός οἱ μεμνῆσθαι, ἐν τῷ κατίζων θρόνῳ δικάζει.

Otanes takes various towns and islands.

XXVI. Οὗτος ὦν ὁ Ὀτάνης, ὁ ἐγκατιζόμενος ἐς
25 τοῦτον τὸν θρόνον, τότε διάδοχος γενόμενος Μεγαβάζῳ
τῆς στρατηγίης Βυζαντίους τε εἷλε καὶ Καλχηδονίους,

εἷλε δὲ Ἄντανδρον τὴν ἐν τῇ Τρῳάδι γῇ, εἷλε δὲ Λαμπώνιον, λαβὼν δὲ παρὰ Λεσβίων νέας εἷλε Λῆμνόν τε καὶ Ἴμβρον, ἀμφοτέρας ἔτι τότε ὑπὸ Πελασγῶν οἰκεομένας. XXVII. Οἱ μὲν δὴ Λήμνιοι καὶ ἐμαχέσαντο εὖ καὶ ἀμυνόμενοι ἀνὰ χρόνον ἐκακώθησαν, τοῖσι δὲ περιεοῦσι αὐτῶν οἱ Πέρσαι ὕπαρχον ἐπιστᾶσι Λυκάρητον τὸν Μαιανδρίου τοῦ βασιλεύσαντος Σάμου ἀδελφεόν. οὗτος ὁ Λυκάρητος ἄρχων ἐν Λήμνῳ τελευτᾷ. αἰτίη δὲ τούτου ἥδε· πάντας ἠνδραποδίζετο καὶ κατεστρέφετο, τοὺς μὲν λιποστρατίης ἐπὶ Σκύθας αἰτιώμενος, τοὺς δὲ σίνεσθαι τὸν Δαρείου στρατὸν τὸν ἀπὸ Σκυθέων ὀπίσω ἀποκομιζόμενον.

After a period of repose, troubles again break out at Naxos and Miletos which eventually involve the Ionians.

XXVIII. Οὗτος μέν νυν τοσαῦτα ἐξεργάσατο στρατηγήσας. μετὰ δὲ οὐ πολλὸν χρόνον ἄνεσις κακῶν ἦν· καὶ ἤρχετο τὸ δεύτερον ἐκ Νάξου τε καὶ Μιλήτου Ἴωσι γίνεσθαι κακά. τοῦτο μὲν γὰρ ἡ Νάξος εὐδαιμονίῃ τῶν νήσων προέφερε, τοῦτο δὲ κατὰ τὸν αὐτὸν χρόνον ἡ Μίλητος αὐτή τε ἑωυτῆς μάλιστα δὴ τότε ἀκμάσασα, καὶ δὴ καὶ τῆς Ἰωνίης ἦν πρόσχημα, κατύπερθε δὲ τούτων ἐπὶ δύο γενεὰς ἀνδρῶν νοσήσασα ἐς τὰ μάλιστα στάσι, μέχρι οὗ μιν Πάριοι κατήρτισαν· τούτους γὰρ καταρτιστῆρας ἐκ πάντων Ἑλλήνων εἵλοντο οἱ Μιλήσιοι.

The award of the Parian arbitrators in the former civil broils at Miletos.

XXIX. Κατήλλαξαν δέ σφεας ὧδε οἱ Πάριοι· ὡς ἀπίκοντο αὐτῶν ἄνδρες οἱ ἄριστοι ἐς τὴν Μίλητον,

ὤρεον γὰρ δή σφεας δεινῶς οἰκοφθορημένους, ἔφασαν
αὐτῶν βούλεσθαι διεξελθεῖν τὴν χώρην. ποιεῦντες
δὲ ταῦτα καὶ διεξιόντες πᾶσαν τὴν Μιλησίην, ὅκως
τινὰ ἴδοιεν ἐν ἀνεστηκυίῃ τῇ χώρῃ ἀγρὸν εὖ ἐξερ-
γασμένον, ἀπεγράφοντο τὸ οὔνομα τοῦ δεσπότεω τοῦ
ἀγροῦ. διεξελάσαντες δὲ πᾶσαν τὴν χώρην καὶ
σπανίους εὑρόντες τούτους, ὡς τάχιστα κατέβησαν
ἐς τὸ ἄστυ, ἁλίην ποιησάμενοι ἀπέδεξαν τούτους μὲν
τὴν πόλιν νέμειν, τῶν εὗρον τοὺς ἀγροὺς εὖ ἐξεργασ-
μένους· δοκέειν γὰρ ἔφασαν καὶ τῶν δημοσίων οὕτω
δή σφεας ἐπιμελήσεσθαι, ὥσπερ τῶν σφετέρων· τοὺς
δὲ ἄλλους Μιλησίους τοὺς πρὶν στασιάζοντας τούτων
ἔταξαν πείθεσθαι.

B.C. 502. *The expelled oligarchs from Naxos take refuge in Miletos and are received by Aristagoras, son-in-law of Histiaios; who offers to get them the support of Artaphernes.*

XXX. Πάριοι μέν νυν οὕτω Μιλησίους κατήρ-
τισαν· τότε δὲ ἐκ τούτων τῶν πολίων ὧδε ἤρχετο
κακὰ γίνεσθαι τῇ Ἰωνίῃ. ἐκ Νάξου ἔφυγον ἄνδρες
τῶν παχέων ὑπὸ τοῦ δήμου, φυγόντες δὲ ἀπίκοντο ἐς
Μίλητον. τῆς δὲ Μιλήτου ἐτύγχανε ἐπίτροπος ἐὼν
Ἀρισταγόρης ὁ Μολπαγόρεω, γαμβρός τε ἐὼν καὶ
ἀνεψιὸς Ἱστιαίου τοῦ Λυσαγόρεω, τὸν ὁ Δαρεῖος ἐν
Σούσοισι κατεῖχε. ὁ γὰρ Ἱστιαῖος τύραννος ἦν
Μιλήτου, καὶ ἐτύγχανε τοῦτον τὸν χρόνον ἐὼν ἐν
Σούσοισι, ὅτε οἱ Νάξιοι ἦλθον, ξεῖνοι πρὶν ἐόντες τῷ
Ἱστιαίῳ. ἀπικόμενοι δὲ οἱ Νάξιοι ἐς τὴν Μίλητον
ἐδέοντο τοῦ Ἀρισταγόρεω, εἴ κως αὐτοῖσι παράσχοι
δύναμίν τινα καὶ κατέλθοιεν ἐς τὴν ἑωυτῶν. ὁ δὲ

ἐπιλεξάμενος, ὡς, ἢν δι' ἑωυτοῦ κατέλθωσι ἐς τὴν
πόλιν, ἄρξει τῆς Νάξου, σκῆψιν δὲ ποιεύμενος τὴν
ξεινίην τὴν Ἱστιαίου, τόνδε σφι τὸν λόγον προσέφερε·
" Αὐτὸς μὲν ὑμῖν οὐ φερέγγυός εἰμι δύναμιν τοσαύτην
" παρασχεῖν ὥστε κατάγειν ἀεκόντων τῶν τὴν πόλιν 5
" ἐχόντων Ναξίων· πυνθάνομαι γὰρ ὀκτακισχιλίην
" ἀσπίδα Ναξίοισι εἶναι καὶ πλοῖα μακρὰ πολλά·
" μηχανήσομαι δὲ πᾶσαν σπουδὴν ποιεύμενος· ἐπι-
" νοέω δὲ τῇδε. Ἀρταφέρνης μοι τυγχάνει ἐὼν φίλος,
" ὁ δὲ Ἀρταφέρνης Ὑστάσπεος μέν ἐστι παῖς, Δαρείου 10
" δὲ τοῦ βασιλέος ἀδελφεός, τῶν δ' ἐπιθαλασσίων
" τῶν ἐν τῇ Ἀσίῃ ἄρχει πάντων, ἔχων στρατιήν τε
" πολλὴν καὶ πολλὰς νέας. τοῦτον ὦν δοκέω τὸν
" ἄνδρα ποιήσειν τῶν ἂν χρηίζωμεν." Ταῦτα ἀκούσαντες οἱ Νάξιοι προσέθεσαν τῷ Ἀρισταγόρῃ πρήσ- 15
σειν τῇ δύναιτο ἄριστα, καὶ ὑπίσχεσθαι δῶρα ἐκέλευον καὶ δαπάνην τῇ στρατιῇ, ὡς αὐτοὶ διαλύσοντες,
ἐλπίδας πολλὰς ἔχοντες, ὅταν ἐπιφανέωσι ἐς τὴν
Νάξον, πάντα ποιήσειν τοὺς Ναξίους τὰ ἂν αὐτοὶ
κελεύωσι, ὡς δὲ καὶ τοὺς ἄλλους νησιώτας· τῶν γὰρ 20
νήσων τούτων τῶν Κυκλάδων οὐδεμία κω ἦν ὑπὸ
Δαρείῳ.

Artaphernes consents to furnish 200 ships to restore the Naxian exiles.

XXXI. Ἀπικόμενος δὲ ὁ Ἀρισταγόρης ἐς τὰς
Σάρδις λέγει πρὸς τὸν Ἀρταφέρνεα, ὡς Νάξος εἴη
νῆσος μεγάθεϊ μὲν οὐ μεγάλη, ἄλλως δὲ καλή τε καὶ 25
ἀγαθὴ καὶ ἀγχοῦ Ἰωνίης, χρήματα δὲ ἔνι πολλὰ καὶ
ἀνδράποδα. " Σὺ ὦν ἐπὶ ταύτην τὴν χώρην στρατη-
" λάτεε, κατάγων ἐς αὐτὴν τοὺς φυγάδας ἐξ αὐτῆς.

"καί τοι ταῦτα ποιήσαντι τοῦτο μὲν ἐστι ἑτοῖμα
"παρ' ἐμοὶ χρήματα μεγάλα πάρεξ τῶν ἀναισιμω-
"μάτων τῇ στρατιῇ (ταῦτα μὲν γὰρ δίκαια ἡμέας
"τοὺς ἄγοντας παρέχειν), τοῦτο δὲ νήσους βασιλέϊ
5 "προσκτήσεαι αὐτήν τε Νάξον καὶ τὰς ἐκ ταύτης
"ἠρτημένας, Πάρον καὶ Ἄνδρον καὶ ἄλλας τὰς
"Κυκλάδας καλευμένας. ἐνθεῦτεν δὲ ὁρμεόμενος
"εὐπετέως ἐπιθήσεαι Εὐβοίῃ, νήσῳ μεγάλῃ τε καὶ
"εὐδαίμονι, οὐκ ἐλάσσονι Κύπρου καὶ κάρτα εὐπετέϊ
10 "αἱρεθῆναι. ἀποχρέουσι δὲ ἑκατὸν νέες ταύτας
"πάσας χειρώσασθαι." Ὁ δὲ ἀμείβετο αὐτὸν τοι-
σίδε· "Σὺ ἐς οἶκον τὸν βασιλέος ἐξηγητὴς γίνεαι
"πρηγμάτων ἀγαθῶν, καὶ ταῦτα εὖ παραινέεις πάντα,
"πλὴν τῶν νεῶν τοῦ ἀριθμοῦ. ἀντὶ δὲ ἑκατὸν νεῶν
15 "διηκόσιαί τοι ἑτοῖμοι ἔσονται ἅμα τῷ ἔαρι. δέει δὲ
"τούτοισι καὶ αὐτὸν βασιλέα συνέπαινον γίνεσθαι."

The king approves, and the fleet is prepared under the command of Megabates.

XXXII. Ὁ μὲν δὴ Ἀρισταγόρης ὡς ταῦτα ἤκουσε, περιχαρὴς ἐὼν ἀπῄιε ἐς Μίλητον, ὁ δὲ Ἀρταφέρνης, ὥς οἱ πέμψαντι ἐς Σοῦσα καὶ ὑπερ-
20 θέντι τὰ ἐκ τοῦ Ἀρισταγόρεω λεγόμενα συνέπαινος καὶ αὐτὸς Δαρεῖος ἐγένετο, παρεσκευάσατο μὲν διηκοσίας τριήρεας, πολλὸν δὲ κάρτα ὅμιλον Περσέων τε καὶ τῶν ἄλλων συμμάχων, στρατηγὸν δὲ τούτων ἀπέδεξε Μεγαβάτην ἄνδρα Πέρσην τῶν Ἀχαιμενι-
25 δέων, ἑωυτοῦ τε καὶ Δαρείου ἀνεψιόν, τοῦ Παυσανίης ὁ Κλεομβρότου Λακεδαιμόνιος, εἰ δὴ ἀληθής γέ ἐστι ὁ λόγος, ὑστέρῳ χρόνῳ τούτων ἡρμόσατο θυγατέρα, ἔρωτα σχὼν τῆς Ἑλλάδος τύραννος γενέσθαι. ἀπο-

δέξας δὲ Μεγαβάτην στρατηγὸν Ἀρταφέρνης ἀπέστειλε τὸν στρατὸν παρὰ τὸν Ἀρισταγόρην.

Megabates and Aristagoras quarrel. The former warns the Naxians, who accordingly prepare to resist.

XXXIII. Παραλαβὼν δὲ ὁ Μεγαβάτης ἐκ τῆς Μιλήτου τόν τε Ἀρισταγόρην καὶ τὴν Ἰάδα στρατιὴν καὶ τοὺς Ναξίους ἔπλεε πρόφασιν ἐπ᾽ Ἑλλησπόντου, ἐπείτε δὲ ἐγένετο ἐν Χίῳ, ἔσχε τὰς νέας ἐς Καύκασα, ὡς ἐνθεῦτεν βορέῃ ἀνέμῳ ἐς τὴν Νάξον διαβάλοι. καὶ οὐ γὰρ ἔδεε τούτῳ τῷ στόλῳ Ναξίους ἀπολέσθαι, πρῆγμα τοιόνδε συνηνείχθη γενέσθαι· περιιόντος Μεγαβάτεω τὰς ἐπὶ τῶν νεῶν φυλακὰς ἐπὶ νεὸς Μυνδίης ἔτυχε οὐδεὶς φυλάσσων· ὁ δὲ δεινόν τι ποιησάμενος ἐκέλευσε τοὺς δορυφόρους ἐξευρόντας τὸν ἄρχοντα ταύτης τῆς νεός, τῷ οὔνομα ἦν Σκύλαξ, τοῦτον δῆσαι διὰ θαλαμίης διελόντας τῆς νεὸς κατὰ τοῦτο, ἔξω μὲν κεφαλὴν ποιεῦντας, ἔσω δὲ τὸ σῶμα. δεθέντος δὲ τοῦ Σκύλακος ἐξαγγέλλει τις τῷ Ἀρισταγόρῃ, ὅτι τὸν ξεῖνόν οἱ τὸν Μύνδιον Μεγαβάτης δήσας λυμαίνοιτο. ὁ δ᾽ ἐλθὼν παραιτέετο τὸν Πέρσην, τυγχάνων δὲ οὐδενὸς τῶν ἐδέετο αὐτὸς ἐλθὼν ἔλυσε. πυθόμενος δὲ κάρτα δεινὸν ἐποιήσατο ὁ Μεγαβάτης, καὶ ἐσπέρχετο τῷ Ἀρισταγόρῃ. ὁ δὲ εἶπε· "Σοὶ δὲ καὶ τούτοισι τοῖσι πρήγμασι τί "ἐστι; οὔ σε ἀπέστειλε Ἀρταφέρνης ἐμέο πείθεσθαι "καὶ πλέειν τῇ ἂν ἐγὼ κελεύω; τί πολλὰ πρήσ- "σεις;" Ταῦτα εἶπε Ἀρισταγόρης. ὁ δὲ θυμωθεὶς τούτοισι, ὡς νὺξ ἐγένετο, ἔπεμπε ἐς Νάξον πλοίῳ ἄνδρας φράσοντας τοῖσι Ναξίοισι πάντα τὰ παρεόντα σφι πρήγματα. XXXIV. Οἱ γὰρ ὦν Νάξιοι οὐδὲν πάντως προσεδέκοντο ἐπὶ σφέας τὸν στόλον τοῦτον ὁρμήσεσθαι. ἐπεὶ μέντοι ἐπύθοντο, αὐτίκα μὲν ἐσηνείκαντο τὰ ἐκ τῶν ἀγρῶν ἐς τὸ τεῖχος, παρεσκευάσαντο δὲ ὡς πολιορκησόμενοι, καὶ σῖτα καὶ ποτὰ κατὰ τάχος ἐσάξαντο. Καὶ οὗτοι μὲν παρεσκευάδατο ὡς παρεσομένου σφι πολέμου, οἱ δ' ἐπείτε διέβαλον ἐκ τῆς Χίου τὰς νέας ἐς τὴν Νάξον, πρὸς πεφραγμένους προσεφέροντο καὶ ἐπολιόρκεον μῆνας τέσσερας. ὡς δὲ τά τε ἔχοντες ἦλθον χρήματα οἱ Πέρσαι, ταῦτα καταδεδαπάνητό σφι, καὶ αὐτῷ τῷ Ἀρισταγόρῃ προσαναισίμωτο πολλά, τοῦ πλεῦνός τε ἐδέετο ἡ πολιορκίη, ἐνθαῦτα τείχεα τοῖσι φυγάσι τῶν Ναξίων οἰκοδομήσαντες ἀπαλλάσσοντο ἐς τὴν ἤπειρον, κακῶς πρήσσοντες.

Aristagoras, failing to put Naxos in the power of the king, meditates a revolt, and is encouraged to provoke one by a message from Histiaios.

XXXV. Ἀρισταγόρης δὲ οὐκ εἶχε τὴν ὑπόσχεσιν τῷ Ἀρταφέρνεϊ ἐκπληρῶσαι· ἅμα δὲ ἐπίεζέ μιν ἡ δαπάνη τῆς στρατιῆς ἀπαιτεομένη, ἀρρώδεέ τε τοῦ στρατοῦ πρήξαντος κακῶς καὶ Μεγαβάτῃ διαβεβλημένος, ἐδόκεέ τε τὴν βασιληΐην τῆς Μιλήτου ἀπαιρεθήσεσθαι. ἀρρωδέων δὲ τούτων ἕκαστα ἐβουλεύετο ἀπόστασιν. συνέπιπτε γὰρ καὶ τὸν ἐστιγμένον τὴν κεφαλὴν ἀπῖχθαι ἐκ Σούσων παρὰ Ἱστιαίου, σημαίνοντα ἀπίστασθαι Ἀρισταγόρῃ ἀπὸ βασιλέος. ὁ γὰρ Ἱστιαῖος βουλόμενος τῷ Ἀρισταγόρῃ σημῆναι ἀποστῆναι ἄλλως μὲν οὐδαμῶς εἶχε ἀσφαλέως σημῆναι ὥστε φυλασσομενέων τῶν ὁδῶν, ὁ δὲ τῶν δούλων τὸν πιστότατον ἀποξυρήσας τὴν

κεφαλὴν ἔστιξε καὶ ἀνέμεινε ἀναφῦναι τὰς τρίχας.
ὡς δὲ ἀνέφυσαν τάχιστα, ἀπέπεμπε ἐς Μίλητον
ἐντειλάμενος αὐτῷ ἄλλο μὲν οὐδέν, ἐπεὰν δὲ ἀπίκηται
ἐς Μίλητον, κελεύειν Ἀρισταγόρην ξυρήσαντά μιν
τὰς τρίχας κατιδέσθαι ἐς τὴν κεφαλήν· τὰ δὲ 5
στίγματα ἐσήμαινε, ὡς καὶ πρότερόν μοι εἴρηται,
ἀπόστασιν. ταῦτα δὲ ὁ Ἱστιαῖος ἐποίεε συμφορὴν
ποιεύμενος μεγάλην τὴν ἑωυτοῦ κατοχὴν τὴν ἐν
Σούσοισι· ἀποστάσιος ὦν γινομένης πολλὰς εἶχε
ἐλπίδας μετήσεσθαι ἐπὶ θάλασσαν, μὴ δὲ νεώτερόν 10
τι ποιεύσης τῆς Μιλήτου οὐδαμὰ ἐς αὐτὴν ἥξειν ἔτι
ἐλογίζετο.

*Aristagoras consults his friends. The prudent advice of
Hekataios is rejected.*

XXXVI. Ἱστιαῖος μέν νυν ταῦτα διανοεύμενος
ἀπέπεμπε τὸν ἄγγελον, Ἀρισταγόρῃ δὲ συνέπιπτε
τοῦ αὐτοῦ χρόνου πάντα ταῦτα συνελθόντα. ἐβου- 15
λεύετο ὦν μετὰ τῶν στασιωτέων, ἐκφήνας τήν τε
ἑωυτοῦ γνώμην καὶ τὰ παρὰ τοῦ Ἱστιαίου ἀπιγμένα.
οἱ μὲν δὴ ἄλλοι πάντες γνώμην κατὰ τὠυτὸ ἐξεφέ-
ροντο, κελεύοντες ἀπίστασθαι, Ἑκαταῖος δὲ ὁ λογο-
ποιὸς πρῶτα μὲν οὐκ ἔα πόλεμον βασιλέϊ τῶν 20
Περσέων ἀναιρέεσθαι, καταλέγων τά τε ἔθνεα πάντα,
τῶν ἦρχε Δαρεῖος, καὶ τὴν δύναμιν αὐτοῦ, ἐπείτε
δὲ οὐκ ἔπειθε, δεύτερα συνεβούλευε ποιέειν, ὅκως
ναυκρατέες τῆς θαλάσσης ἔσονται. ἄλλως μέν νυν
οὐδαμῶς ἔφη λέγων ἐνορᾶν ἐσόμενον τοῦτο (ἐπί- 25
στασθαι γὰρ τὴν δύναμιν τὴν Μιλησίων ἐοῦσαν
ἀσθενέα), εἰ δὲ τὰ χρήματα καταιρεθείη τὰ ἐκ τοῦ
ἱροῦ τοῦ ἐν Βραγχίδῃσι, τὰ Κροῖσος ὁ Λυδὸς ἀνέθηκε,

πολλὰς εἶχε ἐλπίδας ἐπικρατήσειν τῆς θαλάσσης,
καὶ οὕτω αὐτούς τε ἕξειν χρήμασι χρᾶσθαι καὶ τοὺς
πολεμίους οὐ συλήσειν αὐτά. τὰ δὲ χρήματα ἦν
ταῦτα μεγάλα, ὡς δεδήλωταί μοι ἐν τῷ πρώτῳ τῶν
5 λόγων. αὕτη μὲν δὴ οὐκ ἐνίκα ἡ γνώμη, ἐδόκεε δὲ
ὅμως ἀπίστασθαι, ἕνα τε αὐτῶν πλώσαντα ἐς
Μυοῦντα ἐς τὸ στρατόπεδον τὸ ἀπὸ τῆς Νάξου
ἀπελθὸν, ἐὸν ἐνθαῦτα, συλλαμβάνειν πειρᾶσθαι
τοὺς ἐπὶ τῶν νεῶν ἐπιπλέοντας στρατηγούς.

*The first step was to suppress the tyrants of the various
towns; all of whom are allowed by their subjects to
depart in safety, except Koes of Mytilene.*

10   XXXVII. Ἀποπεμφθέντος δὲ Ἰητραγόρεω κατ'
αὐτὸ τοῦτο καὶ συλλαβόντος δόλῳ Ὀλίατον Ἰβανώ-
λιος Μυλασέα καὶ Ἱστιαῖον Τύμνεω Τερμερέα καὶ
Κώην Ἐρξάνδρου, τῷ Δαρεῖος Μυτιλήνην ἐδωρήσατο,
καὶ Ἀρισταγόρην Ἡρακλείδεω Κυμαῖον καὶ ἄλλους
15 συχνούς, οὕτω δὴ ἐκ τοῦ ἐμφανέος ὁ Ἀρισταγόρης
ἀπεστήκεε, πᾶν ἐπὶ Δαρείῳ μηχανεόμενος. Καὶ
πρῶτα μὲν λόγῳ μετεὶς τὴν τυραννίδα ἰσονομίην
ἐποίεε τῇ Μιλήτῳ, ὡς ἂν ἑκόντες αὐτῷ οἱ Μιλήσιοι
συναπισταίατο, μετὰ δὲ καὶ ἐν τῇ ἄλλῃ Ἰωνίῃ τὠυτὸ
20 τοῦτο ἐποίεε, τοὺς μὲν ἐξελαύνων τῶν τυράννων, τοὺς
δ' ἔλαβε τυράννους ἀπὸ τῶν νεῶν τῶν συμπλωσα-
σέων ἐπὶ Νάξον, τούτους δὲ φίλα βουλόμενος ποιέεσθαι τῇσι πόλισι ἐξεδίδου, ἄλλον ἐς ἄλλην πόλιν
παραδιδούς, ὅθεν εἴη ἕκαστος. XXXVIII. Κώην
25 μέν νυν Μυτιληναῖοι ἐπεί τε τάχιστα παρέλαβον,
ἐξαγαγόντες κατέλευσαν, Κυμαῖοι δὲ τὸν σφέτερον
αὐτῶν ἀπῆκαν· ὡς δὲ καὶ ἄλλοι οἱ πλεῦνες ἀπίεσαν.

τυράννων μέν νυν κατάπαυσις ἐγένετο ἀνὰ τὰς
πόλιας, Ἀρισταγόρης δὲ ὁ Μιλήσιος ὡς τοὺς τυράννους κατέπαυσε, στρατηγοὺς ἐν ἑκάστῃ τῶν πολίων
κελεύσας ἑκάστους καταστῆσαι, δεύτερα αὐτὸς ἐς
Λακεδαίμονα τριήρεϊ ἀπόστολος ἐγίνετο· ἔδεε γὰρ 5
δὴ συμμαχίης τινός οἱ μεγάλης ἐξευρεθῆναι.

Sparta. The two wives of King Anaxandridas [B.C.
560—520]. *The second bore Kleomenes, and the first
then bore Dorieus, Leonidas and Kleombrotos.*

XXXIX. Τῆς δὲ Σπάρτης Ἀναξανδρίδης μὲν ὁ
Λέοντος οὐκέτι περιεὼν ἐβασίλευε, ἀλλὰ ἐτετελευ-
τήκεε, Κλεομένης δὲ ὁ Ἀναξανδρίδεω εἶχε τὴν βασιληίην, οὐ κατὰ ἀνδραγαθίην σχὼν, ἀλλὰ κατὰ γένος. 10
Ἀναξανδρίδῃ γὰρ ἔχοντι γυναῖκα ἀδελφεῆς ἑωυτοῦ
θυγατέρα καὶ ἐούσης ταύτης οἱ καταθυμίης παῖδες
οὐκ ἐγίνοντο. τούτου δὲ τοιούτου ἐόντος οἱ ἔφοροι
εἶπαν ἐπικαλεσάμενοι αὐτόν· "Εἴ τοι σύ γε σεωυτοῦ
"μὴ προορᾷς, ἀλλ' ἡμῖν τοῦτό ἐστι οὐ περιοπτέον, 15
"γένος τὸ Εὐρυσθένεος γενέσθαι ἐξίτηλον. σύ νυν
"τὴν μὲν ἔχεις γυναῖκα, ἐπεί τέ τοι οὐ τίκτει, ἔξεο,
"ἄλλην δὲ γῆμον· καὶ ποιέων ταῦτα Σπαρτιήτῃσι
"ἀδήσεις." Ὁ δ' ἀμείβετο φὰς τούτων οὐδέτερα
ποιήσειν, ἐκείνους τε οὐ καλῶς συμβουλεύειν παραι- 20
νέοντας, τὴν ἔχει γυναῖκα, ἐοῦσαν ἀναμάρτητον
ἑωυτῷ, ταύτην ἀπέντα ἄλλην ἐσαγαγέσθαι, οὐδέ σφι
πείσεσθαι. XL. Πρὸς ταῦτα οἱ ἔφοροι καὶ οἱ
γέροντες βουλευσάμενοι προσέφερον Ἀναξανδρίδῃ
τάδε· "Ἐπεὶ τοίνυν περιεχόμενόν σε ὀρέομεν τῆς 25
"ἔχεις γυναικός, σὺ δὲ ταῦτα ποίεε, καὶ μὴ ἀντίβαινε
"τούτοισι, ἵνα μή τι ἀλλοῖον περὶ σεῦ οἱ Σπαρ-

"τιῆται βουλεύσωνται. γυναικὸς μὲν τῆς ἔχεις οὐ
"προσδεόμεθά σευ τῆς ἐξέσιος, σὺ δὲ ταύτῃ τε
"πάντα, ὅσα νῦν παρέχεις, πάρεχε, καὶ ἄλλην πρὸς
"ταύτῃ ἐσάγαγε γυναῖκα τεκνοποιόν." ταῦτά κῃ
λεγόντων συνεχώρησε ὁ Ἀναξανδρίδης, μετὰ δὲ
γυναῖκας ἔχων δύο διξὰς ἱστίας οἴκεε, ποιέων οὐδαμῶς Σπαρτιητικά. XLI. Χρόνου δὲ οὐ πολλοῦ
διελθόντος ἡ ἐσύστερον ἐπελθοῦσα γυνὴ τίκτει τὸν
δὴ Κλεομένεα τοῦτον. καὶ αὕτη τε ἔπεδρον βασιλέα
Σπαρτιήτῃσι ἀπέφαινε, καὶ ἡ προτέρη γυνὴ τὸν
πρότερον χρόνον ἄτοκος ἐοῦσα τότε κως ἐκύησε,
συντυχίῃ ταύτῃ χρησαμένη. ἔχουσαν δὲ αὐτὴν
ἀληθέϊ λόγῳ οἱ τῆς ἐπελθούσης γυναικὸς οἰκήϊοι
πυθόμενοι ὤχλεον, φάμενοι αὐτὴν κομπέειν ἄλλως
βουλομένην ὑποβαλέσθαι. δεινὰ δὲ ποιεύντων
αὐτῶν, τοῦ χρόνου συντάμνοντος, ὑπ' ἀπιστίης οἱ
ἔφοροι τίκτουσαν τὴν γυναῖκα περιιζόμενοι ἐφύλαξαν. ἡ δὲ ὡς ἔτεκε Δωριέα, ἰθέως ἴσχει Λεωνίδην,
καὶ μετὰ τοῦτον ἰθέως ἴσχει Κλεόμβροτον· οἱ δὲ
καὶ διδύμους λέγουσι Κλεόμβροτόν τε καὶ Λεωνίδην
γενέσθαι. ἡ δὲ Κλεομένεα τεκοῦσα καὶ τὸ δεύτερον
ἐπελθοῦσα γυνή, ἐοῦσα θυγάτηρ Πρινητάδεω τοῦ
Δημαρμένου, οὐκέτι ἔτικτε τὸ δεύτερον.

Kleomenes succeeds his father [B.C. 520]; *and Dorieus departs to found a distant colony, first in Libya, and then in Sicily.*

XLII. Ὁ μὲν δὴ Κλεομένης, ὡς λέγεται, ἦν τε
οὐ φρενήρης ἀκρομανής τε, ὁ δὲ Δωριεὺς ἦν τῶν
ἡλίκων πάντων πρῶτος, εὖ τε ἠπίστατο κατ' ἀνδραγαθίην αὐτὸς σχήσων τὴν βασιληίην. ὥστε ἂν

οὕτω φρονέων, ἐπειδὴ ὅ τε Ἀναξανδρίδης ἀπέθανε καὶ οἱ Λακεδαιμόνιοι χρεόμενοι τῷ νόμῳ ἐστήσαντο βασιλέα τὸν πρεσβύτατον Κλεομένεα, ὁ Δωριεὺς δεινόν τε ποιεύμενος καὶ οὐκ ἀξιῶν ὑπὸ Κλεομένεος βασιλεύεσθαι, αἰτήσας λεὼν Σπαρτιήτας ἦγε ἐς ἀποικίην, οὔτε τῷ ἐν Δελφοῖσι χρηστηρίῳ χρησάμενος, ἐς ἥντινα γῆν κτίσων ἴῃ, οὔτε ποιήσας οὐδὲν τῶν νομιζομένων. οἷα δὲ βαρέως φέρων, ἀπίει ἐς τὴν Λιβύην τὰ πλοῖα· κατηγέοντο δέ οἱ ἄνδρες Θηραῖοι. ἀπικόμενος δ᾿ ἐς Κίνυπα οἴκισε χῶρον κάλλιστον τῶν Λιβύων παρὰ ποταμόν. ἐξελαθεὶς δὲ ἐνθεῦτεν τρίτῳ ἔτεϊ ὑπὸ Μακέων τε καὶ Λιβύων καὶ Καρχηδονίων ἀπίκετο ἐς Πελοπόννησον. XLIII. Ἐνθαῦτα δέ οἱ Ἀντιχάρης ἀνὴρ Ἐλεώνιος συνεβούλευσε ἐκ τῶν Λαΐου χρησμῶν Ἡράκλειαν τὴν ἐν Σικελίῃ κτίζειν φὰς τὴν Ἔρυκος χώρην πᾶσαν εἶναι Ἡρακλειδέων αὐτοῦ Ἡρακλέος κτησαμένου. ὁ δὲ ἀκούσας ταῦτα ἐς Δελφοὺς οἴχετο χρησόμενος τῷ χρηστηρίῳ, εἰ αἱρέει ἐπ᾿ ἣν στέλλεται χώρην· ἡ δὲ Πυθίη οἱ χρᾷ αἱρήσειν. παραλαβὼν δὲ ὁ Δωριεὺς τὸν στόλον, τὸν καὶ ἐς Λιβύην ἦγε, ἐκομίζετο παρὰ τὴν Ἰταλίην.

Dorieus in Italy is said to have assisted Kroton against Sybaris.

XLIV. Τὸν χρόνον δὲ τοῦτον, ὥς λέγουσι Συβαρῖται, σφέας τε αὐτοὺς καὶ Τῆλυν τὸν ἑωυτῶν βασιλέα ἐπὶ Κρότωνα μέλλειν στρατεύεσθαι, τοὺς δὲ Κροτωνιήτας περιδεέας γενομένους δεηθῆναι Δωριέος σφίσι τιμωρῆσαι καὶ τυχεῖν δεηθέντας· συστρατεύεσθαί τε δὴ ἐπὶ Σύβαριν Δωριέα καὶ συνελεῖν τὴν Σύβαριν. ταῦτα μέν νυν Συβαρῖται

λέγουσι ποιῆσαι Δωριέα τε καὶ τοὺς μετ' αὐτοῦ·
Κροτωνιῆται δὲ οὐδένα σφίσι φασὶ ξεῖνον προσ-
επιλαβέσθαι τοῦ πρὸς Συβαρίτας πολέμου, εἰ μὴ
Καλλίην τῶν Ἰαμιδέων μάντιν Ἠλεῖον μοῦνον, καὶ
5 τοῦτον τρόπῳ τοιῷδε· παρὰ Τήλυος τοῦ Συβαριτέων
τυράννου ἀποδράντα ἀπικέσθαι παρὰ σφέας, ἐπεί
τέ οἱ τὰ ἱρὰ οὐ προεχώρεε χρηστὰ θυομένῳ ἐπὶ
Κρότωνα. XLV. Ταῦτα δὲ ὦν οὗτοι λέγουσι.
μαρτύρια δὲ τούτων ἑκάτεροι ἀποδεικνύουσι τάδε,
10 Συβαρῖται μὲν τέμενός τε καὶ νηὸν ἐόντα παρὰ τὸν
ξηρὸν Κρᾶθιν, τὸν ἱδρύσασθαι συνελόντα τὴν πόλιν
Δωριέα λέγουσι Ἀθηναίῃ ἐπωνύμῳ Κραθίῃ, τοῦτο
δὲ αὐτοῦ Δωριέος τὸν θάνατον μαρτύριον μέγιστον
ποιεῦνται, ὅτι παρὰ τὰ μεμαντευμένα ποιέων διε-
15 φθάρη· εἰ γὰρ δὴ μὴ παρέπρηξε μηδέν, ἐπ' ὃ δὲ
ἐστάλη ἐποίεε, εἷλε ἂν τὴν Ἐρυκίνην χώρην καὶ
ἑλὼν κατέσχε, οὐδ' ἂν αὐτός τε καὶ ἡ στρατιὴ
διεφθάρη. οἱ δ' αὖ Κροτωνιῆται ἀποδεικνύουσι
Καλλίῃ μὲν τῷ Ἠλείῳ ἐξαίρετα ἐν γῇ τῇ Κροτω-
20 νιήτιδι πολλὰ δοθέντα, τὰ καὶ ἐς ἐμὲ ἔτι ἐνέμοντο
οἱ Καλλίεω ἀπόγονοι, Δωριέϊ δὲ καὶ τοῖσι Δωριέος
ἀπογόνοισι οὐδέν. καίτοι εἰ συνεπελάβετό γε τοῦ
Συβαριτικοῦ πολέμου Δωριεύς, δοθῆναι ἄν οἱ πολλα-
πλήσια ἢ Καλλίῃ. ταῦτα μέν νυν ἑκάτεροι αὐτῶν
25 μαρτύρια ἀποφαίνονται καὶ πάρεστι, ὁκοτέροισί τις
πείθεται αὐτῶν, τούτοισι προσχωρέειν.

*Dorieus falls in Sicily. Euryleon collects the survivors of
the expedition and leads them to Minoa (Heraclea).*

XLVI. Συνέπλεον δὲ Δωριέϊ καὶ ἄλλοι συγκτί-
σται Σπαρτιητέων, Θεσσαλὸς καὶ Παραιβάτης καὶ

Κελέης καὶ Εὐρυλέων, οἳ ἐπείτε ἀπίκοντο παντὶ στόλῳ ἐς τὴν Σικελίην, ἀπέθανον μάχῃ ἑσσωθέντες ὑπό τε Φοινίκων καὶ Ἐγεσταίων· μοῦνος δέ γε Εὐρυλέων τῶν συγκτιστέων περιεγένετο τούτου τοῦ πάθεος. συλλαβὼν δὲ οὗτος τῆς στρατιῆς τοὺς περιγενομένους ἔσχε Μινώην τὴν Σελινουσίων ἀποικίην, καὶ συνηλευθέρου Σελινουσίους τοῦ μουνάρχου Πειθαγόρεω. μετὰ δέ, ὡς τοῦτον κατεῖλε, αὐτὸς τυραννίδι ἐπεχείρησε Σελινοῦντος, καὶ ἐμουνάρχησε χρόνον ἐπ' ὀλίγον· οἱ γάρ μιν Σελινούσιοι ἐπαναστάντες ἀπέκτειναν καταφυγόντα ἐπὶ Διὸς ἀγοραίου βωμόν.

Death of Philip of Kroton.

XLVII. Συνέσπετο δὲ Δωριέϊ καὶ συναπέθανε Φίλιππος ὁ Βουτακίδεω Κροτωνιήτης ἀνὴρ, ὃς ἁρμοσάμενος Τήλυος τοῦ Συβαρίτεω θυγατέρα ἔφυγε ἐκ Κρότωνος, ψευσθεὶς δὲ τοῦ γάμου οἴχετο πλέων ἐς Κυρήνην, ἐκ ταύτης δὲ ὁρμεόμενος συνέσπετο οἰκηΐῃ τε τριήρεϊ καὶ οἰκηΐῃ ἀνδρῶν δαπάνῃ, ἐών τε Ὀλυμπιονίκης καὶ κάλλιστος Ἑλλήνων τῶν κατ' ἑωυτόν. διὰ δὲ τὸ ἑωυτοῦ κάλλος ἠνείκατο παρὰ Ἐγεσταίων τὰ οὐδεὶς ἄλλος· ἐπὶ γὰρ τοῦ τάφου αὐτοῦ ἡρώϊον ἱδρυσάμενοι θυσίῃσι αὐτὸν ἱλάσκονται.

Dorieus was too impatient.

XLVIII. Δωριεὺς μέν νυν τρόπῳ τοιούτῳ ἐτελεύτησε, εἰ δὲ ἠνέσχετο βασιλευόμενος ὑπὸ Κλεομένεος καὶ κατέμενε ἐν Σπάρτῃ, ἐβασίλευε ἂν Λακεδαίμονος· οὐ γάρ τινα πολλὸν χρόνον ἦρξε ὁ Κλεομένης, ἀλλ' ἀπέθανε ἄπαις, θυγατέρα μούνην λιπών, τῇ οὔνομα ἦν Γοργώ.

Aristagoras arrives in Sparta and, showing him a map of Asia, asks Kleomenes to assist the Ionians [B.C. 500].

XLIX. Ἀπικνέεται δ' ὦν ὁ Ἀρισταγόρης ὁ Μιλήτου τύραννος ἐς τὴν Σπάρτην Κλεομένεος ἔχοντος τὴν ἀρχήν, τῷ δὴ ἐς λόγους ἤϊε, ὡς Λακεδαιμόνιοι λέγουσι, ἔχων χάλκεον πίνακα, ἐν τῷ γῆς ἁπάσης περίοδος ἐνετέτμητο καὶ θάλασσά τε πᾶσα καὶ ποταμοὶ πάντες. ἀπικνεόμενος δὲ ἐς λόγους ὁ Ἀρισταγόρης ἔλεγε πρὸς αὐτὸν τάδε· " Κλεόμενες, " σπουδὴν μὲν τὴν ἐμὴν μὴ θωυμάσῃς τῆς ἐνθαῦτα " ἀπίξιος· τὰ γὰρ κατήκοντά ἐστι τοιαῦτα· Ἰώνων " παῖδας δούλους εἶναι ἀντ' ἐλευθέρων ὄνειδος καὶ " ἄλγος μέγιστον μὲν αὐτοῖσι ἡμῖν, ἔτι δὲ τῶν " λοιπῶν ὑμῖν, ὅσῳ προέστατε τῆς Ἑλλάδος. νῦν " ὦν πρὸς θεῶν τῶν Ἑλληνίων ῥύσασθε Ἴωνας ἐκ " δουλοσύνης, ἄνδρας ὁμαίμονας. εὐπετέως δὲ ὑμῖν " ταῦτα οἷά τέ χωρέειν ἐστί· οὔτε γὰρ οἱ βάρβαροι " ἄλκιμοί εἰσι, ὑμεῖς τε τὰ ἐς τὸν πόλεμον ἐς τὰ " μέγιστα ἀνήκετε ἀρετῆς πέρι. ἥ τε μάχη αὐτῶν " ἐστὶ τοιήδε, τόξα καὶ αἰχμὴ βραχέα. ἀναξυρίδας " δὲ ἔχοντες ἔρχονται ἐς τὰς μάχας καὶ κυρβασίας " ἐπὶ τῇσι κεφαλῇσι· οὕτω εὐπετέες χειρωθῆναι εἰσί. " ἔστι δὲ καὶ ἀγαθὰ τοῖσι τὴν ἤπειρον ἐκείνην νεμο- " μένοισι ὅσα οὐδὲ τοῖσι συνάπασι ἄλλοισι, ἀπὸ " χρυσοῦ ἀρξαμένοισι, ἄργυρος καὶ χαλκὸς καὶ ἐσθὴς " ποικίλη καὶ ὑποζύγιά τε καὶ ἀνδράποδα τὰ θυμῷ " βουλόμενοι αὐτοὶ ἂν ἔχοιτε. κατοίκηνται δὲ ἀλλή- " λων ἐχόμενοι ὡς ἐγὼ φράσω. Ἰώνων μὲν τῶνδε " οἵδε Λυδοί, οἰκέοντές τε χώρην ἀγαθὴν καὶ πολυ- " αργυρώτατοι ἐόντες" (δεικνὺς δὲ ἔλεγε ταῦτα ἐς

τῆς γῆς τὴν περίοδον, τὴν ἐφέρετο ἐν τῷ πίνακι
ἐντετμημένην), "Λυδῶν δὲ," ἔφη λέγων ὁ Ἀρισταγόρης, "οἵδε ἔχονται Φρύγες οἱ πρὸς τὴν ἠῶ,
"πολυπροβατώτατοί τε ἐόντες ἁπάντων τῶν ἐγὼ
"οἶδα καὶ πολυκαρπότατοι. Φρυγῶν δὲ ἔχονται 5
"Καππαδόκαι, τοὺς ἡμεῖς Συρίους καλέομεν· τού-
"τοισι δὲ πρόσουροι Κίλικες, κατήκοντες ἐπὶ
"θάλασσαν τήνδε, ἐν τῇ ἥδε Κύπρος νῆσος κέεται,
"οἳ πεντακόσια τάλαντα βασιλέϊ τὸν ἐπέτεον φόρον
"ἐπιτελεῦσι. Κιλίκων δὲ τῶνδε ἔχονται Ἀρμένιοι 10
"οἵδε, καὶ οὗτοι ἐόντες πολυπρόβατοι, Ἀρμενίων δὲ
"Ματιηνοὶ χώρην τήνδε ἔχοντες. ἔχεται δὲ τούτων
"γῆ ἥδε Κισσίη, ἐν τῇ δὴ παρὰ ποταμὸν τόνδε
"Χοάσπεα κείμενά ἐστι τὰ Σοῦσα ταῦτα, ἔνθα
"βασιλεύς τε μέγας δίαιταν ποιέεται, καὶ τῶν 15
"χρημάτων οἱ θησαυροὶ ἐνθαῦτά εἰσι· ἑλόντες δὲ
"ταύτην τὴν πόλιν θαρσέοντες ἤδη τῷ Διὶ πλούτου
"πέρι ἐρίζετε. ἀλλὰ περὶ μὲν χώρης ἄρα οὐ πολλῆς
"οὐδὲ οὕτω χρηστῆς καὶ οὔρων σμικρῶν χρεών ἐστι
"ὑμέας μάχας ἀναβάλλεσθαι πρός τε Μεσσηνίους 20
"ἐόντας ἰσοπαλέας, καὶ Ἀρκάδας τε καὶ Ἀργείους,
"τοῖσι οὔτε χρυσοῦ ἐχόμενόν ἐστι οὐδὲν οὔτε ἀργύρου,
"τῶν πέρι καί τινα ἐνάγει προθυμίη μαχόμενον
"ἀποθνήσκειν· παρέχον δὲ τῆς Ἀσίης πάσης ἄρχειν
"εὐπετέως, ἄλλο τι αἱρήσεσθε;" Ἀρισταγόρης μὲν 25
ταῦτα ἔλεξε, Κλεομένης δὲ ἀμείβετο τοισίδε· "Ὦ
"ξεῖνε Μιλήσιε, ἀναβάλλομαί τοι ἐς τρίτην ἡμέρην
"ὑποκρινέεσθαι."

Kleomenes refuses, then wavers, and finally is induced by his daughter to refuse absolutely.

L. Τότε μὲν ἐς τοσοῦτο ἤλασαν, ἐπεί τε δὲ ἡ κυρίη ἡμέρη ἐγένετο τῆς ὑποκρίσιος καὶ ἦλθον ἐς τὸ συγκείμενον, εἴρετο ὁ Κλεομένης τὸν Ἀρισταγόρην, ὁκόσων ἡμερέων ἀπὸ θαλάσσης τῆς Ἰώνων ὁδὸς εἴη παρὰ βασιλέα. ὁ δὲ Ἀρισταγόρης τἆλλα ἐὼν σοφὸς καὶ διαβάλλων ἐκεῖνον εὖ ἐν τούτῳ ἐσφάλη· χρεὼν γάρ μιν μὴ λέγειν τὸ ἐόν, βουλόμενόν γε Σπαρτιήτας ἐξαγαγεῖν ἐς τὴν Ἀσίην, λέγει δ᾽ ὦν τριῶν μηνῶν φὰς εἶναι τὴν ἄνοδον. ὁ δὲ ὑπαρπάσας τὸν ἐπίλοιπον λόγον, τὸν ὁ Ἀρισταγόρης ὥρμητο λέγειν περὶ τῆς ὁδοῦ, εἶπε· "Ὦ ξεῖνε Μιλήσιε, "ἀπαλλάσσεο ἐκ Σπάρτης πρὸ δύντος ἡλίου· οὐδένα "γὰρ λόγον εὐεπέα λέγεις Λακεδαιμονίοισι, ἐθέλων "σφέας ἀπὸ θαλάσσης τριῶν μηνῶν ὁδὸν ἀγαγεῖν."

LI. ὁ μὲν δὴ Κλεομένης ταῦτα εἴπας ἤϊε ἐς τὰ οἰκία, ὁ δὲ Ἀρισταγόρης λαβὼν ἱκετηρίην ἤϊε ἐς τοῦ Κλεομένεος, ἐσελθὼν δὲ ἔσω ἅτε ἱκετεύων ἐπακοῦσαι ἐκέλευε τὸν Κλεομένεα, ἀποπέμψαντα τὸ παιδίον· προσεστήκεε γὰρ δὴ τῷ Κλεομένεϊ ἡ θυγάτηρ, τῇ οὔνομα ἦν Γοργώ· τοῦτο δέ οἱ καὶ μοῦνον τέκνον ἐτύγχανε ἐὸν ἐτέων ὀκτὼ ἢ ἐννέα ἡλικίην. Κλεομένης δὲ λέγειν μιν ἐκέλευε τὰ βούλεται, μηδὲ ἐπισχεῖν τοῦ παιδίου εἵνεκεν. ἐνθαῦτα δὴ ὁ Ἀρισταγόρης ἤρχετο ἐκ δέκα ταλάντων ὑπισχνεόμενος, ἤν οἱ ἐπιτελέσῃ τῶν ἐδέετο. ἀνανεύοντος δὲ τοῦ Κλεομένεος προέβαινε τοῖσι χρήμασι ὑπερβάλλων ὁ Ἀρισταγόρης, ἐς ὃ πεντήκοντά τε τάλαντα ὑπεδέδεκτο, καὶ τὸ παιδίον αὐδάξατο· "Πάτερ, δια-

"φθερέει σε ὁ ξεῖνος, ἢν μὴ ἀποστὰς ἴῃς." ὅ τε δὴ Κλεομένης ἡσθεὶς τοῦ παιδίου τῇ παραινέσι ἤϊε ἐς ἕτερον οἴκημα· καὶ ὁ Ἀρισταγόρης ἀπαλλάσσετο τὸ παράπαν ἐκ τῆς Σπάρτης, οὐδέ οἱ ἐξεγένετο ἐπὶ πλέον ἔτι σημῆναι περὶ τῆς ἀνόδου τῆς παρὰ βασιλέα.

The road from the coast of Asia Minor to Susa, a three months' journey.

LII. Ἔχει γὰρ ἀμφὶ τῇ ὁδῷ ταύτῃ ὧδε· σταθμοί τε πανταχῇ εἰσὶ βασιλήϊοι καὶ καταλύσιες κάλλισται, διὰ οἰκεομένης τε ἡ ὁδὸς ἅπασα καὶ ἀσφαλέος. διὰ μέν γε Λυδίης καὶ Φρυγίης σταθμοὶ τείνοντες εἴκοσί εἰσι, παρασάγγαι δὲ τέσσερες καὶ ἐνενήκοντα καὶ ἥμισυ. ἐκδέκεται δ᾽ ἐκ τῆς Φρυγίης ὁ Ἅλυς ποταμός, ἐπ᾽ ᾧ πύλαι τε ἔπεισι, τὰς διεξελάσαι πᾶσα ἀνάγκη καὶ οὕτω διεκπερᾶν τὸν ποταμόν, καὶ φυλακτήριον μέγα ἐπ᾽ αὐτῷ. διαβάντι δὲ ἐς τὴν Καππαδοκίην καὶ ταύτῃ πορευομένῳ μέχρι οὔρων τῶν Κιλικίων σταθμοὶ δυῶν δέοντές εἰσι τριήκοντα, παρασάγγαι δὲ τέσσερες καὶ ἑκατόν· ἐπὶ δὲ τοῖσι τούτων οὔροισι διξάς τε πύλας διεξελᾷς καὶ διξὰ φυλακτήρια παραμείψεαι. ταῦτα δὲ διεξελάσαντι καὶ διὰ τῆς Κιλικίης ὁδὸν ποιευμένῳ τρεῖς εἰσὶ σταθμοί, παρασάγγαι δὲ πεντεκαίδεκα καὶ ἥμισυ. οὖρος δὲ Κιλικίης καὶ τῆς Ἀρμενίης ἐστὶ ποταμὸς νηυσιπέρητος, τῷ οὔνομα Εὐφρήτης. ἐν δὲ τῇ Ἀρμενίῃ σταθμοὶ μέν εἰσι καταγωγίων πεντεκαίδεκα, παρασάγγαι δὲ ἓξ καὶ πεντήκοντα καὶ ἥμισυ, καὶ φυλακτήριον ἐν αὐτοῖσι· ἐκ δὲ ταύτης τῆς Ἀρμενίης ἐσβάλλοντι ἐς τὴν Ματιηνὴν γῆν σταθ-

μοί εἰσι τέσσερες [καὶ τριήκοντα, παρασάγγαι δὲ
ἑπτὰ καὶ τριήκοντα καὶ ἑκατόν]. ποταμοὶ δὲ νηυσι-
πέρητοι τέσσερες διὰ ταύτης ῥέουσι, τοὺς πᾶσα
ἀνάγκη διαπορθμεῦσαι ἐστί, πρῶτος μὲν Τίγρις,
5 μετὰ δὲ δεύτερός τε καὶ τρίτος ὡυτὸς ὀνομαζόμενος,
οὐκ ὡυτὸς ἐὼν ποταμὸς οὐδὲ ἐκ τοῦ αὐτοῦ ῥέων· ὁ
μὲν γὰρ πρότερος αὐτῶν καταλεχθεὶς ἐξ Ἀρμενίων
ῥέει, ὁ δὲ ὕστερον ἐκ Ματιηνῶν. ὁ δὲ τέταρτος τῶν
ποταμῶν οὔνομα ἔχει Γύνδης, τὸν Κῦρος διέλαβέ
10 κοτε ἐς διώρυχας ἑξήκοντα καὶ τριηκοσίας. ἐκ δὲ
ταύτης ἐς τὴν Κισσίην χώρην μεταβαίνοντι ἕνδεκα
σταθμοί, παρασάγγαι δὲ δύο καὶ τεσσεράκοντα καὶ
ἥμισύ ἐστι ἐπὶ ποταμὸν Χοάσπην, ἐόντα καὶ τοῦτον
νηυσιπέρητον, ἐπ' ᾧ Σοῦσα πόλις πεπόλισται. οὗτοι
15 οἱ πάντες σταθμοί εἰσι ἕνδεκα καὶ ἑκατόν. καταγωγαὶ
μέν νυν σταθμῶν τοσαῦταί εἰσι ἐκ Σαρδίων ἐς Σοῦσα
ἀναβαίνοντι. LIII. εἰ δὲ ὀρθῶς μεμέτρηται ἡ ὁδὸς
ἡ βασιληίη τοῖσι παρασάγγῃσι καὶ ὁ παρασάγγης
δύναται τριήκοντα στάδια, ὥσπερ οὗτός γε δύναται
20 ταῦτα, ἐκ Σαρδίων στάδιά ἐστι ἐς τὰ βασιλήια τὰ
Μεμνόνια καλεόμενα πεντακόσια καὶ τρισχίλια καὶ
μύρια παρασαγγέων ἐόντων πεντήκοντα καὶ τετρα-
κοσίων. πεντήκοντα δὲ καὶ ἑκατὸν στάδια ἐπ'
ἡμέρῃ ἑκάστῃ διεξιοῦσι ἀναισιμοῦνται ἡμέραι ἀπαρτὶ
25 ἐνενήκοντα. LIV. Οὕτω τῷ Μιλησίῳ Ἀρισταγόρῃ
εἴπαντι πρὸς Κλεομένεα τὸν Λακεδαιμόνιον εἶναι
τριῶν μηνῶν τὴν ἄνοδον τὴν παρὰ βασιλέα ὀρθῶς
εἴρητο. εἰ δέ τις τὸ ἀτρεκέστερον τούτων ἔτι
δίζηται, ἐγὼ καὶ τοῦτο σημανέω· τὴν γὰρ ἐξ Ἐφέσου
30 ἐς Σάρδις ὁδὸν δέει προσλογίσασθαι ταύτῃ. καὶ δὴ
λέγω σταδίους εἶναι τοὺς πάντας ἀπὸ θαλάσσης τῆς

Ἑλληνικῆς μέχρι Σούσων (τοῦτο γὰρ Μεμνόνιον
ἄστυ καλέεται) τεσσεράκοντα καὶ τετρακισχιλίους
καὶ μυρίους· οἱ γὰρ ἐξ Ἐφέσου ἐς Σάρδις εἰσὶ
τεσσεράκοντα καὶ πεντακόσιοι στάδιοι. καὶ οὕτω
τρισὶ ἡμέρῃσι μηκύνεται ἡ τρίμηνος ὁδός. 5

Athens. The death of Hipparchos B.C. 514.

LV. Ἀπελαυνόμενος δὲ ὁ Ἀρισταγόρης ἐκ τῆς
Σπάρτης ἤϊε ἐς τὰς Ἀθήνας γενομένας τυράννων
ὧδε ἐλευθέρας. Ἐπεὶ Ἵππαρχον τὸν Πεισιστράτου,
Ἱππίεω δὲ τοῦ τυράννου ἀδελφεόν, ἰδόντα ὄψιν
ἐνυπνίου τῷ ἑωυτοῦ πάθεϊ ἐναργεστάτην κτείνουσι 10
Ἀριστογείτων καὶ Ἁρμόδιος γένος ἐόντες τὰ ἀνέκαθεν Γεφυραῖοι, μετὰ ταῦτα ἐτυραννεύοντο Ἀθηναῖοι
ἐπ᾽ ἔτεα τέσσερα οὐδὲν ἔσσον, ἀλλὰ καὶ μᾶλλον ἢ
πρὸ τοῦ. LVI. Ἡ μέν νυν ὄψις τοῦ Ἱππάρχου
ἐνυπνίου ἦν ἥδε. ἐν τῇ προτέρῃ νυκτὶ τῶν Παναθη- 15
ναίων ἐδόκεε ὁ Ἵππαρχος ἄνδρα οἱ ἐπιστάντα μέγαν
καὶ εὐειδέα αἰνίσσεσθαι τὰ ἔπεα·

"Τλῆθι λέων ἄτλητα παθὼν τετληότι θυμῷ·
"οὐδεὶς ἀνθρώπων ἀδικῶν τίσιν οὐκ ἀποτίσει."
ταῦτα δέ, ὡς ἡμέρη ἐγένετο τάχιστα, φανερὸς ἦν 20
ὑπερτιθέμενος ὀνειροπόλοισι· μετὰ δὲ ἀπειπάμενος
τὴν ὄψιν ἔπεμπε τὴν πομπήν, ἐν τῇ δὴ τελευτᾷ.

The family of Harmodios and Aristogeiton of Phoenikian origin.

LVII. Οἱ δὲ Γεφυραῖοι, τῶν ἦσαν οἱ φονέες οἱ
Ἱππάρχου, ὡς μὲν αὐτοὶ λέγουσι, ἐγεγόνεσαν ἐξ
Ἐρετρίης τὴν ἀρχήν, ὡς δὲ ἐγὼ ἀναπυνθανόμενος 25
εὑρίσκω, ἦσαν Φοίνικες τῶν σὺν Κάδμῳ ἀπικομένων

Φοινίκων ἐς γῆν τὴν νῦν Βοιωτίην καλεομένην, οἴκεον δὲ τῆς χώρης ταύτης ἀπολαχόντες τὴν Ταναγρικὴν μοῖραν. ἐνθεῦτεν δὲ Καδμείων πρότερον ἐξαναστάντων ὑπ' Ἀργείων οἱ Γεφυραῖοι οὗτοι δεύτερα ὑπὸ Βοιωτῶν ἐξαναστάντες ἐτράποντο ἐπ' Ἀθηνέων. Ἀθηναῖοι δέ σφεας ἐπὶ ῥητοῖσι ἐδέξαντο σφέων αὐτῶν εἶναι πολιήτας, πολλῶν τέων καὶ οὐκ ἀξιαπηγήτων ἐπιτάξαντες ἔργεσθαι.

The Phoenikians introduced letters into Greece, which the Ionians were the first to adopt and modify,—a fact proved by existing Kadmeian inscriptions at Thebes.

LVIII. Οἱ δὲ Φοίνικες οὗτοι οἱ σὺν Κάδμῳ ἀπικόμενοι, τῶν ἦσαν οἱ Γεφυραῖοι, ἄλλα τε πολλὰ οἰκήσαντες ταύτην τὴν χώρην ἐσήγαγον διδασκάλια ἐς τοὺς Ἕλληνας καὶ δὴ καὶ γράμματα, οὐκ ἐόντα πρὶν Ἕλλησι, ὡς ἐμοὶ δοκέειν, πρῶτα μὲν τοῖσι καὶ ἅπαντες χρέονται Φοίνικες, μετὰ δὲ χρόνου προβαίνοντος ἅμα τῇ φωνῇ μετέβαλον καὶ τὸν ῥυθμὸν τῶν γραμμάτων. περιοίκεον δέ σφεας τὰ πολλὰ τῶν χώρων τοῦτον τὸν χρόνον Ἑλλήνων Ἴωνες, οἳ παραλαβόντες διδαχῇ παρὰ τῶν Φοινίκων τὰ γράμματα, μεταρρυθμίσαντές σφεων ὀλίγα ἐχρέωντο, χρεώμενοι δὲ ἐφάτισαν, ὥσπερ καὶ τὸ δίκαιον ἔφερε, ἐσαγαγόντων Φοινίκων ἐς τὴν Ἑλλάδα Φοινικήια κεκλῆσθαι. καὶ τὰς βίβλους διφθέρας καλέουσι ἀπὸ τοῦ παλαιοῦ οἱ Ἴωνες, ὅτι κοτὲ ἐν σπάνι βίβλων ἐχρέωντο διφθέρῃσι αἰγέῃσί τε καὶ οἰέῃσι· ἔτι δὲ καὶ τὸ κατ' ἐμὲ πολλοὶ τῶν βαρβάρων ἐς τοιαύτας διφθέρας γράφουσι. LIX. Εἶδον δὲ καὶ αὐτὸς Καδμήια γράμματα ἐν τῷ ἱρῷ τοῦ Ἀπόλλωνος τοῦ Ἰσμηνίου ἐν Θήβῃσι τῇσι Βοιωτῶν ἐπὶ τρίποσί τισι ἐγκεκολαμμένα, τὰ πολλὰ ὁμοῖα ἐόντα τοῖσι Ἰωνικοῖσι. ὁ μὲν δὴ εἷς τῶν τριπόδων ἐπίγραμμα ἔχει

"Ἀμφιτρύων μ' ἀνέθηκεν ἐὼν ἀπὸ Τηλεβοάων."
ταῦτα ἡλικίην ἂν εἴη κατὰ Λάϊον τὸν Λαβδάκου τοῦ Πολυδώρου τοῦ Κάδμου. LX. Ἕτερος δὲ τρίπους ἐν ἑξαμέτρῳ τόνῳ λέγει·

"Σκαῖος πυγμαχέων με ἑκηβόλῳ Ἀπόλλωνι
"νικήσας ἀνέθηκε τεῒν περικαλλὲς ἄγαλμα."
Σκαῖος δ' ἂν εἴη ὁ Ἱπποκόωντος, εἰ δὴ οὗτός γ' ἐστὶ ὁ ἀναθεὶς καὶ μὴ ἄλλος τὠυτὸ οὔνομα ἔχων τῷ Ἱπποκόωντος, ἡλικίην κατὰ Οἰδίπουν τὸν Λάϊου. LXI. Τρίτος δὲ τρίπους λέγει καὶ οὗτος ἐν ἑξαμέτρῳ·

"Λαοδάμας τρίποδ' αὐτὸς ἐϋσκόπῳ Ἀπόλλωνι
"μουναρχέων ἀνέθηκε τεῒν περικαλλὲς ἄγαλμα."
ἐπὶ τούτου δὴ τοῦ Λαοδάμαντος τοῦ Ἐτεοκλέος μουναρχέοντος ἐξανιστέαται Καδμεῖοι ὑπ' Ἀργείων καὶ τράπονται ἐς τοὺς Ἐγχέλεας, οἱ δὲ Γεφυραῖοι ὑπολειφθέντες ὕστερον ὑπὸ Βοιωτῶν ἀναχωρέουσι ἐς Ἀθήνας· καί σφι ἱρά ἐστι ἐν Ἀθήνῃσι ἱδρυμένα, τῶν οὐδὲν μέτα τοῖσι λοιποῖσι Ἀθηναίοισι, ἄλλα τε κεχωρισμένα τῶν ἄλλων ἱρῶν καὶ δὴ καὶ Ἀχαιίης Δήμητρος ἱρόν τε καὶ ὄργια.

B.C. 510. *The expulsion of Hippias, first attempted unsuccessfully by a Spartan force under Anchimolios, and then successfully by Kleomenes; both invasions being undertaken at the instigation of the Pythian oracle, which was influenced by the Alkmaeonidae.*

LXII. Ἡ μὲν δὴ ὄψις τοῦ Ἱππάρχου ἐνυπνίου, καὶ οἱ Γεφυραῖοι ὅθεν ἐγεγόνεσαν, τῶν ἦσαν οἱ

Ἱππάρχου φονέες, ἀπήγηταί μοι· δέει δὲ πρὸς τούτοισι ἔτι ἀναλαβεῖν τὸν κατ' ἀρχὰς ἤια λέξων λόγον, ὡς τυράννων ἠλευθερώθησαν Ἀθηναῖοι. Ἱππίεω τυραννεύοντος καὶ ἐμπικραινομένου Ἀθηναίοισι διὰ τὸν Ἱππάρχου θάνατον Ἀλκμεωνίδαι γένος ἐόντες Ἀθηναῖοι καὶ φεύγοντες Πεισιστρατίδας, ἐπεί τέ σφι ἅμα τοῖσι ἄλλοισι Ἀθηναίων φυγάσι πειρωμένοισι κατὰ τὸ ἰσχυρὸν οὐ προεχώρεε κάτοδος, ἀλλὰ προσέπταιον μεγάλως πειρώμενοι κατιέναι τε καὶ ἐλευθεροῦν τὰς Ἀθήνας, Λειψύδριον τὸ ὑπὲρ Παιονίης τειχίσαντες, ἐνθαῦτα οἱ Ἀλκμεωνίδαι πᾶν ἐπὶ τοῖσι Πεισιστρατίδῃσι μηχανώμενοι παρ' Ἀμφικτυόνων τὸν νηὸν μισθοῦνται τὸν ἐν Δελφοῖσι, τὸν νῦν ἐόντα, τότε δὲ οὔκω, τοῦτον ἐξοικοδομῆσαι. οἷα δὲ χρημάτων εὖ ἥκοντες καὶ ἐόντες ἄνδρες δόκιμοι ἀνέκαθεν ἔτι, τόν τε νηὸν ἐξεργάσαντο τοῦ παραδείγματος κάλλιον τά τε ἄλλα, καὶ συγκειμένου σφι πωρίνου λίθου ποιέειν τὸν νηὸν Παρίου τὰ ἔμπροσθε αὐτοῦ ἐξεποίησαν. LXIII. Ὡς ὦν δὴ οἱ Ἀθηναῖοι λέγουσι, οὗτοι οἱ ἄνδρες ἐν Δελφοῖσι κατήμενοι ἀνέπειθον τὴν Πυθίην χρήμασι, ὅκως ἔλθοιεν Σπαρτιητέων ἄνδρες εἴτε ἰδίῳ στόλῳ εἴτε δημοσίῳ χρησόμενοι, προφέρειν σφι τὰς Ἀθήνας ἐλευθεροῦν. Λακεδαιμόνιοι δέ, ὥς σφι αἰεὶ τὠυτὸ πρόφαντον ἐγίνετο, πέμπουσι Ἀγχιμόλιον τὸν Ἀστέρος, ἐόντα τῶν ἀστῶν ἄνδρα δόκιμον, σὺν στρατῷ ἐξελῶντα Πεισιστρατίδας ἐξ Ἀθηνέων, ὅμως καὶ ξείνους σφι ἐόντας τὰ μάλιστα· τὰ γὰρ τοῦ θεοῦ πρεσβύτερα ἐποιεῦντο ἢ τὰ τῶν ἀνδρῶν. πέμπουσι δὲ τούτους κατὰ θάλασσαν πλοίοισι. ὁ μὲν δὴ προσσχὼν ἐς Φάληρον τὴν στρατιὴν ἀπέβησε, οἱ δὲ Πεισιστρατίδαι προπυνθανόμενοι ταῦτα ἐπεκα-

λέοντο ἐκ Θεσσαλίης ἐπικουρίην· ἐπεποίητο γάρ σφι συμμαχίη πρὸς αὐτούς. Θεσσαλοὶ δέ σφι δεομένοισι ἀπέπεμψαν κοινῇ γνώμῃ χρεώμενοι χιλίην τε ἵππον καὶ τὸν βασιλέα τὸν σφέτερον Κινέην ἄνδρα Κονιαῖον· τοὺς ἐπεί τε ἔσχον συμμάχους οἱ Πεισιστρα- 5
τίδαι, ἐμηχανέοντο τοιάδε· κείραντες τῶν Φαληρέων τὸ πεδίον καὶ ἱππάσιμον ποιήσαντες τοῦτον τὸν χῶρον ἐπῆκαν τῷ στρατοπέδῳ τὴν ἵππον· ἐμπεσοῦσα δὲ διέφθειρε ἄλλους τε πολλοὺς τῶν Λακεδαιμονίων καὶ δὴ καὶ τὸν Ἀγχιμόλιον, τοὺς δὲ περιγενομένους 10
αὐτῶν ἐς τὰς νέας κατέρξαν. ὁ μὲν δὴ πρῶτος στόλος ἐκ Λακεδαίμονος οὕτω ἀπήλλαξε, καὶ Ἀγχιμολίου εἰσὶ ταφαὶ τῆς Ἀττικῆς Ἀλωπεκῇσι, ἀγχοῦ τοῦ Ἡρακλείου τοῦ ἐν Κυνοσάργεϊ. LXIV. Μετὰ δὲ Λακεδαιμόνιοι μέζω στόλον στείλαντες ἀπέπεμψαν 15
ἐπὶ τὰς Ἀθήνας, στρατηγὸν τῆς στρατιῆς ἀποδέξαντες βασιλέα Κλεομένεα τὸν Ἀναξανδρίδεω, οὐκέτι κατὰ θάλασσαν στείλαντες, ἀλλὰ κατ' ἤπειρον, τοῖσι ἐσβαλοῦσι ἐς τὴν Ἀττικὴν χώρην ἡ τῶν Θεσσαλῶν ἵππος πρώτη προσέμιξε καὶ οὐ μετὰ πολλὸν ἐτρά- 20
πετο, καί σφεων ἔπεσον ὑπὲρ τεσσεράκοντα ἄνδρας· οἱ δὲ περιγενόμενοι ἀπαλλάσσοντο ὡς εἶχον ἰθὺς ἐπὶ Θεσσαλίης. Κλεομένης δὲ ἀπικόμενος ἐς τὸ ἄστυ ἅμα Ἀθηναίων τοῖσι βουλομένοισι εἶναι ἐλευθέροισι ἐπολιόρκεε τοὺς τυράννους ἀπεργμένους ἐν τῷ Πε- 25
λασγικῷ τείχεϊ. LXV. Καὶ οὐδέν τι πάντως ἂν ἐξεῖλον τοὺς Πεισιστρατίδας οἱ Λακεδαιμόνιοι (οὔτε γὰρ ἐπέδρην ἐπενόεον ποιήσασθαι, οἵ τε Πεισιστρατίδαι σίτοισι καὶ ποτοῖσι εὖ παρεσκευάδατο), πολιορκήσαντές τε ἂν ἡμέρας ὀλίγας ἀπαλλάσσοντο ἐς τὴν 30
Σπάρτην. νῦν δὲ συντυχίη τοῖσι μὲν κακὴ ἐπεγένετο,

τοῖσι δὲ ἡ αὐτὴ αὕτη σύμμαχος· ὑπεκτιθέμενοι γὰρ
ἔξω τῆς χώρης οἱ παῖδες τῶν Πεισιστρατιδέων ἥλω-
σαν. τοῦτο δὲ ὡς ἐγένετο, πάντα αὐτῶν τὰ πρήγματα
συνετετάρακτο, παρέστησαν δὲ ἐπὶ μισθῷ τοῖσι
5 τέκνοισι, ἐπ' οἷσι ἐβούλοντο οἱ Ἀθηναῖοι, ὥστε ἐν
πέντε ἡμέρῃσι ἐκχωρῆσαι ἐκ τῆς Ἀττικῆς. μετὰ δὲ
ἐξεχώρησαν ἐς Σίγειον τὸ ἐπὶ τῷ Σκαμάνδρῳ, ἄρξαντες μὲν Ἀθηναίων ἐπ' ἔτεα ἕξ τε καὶ τριήκοντα,
ἐόντες δὲ καὶ οὗτοι ἀνέκαθεν Πύλιοί τε καὶ Νηλεῖδαι,
10 ἐκ τῶν αὐτῶν γεγονότες καὶ οἱ ἀμφὶ Κόδρον τε καὶ
Μέλανθον, οἳ πρότερον ἐπήλυδες ἐόντες ἐγένοντο
Ἀθηναίων βασιλέες. ἐπὶ τούτου δὲ καὶ τὠυτὸ
οὔνομα ἀπεμνημόνευσε Ἱπποκράτης τῷ παιδὶ θέσθαι
τὸν Πεισίστρατον, ἐπὶ τοῦ Νέστορος Πεισιστράτου
15 ποιεύμενος τὴν ἐπωνυμίην. οὕτω μὲν Ἀθηναῖοι
τυράννων ἀπηλλάχθησαν, ὅσα δὲ ἐλευθερωθέντες
ἔρξαν ἢ ἔπαθον ἀξιόχρεα ἀπηγήσιος πρὶν ἢ Ἰωνίην
τε ἀποστῆναι ἀπὸ Δαρείου καὶ Ἀρισταγόρην τὸν
Μιλήσιον ἀπικόμενον ἐς Ἀθήνας χρηΐσαι σφέων
20 βοηθέειν, ταῦτα πρῶτα φράσω.

*The growth of Athenian power after the fall of the
Peisistratidae and the reforms of Kleisthenes.*

LXVI. Ἀθῆναι ἐοῦσαι καὶ πρὶν μεγάλαι, τότε
ἀπαλλαχθεῖσαι τυράννων ἐγίνοντο μέζονες. ἐν δὲ
αὐτῇσι δύο ἄνδρες ἐδυνάστευον, Κλεισθένης τε ἀνὴρ
Ἀλκμεωνίδης, ὅσπερ δὴ λόγον ἔχει τὴν Πυθίην
25 ἀναπεῖσαι, καὶ Ἰσαγόρης ὁ Τισάνδρου οἰκίης μὲν
ἐὼν δοκίμου, ἀτὰρ τὰ ἀνέκαθεν οὐκ ἔχω φράσαι,
θύουσι δὲ οἱ συγγενέες αὐτοῦ Διὶ Καρίῳ. οὗτοι οἱ
ἄνδρες ἐστασίασαν περὶ δυνάμιος, ἑσσούμενος δὲ ὁ

Κλεισθένης τὸν δῆμον προσεταιρίζεται· μετὰ δὲ
τετραφύλους ἐόντας Ἀθηναίους δεκαφύλους ἐποίησε,
τῶν Ἴωνος παίδων Γελέοντος καὶ Αἰγικόρεος καὶ
Ἀργάδεω καὶ Ὅπλητος ἀπαλλάξας τὰς ἐπωνυμίας,
ἐξευρὼν δ' ἑτέρων ἡρώων ἐπωνυμίας ἐπιχωρίων, 5
πάρεξ Αἴαντος· τοῦτον δὲ ἅτε ἀστυγείτονα καὶ
σύμμαχον ξεῖνον ἐόντα προσέθετο.

*Kleisthenes, in the nomenclature of the Attic tribes,
followed the precedent of his grandfather Kleisthenes
of Sikyon.*

LXVII. Ταῦτα δὲ, δοκέειν ἐμοὶ, ἐμιμέετο ὁ
Κλεισθένης οὗτος τὸν ἑωυτοῦ μητροπάτορα Κλεισθένεα τὸν Σικυῶνος τύραννον. Κλεισθένης γὰρ 10
Ἀργείοισι πολεμήσας τοῦτο μὲν ῥαψῳδοὺς ἔπαυσε
ἐν Σικυῶνι ἀγωνίζεσθαι τῶν Ὁμηρείων ἐπέων εἵνεκεν, ὅτι Ἀργεῖοί τε καὶ Ἄργος τὰ πολλὰ πάντα ὑμνέαται, τοῦτο δὲ, ἡρώιον γὰρ ἦν καὶ ἔστι
ἐν αὐτῇ τῇ ἀγορῇ τῶν Σικυωνίων Ἀδρήστου τοῦ 15
Ταλαοῦ, τοῦτον ἐπεθύμησε ὁ Κλεισθένης ἐόντα
Ἀργεῖον ἐκβαλεῖν ἐκ τῆς χώρης. ἐλθὼν δὲ ἐς
Δελφοὺς ἐχρηστηριάζετο, εἰ ἐκβάλλῃ τὸν Ἄδρηστον·
ἡ δὲ Πυθίη οἱ χρᾷ φᾶσα Ἄδρηστον μὲν εἶναι
Σικυωνίων βασιλέα, ἐκεῖνον δὲ λευστῆρα. ἐπεὶ δὲ 20
ὁ θεὸς τοῦτό γε οὐ παρεδίδου, ἀπελθὼν ὀπίσω
ἐφρόντιζε μηχανὴν, τῇ αὐτὸς ὁ Ἄδρηστος ἀπαλ-
λάξεται. ὡς δέ οἱ ἐξευρῆσθαι ἐδόκεε, πέμψας ἐς
Θήβας τὰς Βοιωτίας ἔφη ἐθέλειν ἐπαγαγέσθαι Μελάνιππον τὸν Ἀστακοῦ· οἱ δὲ Θηβαῖοι ἔδοσαν. 25
ἐπαγαγόμενος δὲ ὁ Κλεισθένης τὸν Μελάνιππον
τέμενός οἱ ἀπέδεξε ἐν αὐτῷ τῷ πρυτανηίῳ καί μιν

ἵδρυσε ἐνθαῦτα ἐν τῷ ἰσχυροτάτῳ. ἐπηγάγετο δὲ
τὸν Μελάνιππον ὁ Κλεισθένης (καὶ γὰρ τοῦτο δέει
ἀπηγήσασθαι) ὡς ἔχθιστον ἐόντα Ἀδρήστῳ, ὃς τόν
τε ἀδελφεόν οἱ Μηκιστέα ἀπεκτόνεε καὶ τὸν γαμ-
βρὸν Τυδέα. ἐπείτε δέ οἱ τὸ τέμενος ἀπέδεξε, θυσίας
τε καὶ ὁρτὰς Ἀδρήστου ἀπελόμενος ἔδωκε τῷ Μελανίππῳ. οἱ δὲ Σικυώνιοι ἐώθεσαν μεγαλωστὶ
κάρτα τιμᾶν τὸν Ἄδρηστον· ἡ γὰρ χώρη ἦν αὕτη
Πολύβου, ὁ δὲ Ἄδρηστος ἦν Πολύβου θυγατριδέος,
ἄπαις δὲ Πόλυβος τελευτῶν διδοῖ Ἀδρήστῳ τὴν
ἀρχήν. τά τε δὴ ἄλλα οἱ Σικυώνιοι ἐτίμων τὸν
Ἄδρηστον, καὶ δὴ πρὸς τὰ πάθεα αὐτοῦ τραγικοῖσι
χοροῖσι ἐγέραιρον, τὸν μὲν Διόνυσον οὐ τιμέοντες, τὸν
δὲ Ἄδρηστον. Κλεισθένης δὲ χοροὺς μὲν τῷ Διονύσῳ
ἀπέδωκε, τὴν δὲ ἄλλην θυσίην τῷ Μελανίππῳ.
LXVIII. ταῦτα μὲν ἐς Ἄδρηστόν οἱ ἐπεποίητο,
φυλὰς δὲ τὰς Δωριέων, ἵνα δὴ μὴ αἱ αὐταὶ ἔωσι τοῖσι
Σικυωνίοισι καὶ τοῖσι Ἀργείοισι, μετέβαλε ἐς ἄλλα
οὐνόματα, ἔνθα καὶ πλεῖστον κατεγέλασε τῶν Σικυ-
ωνίων· ἐπὶ γὰρ ὑός τε καὶ ὄνου τὰς ἐπωνυμίας
μετατιθεὶς αὐτὰ τὰ τελευταῖα ἐπέθηκε, πλὴν τῆς
ἑωυτοῦ φυλῆς· ταύτῃ δὲ τὸ οὔνομα ἀπὸ τῆς ἑωυτοῦ
ἀρχῆς ἔθετο. οὗτοι μὲν δὴ Ἀρχέλαοι ἐκαλέοντο,
ἕτεροι δὲ Ὑᾶται, ἄλλοι δὲ Ὀνεᾶται, ἕτεροι δὲ
Χοιρεᾶται. τούτοισι τοῖσι οὐνόμασι τῶν φυλέων
ἐχρέωντο οἱ Σικυώνιοι καὶ ἐπὶ Κλεισθένεος ἄρχοντος
καὶ ἐκείνου τεθνεῶτος ἔτι ἐπ' ἔτεα ἑξήκοντα, μετέπειτεν μέντοι λόγον σφίσι δόντες μετέβαλον ἐς τοὺς
Ὑλλέας καὶ Παμφύλους καὶ Δυμανάτας, τετάρτους δὲ
αὐτοῖσι προσέθεντο ἐπὶ τοῦ Ἀδρήστου παιδὸς Αἰγια-
λέος τὴν ἐπωνυμίην ποιεύμενοι κεκλῆσθαι Αἰγιαλέας.

In introducing his reforms Kleisthenes is opposed by Isagoras, who induced Kleomenes to demand the expulsion of the 'accursed race', the Alkmaeonidae.

LXIX. Ταῦτα μέν νυν ὁ Σικυώνιος Κλεισθένης ἐπεποιήκεε, ὁ δὲ δὴ Ἀθηναῖος Κλεισθένης ἐὼν τοῦ Σικυωνίου τούτου θυγατριδέος καὶ τὸ οὔνομα ἐπὶ τούτου ἔχων, δοκέειν ἐμοὶ καὶ οὗτος ὑπεριδὼν Ἴωνας, ἵνα μὴ σφίσι αἱ αὐταὶ ἔωσι φυλαὶ καὶ Ἴωσι, τὸν ὁμώνυμον Κλεισθένεα ἐμιμήσατο. ὡς γὰρ δὴ τὸν Ἀθηναίων δῆμον πρότερον ἀπωσμένον τότε πάντα πρὸς τὴν ἑωυτοῦ μοῖραν προσεθήκατο, τὰς φυλὰς μετουνόμασε καὶ ἐποίησε πλεῦνας ἐξ ἐλασσόνων. δέκα τε δὴ φυλάρχους ἀντὶ τεσσέρων ἐποίησε, δέκα δὲ καὶ τοὺς δήμους κατένεμε ἐς τὰς φυλάς. ἦν τε τὸν δῆμον προσθέμενος πολλῷ κατύπερθε τῶν ἀντιστασιωτέων. LXX. Ἐν τῷ μέρεϊ δὲ ἐσσούμενος ὁ Ἰσαγόρης ἀντιτεχνᾶται τάδε· ἐπικαλέεται Κλεομένεα τὸν Λακεδαιμόνιον, γενόμενον ἑωυτῷ ξεῖνον ἀπὸ τῆς Πεισιστρατιδέων πολιορκίης. τὸν δὲ Κλεομένεα εἶχε αἰτίη φοιτᾶν παρὰ τοῦ Ἰσαγόρεω τὴν γυναῖκα. τὰ μὲν δὴ πρῶτα πέμπων ὁ Κλεομένης ἐς τὰς Ἀθήνας κήρυκα ἐξέβαλλε Κλεισθένεα καὶ μετ᾽ αὐτοῦ ἄλλους πολλοὺς Ἀθηναίων, τοὺς ἐναγέας ἐπιλέγων. ταῦτα δὲ πέμπων ἔλεγε ἐκ διδαχῆς τοῦ Ἰσαγόρεω· οἱ μὲν γὰρ Ἀλκμεωνίδαι καὶ οἱ συστασιῶται αὐτῶν εἶχον αἰτίην τοῦ φόνου τούτου, αὐτὸς δὲ οὐ μετεῖχε, οὐδ᾽ οἱ φίλοι αὐτοῦ.

The origin of the curse attaching to the Alkmaeonidae.

LXXI. Οἱ δ' ἐναγέες Ἀθηναίων ὧδε οὐνομάσθησαν· ἦν Κύλων τῶν Ἀθηναίων ἀνὴρ Ὀλυμπιονίκης. οὗτος ἐπὶ τυραννίδι ἐκόμησε, προσποιησάμενος δὲ ἑταιρηίην τῶν ἡλικιωτέων καταλαβεῖν τὴν ἀκρόπολιν ἐπειρήθη, οὐ δυνάμενος δὲ ἐπικρατῆσαι ἱκέτης ἵζετο πρὸς τὤγαλμα. τούτους ἀνιστᾶσι μὲν οἱ πρυτάνιες τῶν ναυκράρων, οἵ περ ἔνεμον τότε τὰς Ἀθήνας, ὑπεγγύους πλὴν θανάτου, φονεῦσαι δὲ αὐτοὺς αἰτίη ἔχει Ἀλκμεωνίδας. ταῦτα πρὸ τῆς Πεισιστράτου ἡλικίης ἐγένετο.

Kleomenes invades Attica, attempts to destroy the new constitution of Athens, and seizes the Akropolis, but is compelled to retire.

LXXII. Κλεομένης δὲ ὡς πέμπων ἐξέβαλλε Κλεισθένεα καὶ τοὺς ἐναγέας, Κλεισθένης μὲν αὐτὸς ὑπεξέσχε, μετὰ δὲ οὐδὲν ἔσσον παρῆν ἐς τὰς Ἀθήνας ὁ Κλεομένης οὐ σὺν μεγάλῃ χειρί, ἀπικόμενος δὲ ἀγηλατέει ἑπτακόσια ἐπίστια Ἀθηναίων, τά οἱ ὑπέθετο ὁ Ἰσαγόρης. ταῦτα δὲ ποιήσας δεύτερα τὴν βουλὴν καταλύειν ἐπειρᾶτο, τριηκοσίοισι δὲ τοῖσι Ἰσαγόρεω στασιώτῃσι τὰς ἀρχὰς ἐνεχείριζε. ἀντισταθείσης δὲ τῆς βουλῆς καὶ οὐ βουλομένης πείθεσθαι ὅ τε Κλεομένης καὶ ὁ Ἰσαγόρης καὶ οἱ στασιῶται αὐτοῦ καταλαμβάνουσι τὴν ἀκρόπολιν. Ἀθηναίων δὲ οἱ λοιποὶ τὰ αὐτὰ φρονήσαντες ἐπολιόρκεον αὐτοὺς ἡμέρας δύο· τῇ δὲ τρίτῃ ὑπόσπονδοι ἐξέρχονται ἐκ τῆς χώρης ὅσοι ἦσαν αὐτῶν Λακεδαιμόνιοι. ἐπετελέετο δὲ τῷ Κλεομένεϊ ἡ φήμη· ὡς γὰρ ἀνέβη ἐς τὴν ἀκρόπολιν μέλλων δὴ αὐτὴν κατασχήσειν, ἤιε ἐς τὸ ἄδυτον τῆς θεοῦ ὡς προσερέων· ἡ δὲ ἵρεια ἐξαναστᾶσα ἐκ τοῦ θρόνου πρὶν ἢ τὰς θύρας αὐτὸν ἀμεῖψαι εἶπε· "Ὦ ξεῖνε Λακεδαιμόνιε, "πάλιν χώρει μηδ᾽ ἔσιθι ἐς τὸ ἱρόν· οὐ γὰρ θεμιτὸν 5 "Δωριεῦσι παριέναι ἐνθαῦτα." ὁ δὲ εἶπε· "Ὦ γύναι, "ἀλλ᾽ οὐ Δωριεύς εἰμι, ἀλλ᾽ Ἀχαιός." ὁ μὲν δὴ τῇ κληδόνι οὐδὲν χρεώμενος ἐπεχείρησέ τε καὶ τότε πάλιν ἐξέπιπτε μετὰ τῶν Λακεδαιμονίων, τοὺς δὲ ἄλλους Ἀθηναῖοι κατέδησαν τὴν ἐπὶ θανάτῳ, ἐν δὲ 10 αὐτοῖσι καὶ Τιμησίθεον τὸν Δελφόν, τοῦ ἔργα χειρῶν τε καὶ λήματος ἔχοιμ᾽ ἂν μέγιστα καταλέξαι. οὗτοι μέν νυν δεδεμένοι ἐτελεύτησαν,

Kleisthenes is recalled. The Athenians propose an alliance with Persia.

LXXIII. Ἀθηναῖοι δὲ μετὰ ταῦτα Κλεισθένεα καὶ τὰ ἑπτακόσια ἐπίστια τὰ διωχθέντα ὑπὸ Κλεομέ- 15 νεος μεταπεμψάμενοι πέμπουσι ἀγγέλους ἐς Σάρδις, συμμαχίην βουλόμενοι ποιήσασθαι πρὸς Πέρσας· ἠπιστέατο γάρ σφι [πρὸς] Λακεδαιμονίους τε καὶ Κλεομένεα ἐκπεπολεμῶσθαι. ἀπικομένων δὲ τῶν ἀγγέλων ἐς τὰς Σάρδις καὶ λεγόντων τὰ ἐντεταλμένα 20 Ἀρταφέρνης ὁ Ὑστάσπεος Σαρδίων ὕπαρχος ἐπειρώτα, τίνες ἐόντες ἄνθρωποι καὶ κῇ γῆς οἰκημένοι δεοίατο Περσέων σύμμαχοι γενέσθαι, πυθόμενος δὲ πρὸς τῶν ἀγγέλων ἀπεκορύφου σφι τάδε· Εἰ μὲν διδοῦσι βασιλέι Δαρείῳ Ἀθηναῖοι γῆν τε καὶ ὕδωρ, 25 ὁ δὲ συμμαχίην σφι συνετίθετο, εἰ δὲ μὴ διδοῦσι, ἀπαλλάσσεσθαι αὐτοὺς ἐκέλευε. οἱ δὲ ἄγγελοι ἐπὶ σφέων αὐτῶν βαλόμενοι διδόναι ἔφασαν, βουλόμενοι τὴν συμμαχίην ποιήσασθαι. οὗτοι μὲν δὴ ἀπελθόντες ἐς τὴν ἑωυτῶν αἰτίας μεγάλας εἶχον.

Kleomenes prepares another invasion of Attica in the interests of the Peisistratidae, B.C. 506,

LXXIV. Κλεομένης δὲ ἐπιστάμενος περιυβρίσθαι ἔπεσι καὶ ἔργοισι ὑπ' Ἀθηναίων συνέλεγε ἐκ πάσης Πελοποννήσου στρατὸν, οὐ φράζων ἐς τὸ συλλέγει, τίσασθαι δὲ ἐθέλων τὸν δῆμον τῶν Ἀθηναίων καὶ Ἰσαγόρην βουλόμενος τύραννον καταστῆσαι· συνεξῆλθε γάρ οἱ οὗτος ἐκ τῆς ἀκροπόλιος. Κλεομένης τε δὴ στόλῳ μεγάλῳ ἐσέβαλε ἐς Ἐλευσῖνα, καὶ οἱ Βοιωτοὶ ἀπὸ συνθήματος Οἰνόην αἱρέουσι καὶ Ὑσιάς, δήμους τοὺς ἐσχάτους τῆς Ἀττικῆς, Χαλκιδέες τε ἐπὶ τὰ ἕτερα ἐσίνοντο ἐπιόντες χώρους τῆς Ἀττικῆς. Ἀθηναῖοι δὲ, καί περ ἀμφιβολίῃ ἐχόμενοι, Βοιωτῶν μὲν καὶ Χαλκιδέων ἐσύστερον ἔμελλον μνήμην ποιήσεσθαι, Πελοποννησίοισι δὲ ἐοῦσι ἐν Ἐλευσῖνι ἀντία ἔθεντο τὰ ὅπλα.

but is deserted by the Korinthians, and his fellow king Demaratos.

LXXV. Μελλόντων δὲ συνάψειν τὰ στρατόπεδα ἐς μάχην Κορίνθιοι μὲν πρῶτοι σφίσι αὐτοῖσι δόντες λόγον, ὡς οὐ ποιοῖεν τὰ δίκαια, μετεβάλλοντό τε καὶ ἀπαλλάσσοντο, μετὰ δὲ Δημάρητος ὁ Ἀρίστωνος, ἐὼν καὶ οὗτος βασιλεὺς Σπαρτιητέων, καὶ συνεξαγαγών τε τὴν στρατιὴν ἐκ Λακεδαίμονος καὶ οὐκ ἐὼν διάφορος ἐν τῷ πρόσθε χρόνῳ Κλεομένεϊ. ἀπὸ δὲ ταύτης τῆς διχοστασίης ἐτέθη νόμος ἐν Σπάρτῃ, μὴ ἐξεῖναι ἕπεσθαι ἀμφοτέρους τοὺς βα-

σιλέας ἐξιούσης τῆς στρατιῆς (τέως γὰρ ἀμφότεροι
εἵποντο), παραλυομένου δὲ τούτων τοῦ ἑτέρου καταλείπεσθαι καὶ τῶν Τυνδαριδέων τὸν ἕτερον· πρὸ τοῦ
γὰρ δὴ καὶ οὗτοι ἀμφότεροι ἐπίκλητοί σφι ἐόντες
εἵποντο. τότε δὴ ἐν τῇ Ἐλευσῖνι ὁρέοντες οἱ λοιποὶ 5
τῶν συμμάχων τούς τε βασιλέας τῶν Λακεδαιμονίων
οὐκ ὁμολογέοντας καὶ Κορινθίους ἐκλιπόντας τὴν
τάξιν οἴχοντο καὶ αὐτοὶ ἀπαλλασσόμενοι.

Previous invasions of Attica by Dorians.

LXXVI. Τέταρτον δὴ τοῦτο ἐπὶ τὴν Ἀττικὴν
ἀπικόμενοι Δωριέες, δίς τε ἐπὶ πολέμῳ ἐσβαλόντες, 10
καὶ δὶς ἐπ' ἀγαθῷ τοῦ πλήθεος τοῦ Ἀθηναίων,
πρῶτον μὲν, ὅτε καὶ Μέγαρα κατοίκισαν (οὗτος ὁ
στόλος ἐπὶ Κόδρου βασιλεύοντος Ἀθηναίων ὀρθῶς
ἂν καλέοιτο), δεύτερον δὲ καὶ τρίτον, ὅτε ἐπὶ Πεισιστρατιδέων ἐξέλασιν ὁρμηθέντες ἐκ Σπάρτης ἀπί- 15
κοντο, τέταρτον δὲ τότε, ὅτε ἐς Ἐλευσῖνα Κλεομένης
ἄγων Πελοποννησίους ἐσέβαλε, οὕτω τέταρτον τότε
Δωριέες ἐσέβαλον ἐς Ἀθήνας.

The Athenians retaliate by an attack upon the Chalkidians, who are supported by the Boeotians.

LXXVII. Διαλυθέντος ὦν τοῦ στόλου τούτου ἀκλεῶς ἐνθαῦτα Ἀθηναῖοι τίνυσθαι βουλόμενοι 20
πρῶτα στρατηίην ποιεῦνται ἐπὶ Χαλκιδέας. Βοιωτοὶ
δὲ τοῖσι Χαλκιδεῦσι βοηθέουσι ἐπὶ τὸν Εὔριπον.
Ἀθηναίοισι δὲ ἰδοῦσι τοὺς βοηθοὺς ἔδοξε πρότερον
τοῖσι Βοιωτοῖσι ἢ τοῖσι Χαλκιδεῦσι ἐπιχειρέειν.
συμβάλλουσί τε δὴ τοῖσι Βοιωτοῖσι οἱ Ἀθηναῖοι 25
καὶ πολλῷ ἐκράτησαν, κάρτα δὲ πολλοὺς φονεύ-

σαντες ἑπτακοσίους αὐτῶν ἐζώγρησαν. τῆς δὲ
αὐτῆς ταύτης ἡμέρης οἱ Ἀθηναῖοι διαβάντες ἐς τὴν
Εὔβοιαν συμβάλλουσι καὶ τοῖσι Χαλκιδεῦσι, νική-
σαντες δὲ καὶ τούτους τετρακισχιλίους κληρούχους
ἐπὶ τῶν ἱπποβοτέων τῇ χώρῃ λείπουσι· οἱ δ' ἱπποβόται ἐκαλέοντο οἱ παχέες τῶν Χαλκιδέων. ὅσους
δὲ καὶ τούτων ἐζώγρησαν, ἅμα τοῖσι Βοιωτῶν ἐζω-
γρημένοισι εἶχον ἐν φυλακῇ, ἐν πέδαις δήσαντες·
χρόνῳ δὲ ἔλυσάν σφεας δίμνεως ἀποτιμησάμενοι.
τὰς δὲ πέδας αὐτῶν, ἐν τῇσι ἐδεδέατο, ἀνεκρέμασαν
ἐς τὴν ἀκρόπολιν, αἵ περ ἔτι καὶ ἐς ἐμὲ ἦσαν περι-
εοῦσαι, κρεμάμεναι ἐκ τειχέων περιπεφλευσμένων
πυρὶ ὑπὸ τοῦ Μήδου, ἀντίον δὲ τοῦ μεγάρου τοῦ πρὸς
ἑσπέρην τετραμμένου. καὶ τῶν λύτρων τὴν δεκάτην
ἀνέθηκαν, ποιησάμενοι τέθριππον χάλκεον· τὸ δὲ
ἀριστερῆς χειρὸς ἕστηκε πρῶτον ἐσιόντι ἐς τὰ προπύλαια τὰ ἐν τῇ ἀκροπόλι· ἐπιγέγραπται δέ οἱ τάδε·

"Ἔθνεα Βοιωτῶν καὶ Χαλκιδέων δαμάσαντες
"παῖδες Ἀθηναίων ἔργμασιν ἐν πολέμου
"δεσμῷ ἐν ἀχλυόεντι σιδηρέῳ ἔσβεσαν ὕβριν·
"τῶν ἵππους δεκάτην Παλλάδι τάσδ' ἔθεσαν."

The rising prosperity of Athens after the expulsion of the tyrants shows the advantages of liberty.

LXXVIII. Ἀθηναῖοι μέν νυν αὔξηντο, δηλοῖ
δὲ οὐ κατ' ἓν μοῦνον, ἀλλὰ πανταχῇ ἡ ἰσηγορίη ὡς
ἐστὶ χρῆμα σπουδαῖον, εἰ καὶ Ἀθηναῖοι τυραννευό-
μενοι μὲν οὐδαμῶν τῶν σφέας περιοικεόντων ἦσαν
τὰ πολέμια ἀμείνους, ἀπαλλαχθέντες δὲ τυράννων
μακρῷ πρῶτοι ἐγένοντο· δηλοῖ ὦν ταῦτα, ὅτι κατεχόμενοι μὲν ἐθελοκάκεον ὡς δεσπότῃ ἐργαζόμενοι,

ἐλευθερωθέντων δὲ αὐτὸς ἕκαστος ἑωυτῷ προεθυμέετο κατεργάζεσθαι.

The Boeotians in revenge for their defeat in the Chalkidian war make an attack upon Attica, and, being repulsed, obtain the help of the Aeginetans who harry the Attic coast.

LXXIX. οὗτοι μέν νυν ταῦτα ἔπρησσον, Θηβαῖοι δὲ μετὰ ταῦτα ἐς θεὸν ἔπεμπον, βουλόμενοι τίσασθαι Ἀθηναίους. ἡ δὲ Πυθίη ἀπὸ σφέων μὲν αὐτῶν οὐκ ἔφη αὐτοῖσι εἶναι τίσιν, ἐς πολύφημον δὲ ἐξενείκαντας ἐκέλευε τῶν ἄγχιστα δέεσθαι. ἀπελθόντων ὦν τῶν θεοπρόπων ἐξέφερον τὸ χρηστήριον ἀλίην ποιησάμενοι· ὡς ἐπυνθάνοντο δὲ λεγόντων αὐτῶν τῶν ἄγχιστα δέεσθαι, εἶπαν οἱ Θηβαῖοι ἀκούσαντες τούτων· "οὐκ ὦν ἄγχιστα ἡμέων οἰκέουσι "Ταναγραῖοί τε καὶ Κορωναῖοι καὶ Θεσπιέες, καὶ " οὗτοί γε ἅμα ἡμῖν αἰεὶ μαχόμενοι προθύμως συνδια- "φέρουσι τὸν πόλεμον. τί δέει τούτων γε δέεσθαι; "ἀλλὰ μᾶλλον μὴ οὐ τοῦτο ᾖ τὸ χρηστήριον." LXXX. Τοιαῦτα δὴ ἐπιλεγομένων εἶπε δή κοτε μαθών τις· "Ἐγώ μοι δοκέω συνιέναι τὸ ἐθέλει λέγειν "ἡμῖν τὸ μαντήιον. Ἀσωποῦ λέγονται γενέσθαι θυ- "γατέρες Θήβη τε καὶ Αἴγινα· τούτων ἀδελφεῶν "ἐουσέων δοκέω ἡμῖν Αἰγινητέων δέεσθαι τὸν θεὸν "χρῆσαι τιμωρητήρων γενέσθαι." καὶ οὐ γάρ τις ταύτης ἀμείνων γνώμη ἐδόκεε φαίνεσθαι, αὐτίκα πέμψαντες ἐδέοντο Αἰγινητέων, ἐπικαλεόμενοι κατὰ τὸ χρηστήριόν σφι βοηθέειν, ὡς ἐόντων ἀγχιστέων, οἱ δέ σφι αἰτέουσι ἐπικουρίην τοὺς Αἰακίδας συμπέμπειν ἔφασαν. LXXXI. Πειρησαμένων δὲ τῶν

Θηβαίων κατὰ τὴν συμμαχίην τῶν Αἰακιδέων καὶ
τρηχέως περιεφθέντων ὑπὸ τῶν Ἀθηναίων αὖτις
οἱ Θηβαῖοι πέμψαντες τοὺς μὲν Αἰακίδας σφι
ἀπεδίδοσαν, τῶν δὲ ἀνδρῶν ἐδέοντο. Αἰγινῆται δὲ
5 εὐδαιμονίῃ τε μεγάλῃ ἐπαερθέντες καὶ ἔχθρης παλαιῆς ἀναμνησθέντες ἐχούσης ἐς Ἀθηναίους τότε
Θηβαίων δεηθέντων πόλεμον ἀκήρυκτον Ἀθηναίοισι
ἐπέφερον. ἐπικειμένων γὰρ αὐτῶν Βοιωτοῖσι ἐπιπλώσαντες μακρῇσι νηυσὶ ἐς τὴν Ἀττικὴν κατὰ
10 μὲν ἔσυραν Φάληρον, κατὰ δὲ τῆς ἄλλης παραλίης
πολλοὺς δήμους, ποιεῦντες δὲ ταῦτα μεγάλως Ἀθηναίους ἐσίνοντο.

The enmity between Aegina and Athens began on account of the seizure by the Aeginetans of the sacred images in Epidauros, made of Attic olive-wood. The Athenian version of the story.

LXXXII. Ἡ δὲ ἔχθρη ἡ προοφειλομένη ἐς
Ἀθηναίους ἐκ τῶν Αἰγινητέων ἐγένετο ἐξ ἀρχῆς
15 τοιῆσδε. Ἐπιδαυρίοισι ἡ γῆ καρπὸν οὐδένα ἀνεδίδου.
περὶ ταύτης ὦν τῆς συμφορῆς οἱ Ἐπιδαύριοι ἐχρέοντο ἐν Δελφοῖσι· ἡ δὲ Πυθίη σφέας ἐκέλευε Δαμίης
τε καὶ Αὐξησίης ἀγάλματα ἱδρύσασθαι καί σφι
ἱδρυσαμένοισι ἄμεινον συνοίσεσθαι. ἐπειρώτεον ὦν
20 οἱ Ἐπιδαύριοι, κότερα χαλκοῦ ποιέωνται τὰ ἀγάλματα ἢ λίθου· ἡ δὲ Πυθίη οὐδέτερα τούτων ἔα,
ἀλλὰ ξύλου ἡμέρης ἐλαίης. ἐδέοντο ὦν οἱ Ἐπιδαύριοι Ἀθηναίων ἐλαίην σφι δοῦναι ταμέσθαι,
ἱροτάτας δὴ ἐκείνας νομίζοντες εἶναι· λέγεται δὲ
25 καὶ ὡς ἐλαῖαι ἦσαν ἄλλοθι γῆς οὐδαμοῦ κατὰ χρόνον
ἐκεῖνον ἢ ἐν Ἀθήνῃσι. οἱ δὲ ἐπὶ τοισίδε δώσειν

ἔφασαν, ἐπ' ᾧ ἀπάξουσι ἔτεος ἑκάστου τῇ Ἀθηναίῃ
τε τῇ πολιάδι ἱρὰ καὶ τῷ Ἐρεχθεῖ· καταινέσαντες
δ' ἐπὶ τούτοισι οἱ Ἐπιδαύριοι τῶν τε ἐδέοντο ἔτυχον,
καὶ ἀγάλματα ἐκ τῶν ἐλαιέων τούτων ποιησάμενοι
ἱδρύσαντο· καὶ ἥ τε γῆ σφι ἔφερε καρπόν, καὶ Ἀθηναίοισι ἐπετέλεον τὰ συνέθεντο. LXXXIII. Τοῦτον
δ' ἔτι τὸν χρόνον καὶ πρὸ τοῦ Αἰγινῆται Ἐπιδαυρίων
ἤκουον, τά τε ἄλλα καὶ δίκας διαβαίνοντες ἐς Ἐπί-
δαυρον ἐδίδοσάν τε καὶ ἐλάμβανον παρ' ἀλλήλων
οἱ Αἰγινῆται. τὸ δὲ ἀπὸ τοῦδε νέας τε πηξάμενοι
καὶ ἀγνωμοσύνῃ χρησάμενοι ἀπέστησαν ἀπὸ τῶν
Ἐπιδαυρίων. ἅτε δὲ ἐόντες διάφοροι, ἐδηλέοντο
αὐτοὺς ὥστε δὴ θαλασσοκράτορες ἐόντες, καὶ δὴ καὶ
τὰ ἀγάλματα ταῦτα τῆς τε Δαμίης καὶ τῆς Αὐξησίης
ὑπαιρέονται αὐτῶν, καί σφεα ἐκόμισάν τε καὶ ἱδρύσαντο τῆς σφετέρης χώρης ἐς τὴν μεσόγαιαν, τῇ
Οἴη μέν ἐστι οὔνομα, στάδια δὲ μάλιστά κῃ ἀπὸ
τῆς πόλιος ὡς εἴκοσι ἀπέχει. ἱδρυσάμενοι δὲ ἐν
τούτῳ τῷ χώρῳ θυσίῃσί τέ σφεα καὶ χοροῖσι γυναι-
κηίοισι κερτόμοισι ἱλάσκοντο, χορηγῶν ἀποδεικνυ-
μένων ἑκατέρῃ τῶν δαιμόνων δέκα ἀνδρῶν· κακῶς
δὲ ἠγόρευον οἱ χοροὶ ἄνδρα μὲν οὐδένα, τὰς δὲ ἐπι-
χωρίας γυναῖκας. ἦσαν δὲ καὶ τοῖσι Ἐπιδαυρίοισι
αἱ τοιαῦται ἱρουργίαι· εἰσὶ δέ σφι καὶ ἄρρητοι
ἱρουργίαι. LXXXIV. Κλεφθέντων δὲ τῶνδε τῶν
ἀγαλμάτων οἱ Ἐπιδαύριοι τοῖσι Ἀθηναίοισι τὰ
συνέθεντο οὐκ ἐπετέλεον. πέμψαντες δὲ οἱ Ἀθηναῖοι
ἐμήνιον τοῖσι Ἐπιδαυρίοισι· οἱ δὲ ἀπέφαινον λόγῳ,
ὡς οὐκ ἀδικοῖεν· ὅσον μὲν γὰρ χρόνον εἶχον τὰ
ἀγάλματα ἐν τῇ χώρῃ, ἐπιτελέειν τὰ συνέθεντο,
ἐπεὶ δὲ ἐστερῆσθαι αὐτῶν, οὐ δίκαιοι εἶναι ἀποφέρειν

ἔτι, ἀλλὰ τοὺς ἔχοντας αὐτὰ Αἰγινήτας πρήσσεσθαι ἐκέλευον. πρὸς ταῦτα οἱ Ἀθηναῖοι ἐς Αἴγιναν πέμψαντες ἀπαίτεον τὰ ἀγάλματα· οἱ δὲ Αἰγινῆται ἔφασαν σφίσι τε καὶ Ἀθηναίοισι εἶναι οὐδὲν πρῆγμα.
LXXXV. Ἀθηναῖοι μέν νυν λέγουσι μετὰ τὴν ἀπαίτησιν ἀποσταλῆναι τριήρεϊ μιῇ τῶν ἀστῶν τούτους, οἳ ἀποπεμφθέντες ἀπὸ τοῦ κοινοῦ καὶ ἀπικόμενοι ἐς Αἴγιναν τὰ ἀγάλματα ταῦτα ὡς σφετέρων ξύλων ἐόντα ἐπειρῶντο ἐκ τῶν βάθρων ἐξανασπᾶν, ἵνα σφέα ἀνακομίσωνται. οὐ δυναμένους δὲ τούτῳ τῷ τρόπῳ αὐτῶν κρατῆσαι, περιβαλόντας σχοινία ἕλκειν τὰ ἀγάλματα, καί σφι ἕλκουσι βροντήν τε καὶ ἅμα τῇ βροντῇ σεισμὸν ἐπιγενέσθαι· τοὺς δὲ τριηρίτας τοὺς ἕλκοντας ὑπὸ τούτων ἀλλοφρονῆσαι, παθόντας δὲ τοῦτο κτείνειν ἀλλήλους ἅτε πολεμίους, ἐς ὃ ἐκ πάντων ἕνα λειφθέντα ἀνακομισθῆναι αὐτὸν ἐς Φάληρον.

The Aeginetan version. The interference of the Argives.

LXXXVI. Ἀθηναῖοι μέν νυν οὕτω λέγουσι γενέσθαι, Αἰγινῆται δὲ οὐ μιῇ νηῒ ἀπικέσθαι Ἀθηναίους (μίαν μὲν γὰρ καὶ ὀλίγῳ πλεῦνας μιῆς, καὶ εἴ σφι μὴ ἔτυχον ἐοῦσαι νέες, ἀπαμύνασθαι ἂν εὐπετέως), ἀλλὰ πολλῇσι νηυσὶ ἐπιπλέειν σφι ἐπὶ τὴν χώρην, αὐτοὶ δέ σφι εἶξαι καὶ οὐ ναυμαχῆσαι. οὐκ ἔχουσι δὲ τοῦτο διασημῆναι ἀτρεκέως, οὔτε εἰ ἥσσονες συγγινωσκόμενοι εἶναι τῇ ναυμαχίῃ κατὰ τοῦτο εἶξαν, οὔτε εἰ βουλόμενοι ποιῆσαι οἷόν τι καὶ ἐποίησαν. Ἀθηναίους μέν νυν, ἐπεί τέ σφι οὐδεὶς ἐς μάχην κατίστατο, ἀποβάντας ἀπὸ τῶν νεῶν τραπέσθαι πρὸς τὰ ἀγάλματα, οὐ δυναμένους δὲ ἀνασπάσαι ἐκ τῶν βάθρων αὐτὰ οὕτω δὴ περιβαλομένους σχοινία ἕλκειν, ἐς ὃ ἑλκόμενα τὰ ἀγάλματα ἀμφότερα τὠυτὸ ποιῆσαι, ἐμοὶ μὲν οὐ πιστὰ λέγοντες, ἄλλῳ δέ τεῳ· ἐς γούνατα γάρ σφι αὐτὰ πεσεῖν, καὶ τὸν ἀπὸ τούτου χρόνον διατελέειν οὕτω ἔχοντα. 5 Ἀθηναίους μὲν δὴ ταῦτα ποιέειν, σφέας δὲ Αἰγινῆται λέγουσι πυθομένους τοὺς Ἀθηναίους ὡς μέλλοιεν ἐπὶ σφέας στρατεύεσθαι, ἑτοίμους Ἀργείους ποιέεσθαι. τούς τε δὴ Ἀθηναίους ἀποβεβάναι ἐς τὴν Αἰγιναίην, καὶ παρεῖναι βοηθέοντάς σφι τοὺς Ἀργείους, καὶ 10 λαθεῖν τε ἐξ Ἐπιδαύρου διαβάντας ἐς τὴν νῆσον καὶ οὐ προακηκοόσι τοῖσι Ἀθηναίοισι ἐπιπεσεῖν ὑποταμομένους τὸ ἀπὸ τῶν νεῶν, ἅμα τε ἐν τούτῳ τὴν βροντήν τε γενέσθαι καὶ τὸν σεισμὸν αὐτοῖσι.

The sole survivor of the Athenian expedition into Aegina murdered by Attic women.

LXXXVII. Λέγεται μέν νυν ὑπ' Ἀργείων τε 15 καὶ Αἰγινητέων τάδε, ὁμολογέεται δὲ καὶ ὑπ' Ἀθηναίων ἕνα μοῦνον τὸν ἀποσωθέντα αὐτῶν ἐς τὴν Ἀττικὴν γενέσθαι· πλὴν Ἀργεῖοι μὲν λέγουσι αὐτῶν τὸ Ἀττικὸν στρατόπεδον διαφθειράντων τὸν ἕνα τοῦτον περιγενέσθαι, Ἀθηναῖοι δὲ τοῦ δαιμονίου· 20 περιγενέσθαι μέντοι οὐδὲ τοῦτον τὸν ἕνα, ἀλλ' ἀπολέσθαι τρόπῳ τοιῷδε. κομισθεὶς ἄρα ἐς τὰς Ἀθήνας ἀπήγγειλε τὸ πάθος· πυθομένας δὲ τὰς γυναῖκας τῶν ἐπ' Αἴγιναν στρατευσαμένων ἀνδρῶν, δεινόν τι ποιησαμένας ἐκεῖνον μοῦνον ἐξ ἁπάντων σωθῆναι, 25 πέριξ τὸν ἄνθρωπον τοῦτον λαβούσας καὶ κεντεύσας τῇσι περόνῃσι τῶν ἱματίων εἰρωτᾶν ἑκάστην αὐτέων, ὅκῃ εἴη ὁ ἑωυτῆς ἀνήρ. καὶ τοῦτον μὲν οὕτω δια-

φθαρῆναι, Ἀθηναίοισι δὲ ἔτι τοῦ πάθεος δεινότερόν
τι δόξαι εἶναι τὸ τῶν γυναικῶν ἔργον. ἄλλῳ μὲν δὴ
οὐκ ἔχειν ὅτεῳ ζημιώσωσι τὰς γυναῖκας, τὴν δὲ
ἐσθῆτα μετέβαλον αὐτέων ἐς τὴν Ἰάδα· ἐφόρεον γὰρ
5 δὴ πρὸ τοῦ αἱ τῶν Ἀθηναίων γυναῖκες ἐσθῆτα
Δωρίδα, τῇ Κορινθίῃ παραπλησιωτάτην· μετέβαλον
ὦν ἐς τὸν λίνεον κιθῶνα, ἵνα δὴ περόνῃσι μὴ χρέωνται. LXXXVIII. Ἔστι δὲ ἀληθέϊ λόγῳ χρεωμένοισι οὐκ Ἰὰς αὕτη ἡ ἐσθὴς τὸ παλαιόν, ἀλλὰ
10 Κάειρα, ἐπεὶ ἥ γε Ἑλληνικὴ ἐσθὴς πᾶσα ἡ ἀρχαίη
τῶν γυναικῶν ἡ αὐτὴ ἦν, τὴν νῦν Δωρίδα καλέομεν.
τοῖσι δὲ Ἀργείοισι καὶ τοῖσι Αἰγινήτῃσι καὶ πρὸς
ταῦτα ἔτι τόδε ποιῆσαι νόμον εἶναι παρὰ σφίσι
ἑκατέροισι, τὰς περόνας ἡμιολίας ποιέεσθαι τοῦ τότε
15 κατεστεῶτος μέτρου, καὶ ἐς τὸ ἱρὸν τῶν θεῶν τούτων
περόνας μάλιστα ἀνατιθέναι τὰς γυναῖκας, Ἀττικὸν
δὲ μήτε τι ἄλλο προσφέρειν πρὸς τὸ ἱρὸν μήτε
κέραμον, ἀλλ' ἐκ χυτρίδων ἐπιχωρίων νόμον τὸ
λοιπὸν αὐτόθι εἶναι πίνειν. Ἀργείων μέν νυν καὶ
20 Αἰγινητέων αἱ γυναῖκες ἐκ τότε κατ' ἔριν τῶν
Ἀθηναίων περόνας ἔτι καὶ ἐς ἐμὲ ἐφόρεον μέζονας ἢ
πρὸ τοῦ.

*The Aeginetans, being thus hostile to the Athenians, join
the Boeotians in their attack upon Attica. The
Athenians are told by the oracle to wait thirty years
before attacking Aegina.*

LXXXIX. Τῆς δὲ ἔχθρης τῆς πρὸς Αἰγινήτας
Ἀθηναίοισι γενομένης ἀρχὴ κατὰ εἴρηται ἐγένετο.
25 τότε δὴ Θηβαίων ἐπικαλεομένων προθύμως τῶν περὶ
τὰ ἀγάλματα γενομένων ἀναμιμνησκόμενοι οἱ Αἰγι-

νῆται ἐβοήθεον τοῖσι Βοιωτοῖσι. Αἰγινῆταί τε δὴ
ἐδηίουν τῆς Ἀττικῆς τὰ παραθαλάσσια, καὶ Ἀθηναίοισι ὁρμεομένοισι ἐπ' Αἰγινήτας στρατεύεσθαι
ἦλθε μαντήιον ἐκ Δελφῶν, ἐπισχόντας ἀπὸ τοῦ
Αἰγινητέων ἀδικίου τριήκοντα ἔτεα τῷ ἑνὶ καὶ τριη- 5
κοστῷ Αἰακῷ τέμενος ἀποδέξαντας ἄρχεσθαι τοῦ
πρὸς Αἰγινήτας πολέμου καί σφι χωρήσειν τὰ
βούλονται· ἢν δὲ αὐτίκα ἐπιστρατεύωνται, πολλὰ
μέν σφεας ἐν τῷ μεταξὺ τοῦ χρόνου πείσεσθαι,
πολλὰ δὲ καὶ ποιήσειν, τέλος μέντοι καταστρέψε- 10
σθαι. ταῦτα ὡς ἀπενειχθέντα ἤκουσαν οἱ Ἀθηναῖοι,
τῷ μὲν Αἰακῷ τέμενος ἀπέδεξαν τοῦτο, τὸ νῦν ἐπὶ
τῆς ἀγορῆς ἵδρυται, τριήκοντα δὲ ἔτεα οὐκ ἀνέσχοντο
ἀκούσαντες, ὅκως χρεὸν εἴη ἐπισχεῖν πεπονθότας
πρὸς Αἰγινητέων ἀνάρσια. 15

The Athenians, though unwilling to obey, are hindered by fresh acts of hostility from Sparta, caused by Kleomenes discovering that the oracle had been tampered with by the Alkmaeonidae when it ordered the Spartans to drive out Hippias. The Spartans send for Hippias and summon a congress of allies.

XC. Ἐς τιμωρίην δὲ παρασκευαζομένοισι αὐτοῖσι ἐκ Λακεδαιμονίων πρῆγμα ἐγειρόμενον ἐμπόδιον ἐγένετο. πυθόμενοι γὰρ οἱ Λακεδαιμόνιοι τὰ ἐκ
τῶν Ἀλκμαιωνιδέων ἐς τὴν Πυθίην μεμηχανημένα
καὶ τὰ ἐκ τῆς Πυθίης ἐπὶ σφέας τε καὶ τοὺς Πει- 20
σιστρατίδας συμφορὴν ἐποιεῦντο διπλόην, ὅτι τε
ἄνδρας ξείνους σφι ἐόντας ἐξεληλάκεσαν ἐκ τῆς
ἐκείνων, καὶ ὅτι ταῦτα ποιήσασι χάρις οὐδεμία
ἐφαίνετο πρὸς τῶν Ἀθηναίων. ἔτι τε πρὸς τού-

τοῖσι ἐνῆγόν σφεας οἱ χρησμοὶ λέγοντες πολλά τε
καὶ ἀνάρσια ἔσεσθαι αὐτοῖσι ἐξ Ἀθηναίων, τῶν
πρότερον μὲν ἦσαν ἀδαέες, τότε δὲ Κλεομένεος
κομίσαντος ἐς Σπάρτην ἐξέμαθον. ἐκτήσατο δὲ ὁ
5 Κλεομένης ἐκ τῆς Ἀθηναίων ἀκροπόλιος τοὺς χρησμούς, τοὺς ἔκτηντο μὲν πρότερον οἱ Πεισιστρατίδαι,
ἐξελαυνόμενοι δὲ ἔλιπον ἐν τῷ ἱρῷ, καταλειφθέντας
δὲ ὁ Κλεομένης ἀνέλαβε. XCI. Τότε δὲ ὡς ἀνέλαβον οἱ Λακεδαιμόνιοι τοὺς χρησμοὺς καὶ τοὺς Ἀθη-
10 ναίους ὥρεον αὐξομένους καὶ οὐδαμῶς ἑτοίμους ἐόντας
πείθεσθαι σφίσι, νόῳ λαβόντες, ὡς ἐλεύθερον μὲν ἐὸν
τὸ γένος τὸ Ἀττικὸν ἰσόρροπον τῷ ἑωυτῶν ἂν γίνοιτο,
κατεχόμενον δὲ ὑπὸ τυραννίδος ἀσθενὲς καὶ πειθαρχέ-
εσθαι ἑτοῖμον, μαθόντες δὲ τούτων ἕκαστα μετεπέμ-
15 ποντο Ἱππίην τὸν Πεισιστράτου ἀπὸ Σιγείου τοῦ
ἐν Ἑλλησπόντῳ, ἐς τὸ καταφεύγουσι οἱ Πεισιστρατίδαι. ἐπείτε δέ σφι Ἱππίης καλεόμενος ἧκε,
μεταπεμψάμενοι καὶ τῶν ἄλλων συμμάχων ἀγγέλους
ἔλεγόν σφι Σπαρτιῆται τάδε· "Ἄνδρες σύμμαχοι,
20 "συγγινώσκομεν αὐτοῖσι ἡμῖν οὐ ποιήσασι ὀρθῶς·
"ἐπαερθέντες γὰρ κιβδήλοισι μαντηίοισι ἄνδρας ξεί-
"νους ἐόντας ἡμῖν τὰ μάλιστα καὶ ἀναδεκομένους
"ὑποχειρίας παρέξειν τὰς Ἀθήνας, τούτους ἐκ τῆς
"πατρίδος ἐξηλάσαμεν, καὶ ἔπειτα ποιήσαντες ταῦτα
25 "δήμῳ ἀχαρίστῳ παρεδώκαμεν τὴν πόλιν, ὃς ἐπείτε
"δι' ἡμέας ἐλευθερωθεὶς ἀνέκυψε, ἡμέας μὲν καὶ
"τὸν βασιλέα ἡμέων περιυβρίσας ἐξέβαλε, δόξαν δὲ
"φύσας αὐξάνεται, ὥστε ἐκμεμαθήκασι μάλιστα μὲν
"οἱ περίοικοι αὐτῶν Βοιωτοὶ καὶ Χαλκιδέες, τάχα
30 "δέ τις καὶ ἄλλος ἐκμαθήσεται ἁμαρτών. ἐπείτε
"δὲ ἐκεῖνα ποιήσαντες ἡμάρτομεν, νῦν πειρησόμεθά

"σφέας ἅμα ὑμῖν ἀκεόμενοι· αὐτοῦ γὰρ τούτου
"εἵνεκεν τόνδε τε τὸν Ἱππίην μετεπεμψάμεθα καὶ
"ὑμέας ἀπὸ τῶν πολίων, ἵνα κοινῷ τε λόγῳ καὶ
"κοινῷ στόλῳ ἐσαγαγόντες αὐτὸν ἐς τὰς Ἀθήνας
"ἀποδῶμεν τά καὶ ἀπειλόμεθα."

The Korinthian Sosikles protests against Hellenic forces being used to set up a tyranny in Athens. The story of the Kypselid tyrants at Korinth.

XCII. Οἱ μὲν ταῦτα ἔλεγον, τῶν δὲ συμμάχων τὸ πλῆθος οὐκ ἐνεδέκετο τοὺς λόγους. οἱ μέν νυν ἄλλοι ἡσυχίην ἦγον, Κορίνθιος δὲ Σωσικλέης ἔλεξε τάδε·

§ 1. "Ἦ δὴ ὅ τε οὐρανὸς ἔσται ἔνερθε τῆς γῆς
"καὶ ἡ γῆ μετέωρος ὑπὲρ τοῦ οὐρανοῦ καὶ οἱ
"ἄνθρωποι νομὸν ἐν θαλάσσῃ ἕξουσι καὶ οἱ ἰχθύες
"τὸν πρότερον ἄνθρωποι, ὅτε γε ὑμεῖς, ὦ Λακε-
"δαιμόνιοι, ἰσοκρατίας καταλύοντες τυραννίδας ἐς
"τὰς πόλις κατάγειν παρασκευάζεσθε, τοῦ οὔτε
"ἀδικώτερον οὐδέν ἐστι κατ᾽ ἀνθρώπους οὔτε μιαι-
"φονώτερον. εἰ γὰρ δὴ τοῦτό γε δοκέει ὑμῖν εἶναι
"χρηστὸν ὥστε τυραννεύεσθαι τὰς πόλις, αὐτοὶ
"πρῶτοι τύραννον καταστησάμενοι παρὰ σφίσι
"αὐτοῖσι οὕτω καὶ τοῖσι ἄλλοισι δίζησθε κατιστάναι·
"νῦν δὲ αὐτοὶ ἄπειροι ἐόντες τυράννων καὶ φυλάσ-
"σοντες δεινότατα τοῦτο ἐν τῇ Σπάρτῃ μὴ γενέσθαι
"παραχρᾶσθε ἐς τοὺς συμμάχους· εἰ δὲ αὐτοὶ
"ἔμπειροι ἔατε, κατά περ ἡμεῖς, εἴχετε ἂν περὶ
"αὐτοῦ γνώμας ἀμείνονας συμβαλέσθαι ἤ περ νῦν.

The rule of the Bakchiadae at Korinth threatened by the birth of Labda's son.

§ 2. "Κορινθίοισι γὰρ ἦν πόλιος κατάστασις
"τοιήδε· ἦν ὀλιγαρχίη, καὶ οὗτοι Βακχιάδαι καλεό-
"μενοι ἔνεμον τὴν πόλιν, ἐδίδοσαν δὲ καὶ ἤγοντο ἐξ
"ἀλλήλων, Ἀμφίονι δὲ ἐόντι τούτων τῶν ἀνδρῶν
5 "γίνεται θυγάτηρ χωλή· οὔνομα δέ οἱ ἦν Λάβδα.
"ταύτην Βακχιαδέων γὰρ οὐδεὶς ἤθελε γῆμαι, ἴσχει
"Ἠετίων ὁ Ἐχεκράτεος, δήμου μὲν ἐκ Πέτρης ἐών,
"ἀτὰρ τὰ ἀνέκαθεν Λαπίθης τε καὶ Καινείδης. ἐκ
"δέ οἱ ταύτης τῆς γυναικὸς οὐδ' ἐξ ἄλλης παῖδες
10 "ἐγίνοντο. ἐστάλη ὧν ἐς Δελφοὺς περὶ γόνου.
"ἐσιόντα δὲ αὐτὸν ἰθέως ἡ Πυθίη προσαγορεύει
"τοισίδε τοῖσι ἔπεσι·

"Ἠετίων, οὔτις σε τίει πολύτιτον ἐόντα.
"Λάβδα κύει, τέξει δ' ὀλοοίτροχον· ἐν δὲ πεσεῖται
15 "ἀνδράσι μουνάρχοισι, δικαιώσει δὲ Κόρινθον.
"ταῦτα χρησθέντα τῷ Ἠετίωνι ἐξαγγέλλεταί κως
"τοῖσι Βακχιάδῃσι, τοῖσι τὸ μὲν πρότερον γενόμενον
"χρηστήριον ἐς Κόρινθον ἦν ἄσημον, φέρον τε ἐς
"τὠυτὸ καὶ τὸ τοῦ Ἠετίωνος, καὶ λέγον ὧδε·
20 "αἰετὸς ἐν πέτρῃσι κύει, τέξει δὲ λέοντα
"καρτερὸν ὠμηστήν· πολλῶν δ' ὑπὸ γούνατα λύσει.
"ταῦτά νυν εὖ φράζεσθε, Κορίνθιοι, οἳ περὶ καλὴν
"Πειρήνην οἰκεῖτε καὶ ὀφρυόεντα Κόρινθον.

They determine to destroy the babe.

§ 3. "Τοῦτο μὲν δὴ τοῖσι Βακχιάδῃσι πρότερον
25 "γενόμενον ἦν ἀτέκμαρτον, τότε δὲ τὸ Ἠετίωνι γενό-
"μενον ὡς ἐπύθοντο, αὐτίκα καὶ τὸ πρότερον συνῆκαν

"ἐὸν συνῳδὸν τῷ Ἠετίωνος. συνέντες δὲ καὶ τοῦτο
"εἶχον ἐν ἡσυχίῃ, ἐθέλοντες τὸν μέλλοντα Ἠετίωνι
"γίνεσθαι γόνον διαφθεῖραι. ὡς δὲ ἔτεκε ἡ γυνὴ τά-
"χιστα, πέμπουσι σφέων αὐτῶν δέκα ἐς τὸν δῆμον, ἐν
"τῷ κατοίκητο ὁ Ἠετίων, ἀποκτενέοντας τὸ παιδίον. 5
"ἀπικόμενοι δὲ οὗτοι ἐς τὴν Πέτρην καὶ παρελθόντες
"ἐς τὴν αὐλὴν τὴν Ἠετίωνος αἴτεον τὸ παιδίον· ἡ δὲ
"Λάβδα εἰδυῖά τε οὐδὲν τῶν εἵνεκεν ἐκεῖνοι ἀπικοίατο
"καὶ δοκέουσά σφεας φιλοφροσύνης τοῦ πατρὸς εἵνεκεν
"αἰτέειν φέρουσα ἐνεχείρισε αὐτῶν ἑνί. τοῖσι δὲ ἄρα 10
"ἐβεβούλευτο κατ' ὁδὸν τὸν πρῶτον αὐτῶν λαβόντα
"τὸ παιδίον προσουδίσαι. ἐπείτε ὦν ἔδωκε φέρουσα
"ἡ Λάβδα, τὸν λαβόντα τῶν ἀνδρῶν θείῃ τύχῃ
"προσεγέλασε τὸ παιδίον, καὶ τὸν φρασθέντα τοῦτο
"οἰκτός τις ἴσχει ἀποκτεῖναι, κατοικτείρας δὲ παρα- 15
"διδοῖ τῷ δευτέρῳ, ὁ δὲ τῷ τρίτῳ. οὕτω δὲ διεξῆλθε
"διὰ πάντων τῶν δέκα παραδιδόμενον οὐδενὸς βουλο-
"μένου διεργάσασθαι. ἀποδόντες ὦν ὀπίσω τῇ τε-
"κούσῃ τὸ παιδίον καὶ ἐξελθόντες ἔξω ἑστεῶτες ἐπὶ
"τῶν θυρέων ἀλλήλων ἅπτοντο καταιτιώμενοι, καὶ 20
"μάλιστα τοῦ πρώτου λαβόντος, ὅτι οὐκ ἐποίησε κατὰ
"τὰ δεδογμένα, ἐς ὃ δή σφι χρόνου ἐγγινομένου ἔδοξε
"αὖτις παρελθόντας πάντας τοῦ φόνου μετίσχειν.

Labda hides the child in a chest (κυψέλη).

§ 4. "Ἔδεε δὲ ἐκ τοῦ Ἠετίωνος γόνου Κορίνθῳ
"κακὰ ἀναβλαστεῖν. ἡ Λάβδα γὰρ πάντα ταῦτα 25
"ἤκουε ἑστεῶσα πρὸς αὐτῇσι τῇσι θύρῃσι· δείσασα
"δὲ, μή σφι μεταδόξῃ καὶ τὸ δεύτερον λαβόντες τὸ
"παιδίον ἀποκτείνωσι, φέρουσα κατακρύπτει ἐς τὸ
"ἀφραστότατόν οἱ ἐφαίνετο εἶναι, ἐς κυψέλην, ἐπι-

"σταμένη, ὡς, εἰ ὑποστρέψαντες ἐς ζήτησιν ἀπι-
"κοίατο, πάντα ἐρευνήσειν μέλλοιεν, τὰ δὴ καὶ
"ἐγένετο. ἐλθοῦσι δὲ καὶ διζημένοισι αὐτοῖσι ὡς
"οὐκ ἐφαίνετο, ἐδόκεε ἀπαλλάσσεσθαι καὶ λέγειν
5 "πρὸς τοὺς ἀποπέμψαντας, ὡς πάντα ποιήσειαν, τὰ
"ἐκεῖνοι ἐνετείλαντο.

Kypselos grows up and becomes tyrant of Korinth.

§ 5. "οἱ μὲν δὴ ἀπελθόντες ἔλεγον ταῦτα, Ἠετίωνι
"δὲ μετὰ ταῦτα ὁ παῖς αὐξάνετο καὶ οἱ διαφυγόντι
"τοῦτον τὸν κίνδυνον ἀπὸ τῆς κυψέλης ἐπωνυμίην
10 "Κύψελος οὔνομα ἐτέθη. ἀνδρωθέντι δὲ καὶ μαν-
"τευομένῳ Κυψέλῳ ἐγένετο ἀμφιδέξιον χρηστήριον
"ἐν Δελφοῖσι, τῷ πίσυνος γενόμενος ἐπεχείρησέ τε
"καὶ ἔσχε Κόρινθον. ὁ δὲ χρησμὸς ὅδε ἦν·
"ὄλβιος οὗτος ἀνήρ, ὃς ἐμὸν δόμον ἐσκαταβαίνει,
15 "Κύψελος Ἠετίδης, βασιλεὺς κλειτοῖο Κορίνθου,
"αὐτὸς καὶ παῖδες, παίδων γε μὲν οὐκέτι παῖδες.
"τὸ μὲν δὴ χρηστήριον τοῦτο ἦν, τυραννεύσας δὲ ὁ
"Κύψελος τοιοῦτος δή τις ἀνὴρ ἐγένετο· πολλοὺς
"μὲν Κορινθίων ἐδίωξε, πολλοὺς δὲ χρημάτων ἀπε-
20 "στέρησε, πολλῷ δ' ἔτι πλείστους τῆς ψυχῆς.

*He is succeeded by Periander, who sends to Thrasybulus
of Miletos for advice.*

§ 6. "Ἄρξαντος δὲ τούτου ἐπὶ τριήκοντα ἔτεα
"καὶ διαπλέξαντος τὸν βίον εὖ διάδοχός οἱ τῆς τυραν-
"νίδος ὁ παῖς Περίανδρος γίνεται. ὁ τοίνυν Περίαν-
"δρος κατ' ἀρχὰς μὲν ἦν ἠπιώτερος τοῦ πατρός, ἐπείτε
25 "δὲ ὡμίλησε δι' ἀγγέλων Θρασυβούλῳ τῷ Μιλήτου
"τυράννῳ, πολλῷ ἔτι ἐγένετο Κυψέλου μιαιφονώτερος·
"πέμψας γὰρ παρὰ Θρασύβουλον κήρυκα ἐπυνθάνετο,

"ὅντινα ἂν τρόπον ἀσφαλέστατον καταστησάμενος
"τῶν πρηγμάτων κάλλιστα τὴν πόλιν ἐπιτροπεύοι.
"Θρασύβουλος δὲ τὸν ἐλθόντα παρὰ τοῦ Περιάνδρου
"ἐξῆγε ἔξω τοῦ ἄστεος, ἐσβὰς δὲ ἐς ἄρουραν ἐσπαρ-
"μένην ἅμα τε διεξήϊε τὸ λήϊον ἐπειρωτῶν τε καὶ 5
"ἀναποδίζων τὸν κήρυκα κατὰ τὴν ἀπὸ Κορίνθου
"ἄπιξιν, καὶ ἐκόλουε αἰεί, ὅκως τινὰ ἴδοι τῶν ἀστα-
"χύων ὑπερέχοντα, κολούων δὲ ἔρριπτε, ἐς ὃ τοῦ
"ληΐου τὸ κάλλιστόν τε καὶ βαθύτατον διέφθειρε
"τρόπῳ τοιούτῳ· διεξελθὼν δὲ τὸ χωρίον καὶ ὑποθέ- 10
"μενος ἔπος οὐδὲν ἀποπέμπει τὸν κήρυκα. νοστή-
"σαντος δὲ τοῦ κήρυκος ἐς τὴν Κόρινθον ἦν πρόθυμος
"πυνθάνεσθαι τὴν ὑποθήκην ὁ Περίανδρος. ὁ δὲ
"οὐδέν οἱ ἔφη Θρασύβουλον ὑποθέσθαι, θωυμάζειν
"τε αὐτοῦ, παρ' οἷόν μιν ἄνδρα ἀποπέμψειε, ὡς 15
"παραπλῆγά τε καὶ τῶν ἑωυτοῦ σινάμωρον, ἀπη-
"γεόμενος τά περ πρὸς Θρασυβούλου ὀπώπεε.

Periander's cruelty.

§ 7. "Περίανδρος δὲ συνεὶς τὸ ποιηθέν, καὶ νόῳ
"σχών, ὥς οἱ ὑπετίθετο Θρασύβουλος τοὺς ὑπερόχους
"τῶν ἀστῶν φονεύειν, ἐνθαῦτα δὴ πᾶσαν κακότητα 20
"ἐξέφαινε ἐς τοὺς πολιήτας. ὅσα γὰρ Κύψελος
"ἀπέλιπε κτείνων τε καὶ διώκων, Περίανδρός σφεα
"ἀπετέλεσε, μιῇ δὲ ἡμέρῃ ἀπέδυσε πάσας τὰς Κο-
"ρινθίων γυναῖκας διὰ τὴν ἑωυτοῦ γυναῖκα Μέλισσαν.
"πέμψαντι γάρ οἱ ἐς Θεσπρωτοὺς ἐπ' Ἀχέροντα 25
"ποταμὸν ἀγγέλους ἐπὶ τὸ νεκυομαντήϊον παρακατα-
"θήκης πέρι ξεινικῆς οὔτε σημανέειν ἔφη ἡ Μέλισσα
"ἐπιφανεῖσα οὔτε κατερέειν ἐν τῷ κέεται χώρῳ ἡ
"παρακαταθήκη· ῥιγοῦν τε γὰρ καὶ εἶναι γυμνή· τῶν

"γάρ οἱ συγκατέθαψε εἱμάτων ὄφελος εἶναι οὐδὲν οὐ
"κατακαυθέντων· μαρτύριον δέ οἱ εἶναι, ὡς ἀληθέα
"ταῦτα λέγει, ὅτι ἐπὶ ψυχρὸν τὸν ἰπνὸν Περίανδρος
"τοὺς ἄρτους ἐπέβαλε. ταῦτα δὲ ὡς ὀπίσω ἀπηγ-
5 "γέλθη τῷ Περιάνδρῳ (πιστὸν γάρ οἱ ἦν τὸ συμ-
"βόλαιον, ὃς νεκρῷ ἐούσῃ Μελίσσῃ ἐμίγη), ἰθέως δὴ
"μετὰ τὴν ἀγγελίην κήρυγμα ἐποιήσατο ἐς τὸ Ἡραῖον
"ἐξιέναι πάσας τὰς Κορινθίων γυναῖκας. αἱ μὲν δὴ
"ὡς ἐς ὁρτὴν ἤισαν κόσμῳ τῷ καλλίστῳ χρεόμεναι,
10 "ὁ δ᾽ ὑποστήσας τοὺς δορυφόρους ἀπέδυσέ σφεας
"πάσας ὁμοίως, τάς τ᾽ ἐλευθέρας καὶ τὰς ἀμφιπόλους,
"συμφορήσας δὲ ἐς ὄρυγμα Μελίσσῃ ἐπευχόμενος
"κατέκαιε. ταῦτα δέ οἱ ποιήσαντι καὶ τὸ δεύτερον
"πέμψαντι ἔφρασε τὸ εἴδωλον τὸ Μελίσσης ἐς τὸν
15 "κατέθηκε χῶρον τοῦ ξείνου τὴν παρακαταθήκην.
"Τοιοῦτο μέν ἐστι ὑμῖν ἡ τυραννίς, ὦ Λακεδαιμόνιοι,
"καὶ τοιούτων ἔργων. ἡμέας δὲ τοὺς Κορινθίους τό
"τε αὐτίκα θῶυμα μέγα εἶχε, ὅτε ὑμέας εἴδομεν
"μεταπεμπομένους Ἱππίην, νῦν τε δὴ καὶ μεζόνως
20 "θωυμάζομεν λέγοντας ταῦτα, ἐπιμαρτυρόμεθά τε
"ἐπικαλεόμενοι ὑμῖν θεοὺς τοὺς Ἑλληνίους, μὴ κατι-
"στάναι τυραννίδας ἐς τὰς πόλις. οὐκ ὦν παύσεσθε,
"ἀλλὰ πειρήσεσθε παρὰ τὸ δίκαιον κατάγοντες Ἱπ-
"πίην, ἴστε ὑμῖν Κορινθίους γε οὐ συναινέοντας."

*Hippias, protesting that the Korinthians would repent their
action, retires to Sigeium, formerly taken by Peisistratos.*

25 XCIII. Σωσικλέης μὲν ἀπὸ Κορίνθου πρεσ-
βεύων ἔλεξε τάδε, Ἱππίης δὲ αὐτὸν ἀμείβετο τοὺς
αὐτοὺς ἐπικαλέσας θεοὺς ἐκείνῳ, ἦ μὲν Κορινθίους
μάλιστα πάντων ἐπιποθήσειν Πεισιστρατίδας, ὅταν

σφι ἥκωσι ἡμέραι αἱ κύριαι ἀνιᾶσθαι ὑπ' Ἀθηναίων. Ἱππίης μὲν τούτοισι ἀμείψατο οἷά τε τοὺς χρησμοὺς ἀτρεκέστατα ἀνδρῶν ἐξεπιστάμενος, οἱ δὲ λοιποὶ τῶν συμμάχων τέως μὲν εἶχον ἐν ἡσυχίῃ σφέας αὐτούς, ἐπείτε δὲ Σωσικλέος ἤκουσαν εἴπαντος 5 ἐλευθέρως, ἅπας τις αὐτῶν φωνὴν ῥήξας αἱρέετο τοῦ Κορινθίου τὴν γνώμην, Λακεδαιμονίοισί τε ἐπεμαρτύροντο μὴ ποιέειν μηδὲν νεώτερον περὶ πόλιν Ἑλλάδα. XCIV. οὕτω μὲν ταῦτα ἐπαύθη, Ἱππίῃ δὲ ἐνθεῦτεν ἀπελαυνομένῳ ἐδίδου μὲν Ἀμύντης ὁ 10 Μακεδὼν Ἀνθεμοῦντα, ἐδίδοσαν δὲ Θεσσαλοὶ Ἰωλκόν. ὁ δὲ τούτων μὲν οὐδέτερα αἱρέετο, ἀνεχώρεε δὲ ὀπίσω ἐς Σίγειον, τὸ εἷλε Πεισίστρατος αἰχμῇ παρὰ Μυτιληναίων, κρατήσας δὲ αὐτοῦ κατέστησε τύραννον εἶναι παῖδα τὸν ἑωυτοῦ νόθον Ἡγησίστρα- 15 τον, γεγονότα ἐξ Ἀργείης γυναικός, ὃς οὐκ ἀμαχητὶ εἶχε τὰ παρέλαβε παρὰ Πεισιστράτου.

The son of Peisistratos has to fight for Sigeium, which he eventually secures by the arbitration of Periander.

ἐπολέμεον γὰρ ἔκ τε Ἀχιλληΐου πόλιος ὁρμεόμενοι καὶ Σιγείου χρόνον ἐπὶ συχνὸν Μυτιληναῖοί τε καὶ Ἀθηναῖοι, οἱ μὲν ἀπαιτέοντες τὴν χώρην, Ἀθηναῖοι 20 δὲ οὔτε συγγινωσκόμενοι, ἀποδεικνύντες τε λόγῳ οὐδὲν μᾶλλον Αἰολεῦσι μετεὸν τῆς Ἰλιάδος χώρης ἢ οὐ καὶ σφίσι καὶ τοῖσι ἄλλοισι, ὅσοι Ἑλλήνων συνεπρήξαντο Μενέλεῳ τὰς Ἑλένης ἁρπαγάς. XCV. Πολεμεόντων δέ σφεων παντοῖα καὶ ἄλλα ἐγένετο 25 ἐν τῇσι μάχῃσι, ἐν δὲ δὴ καὶ Ἀλκαῖος ὁ ποιητὴς συμβολῆς γενομένης καὶ νικώντων Ἀθηναίων αὐτὸς μὲν φεύγων ἐκφεύγει, τὰ δέ οἱ ὅπλα ἴσχουσι Ἀθη-

ναῖοι, καί σφεα ἀνεκρέμασαν πρὸς τὸ Ἀθήναιον τὸ
ἐν Σιγείῳ. ταῦτα δὲ Ἀλκαῖος ἐν μέλεϊ ποιήσας
ἐπιτιθεῖ ἐς Μυτιλήνην, ἐξαγγελλόμενος τὸ ἑωυτοῦ
πάθος Μελανίππῳ ἀνδρὶ ἑταίρῳ. Μυτιληναίους δὲ
5 καὶ Ἀθηναίους κατήλλαξε Περίανδρος ὁ Κυψέλου·
τούτῳ γὰρ διαιτητῇ ἐπετράποντο· κατήλλαξε δὲ
ὧδε, νέμεσθαι ἑκατέρους τὴν ἔχουσι. Σίγειον μέν
νυν οὕτω ἐγένετο ὑπ' Ἀθηναίοισι.

*Hippias does all he can to stir up the Persians against
Athens.* B.C. 505—1.

XCVI. Ἱππίης δὲ ἐπεί τε ἀπίκετο ἐκ τῆς
10 Λακεδαίμονος ἐς τὴν Ἀσίην, πᾶν χρῆμα ἐκίνεε,
διαβάλλων τε τοὺς Ἀθηναίους πρὸς τὸν Ἀρταφέρνεα
καὶ ποιέων ἅπαντα, ὅκως αἱ Ἀθῆναι γενοίατο ὑπ'
ἑωυτῷ τε καὶ Δαρείῳ. Ἱππίης τε δὴ ταῦτα ἔπρησσε,
καὶ οἱ Ἀθηναῖοι πυθόμενοι ταῦτα πέμπουσι ἐς Σάρδις
15 ἀγγέλους, οὐκ ἐῶντες τοὺς Πέρσας πείθεσθαι Ἀθηναίων τοῖσι φυγάσι· ὁ δὲ Ἀρταφέρνης ἐκέλευέ σφεας,
εἰ βουλοίατο σῶοι εἶναι, καταδέκεσθαι ὀπίσω Ἱππίην.
οὐκ ὦν δὴ ἐνεδέκοντο τοὺς λόγους ἀποφερομένους οἱ
Ἀθηναῖοι· οὐκ ἐνδεκομένοισι δέ σφι ἐδέδοκτο ἐκ τοῦ
20 φανεροῦ τοῖσι Πέρσῃσι πολεμίους εἶναι.

*When Aristagoras, therefore, appeared before the Athenians,
in* B.C. 501, *asking help for the Ionians against Persia,
he was readily listened to.*

XCVII. Νομίζουσι δὴ ταῦτα καὶ διαβεβλημένοισι ἐς τοὺς Πέρσας ἐν τούτῳ δὴ τῷ καιρῷ ὁ
Μιλήσιος Ἀρισταγόρης ὑπὸ Κλεομένεος τοῦ Λακε-
δαιμονίου ἐξελαθεὶς ἐκ τῆς Σπάρτης ἀπίκετο ἐς
25 Ἀθήνας· αὕτη γὰρ ἡ πόλις τῶν λοιπέων ἐδυνάστευε

μέγιστον. ἐπελθὼν δὲ ἐπὶ τὸν δῆμον ὁ Ἀρισταγόρης ταὐτὰ ἔλεγε τά καὶ ἐν τῇ Σπάρτῃ περὶ τῶν ἀγαθῶν τῶν ἐν τῇ Ἀσίῃ καὶ τοῦ πολέμου τοῦ Περσικοῦ, ὡς οὔτε ἀσπίδα οὔτε δόρυ νομίζουσι, εὐπετέες τε χειρωθῆναι εἴησαν. ταῦτά τε δὴ ἔλεγε 5 καὶ πρὸς τοῖσι τάδε, ὡς οἱ Μιλήσιοι τῶν Ἀθηναίων εἰσὶ ἄποικοι, καὶ οἰκός σφεας εἴη ῥύεσθαι δυναμένους μέγα. καὶ οὐδὲν ὅ τι οὐκ ὑπίσχετο οἷα κάρτα δεόμενος, ἐς ὃ ἀνέπεισέ σφεας. πολλοὺς γὰρ οἶκε εἶναι εὐπετέστερον διαβάλλειν ἢ ἕνα, εἰ Κλεομένεα 10 μὲν τὸν Λακεδαιμόνιον μοῦνον οὐκ οἷός τε ἐγένετο διαβαλεῖν, τρεῖς δὲ μυριάδας Ἀθηναίων ἐποίησε τοῦτο. Ἀθηναῖοι μὲν δὴ ἀναπεισθέντες ἐψηφίσαντο εἴκοσι νέας ἀποστεῖλαι βοηθοὺς Ἴωσι, στρατηγὸν ἀποδέξαντες αὐτῶν εἶναι Μελάνθιον ἄνδρα τῶν 15 ἀστῶν ἐόντα τὰ πάντα δόκιμον. αὗται δὲ αἱ νέες ἀρχὴ κακῶν ἐγένοντο Ἕλλησί τε καὶ βαρβάροισι.

Aristagoras returns to Miletos and begins acting against Persia by inducing the Paeonians (see cc. 12—16) to return to their native land.

XCVIII. Ἀρισταγόρης δὲ προπλώσας καὶ ἀπικόμενος ἐς τὴν Μίλητον, ἐξευρὼν βούλευμα, ἀπ' οὗ Ἴωσι μὲν οὐδεμία ἔμελλε ὠφελείη ἔσεσθαι (οὐδ' ὦν 20 οὐδὲ τούτου εἵνεκεν ἐποίεε, ἀλλ' ὅκως βασιλέα Δαρεῖον λυπήσειε), ἔπεμψε ἐς τὴν Φρυγίην ἄνδρα ἐπὶ τοὺς Παίονας τοὺς ἀπὸ Στρυμόνος ποταμοῦ αἰχμαλώτους γενομένους ὑπὸ Μεγαβάζου, οἰκέοντας δὲ τῆς Φρυγίης χῶρόν τε καὶ κώμην ἐπ' ἑωυτῶν, ὃς 25 ἐπειδὴ ἀπίκετο ἐς τοὺς Παίονας, ἔλεγε τάδε· "Ἄνδρες "Παίονες, ἔπεμψέ με Ἀρισταγόρης ὁ Μιλήτου τύραν-

"νος σωτηρίην ὑμῖν ὑποθησόμενον, ἤν περ βούλησθε
"πείθεσθαι. νῦν γὰρ Ἰωνίη πᾶσα ἀπέστηκε ἀπὸ
"βασιλέος, καὶ ὑμῖν παρέχει σώζεσθαι ἐπὶ τὴν ὑμετέ-
"ρην αὐτῶν. μέχρι μὲν θαλάσσης αὐτοῖσι ὑμῖν, τὸ
5 "δὲ ἀπὸ τούτου ἡμῖν ἤδη μελήσει." ταῦτα δὲ ἀκούσαντες οἱ Παίονες κάρτα τε ἀσπαστὸν ἐποιήσαντο,
καὶ ἀναλαβόντες παῖδάς τε καὶ γυναῖκας ἀπεδίδρησκον ἐπὶ θάλασσαν· οἱ δέ τινες αὐτῶν καὶ κατέ-
μειναν ἀρρωδήσαντες αὐτοῦ. ἐπείτε δὲ οἱ Παίονες
10 ἀπίκοντο ἐπὶ θάλασσαν, ἐνθεῦτεν ἐς Χίον διέβησαν.
ἐόντων δὲ ἤδη ἐν Χίῳ κατὰ πόδας ἐληλύθεε Περσέων
ἵππος πολλὴ διώκουσα τοὺς Παίονας· ὡς δὲ οὐ
κατέλαβον, ἐπηγγέλλοντο ἐς τὴν Χίον τοῖσι Παίοσι,
ὅκως ἂν ὀπίσω ἀπέλθοιεν. οἱ δὲ Παίονες τοὺς
15 λόγους οὐκ ἐνεδέκοντο, ἀλλ᾽ ἐκ Χίου μὲν Χῖοί σφεας
ἐς Λέσβον ἤγαγον, Λέσβιοι δὲ ἐς Δορίσκον ἐκόμι-
σαν· ἐνθεῦτεν δὲ πεζῇ κομιζόμενοι ἀπίκοντο ἐς
Παιονίην.

*The Ionians, assisted by the Athenians and Eretrians,
enter and burn Sardis;*

XCIX. Ἀρισταγόρης δέ, ἐπειδὴ οἵ τε Ἀθηναῖοι
20 ἀπίκοντο εἴκοσι νηυσί, ἅμα ἀγόμενοι Ἐρετριέων
πέντε τριήρεας, οἳ οὐ τὴν Ἀθηναίων χάριν ἐστρα-
τεύοντο, ἀλλὰ τὴν αὐτῶν Μιλησίων, ὀφειλόμενά σφι
ἀποδιδόντες (οἱ γὰρ δὴ Μιλήσιοι πρότερον τοῖσι
Ἐρετριεῦσι τὸν πρὸς Χαλκιδέας πόλεμον συνδιή-
25 νεικαν, ὅτε περ καὶ Χαλκιδεῦσι ἀντία Ἐρετριέων
καὶ Μιλησίων Σάμιοι ἐβοήθεον), οὗτοι ὦν ἐπείτε
σφι ἀπίκοντο καὶ οἱ ἄλλοι σύμμαχοι παρῆσαν,
ἐποιέετο στρατηίην ὁ Ἀρισταγόρης ἐς Σάρδις. αὐτὸς

μὲν δὴ οὐκ ἐστρατεύετο, ἀλλ' ἔμενε ἐν Μιλήτῳ, στρατηγοὺς δὲ ἄλλους ἀπέδεξε Μιλησίων εἶναι, τὸν ἑωυτοῦ τε ἀδελφεὸν Χαροπῖνον καὶ τῶν ἄλλων ἀστῶν Ἑρμόφαντον. C. Ἀπικόμενοι δὲ τῷ στόλῳ τούτῳ Ἴωνες ἐς Ἔφεσον πλοῖα μὲν κατέλιπον ἐν Κορησσῷ τῆς Ἐφεσίης, αὐτοὶ δὲ ἀνέβαινον χειρὶ πολλῇ ποιεύμενοι Ἐφεσίους ἡγεμόνας. πορευόμενοι δὲ παρὰ ποταμὸν Καΰστριον, ἐνθεῦτεν ἐπείτε ὑπερβάντες τὸν Τμῶλον ἀπίκοντο, αἱρέουσι Σάρδις οὐδενός σφι ἀντιωθέντος, αἱρέουσι δὲ χωρὶς τῆς ἀκροπόλιος τἆλλα πάντα· τὴν δὲ ἀκρόπολιν ἐρρύετο αὐτὸς Ἀρταφέρνης, ἔχων δύναμιν ἀνδρῶν οὐκ ὀλίγην. CI. Τὸ δὲ μὴ λεηλατῆσαι ἑλόντας σφέας τὴν πόλιν ἔσχε τόδε. ἦσαν ἐν τῇσι Σάρδισι οἰκίαι αἱ μὲν πλεῦνες καλάμιναι, ὅσαι δ' αὐτέων καὶ πλίνθιναι ἦσαν, καλάμου εἶχον τὰς ὀροφάς. τούτων δὴ μίαν τῶν τις στρατιωτέων ὡς ἐνέπρησε, αὐτίκα ἀπ' οἰκίης ἐς οἰκίην ἰὸν τὸ πῦρ ἐπενέμετο τὸ ἄστυ πᾶν. καιομένου δὲ τοῦ ἄστεος οἱ Λυδοί τε καὶ ὅσοι Περσέων ἐνῆσαν ἐν τῇ πόλι, ἀπολαμφθέντες πάντοθεν ὥστε τὰ περιέσχατα νεμομένου τοῦ πυρὸς καὶ οὐκ ἔχοντες ἐξήλυσιν ἐκ τοῦ ἄστεος, συνέρρεον ἔς τε τὴν ἀγορὴν καὶ ἐπὶ τὸν Πακτωλὸν ποταμόν, ὅς σφι ψῆγμα χρυσοῦ καταφορέων ἐκ τοῦ Τμώλου διὰ μέσης τῆς ἀγορῆς ῥέει καὶ ἔπειτα ἐς τὸν Ἕρμον ποταμὸν ἐκδιδοῖ, ὁ δὲ ἐς θάλασσαν· ἐπὶ τοῦτον δὴ τὸν Πακτωλὸν καὶ ἐς τὴν ἀγορὴν ἀθροιζόμενοι οἵ τε Λυδοὶ καὶ οἱ Πέρσαι ἠναγκάζοντο ἀμύνεσθαι. οἱ δὲ Ἴωνες ὁρέοντες τοὺς μὲν ἀμυνομένους τῶν πολεμίων, τοὺς δὲ σὺν πλήθεϊ πολλῷ προσφερομένους ἐξανεχώρησαν δείσαντες πρὸς τὸ οὖρος τὸν Τμῶλον καλεόμενον, ἐνθεῦτεν δὲ ὑπὸ νύκτα ἀπαλλάσσοντο ἐπὶ τὰς νέας.

but on their return are overtaken by a Persian force and suffer severely.

CII. Καὶ Σάρδιες μὲν ἐνεπρήσθησαν, ἐν δὲ αὐτῇσι καὶ ἱρὸν ἐπιχωρίης θεοῦ Κυβήβης, τὸ σκηπτόμενοι οἱ Πέρσαι ὕστερον ἀντενεπίμπρασαν τὰ ἐν Ἕλλησι ἱρά. τότε δὲ οἱ Πέρσαι οἱ ἐντὸς Ἅλυος ποταμοῦ νομοὺς ἔχοντες προπυνθανόμενοι ταῦτα συνηλίζοντο καὶ ἐβοήθεον τοῖσι Λυδοῖσι. καί κως ἐν μὲν Σάρδισι οὐκέτι ἐόντας τοὺς Ἴωνας εὑρίσκουσι, ἑπόμενοι δὲ κατὰ στίβον αἱρέουσι αὐτοὺς ἐν Ἐφέσῳ. καὶ ἀντετάχθησαν μὲν οἱ Ἴωνες, συμβαλόντες δὲ πολλὸν ἑσσώθησαν. καὶ πολλοὺς αὐτῶν οἱ Πέρσαι φονεύουσι, ἄλλους τε ὀνομαστούς, ἐν δὲ δὴ καὶ Εὐαλκίδην στρατηγέοντα Ἐρετριέων, στεφανηφόρους τε ἀγῶνας ἀναραιρηκότα καὶ ὑπὸ Σιμωνίδεω τοῦ Κηίου πολλὰ αἰνεθέντα. οἳ δὲ αὐτῶν ἀπέφυγον τὴν μάχην, ἐσκεδάσθησαν ἀνὰ τὰς πόλιας.

The Athenians return home: but the Ionians continue their operations (1) in the Hellespont.

CIII. Τότε μὲν δὴ οὕτω ἠγωνίσαντο, μετὰ δὲ Ἀθηναῖοι μὲν τὸ παράπαν ἀπολιπόντες τοὺς Ἴωνας ἐπικαλεομένου σφέας πολλὰ δι' ἀγγέλων Ἀρισταγόρεω οὐκ ἔφασαν τιμωρήσειν σφι. Ἴωνες δὲ τῆς Ἀθηναίων συμμαχίης στερηθέντες (οὕτω γάρ σφι ὑπῆρχε πεποιημένα ἐς Δαρεῖον) οὐδὲν δὴ ἧσσον τὸν πρὸς βασιλέα πόλεμον ἐσκευάζοντο. πλώσαντες δὲ

ἐς τὸν Ἑλλήσποντον Βυζάντιόν τε καὶ τὰς ἄλλας πόλις ἁπάσας τὰς ταύτῃ ὑπ' ἑωυτοῖσι ἐποιήσαντο, ἐκπλώσαντές τε ἔξω τὸν Ἑλλήσποντον Καρίης τὴν πολλὴν προσεκτήσαντο σφίσι σύμμαχον εἶναι· καὶ γὰρ τὴν Καῦνον πρότερον οὐ βουλομένην συμμα- 5
χέειν, ὡς ἐνέπρησαν τὰς Σάρδις, τότε σφι καὶ αὕτη προσεγένετο.

(2) *in Kypros.*

CIV. Κύπριοι δὲ ἐθελονταί σφι πάντες προσεγένοντο πλὴν Ἀμαθουσίων· ἀπέστησαν γὰρ καὶ οὗτοι ὧδε ἀπὸ Μήδων. ἦν Ὀνήσιλος Γόργου μὲν 10
τοῦ Σαλαμινίων βασιλέος ἀδελφεὸς νεώτερος, Χέρσιος δὲ τοῦ Σιρώμου τοῦ Εὐέλθοντος παῖς. οὗτος ὡνὴρ πολλάκις μὲν καὶ πρότερον τὸν Γόργον παρηγορέετο ἀπίστασθαι ἀπὸ βασιλέος, τότε δ', ὡς καὶ τοὺς Ἴωνας ἐπύθετο ἀπεστάναι, πάγχυ ἐπικείμενος 15
ἐνῆγε. ὡς δὲ οὐκ ἔπειθε τὸν Γόργον, ἐνθαῦτά μιν φυλάξας ἐξελθόντα τὸ ἄστυ τὸ Σαλαμινίων ὁ Ὀνήσιλος ἅμα τοῖσι ἑωυτοῦ στασιώτῃσι ἀπεκλήισε τῶν πυλέων. Γόργος μὲν δὴ στερηθεὶς τῆς πόλιος ἔφευγε ἐς Μήδους, Ὀνήσιλος δὲ ἦρχε Σαλαμῖνος καὶ ἀνέ- 20
πειθε πάντας Κυπρίους συναπίστασθαι. τοὺς μὲν δὴ ἄλλους ἀνέπεισε, Ἀμαθουσίους δὲ οὐ βουλομένους οἱ πείθεσθαι ἐπολιόρκεε προσκατήμενος.

*The wrath of Darius at hearing of the burning of Sardis;
and his vow of vengeance.*

CV. Ὀνήσιλος μέν νυν ἐπολιόρκεε Ἀμαθοῦντα, βασιλέϊ δὲ Δαρείῳ ὡς ἐξηγγέλθη Σάρδις ἁλούσας 25
ἐμπεπρῆσθαι ὑπό τε Ἀθηναίων καὶ Ἰώνων, τὸν δὲ

ἡγεμόνα γενέσθαι τῆς συλλογῆς, ὥστε ταῦτα συνυφανθῆναι, τὸν Μιλήσιον Ἀρισταγόρην, πρῶτα μὲν
λέγεται αὐτὸν, ὡς ἐπύθετο ταῦτα, Ἰώνων οὐδένα
λόγον ποιησάμενον, εὖ εἰδότα, ὡς οὗτοί γε οὐ καταπροΐξονται ἀποστάντες, εἴρεσθαι οἵτινες εἶεν οἱ
Ἀθηναῖοι, μετὰ δὲ πυθόμενον αἰτῆσαι τὸ τόξον,
λαβόντα δὲ καὶ ἐπιθέντα ὀιστὸν ἄνω ἐς τὸν οὐρανὸν
ἀπεῖναι, καί μιν ἐς τὸν ἠέρα βάλλοντα εἰπεῖν· "Ὦ
"Ζεῦ, ἐκγενέσθαι μοι Ἀθηναίους τίσασθαι," εἴπαντα
δὲ ταῦτα προστάξαι ἑνὶ τῶν θεραπόντων δείπνου
προκειμένου αὐτῷ ἐς τρὶς ἑκάστοτε εἰπεῖν· "Δέσποτα,
"μέμνεο τῶν Ἀθηναίων."

Darius accuses Histiaios of being privy to the Ionian revolt; but is overpersuaded by him and sends him down to put an end to it.

CVI. Προστάξας δὲ ταῦτα εἶπε, καλέσας ἐς
ὄψιν Ἱστιαῖον τὸν Μιλήσιον, τὸν ὁ Δαρεῖος κατεῖχε
χρόνον ἤδη πολλόν· "Πυνθάνομαι, Ἱστιαῖε, ἐπίτροπον
"τὸν σὸν, τῷ σὺ Μίλητον ἐπέτρεψας, νεώτερα ἐς
"ἐμὲ πεποιηκέναι πρήγματα· ἄνδρας γάρ μοι ἐκ τῆς
"ἑτέρης ἠπείρου ἐπαγαγὼν καὶ Ἴωνας σὺν αὐτοῖσι
"τοὺς δώσοντας ἐμοὶ δίκην τῶν ἐποίησαν, τούτους
"ἀναγνώσας ἅμα ἐκείνοισι ἕπεσθαι Σαρδίων με
"ἀπεστέρηκε. νῦν ὦν κῶς τοι ταῦτα φαίνεται ἔχειν
"καλῶς; κῶς δ' ἄνευ τῶν σῶν βουλευμάτων τοιοῦτό
"τι ἐπρήχθη; ὅρα, μὴ ἐξ ὑστέρης σεωυτὸν ἐν αἰτίῃ
"σχῇς." εἶπε πρὸς ταῦτα ὁ Ἱστιαῖος· "Βασιλεῦ,
"κοῖον ἐφθέγξαο ἔπος; ἐμὲ βουλεῦσαι πρῆγμα, ἐκ τοῦ
"σοί τι ἢ μέγα ἢ σμικρὸν ἔμελλε λυπηρὸν ἀνασχή-
"σειν; τί δ' ἂν ἐπιδιζήμενος ποιέοιμι ταῦτα, τεῦ δὲ

"ἐνδεὴς ἐών; τῷ πάρα μὲν πάντα ὅσα περ σοί, πάντων
" δὲ πρὸς σέο βουλευμάτων ἐπακούειν ἀξιεῦμαι. ἀλλ᾽
" εἴπερ τι τοιοῦτο, οἷον σὺ εἴρηκας, πρήσσει ὁ ἐμὸς
" ἐπίτροπος, ἴσθι αὐτὸν ἐπ᾽ ἑωυτοῦ βαλλόμενον πεπρη-
" χέναι. ἀρχὴν δὲ ἔγωγε οὐδὲ ἐνδέκομαι τὸν λόγον, 5
" ὅκως τι Μιλήσιοι καὶ ὁ ἐμὸς ἐπίτροπος νεώτερον
" πρήσσουσι περὶ πρήγματα τὰ σά· εἰ δ᾽ ἄρα τι
" τοιοῦτο ποιεῦσι καὶ σὺ τὸ ἐὸν ἀκήκοας, ὦ βασιλεῦ,
" μάθε, οἷον πρῆγμα ἐργάσαο ἐμὲ ἀπὸ θαλάσσης
" ἀνάσπαστον ποιήσας. Ἴωνες γὰρ οἴκασι ἐμεῦ ἐξ 10
" ὀφθαλμῶν σφι γενομένου ποιῆσαι τῶν πάλαι ἵμερον
" εἶχον· ἐμέο δ᾽ ἂν ἐόντος ἐν Ἰωνίῃ οὐδεμία πόλις
" ὑπεκίνησε. νῦν ὦν ὡς τάχος ἄπες με πορευθῆναι
" ἐς Ἰωνίην, ἵνα τοι ἐκεῖνά τε πάντα καταρτίσω ἐς
" τὠυτὸ, καὶ τὸν Μιλήτου ἐπίτροπον τοῦτον τὸν ταῦ- 15
" τα μηχανησάμενον ἐγχειρίθετον παραδῶ. ταῦτα
" δὲ κατὰ νόον τὸν σὸν ποιήσας θεοὺς ἐπόμνυμι τοὺς
" βασιληίους μὴ μὲν πρότερον ἐκδύσεσθαι τὸν ἔχων
" κιθῶνα καταβήσομαι ἐς Ἰωνίην, πρὶν ἄν τοι Σαρδὼ
" νῆσον τὴν μεγίστην δασμοφόρον ποιήσω." CVII. 20
Ἱστιαῖος μὲν δὴ λέγων ταῦτα διέβαλε, Δαρεῖος δὲ
ἐπείθετο καί μιν ἀπίει, ἐντειλάμενος, ἐπεὰν τὰ
ὑπέσχετό οἱ ἐπιτελέα ποιήσῃ, παραγίνεσθαί οἱ
ὀπίσω ἐς τὰ Σοῦσα.

Meanwhile the war is carried on vigorously in Kypros,
B.C. 501.

CVIII. Ἐν ᾧ δὲ ἡ ἀγγελίη τε περὶ τῶν Σαρδίων 25
παρὰ βασιλέα ἀνήιε καὶ Δαρεῖος τὰ περὶ τὸ τόξον
ποιήσας Ἱστιαίῳ ἐς λόγους ἦλθε καὶ Ἱστιαῖος
μεμετιμένος ὑπὸ Δαρείου ἐκομίζετο ἐπὶ θάλασσαν,

ἐν τούτῳ παντὶ τῷ χρόνῳ ἐγίνετο τάδε· πολιορκέοντι τῷ Σαλαμινίῳ Ὀνησίλῳ Ἀμαθουσίους ἐξαγγέλλεται νηυσὶ στρατιὴν πολλὴν ἄγοντα Περσικὴν Ἀρτύβιον ἄνδρα Πέρσην προσδόκιμον ἐς τὴν Κύπρον εἶναι. 5 πυθόμενος δὲ ταῦτα ὁ Ὀνήσιλος κήρυκας διέπεμπε ἐς τὴν Ἰωνίην, ἐπικαλεύμενός σφεας. Ἴωνες δὲ οὐκ ἐς μακρὴν βουλευσάμενοι ἧκον πολλῷ στόλῳ. Ἴωνές τε δὴ παρῆσαν ἐς τὴν Κύπρον, καὶ οἱ Πέρσαι νηυσὶ διαβάντες ἐκ τῆς Κιλικίης ἤϊσαν ἐπὶ τὴν Σαλαμῖνα 10 πεζῇ· τῇσι δὲ νηυσὶ οἱ Φοίνικες περιέπλωον τὴν ἄκρην, αἳ καλεῦνται Κληῖδες τῆς Κύπρου.

The Ionians and the Kyprians under Onesilos arrange their dispositions for the battle.

CIX. Τούτου δὲ τοιούτου γινομένου ἔλεξαν οἱ τύραννοι τῆς Κύπρου, συγκαλέσαντες τῶν Ἰώνων τοὺς στρατηγούς· "Ἄνδρες Ἴωνες, αἵρεσιν ὑμῖν δίδο- 15 "μεν ἡμεῖς οἱ Κύπριοι, ὁκοτέροισι βούλεσθε προσφέ- "ρεσθαι, ἢ Πέρσῃσι ἢ Φοίνιξι. εἰ μὲν γὰρ πεζῇ "βούλεσθε ταχθέντες Περσέων διαπειρᾶσθαι, ὥρη "ἂν εἴη ὑμῖν ἐκβάντας ἐκ τῶν νεῶν τάσσεσθαι πεζῇ, "ἡμέας δὲ ἐς τὰς νέας ἐμβαίνειν τὰς ὑμετέρας Φοίνιξι 20 "ἀνταγωνιευμένους· εἰ δὲ Φοινίκων μᾶλλον βούλεσθε "διαπειρᾶσθαι, ποιέειν χρεόν ἐστι ὑμέας, ὁκότερα ἂν "δὴ τούτων ἕλησθε, ὅκως τὸ κατ' ὑμέας ἔσται ἥ τε "Ἰωνίη καὶ ἡ Κύπρος ἐλευθέρη." Εἶπαν οἱ Ἴωνες πρὸς ταῦτα· "Ἡμέας ἀπέπεμψε τὸ κοινὸν τῶν Ἰώνων 25 "φυλάξοντας τὴν θάλασσαν, ἀλλ' οὐκ ἵνα Κυπρίοισι "τὰς νέας παραδόντες αὐτοὶ Πέρσῃσι πεζῇ προσφε- "ρώμεθα. ἡμεῖς μέν νυν ἐπ' οὗ ἐτάχθημεν, ταύτῃ "πειρησόμεθα εἶναι χρηστοί, ὑμέας δὲ χρεόν ἐστι

"ἀναμνησθέντας, οἷα ἐπάσχετε δουλεύοντες πρὸς
"τῶν Μήδων, γίνεσθαι ἄνδρας ἀγαθούς." Ἴωνες
μὲν τούτοισι ἀμείψαντο, CX. μετὰ δὲ ἡκόντων ἐς
τὸ πεδίον τὸ Σαλαμινίων τῶν Περσέων διέτασσον οἱ
βασιλέες τῶν Κυπρίων τοὺς μὲν ἄλλους Κυπρίους
κατὰ τοὺς ἄλλους στρατιώτας ἀντιτάσσοντες, Σαλαμινίων δὲ καὶ Σολίων ἀπολέξαντες τὸ ἄριστον ἀντέ-
τασσον Πέρσῃσι. Ἀρτυβίῳ δὲ τῷ στρατηγῷ τῶν
Περσέων ἐθελοντὴς ἀντετάσσετο Ὀνήσιλος.

Artybios and his rearing horse.

CXI. Ἤλαυνε δὲ ἵππον ὁ Ἀρτύβιος δεδιδαγ-
μένον πρὸς ὁπλίτην ἵστασθαι ὀρθόν. πυθόμενος ὧν
ταῦτα ὁ Ὀνήσιλος, ἦν γάρ οἱ ὑπασπιστὴς γένος
μὲν Κὰρ, τὰ δὲ πολέμια κάρτα δόκιμος καὶ ἄλλως
λήματος πλέος, εἶπε πρὸς τοῦτον· "Πυνθάνομαι τὸν
"Ἀρτυβίου ἵππον ἱστάμενον ὀρθὸν καὶ ποσὶ καὶ
"στόματι κατεργάζεσθαι πρὸς τὸν ἂν προσενειχθῇ.
"σὺ ὧν βουλευσάμενος αὐτίκα εἰπὲ, ὁκότερον βούλεαι
"φυλάξας πλῆξαι, εἴτε τὸν ἵππον εἴτε αὐτὸν Ἀρτύ-
"βιον." Εἶπε πρὸς ταῦτα ὁ ὀπέων αὐτοῦ· "Ὦ
"βασιλεῦ, ἕτοιμος μὲν ἐγώ εἰμι ποιέειν καὶ ἀμφότερα
"καὶ τὸ ἕτερον αὐτῶν, καὶ πάντως τὸ ἂν ἐπιτάσσῃς
"σύ· ὡς μέντοι ἔμοιγε δοκέει εἶναι τοῖσι σοῖσι πρήγ-
"μασι προσφερέστερον, φράσω. βασιλέα μὲν καὶ
"στρατηγὸν χρεόν εἶναί φημι βασιλέϊ τε καὶ στρα-
"τηγῷ προσφέρεσθαι· ἤν τε γὰρ κατέλῃς ἄνδρα
"στρατηγὸν, μέγα τοι γίνεται, καὶ δεύτερα, ἢν σὲ
"ἐκεῖνος, τὸ μὴ γένοιτο, ὑπ᾽ ἀξιόχρεω καὶ ἀποθανεῖν
"ἡμίσεα συμφορή· ἡμέας δὲ τοὺς ὑπηρέτας ἑτέροισί
"τε ὑπηρέτῃσι προσφέρεσθαι καὶ πρὸς ἵππον, τοῦ

"σὺ τὰς μηχανὰς μηδὲν φοβηθῇς· ἐγὼ γάρ τοι ὑπο-
"δέκομαι μή μιν ἀνδρὸς ἔτι γε μηδενὸς στήσεσθαι
"ἐναντίον."

The Ionians conquer at sea.

CXII. Ταῦτα εἶπε, καὶ μεταυτίκα συνέμισγε τὰ στρατόπεδα πεζῇ καὶ νηυσί· νηυσὶ μέν νυν Ἴωνες ἄκροι γενόμενοι ταύτην τὴν ἡμέρην ὑπερεβάλοντο τοὺς Φοίνικας, καὶ τούτων Σάμιοι ἠρίστευσαν, πεζῇ δὲ, ὡς συνῆλθον τὰ στρατόπεδα, συμπεσόντα ἐμάχοντο, κατὰ δὲ τοὺς στρατηγοὺς ἀμφοτέρους τάδε ἐγίνετο· ὡς προσεφέρετο πρὸς τὸν Ὀνήσιλον ὁ Ἀρτύβιος ἐπὶ τοῦ ἵππου κατήμενος, ὁ Ὀνήσιλος, κατὰ συνεθήκατο τῷ ὑπασπιστῇ, παίει προσφερόμενον αὐτὸν τὸν Ἀρτύβιον, ἐπιβαλόντος δὲ τοῦ ἵππου τοὺς πόδας ἐπὶ τὴν Ὀνησίλου ἀσπίδα, ἐνθαῦτα ὁ Κὰρ δρεπάνῳ πλήξας ἀπαράσσει τοῦ ἵππου τοὺς πόδας. Ἀρτύβιος μὲν δὴ ὁ στρατηγὸς τῶν Περσέων ὁμοῦ τῷ ἵππῳ πίπτει αὐτοῦ ταύτῃ,

But the Kyprians, weakened by desertions, are beaten on land, and Onesilos falls.

CXIII. Μαχομένων δὲ καὶ τῶν ἄλλων Στησήνωρ, τύραννος ἐὼν Κουρίου, προδιδοῖ ἔχων δύναμιν ἀνδρῶν περὶ ἑωυτὸν οὐ σμικρήν. οἱ δὲ Κουριέες οὗτοι λέγονται εἶναι Ἀργείων ἄποικοι. προδόντων δὲ τῶν Κουριέων αὐτίκα καὶ τὰ Σαλαμινίων πολεμιστήρια ἅρματα τὠυτὸ τοῖσι Κουριεῦσι ἐποίεον. γινομένων δὲ τούτων κατυπέρτεροι ἦσαν οἱ Πέρσαι τῶν Κυπρίων. τετραμμένου δὲ τοῦ στρατοπέδου ἄλλοι τε ἔπεσον πολλοὶ καὶ δὴ καὶ Ὀνήσιλός τε ὁ Χέρσιος, ὅς περ τὴν Κυπρίων ἀπόστασιν ἔπρηξε, καὶ ὁ Σολίων βασιλεὺς Ἀριστόκυπρος ὁ Φιλοκύπρου, Φιλοκύπρου δὲ τούτου, τὸν Σόλων ὁ Ἀθηναῖος ἀπικόμενος ἐς Κύπρον ἐν ἔπεσι αἴνεσε τυράννων μάλιστα.

The Ionian fleet returns home, and Kypros is reduced.

CXIV. Ὀνησίλου μέν νυν Ἀμαθούσιοι, ὅτι σφέας ἐπολιόρκησε, ἀποταμόντες τὴν κεφαλὴν ἐκόμισαν ἐς Ἀμαθοῦντα καί μιν ἀνεκρέμασαν ὑπὲρ τῶν πυλέων. κρεμαμένης δὲ τῆς κεφαλῆς καὶ ἐούσης ἤδη κοίλης ἐσμὸς μελισσέων ἐσδὺς ἐς αὐτὴν κηρίων μιν ἐνέπλησαν. τούτου δὲ γενομένου τοιούτου, ἐχρέοντο γὰρ περὶ αὐτῆς οἱ Ἀμαθούσιοι, ἐμαντεύθη σφι τὴν μὲν κεφαλὴν κατελόντας θάψαι, Ὀνησίλῳ δὲ θύειν ὡς ἥρωϊ ἀνὰ πᾶν ἔτος, καί σφι ποιεῦσι ταῦτα ἄμεινον συνοίσεσθαι.

The Persian commanders proceed to reduce the Greek cities in Asia.

CXV. Ἀμαθούσιοι μέν νυν ἐποίευν ταῦτα καὶ τὸ μέχρι ἐμεῦ· Ἴωνες δὲ οἱ ἐν Κύπρῳ ναυμαχήσαντες ἐπείτε ἔμαθον τὰ πρήγματα τὰ Ὀνησίλου διεφθαρμένα καὶ τὰς πόλιας τῶν Κυπρίων πολιορκευμένας τὰς ἄλλας πλὴν Σαλαμῖνος, ταύτην δὲ Γόργῳ τῷ προτέρῳ βασιλέϊ τοὺς Σαλαμινίους παραδόντας, αὐτίκα μαθόντες οἱ Ἴωνες ταῦτα ἀπέπλωον ἐς τὴν Ἰωνίην. τῶν δὲ ἐν Κύπρῳ πολίων ἀντέσχε χρόνον ἐπὶ πλεῖστον πολιορκευμένη Σόλοι, τὴν πέριξ ὑπορύσσοντες τὸ τεῖχος πέμπτῳ μηνὶ εἷλον οἱ Πέρσαι. CXVI. Κύπριοι μὲν δὴ ἐνιαυτὸν ἐλεύθεροι γενόμενοι αὖτις ἐκ νέης κατεδεδούλωντο· Δαυ-

ρίσης δὲ ἔχων Δαρείου θυγατέρα καὶ Ὑμέης τε καὶ
Ὀτάνης καὶ ἄλλοι Πέρσαι στρατηγοί, ἔχοντες καὶ
οὗτοι Δαρείου θυγατέρας, ἐπιδιώξαντες τοὺς ἐς Σάρδις στρατευσαμένους Ἰώνων καὶ ἐσαράξαντές σφεας
ἐς τὰς νέας, τῇ μάχῃ ὡς ἐπεκράτησαν, τὸ ἐνθεῦτεν
ἐπιδιελόμενοι τὰς πόλις ἐπόρθεον. CXVII. Δαυρίσης μὲν τραπόμενος πρὸς τὰς ἐν Ἑλλησπόντῳ
πόλις εἷλε μὲν Δάρδανον, εἷλε δὲ Ἄβυδόν τε καὶ
Περκώτην καὶ Λάμψακον καὶ Παισόν· ταύτας μὲν
ἐπ' ἡμέρης ἑκάστην αἵρεε, ἀπὸ δὲ Παισοῦ ἐλαύνοντί
οἱ ἐπὶ Πάριον πόλιν ἦλθε ἀγγελίη τοὺς Κᾶρας
τὠυτὸ Ἴωσι φρονήσαντας ἀπεστάναι ἀπὸ Περσέων.
ἀποστρέψας ὦν ἐκ τοῦ Ἑλλησπόντου ἤλαυνε τὸν
στρατὸν ἐπὶ τὴν Καρίην.

The Karians collect an army, but are defeated by the Persians in a battle on the river Marsyas.

CXVIII. Καί κως ταῦτα τοῖσι Καρσὶ ἐξηγγέλθη πρότερον πρὶν ἢ τὸν Δαυρίσην ἀπικέσθαι.
πυθόμενοι δὲ οἱ Κᾶρες συνελέγοντο ἐπὶ Λευκάς τε
στήλας καλεομένας καὶ ποταμὸν Μαρσύην, ὃς ῥέων
ἐκ τῆς Ἰδριάδος χώρης ἐς τὸν Μαίανδρον ἐκδιδοῖ.
συλλεχθέντων δὲ τῶν Καρῶν ἐνθαῦτα ἐγίνοντο
βουλαὶ ἄλλαι τε πολλαὶ καὶ ἀρίστη γε δοκέουσα
εἶναι ἐμοὶ Πιξωδάρου τοῦ Μαυσώλου ἀνδρὸς Κιν-
δυέος, ὃς τοῦ Κιλίκων βασιλέος Συεννέσιος εἶχε
θυγατέρα. τούτου τοῦ ἀνδρὸς ἡ γνώμη ἔφερε διαβάντας τὸν Μαίανδρον τοὺς Κᾶρας καὶ κατὰ νώτου
ἔχοντας τὸν ποταμὸν οὕτω συμβάλλειν, ἵνα μὴ
ἔχοντες ὀπίσω φεύγειν οἱ Κᾶρες αὐτοῦ τε μένειν
ἀναγκαζόμενοι γενοίατο ἔτι ἀμείνονες τῆς φύσιος.

αὕτη μέν νυν οὐκ ἐνίκα ἡ γνώμη, ἀλλὰ τοῖσι Πέρσῃσι κατὰ νώτου γίνεσθαι τὸν Μαίανδρον μᾶλλον ἢ σφίσι, δηλαδὴ, ἢν φυγὴ τῶν Περσέων γένηται καὶ ἑσσωθέωσι τῇ συμβολῇ, ὡς οὐκ ἀπονοστήσουσι ἐς τὸν ποταμὸν ἐσπίπτοντες. CXIX. Μετὰ δὲ παρεόντων καὶ διαβάντων τὸν Μαίανδρον τῶν Περσέων ἐνθαῦτα ἐπὶ τῷ Μαρσύῃ ποταμῷ συνέβαλόν τε τοῖσι Πέρσῃσι οἱ Κᾶρες καὶ μάχην ἐμαχέσαντο ἰσχυρὴν καὶ ἐπὶ χρόνον πολλὸν, τέλος δὲ ἐσσώθησαν διὰ πλῆθος. Περσέων μὲν δὴ ἔπεσον ἄνδρες ἐς δισχιλίους, Καρῶν δὲ ἐς μυρίους. ἐνθεῦτεν δὲ οἱ διαφυγόντες αὐτῶν κατειλήθησαν ἐς Λάβρανδα ἐς Διὸς στρατίου ἱρὸν, μέγα τε καὶ ἅγιον ἄλσος πλατανίστων. μοῦνοι δὲ τῶν ἡμεῖς ἴδμεν Κᾶρές εἰσι, οἳ Διὶ στρατίῳ θυσίας ἀνάγουσι. κατειληθέντες δὲ ὦν οὗτοι ἐνθαῦτα ἐβουλεύοντο περὶ σωτηρίης, ὁκότερα ἢ παραδόντες σφέας αὐτοὺς Πέρσῃσι ἢ ἐκλιπόντες τὸ παράπαν τὴν Ἀσίην ἄμεινον πρήξουσι.

Reinforced by the Milesians and their allies the Karians resolve to fight once more, but are again beaten.

CXX. Βουλευομένοισι δέ σφι ταῦτα παραγίνονται βοηθέοντες Μιλήσιοί τε καὶ οἱ τούτων σύμμαχοι. ἐνθαῦτα δὲ τὰ μὲν πρότερον οἱ Κᾶρες ἐβουλεύοντο μετῆκαν, οἱ δὲ αὖτις πολεμεῖν ἐξ ἀρχῆς ἀρτέοντο. καὶ ἐπιοῦσί τε τοῖσι Πέρσῃσι συμβάλουσι καὶ μαχεσάμενοι ἐπὶ πλεῦν ἢ πρότερον ἐσσώθησαν· πεσόντων δὲ τῶν πάντων πολλῶν Μιλήσιοι μάλιστα ἐπλήγησαν.

The Karians shortly afterwards succeed, by lying in ambush, in inflicting a severe blow on the Persian army and killing Daurises, Amorges, and Sisimakes.

CXXI. Μετὰ δὲ τοῦτο τὸ τρῶμα ἀνέλαβόν τε καὶ ἀνεμαχέσαντο οἱ Κᾶρες. πυθόμενοι γὰρ, ὡς στρατεύεσθαι ἑρμέαται οἱ Πέρσαι ἐπὶ τὰς πόλις σφέων, ἐλόχησαν τὴν ἐν Πηδάσῳ ὁδὸν, ἐς τὴν ἐμπε-
5 σόντες οἱ Πέρσαι νυκτὸς διεφθάρησαν καὶ αὐτοὶ καὶ οἱ στρατηγοὶ αὐτῶν, Δαυρίσης καὶ Ἀμόργης καὶ Σισιμάκης, σὺν δέ σφι ἀπέθανε καὶ Μύρσος ὁ Γύγεω. τοῦ δὲ λόχου τούτου ἡγεμὼν ἦν Ἡρακλείδης Ἰβανώ-λιος ἀνὴρ Μυλασεύς. οὗτοι μέν νυν τῶν Περσέων
10 οὕτω διεφθάρησαν,

Meanwhile the Persians, under Hymeas, overran the Troad.

CXXII. Ὑμέης δὲ καὶ αὐτὸς ἐὼν τῶν ἐπιδιω-ξάντων τοὺς ἐς Σάρδις στρατευσαμένους Ἰώνων, τραπόμενος ἐς τὴν Προποντίδα εἷλε Κίον τὴν Μυσίην. ταύτην δὲ ἐξελὼν, ὡς ἐπύθετο τὸν Ἑλλήσ-
15 ποντον ἐκλελοιπέναι Δαυρίσην καὶ στρατεύεσθαι ἐπὶ Καρίης, καταλιπὼν τὴν Προποντίδα ἐπὶ τὸν Ἑλλήσποντον ἦγε τὸν στρατὸν, καὶ εἷλε μὲν Αἰολέας πάντας, ὅσοι τὴν Ἰλιάδα νέμονται, εἷλε δὲ Γέργιθας τοὺς ὑπολειφθέντας τῶν ἀρχαίων Τευκρῶν. αὐτός
20 τε Ὑμέης αἱρέων ταῦτα τὰ ἔθνεα νούσῳ τελευτᾷ ἐν τῇ Τρῳάδι.

After the death of Hymeas, Artaphernes and Otanes took Klazomenae and Kyme.

CXXIII. Οὗτος μὲν δὴ οὕτω ἐτελεύτησε, Ἀρταφέρνης δὲ ὁ Σαρδίων ὕπαρχος καὶ Ὀτάνης ὁ τρίτος στρατηγὸς ἐτάχθησαν ἐπὶ τὴν Ἰωνίην καὶ τὴν προσεχέα Αἰολίδα στρατεύεσθαι. Ἰωνίης μέν νυν Κλαζομενὰς αἱρέουσι, Αἰολέων δὲ Κύμην. 5

Aristagoras thereupon, becoming alarmed, determined, in spite of the advice of Hekataios, to fly to Myrkinos, where he perished in a battle with the native Thrakians.

CXXIV. Ἁλισκομενέων δὲ τῶν πολίων, ἦν γάρ, ὡς διέδεξε, Ἀρισταγόρης ὁ Μιλήσιος ψυχὴν οὐκ ἄκρος, ὃς ταράξας τὴν Ἰωνίην καὶ ἐγκερασάμενος πρήγματα μεγάλα δρησμὸν ἐβούλευε, ὁρέων ταῦτα, πρὸς δέ οἱ καὶ ἀδύνατα ἐφαίνετο βασιλέα Δαρεῖον 10 ὑπερβαλέσθαι, πρὸς ταῦτα δὴ ὦν συγκαλέσας τοὺς συστασιώτας ἐβουλεύετο, λέγων, ὡς ἄμεινον σφίσι εἴη κρησφύγετόν τι ὕπαρχον εἶναι, ἢν ἄρα ἐξωθέωνται ἐκ τῆς Μιλήτου, εἴτε δὴ ὦν ἐς Σαρδὼ ἐκ τοῦ τόπου τούτου ἄγοι ἐς ἀποικίην εἴτε ἐς Μύρκινον τὴν 15 Ἠδωνῶν, τὴν Ἱστιαῖος ἐτείχεε παρὰ Δαρείου δωρεὴν λαβών. ταῦτα ἐπειρώτα ὁ Ἀρισταγόρης. CXXV. Ἑκαταίου μέν νυν τοῦ Ἡγησάνδρου, ἀνδρὸς λογοποιοῦ, τούτων μὲν ἐς οὐδετέρην στέλλειν ἔφερε ἡ γνώμη, ἐν Λέρῳ δὲ τῇ νήσῳ τεῖχος οἰκοδομησάμενον ἡσυχίην 20 ἄγειν, ἢν ἐκπέσῃ ἐκ τῆς Μιλήτου· ἔπειτα δὲ ἐκ ταύτης ὁρμεόμενον κατελεύσεσθαι ἐς τὴν Μίλητον. CXXVI. ταῦτα μὲν δὴ Ἑκαταῖος συνεβούλευε,

αὐτῷ δὲ Ἀρισταγόρῃ ἡ πλείστη γνώμη ἦν ἐς τὴν
Μύρκινον ἀπάγειν. τὴν μὲν δὴ Μίλητον ἐπιτράπει
Πυθαγόρῃ ἀνδρὶ τῶν ἀστῶν δοκίμῳ, αὐτὸς δὲ παραλαβὼν πάντα τὸν βουλόμενον ἔπλεε ἐς τὴν Θρηίκην,
5 καὶ ἔσχε τὴν χώρην, ἐπ᾽ ἣν ἐστάλη. ἐκ δὲ ταύτης
ὁρμεόμενος ἀπόλλυται ὑπὸ Θρηίκων αὐτός τε ὁ
Ἀρισταγόρης καὶ ὁ στρατὸς αὐτοῦ, πόλιν περικατήμενος καὶ βουλομένων τῶν Θρηίκων ὑποσπόνδων
ἐξιέναι.

NOTES.

NOTES.

[*For names of persons and places see Historical and Geographical Index. G. stands for Goodwin's Greek Grammar. App. for Appendix on the Ionic dialect in Book IX. Clyde for Clyde's Greek Syntax. Madvig for Madvig's Greek Syntax, Eng. Transl.*]

CHAPTER I.

1. ἐν Εὐρώπῃ...καταλειφθέντες. That is, the 80,000 men left by Darius when he crossed back into Asia after his Skythian expedition. See 4, 142—4.

4. περιεφθέντας τρηχέως 'who had been roughly handled already', cp. p. 48, l. 2; 1, 73 αὐτοὺς...τρηχέως κάρτα περιέσπε ἀεικείῃ. 6, 15 περιέφθησαν τρηχύτατα.

6. χρήσαντος τοῦ θεοῦ 'upon *their* god having bidden them in an oracle'.

7. ἐπικαλέσωνται 'call out to', not 'challenge' (προκαλέεσθαι), as is shown by the context. Cp. 9, 61, 62 ἐπικαλέσασθαι τὴν θεόν.

8. τοὺς δὲ 'that then they should attack'. For δὲ in apodosis see p. 22, l. 20.

12. ἐκ προκλήσιος 'in consequence of a challenge', 'on challenge'. Cp. 9, 75 and p. 41, l. 21 ταῦτα ἔλεγε ἐκ διδαχῆς.

14. τὰ δύο sc. 'in two of the three contests'.

ἐπαιώνιζον 'they began singing their Paean', they called out Παίων ἰὼ Παίων, which the *Paeonians* took as a calling them by name, and so fulfilling the oracle. A different Paean was in use among different Hellenes (Thucyd. 7, 44, 6), and also before and after battle (Thucyd. 1, 50, 6).

15. τὸ χρηστήριον αὐτὸ τοῦτο εἶναι 'that this was exactly what the oracle referred to'. For such quibbling oracles, see on 6, 76.

1. ἂν εἴη...ἐπιτελεόμενος 'must be in the act of fulfilment',—the optative expresses a less confident feeling than the indicative.

νῦν ἡμέτερον τὸ ἔργον 'now is our time to act'. St. quotes Arist.

Pax 427 ὑμέτερον ἐντεῦθεν ἔργον, ὤνδρες· ἀλλὰ ταῖς ἅμαις εἰσιόντες ὡς τάχιστα τοὺς λίθους ἀφέλκετε.

3, 4. **πολλὸν** adverbial, cp. 6, 82. **σφέων** = αὐτῶν App. C. II. (d).

CHAPTER II.

4. **δή** resumptive. **ἀπὸ Παιόνων** 'at the hands of the Paeonians'. Cp. 6, 98 τὰ μὲν ἀπὸ τῶν Περσέων γενόμενα τὰ δὲ ἀπὸ αὐτῶν κορυφαίων.

5. **τότε δὲ** 'on this occasion', when attacked by the Persians: opposed to πρότερον.

9. **διὰ τῆς Θρηίκης** that is, from East to West (Stein).

10. **ἡμερούμενος** 'subduing', lit. 'rendering tame' or submissive. Cp. 4, 118 τοὺς αἰεὶ ἐμποδὼν γινομένους ἡμεροῦται.

CHAPTER III.

13. **μετά γε Ἰνδούς** 'next of course to the Indians'. Cp. Pausan. I, 9, 5 Θρᾳκῶν τῶν πάντων οὐδένες πλείους εἰσὶ τῶν ἀνθρώπων, ὅτι μὴ Κελτοί, πρὸς ἄλλο ἔθνος ἐν ἀντεξετάζοντι. Her. 3, 94 Ἰνδῶν δὲ πλῆθος πολλῷ πλεῖστον πάντων τῶν ἡμεῖς ἴδμεν ἀνθρώπων. Strabo counted 22 Thrakian tribes (fr. vii. 46). Herodotos mentions 18. Hekataeos gives 10 additional names; Thucydides (2, 96) 3 more; Pliny 20. The whole number of known names of Thrakian tribes amounts to 50 (Rawl.).

15. **φρονέοι κατὰ τὠυτό** 'were in union', cp. p. 42, l. 22; 1, 60 μετὰ δὲ οὐ πολλὸν χρόνον τὠυτὸ φρονήσαντες...ἐξελαύνουσί μιν.

17. **ἀλλὰ γάρ** 'but as it is hopeless and impossible for this to take place'...**εἰσὶ δή** 'they accordingly are'. The reason is introduced by **γάρ** before the fact. See p. 10, l. 20, and on 6, 11.

ἀμήχανον μή...ἐγγένηται 'it is impossible that this should happen'. By a somewhat remarkable extension ἀμήχανον takes the construction of verbs of fearing or caution, as though it = οὐ δέος or οὐ κίνδυνός ἐστι μὴ ἐγγένηται. Cp. οὐ μὴ γένηται 'it will certainly not happen'. **κατὰ τοῦτο** 'on that account', or 'for that reason'. Cp. 6, 1 κατὰ κοῖόν τι δοκέοι Ἴωνας ἀπεστάναι. See on p. 19, l. 14.

19. **κατὰ χώρας** 'in their various places of residence', 'according to the districts occupied by them'.

CHAPTER IV.

22. **οἱ ἀθανατίζοντες** 'who believe in their immortality'. See 4, 93—4. They believed that after death they went to their god Zalmoxis.

24. ἐπιτελέουσι 'they practise'. The verb applies to various things, to religious rites 2, 63; 4, 186: to professions c. 60: to injunctions of authority 1, 90, 115.

27. ὀλοφύρονται cp. a fragment of Euripides from his play of Kresphontes, fr. xiii. (Nauck 452):

ἐχρῆν γὰρ ἡμᾶς σύλλογον ποιουμένους
τὸν φύντα θρηνεῖν, εἰς ὅσ' ἔρχεται κακά,
τὸν δ' αὖ θανόντα καὶ πόνων πεπαυμένον
χαίροντας εὐφημοῦντας ἐκπέμπειν δόμων.

ἀναπλῆσαι 'to endure', cp. 6, 12 τίνα δαιμόνων παραβάντες τάδε ἀναπίμπλαμεν; 9, 87 γῆ ἡ Βοιωτίη πλέω μὴ ἀναπλήσῃ.

1. τὸν ἀπογενόμενον 'the dead', cp. 2, 85 τοῖσι ἂν ἀπογένηται ἐκ 3 τῶν οἰκίων ἄνθρωπος.

3. ἐπιλέγοντες 'saying besides', 'adding at the same time'. Cp. 4, 65 τὰς κεφαλὰς ταύτας παραφέρει καὶ ἐπιλέγει ὥς οἱ κ.τ.λ.

CHAPTER V.

6. κρίσις μεγάλη τῶν γυναικῶν 'a great contest between the women'. Cp. 7, 26 ἐς κρίσιν τούτου πέρι ἐλθόντας.

10. σφάζεται ἐς τὸν τάφον 'is slaughtered over the grave' i.e. so that the blood runs into it. Cp. 4, 62 ἀποσφάζουσι τοὺς ἀνθρώπους ἐς ἄγγος.

12. συμφορὴν μεγάλην ποιεῦνται 'regard it as a great misfortune', 'mourn vehemently'. Cp. c. 90; 6, 61 συμφορὴν τὸ εἶδος αὐτῆς ποιεύμενος. 9, 77 συμφορὴν ἐποιεῦντο μεγάλην. It is one of the numerous phrases, particularly common in Herodotos, in which ποιεῖσθαι with a substantive takes the place of a simple verb.

The analogy of this custom to the Indian *Suttee* is obvious, and similar customs are said to have existed among Teutonic, Slavonian and Scandinavian tribes. It seems generally connected with polygamy.

CHAPTER VI.

15. πωλεῦσι τὰ τέκνα. A custom still prevalent among the Circassians. ἐπ' ἐξαγωγῇ 'for exportation', 'for the foreign market'. Cp. 7, 156 τούτους...ἀπέδοτο ἐπ' ἐξαγωγῇ ἐκ Σικελίας.

18. ὠνέονται τὰς γυναῖκας. The obtaining wives by purchase had been a Greek custom in Heroic times, cp. the explanation of παρθένοι ἀλφεσίβοιαι 'maidens who bring in presents of cattle from their suitors',

Homer, Il. 18, 593; Hymn in Vener. 119; but this was gradually supplanted by the custom of the father giving his daughter a portion, φερνή. See Euripid. Hippol. 625—6. The older custom long prevailed apparently among the Thrakians and probably among the Skythae also. Stein quotes Xenoph. Anab. 7, 2, 38 σοὶ δὲ, ὦ Ξενοφῶν, καὶ θυγατέρα δώσω, καὶ εἴ τίς σοι ἐστὶ θυγάτηρ ὠνήσομαι Θρᾳκίῳ νόμῳ.

19. τὸ ἐστίχθαι 'to be tattooed'. Xenophon (Anab. 5, 4, 31) saw some tattooed people on the coast of the Pontus, and the tattooing of the Thrakes is noticed by Cicero (de off. 2, 25) and Strabo 7, 5, 4. Hence the term στιμαγτίας for a slave in the later Attic writers, at a time when many Thracian slaves were kept in Greece. (Xenoph. Hell. 5, 3, 24. Cp. Aristoph. Lysist. 331.) See for a representation *Journ. of Hellen. Stud.* vol. ix, p. 145, plate vi.

21. ἀργὸν...ἀτιμότατον. It is a common characteristic of barbarians to look upon manual labour as degrading, and to regard war as the only honourable employment. ἀργός = ἄεργος 'free from agricultural labour'. The same peculiarity is noticed by Tacitus as to the Germans, *nec arare terram aut exspectare annum tam facile persuaseris quam vocare hostem et vulnera mereri. Pigrum quin immo et iners videtur sudore adquirere quod possis sanguine parare. Quotiens bella non ineunt multum venatibus, plus per otium transigunt, dediti somno ciboque, fortissimus quisque ac bellicosissimus nihil agens, delegata domus et penatium et agrorum cura feminis senibusque.* German. 14—15. Cp. Caes. B. G. 6, 21—2.

22. ἀπὸ πολέμου καὶ ληϊστύος 'on war and plunder'. So the Skythae of the Tauric Chersonese ζώουσι ἀπὸ ληΐης τε καὶ πολέμου. Cp. Thucydides' account of the early habits of the Greeks themselves in regard to plunder and piracy, 1, 5.

CHAPTER VII.

24. Ἄρεα...Διόνυσον...Ἄρτεμιν. These represent War, Wine and the Chase. The worship of Dionysus in Thrace was famous. They called him Sabazius (schol. Arist. Vesp. 9; Aves 875), and a temple and oracle of his are mentioned in 7, 111. The legends of Orpheus and Lykurgos were connected with this worship.

The Thracian worship of Artemis is mentioned again in 4, 33. The name of the goddess with them was Bendis; and the connexion of Athens and Thrace, which begun early, is illustrated by the fact that a shrine and temenos sacred to Artemis existed in Munychia, the latter of which was called the *Bendideium*, a festival called the *Bendideia* being celebrated there. [See Xenoph. Hellen. 2, 4, 11. Plato Rep. 354 A. Demosth. de Cor. § 107. Livy, 38, 41.] Another name for Bendis seems to have been *Cotys* or *Cotytto*; see Strabo (10, 3, 16) who quotes a passage from Aeschylos' play of the Edoni

σεμνὰ Κότυς, ἐν τοῖς Ἠδωνοῖς,
ὄρεια δ' ὄργαν' ἔχοντες.

26. **πάρεξ τῶν ἄλλων** 'separately from other citizens'. Another analogy with the Germans (Tac. Germ. 9) and Gauls (Caes. B.G. 6, 17 *Deum maxime Mercurium colunt. Hujus sunt plurima simulacra; hunc omnium inventorem artium ferunt; hunc viarum atque itinerum ducem; hunc ad quaestus pecuniae mercaturasque habere vim maximam arbitrantur*).

CHAPTER VIII.

3. **ταφαί** 'funeral ceremonies'.
6. **θάπτουσι** 'they perform the obsequies'.

ἄλλως 'simply', cp. 3, 139 ἐγὼ ταύτην πωλέω μὲν οὐδενὸς χρήματος, δίδωμι δὲ ἄλλως, εἴπερ τοῦτο δεῖ γενέσθαι. Others explain ἄλλως as in apposition to γῇ κρύψαντες 'or in another way, namely by burying it'. But cp. Thucyd. 8, 78 ἄλλως ὄνομα καὶ οὐκ ἔργον. Demosth. de F. L. § 24 ὄχλος ἄλλως καὶ βασκανία.

7. **χέαντες** 'having heaped up', an Epic usage=χώσαντες. Il. 7, 336 τύμβον δ' ἀμφὶ πυρὴν ἕνα χεύομεν. 24, 799 σῆμα χεύαντες.
8. **παντοῖον** 'of all sorts', like the funeral games in Il. 22, 262 f.

κατὰ λόγον μουνομαχίης 'in the way of single combat': so ἐν ἀνδραπόδων λόγῳ 6, 19; ἐν συμμάχων λόγῳ 8, 68, 3. Herodotos uses λόγος in a great variety of connexions and meanings, some of which will be found in the index. He here means that the games, though of all sorts, consisted of several contests between pairs of combatants.

CHAPTER IX.

11. **τὸ πρὸς βορέω ἔτι** 'still further North', 'what lies beyond this country to the Northward'. πρός with the genitive, in a local reference is 'on the side of', cp. τὸ πρὸς ἑσπέρης 4, 100.
12. **οὐδεὶς ἔχει φράσαι τὸ ἀτρεκές** nearly three centuries later Polybius (3, 38) asserted that the same ignorance prevailed concerning this Northern district.
14. **ἄπειρος** 'without any (known) limit'.

18. **λασίους** 'with long coats', like Shetland ponies. It has been noticed that Strabo in describing the Sigynni, a tribe on the Caspian, gives the same account of their horses (11. 11, 8).

ἐπὶ...δακτύλους 'to the depth of five fingers'. For ἐπὶ with the notion of extent cp. 9, 15 ἐπὶ δέκα σταδίους.

19. **σιμούς** 'short-faced' or 'snub-nosed', as the wild horses of the Steppes.

23. **Μήδων ἀποίκους.** That is, probably, the Sigynnae retained some recollection of their Aryan origin, common to them and the Medes, and of their subsequent wandering westward.

26. **σιγύννας.** The word is well attested by later writers as in use in Kypros for a 'spear'; but no other instance of its alleged use in Liguria for κάπηλος ('trader') is known. According to some it is a Makedonian word for 'a spear'. Some critics condemn the whole passage σιγύννας—δόρατα as a later addition or explanation.

δ' ὦν 'however that may be'.

CHAPTER X.

1. **μέλισσαι.** Herodotos' criticism on this legend is doubtless just; yet it is pointed out that the valley of the Danube is infested with mosquitos, which may have given rise to the story: nor do the anecdotes told of wild swarms of bees disagree with the idea of their making a journey dangerous.

5. **δύσριγα** 'incapable of bearing cold'.

7. **δ' ὦν**, see p. 4, l. 26.

CHAPTER XI.

9. **Δαρεῖος δὲ ὡς.** The story is resumed from 4, 143 in which it is mentioned that Darius crossed from Sestos to Asia on his return from his Skythian expedition.

11. **εὐεργεσίης** in preventing the destruction of the bridge over the Danube 4, 137; 6, 30. The word is a technical one both for the good service and the claim on a reward which it established. Cp. Thucyd. 1, 129 κεῖταί σοι εὐεργεσία ἐν τῷ ἡμετέρῳ οἴκῳ ἐσαεὶ ἀνάγραπτος, and note to Herod. 8, 85.

16. **δὴ** 'as I say', summing up a statement.

17. **τε οὐ...τε**, cp. p. 24, l. 25.

18. **δημότης** *civis* 'a private citizen', he was στρατηγὸς Μυτιληναίων

(4, 97) in command of the Mitylenean contingent in Darius' army, but not a ruler at home.

19. **κατά** for κατὰ τά (6, 54).

20. **ἐτράποντο** 'turned their attention', 'were set upon the objects of their choice', p. 7, l. 25. Cp. Thucyd. 5, 9, 3 κατὰ θέαν τετραμμένους 'set on looking about them'.

CHAPTER XII.

21. **ἰδόμενον** = ἰδόντα, only in composition with a preposition in Attic prose. It seems peculiar to Herodotos, not occurring in Homer.

23. **ἀνασπάστους ποιῆσαι** 'to forcibly remove'. Cp. 4, 204 τούτους ἐκ τῆς Αἰγύπτου ἀνασπάστους ἐποίησαν παρὰ βασιλέα.

4. **φυλάξαντες** 'having watched for'. Cp. 6, 52.

5. **προκατιζόμενον ἐς τὸ προάστειον** 'when he was sitting on the seat of justice in the suburb of the Lydians'. Notice the pregnant use of ἐς, he came down *into* the suburb of Sardis and was there sitting in state to administer justice. Cp. παρῆν ἐς, συλλέγεσθαι ἐς 6, 1, 7. For this meaning of προκατίζεσθαι cp. 1, 14 ἀνέθηκε Μίδης τὸν βασιλήιον θρόνον, ἐς τὸν προκατίζων ἐδίκαζε. The προάστειον at Sardis seems to mean some open space in the lower town, in distinction to the citadel, where the king sat to administer justice. We find that the later kings of Egypt, who probably followed eastern usages, did this in a porch or gate-house (πυλών) of the Palace [Polyb. 15, 31]. Herod. describes it as τὸ τῶν Λυδῶν, for the citadel was in the hands of the Persians.

7. **ἐπ' ὕδωρ** 'to fetch water'. Cp. 9, 44 ἔθεον ἐπὶ τοὺς στρατηγούς.

8. **ἐκ τοῦ βραχίονος** 'by her arm', the rein was over her arm.

9. **κλώθουσαν** 'spinning flax'. Her right hand would hold the spindle (ἄτρακτος), the distaff (ἠλακάτη) being held in the left; the end of the latter being secured in some way in her girdle.

10. **ἐπιμελὲς...ἐγένετο** 'it attracted the attention of Darius'. Cp. 1, 89 τῷ Κύρῳ ἐπιμελὲς ἐγένετο τὰ Κροῖσος εἶπε.

11. **ἐκ τῆς γυναικός.** For ἐκ with the agent, which is very common in Herodotos, see 6, 13 τὰ γινόμενα ἐκ τῶν Ἰώνων, cp. id. cc. 22, 42 etc.

16. **ἦρσε** 'watered', 'gave to drink', ἐπότισε. Cp. 7, 109 ταύτην τὴν λίμνην τὰ ὑποζύγια μοῦνα ἀρδόμενα ἀνεξήρηνε.

CHAPTER XIII.

23. **σκοπιὴν ἔχοντες** 'watching', an Homeric expression, see Odyss. 8, 302 Ἠέλιος γάρ οἱ σκοπιὴν ἔχε εἶπέ τε μῦθον.

24. ὁποδαπή 'of what country'.

27. εἰσι...ἔλθοιεν, as usual in indirect questions of two clauses Herodotos varies the moods of the verbs from the dramatic indicative to the historic optative. Cp. infr. c. 97; 6, 3 εἰρωτεόμενος...κατ' ὅ τι ἐπέστειλε Ἀρισταγόρη ἀπίστασθαι καὶ κακὸν τοσοῦτο εἴη Ἴωνας ἐξεργασμένος. Both constructions are good Greek, and the change seems only for the sake of variety; the first part of the question being put as though direct, the second as indirect.

29, 30. ἔλθοιεν...εἴη πεπολισμένη. Notice the difference of tenses; their coming was a single act, the country *is* and has always been as they describe it.

πεπολισμένη 'established a settled state', generally οἰκημένη.

7 2. καὶ πᾶσαι 'all others as well as your sister'.

4. προθύμως, join to ἔφασαν 'they said earnestly'.

αὐτοῦ γὰρ ὦν τούτου εἵνεκεν 'for this was the precise motive of the transaction', i.e. that Darius might ask them the question.

CHAPTER XIV.

8. ἠθέων 'their accustomed haunts', 'their homes'. Cp. 6, 3, where a similar measure is attributed to the King as in contemplation for the Ionians.

καὶ αὐτοὺς καὶ τὰ τέκνα τε καὶ τὰς γυναῖκας. Notice the reiterated conjunctions which, like brackets, mark groups. The τε καί connect τέκνα and γυναῖκας as a separate group connected with αὐτοὺς by the preceding καί.

10. ἔθεε 'started at speed', like a royal courier (ἄγγαρος).

12. ἐπιλεξάμενος 'having read it', often in Herodotos for ἀναγιγνώσκειν, cp. 1, 124; 2, 125; 3, 41.

CHAPTER XV.

15. πρὸς θαλάσσης 'by the coast-road', so as to hold the road from Abdera by Datum (Neapolis, the port of Crenides) and Skaptesyle. For the sense of πρός not 'towards', but 'in the direction of' cp. p. 4, l. 11 πρὸς βορέω. ταύτῃ 'by this road' which passed between Mt Pangaeum and the sea (τὴν πρὸς θαλάσσης ἐσβολὴν) leading into the plain of the Strymon. The Persians seem to have come by the more northern and inland route (τὴν ἄνω ὁδὸν) which led by Crenides (Philippi) over the hills (Symbolon) into this plain. These are the two points held by

Brutus and Cassius in B.C. 42. See Appian, B.C. 41, 87, Dio. Cass. 47, 35.

21. **λαθόντες.** The Paeonians being in the lower road by the sea did not perceive that the Persians had passed them by the upper road, and so got between them and their own country.

22. **οἷα...ἐπιπεσόντες** 'seeing that they had thus made their way into their towns'.

25. **κατ' ἑωυτοὺς ἕκαστοι ἐτράποντο** 'each contingent turned its attention to its own safety'. Cp. p. 5, l. 20.

παρεδίδοσαν 'began making offers of surrender', the imperfect, because it was a series of separate movements.

28. **ἐξαναστάντες** (ἐξανάστατοι γενόμενοι) 'being forced to remove'.

CHAPTER XVI.

4. **τοὺς ἐν τῇ λίμνῃ κατοικημένους.** The discovery of remains of 8 lake dwellings in Switzerland and Germany, as well as in Scotland and Ireland, have gone far to confirm this description of Herodotos. Keller says (*Lake Dwellings*, p. 290) 'the piles were from the commencement 'driven into the actual bed of the lake; and they were so long that 'their heads stood a few feet above the water, whatever might be its 'level. They stood in close rows, and when covered with horizontal 'timbers and boards formed a firm scaffolding, a foundation for the 'erection of the dwellings themselves. These abodes were therefore 'like the fishermen's huts which were found in earlier times, and 'perhaps even now are to be seen, on several of the Swiss lakes'. Hippocrates (born about 50 years before Herodotos) has a reference to them also (*de acribus* 37). 'Concerning the people on the Phasis '(*Rioni*), that region is marshy and hot, and full of water and woody; 'and at every season frequent and violent rains fall there. The inhabi-'tants live in the marshes, and have houses of timber and reeds 'constructed in the midst of the waters; and they seldom go out to the 'city or the market, but sail up and down in boats made out of a single 'tree-trunk; for there are numerous canals in that region'. For later references see Keller, p. 315—7.

5. **ἐξαιρέειν** 'to take and remove'. Cp. 6, 33, 133.

ἴκρια are the 'platforms' mentioned in the previous note, σταυροί are the 'piles'. **ἐζευγμένα** 'clamped together'.

9. **μετὰ δέ** 'but subsequently', i.e. after the original staking was completed.

11—13. κατὰ γυναῖκα ἑκάστην each man drives in three piles for each wife. ἄγεται *ducit;* notice the middle, ἄγεσθαι γυναῖκα 'to take to his own house'=γαμεῖν. So 6, 63 ἐσηγάγετο γυναῖκα, id. 69 ὥς με ἠγάγετο Ἀρίστων ἐς ἑωυτοῦ. κρατέων 'being in possession of'; the singular with the distributive. ἕκαστος explains the subject of οἰκέουσι.

14. καλύβης 'a hut', see on l. 4.

15. θύρης καταπακτῆς 'a trap-door', lit. a door that shuts down tight (πήγνυμι).

17. τοῦ ποδός 'by the foot'. G. § 171, note.

19. χόρτον 'as fodder'.

21. ἀνακλίνῃ 'he opens it' by raising and throwing it back.

σπυρίδα κεινήν 'an empty basket' like the eel-traps on the Thames. The large number of fish-bones and fish-skeletons found among the remains of the lake dwellings, as well as some of the nets and hooks, show that the inhabitants of these places carried on fishing with constant success. Keller, p. 297. A recent discovery near Milan seems to shew that these dwellings were sometimes anterior even to this mode of supplying food. Standard, 19 Nov., 1889.

24. πάπρακάς τε καὶ τίλωνας. These fish have not been identified. Skulls of pike have been found in lake villages, and carp and eels would doubtless be taken also.

CHAPTER XVII.

4. γῆν τε καὶ ὕδωρ the symbols of the submission of the entire country. See 6, 48; 7, 13; 8, 46; p. 43, l. 25.

5. σύντομος sc. ὁδός. Cp. 7, 121 ταύτῃ γὰρ ἐπυνθάνετο συντομώτατον εἶναι. 4, 136 τὰ σύντομα τῆς ὁδοῦ ἐπιστάμενος. The Macedonia here referred to is the district between the Axius and Strymon, which Thucydides (2, 99, 3) calls τὴν παρὰ θάλασσαν νῦν Μακεδονίαν.

6. ἔχεται 'comes next to', cp. 6, 8 εἴχοντο δὲ τούτων Πριηνέες.

7. τὸ μέταλλον the gold and silver mines of this district were long a source of wealth to Makedonian kings, see 6, 46; 9, 75.

9. ἐφοίτα 'used to come in' as revenue. Cp. 3, 90 τὰ δὲ τριηκόσια καὶ ἑξήκοντα (τάλαντα) Δαρείῳ ἐφοίτα.

μετὰ δὲ...εἶναι 'and after the mine, upon passing the mountain called Dysorum, one is in Makedonia'. The infinitive εἶναι seems to depend on the notion contained in σύντομος, 'it is a short road, so that one is in Macedonia after etc.'. Abicht reads ὑπερβάντι and explains the dative as depending on ἔστι or ἔξεστι understood, comparing l. 104.

CHAPTER XVIII.

11. **οἱ ὦν.** The ὦν resumes the narrative broken by the clause ἔστι δὲ—Μακεδονίῃ.

14. **ἐδίδου...καλέει** 'he was for giving it', 'he at once consented to give it', imperfect, 'and he invited them', present for historic aorist. Herodotos often thus combines the tenses cp. 6, 34 τὴν ἱρὴν ὁδὸν ᾔισαν καί σφεας ὡς οὐδεὶς ἐκάλεε ἐκτράπονται ἐπ' Ἀθηνέων.

16. **ὡς ἀπὸ δείπνου ἐγένοντο** 'when they had finished eating', i.e. when the wine was to be handed round. Cp. 6, 129; 9, 16 ὡς δὲ ἀπὸ δείπνου ἦσαν, cp. 1, 127.

17. **διαπίνοντες** 'as they were drinking to each other'. See on 9, 16. To the examples there quoted add Pollux 6, 19 προπίνειν διαπίνειν, διαμιλλᾶσθαι ἐν τῷ πότῳ. The force of the word is properly therefore 'to drink against each other', as in the compounds διακοντίζεσθαι, διαείδειν.

20. **κουριδίας γυναῖκας** 'wedded wives', opposed to παλλακὰς 'concubines' again in 6, 138; 1, 135.

ἐσάγεσθαι 'to introduce into our company'. For the middle see p. 8, l. 12.

22. **διδοῖς** 'are willing to give', 'are ready to give', cp. ἐδίδου above.

3. **φάμενοι** Homeric and Ionic, rare in Attic. For ἔλεγον φάμενοι 10 cp. c. 36 ἔφη λέγων, 6, 67 εἶπε φάς.

4. **ἀρχῆθεν** 'at all', 'to begin with', = ἀρχήν.

6. **ἀλγηδόνας...ὀφθαλμῶν** 'irritations to the sight', we should perhaps say 'to make their mouths water'. Cp. Terence, Phorm. sub fin., *Vin primum hodie facere quod ego gaudeam, Nausistrata, Et quod tuo viro oculi doleant?*

9. **πλεόνως,** cp. μειζόνως 3, 128 for the Attic πλέον and μεῖζον.

CHAPTER XIX.

13. **κακῶν ἀπαθής** 'having had no experience of misfortune' to teach him to submit to the insolence of the strangers. For the phrase see 7, 184. Stein quotes Soph. Antig. 1191 κακῶν γὰρ οὐκ ἄπειρος οὖσ' ἀκούσομαι. Cp. also Eurip. Alc. 926 παρ' εὐτυχῆ σοι πότμον ἦλθεν ἀπειροκάκῳ τόδ' ἄλγος.

14. **κατέχειν** 'to restrain himself'. 8, 114 ὁ δὲ γελάσας τε καὶ

κατασχὼν πολλὸν χρόνον. Cp. 6, 39 εἶχε κατ' οἴκους 'kept himself indoors'.

16. εἶκε τῇ ἡλικίῃ 'give away to the desire for rest natural to your time of life', so in 7, 18 εἴκειν τῇ ἡλικίᾳ is 'to give way to the natural ambition of your youth'.

λιπάρεε τῇ πόσι 'persist in remaining at the wine drinking', cf. 9, 45 λιπαρέετε μένοντες.

19. πρήξειν μέλλοι, for construction of μέλλω with present or future infinitive (not aorist) see G. § 202, 3. [And for exceptions see Rutherford *New Phrynichus*, p. 420.]

20. σχεδὸν γάρ. For the γάρ anticipatory see p. 2, l. 17. σχεδόν 'almost' or 'pretty well' is a *litotes* for σαφῶς 'quite well', often used with a certain ironical force. Soph. Ant. 470 σχεδόν τι μώρῳ μωρίαν ὀφλισκάνω. Trach. 43 σχεδὸν δ' ἐπίσταμαί τι πῆμ' ἔχοντά νιν. Eurip. Troad. 898 σχεδὸν οἶδά σοι μισουμένη.

21. ἀνακαιομένου 'burning with indignation', 'flaring up into wrath'. A rare usage of the word. St. compares Eurip. Or. 609 μᾶλλόν μ' ἀνάψεις ἐπὶ σὸν ἐξελθεῖν φόνον.

ὅτι...νεώτερον 'namely, that you wish to send me out of the way before striking some blow'.

24. ἐξεργάσῃ 'ruin', cp. 4, 134 τὸ ἡμέας οἷόν τε ἔσται ἐξεργάσασθαι.
ἀνέχεο, cp. p. 27, l. 22 ἠνέσχετο βασιλευόμενος.

CHAPTER XX.

26. χρηΐσας τούτων 'having made this request', cp. p. 17, l. 14 τῶν ἂν χρηΐζωμεν.

28. εὐπέτεια 'complete control over', 'free use of', *copia*. Cf. Xen. Oecon. 5, 5 τροφῆς εὐπέτεια. Plato LL. 718 D τῶν προθυμουμένων εὐπέτεια. (L. and Sc.)

2. ἀποσημανέετε 'you have only to signify your wishes'. The future as polite imperative, Clyde § 35. Hom. Od. 2, 270 Τηλέμαχ' οὐδ' ὄπιθεν κακὸς ἔσσεαι, οὐδ' ἀνοήμων. For ἀποσημαίνειν 'to point to', 'indicate', cp. Thucyd. 4, 27, 5 ἐς Νικίαν...ἀπεσήμαινε. In 9, 71 ἀποσημήνασθαι 'to derive an opinion', 'to have proved to myself'.

4. καλῶς ἔχοντας...μέθης 'have had enough wine', lit. 'are well off in respect to drinking', cp. 1, 32 πολλοὶ δὲ μετρίως ἔχοντες βίου.

12. πανδαισίη 'luxuriousness', a banquet of every kind of dainty. Cp. Arist. Pax 565 τὸ στῖφος αὐτῶν φαίνεται | καὶ πυκνὸν καὶ γοργὸν ὥσπερ μᾶζα καὶ πανδαισία.

13. πρός adv. 'besides', p. 12, l. 12.
14. τὰ οἷά τε...παρέχειν 'whatever we could by diligent search supply you with'. οἷά τε = οἷόν τε, as δῆλα and other plurals are used by Herodotos.
15. καὶ δὴ καὶ 'and to cap all'.
16. ἐπιδαψιλευόμεθα 'we lavish upon you'.
17. τιμεόμενοι App. D. III. 2 (a).
18. τῶν πέρ ἐστε ἄξιοι. There is a tragical irony in the words, in view of what was to happen to the men; cp. the use of μέμφεσθαι in 8, 106 ὥστε σε μὴ μέμψασθαι τὴν ἀπ' ἐμέο τοι ἐσομένην δίκην.
19. ἀνὴρ Ἕλλην. Alexander calls himself a Greek, because his family the Temenidae claimed descent from Temenos of Argos, see c. 22; 8, 137. Thucyd. 2, 99.
22. τῷ λόγῳ 'in pretence', generally opposed to ἔργῳ.

CHAPTER XXI.

25. ἡ θεραπηίη = οἱ θεράποντες: so ἡ δουλεία for οἱ δοῦλοι Thucyd. 5, 23, 4; φυγή = φυγάδες id. 8, 64, 4; Herod. 3, 138; ἡ ἀρχή = οἱ ἄρχοντες Lys. 9 § 16.
26. ἡ πᾶσα πολλή 'all the lavish equipment'—which Persians usually had.
28. μετὰ δέ adverbial, cp. p. 8, l. 9.
29. ἐκ of the agent, see p. 6, l. 11.
1. καί 'however'. κατέλαβε 'stopped them' from prosecuting the search, cp. 9, 2 οἱ Θηβαῖοι κατελάμβανον τὸν Μαρδόνιον 'tried to prevent his going on'.
3. δοὺς δέ...τῷ στρατηγῷ 'and so Alexander stopped the enquiry by giving these things to a Persian named Bubares, who was the leader of the party that was searching for the dead men'.
6. καταλαμφθείς [App. E. 2 (b)] ἐσιγήθη 'was hushed up'.

CHAPTER XXII.

9. κατά περ, see p. 5, l. 19.
10. ἐν τοῖσι ὄπισθε λόγοισι, see 7, 137.
12. πρὸς δέ 'and besides', p. 11, l. 13.
οἱ...διέποντες. The managers (ἀγωνοθέται) of the Olympic games were Eleans, who from time immemorial had had that privilege, with

the exception of a brief period during which Pheidon of Argos deprived them of it. Cp. 6, 127. From the 50th Olympiad (B.C. 580) to the 75th (B.C. 480) two such Agonothetae were appointed to this office by lot from among the Eleans. After that time Hellanodikae were appointed every Olympiad, varying in numbers from nine to eight and ten at different periods. They acted as a court of reference on all disputed points, and especially as to the admission of competitors, who were bound to be of Greek blood; hence ἔγνωσαν 'they decided'. See 2, 160; Pausan. 4, 9, 4—6.

14. ἀεθλεύειν a general word applicable to all contests, 'to enter for the prize'.

ἑλομένου 'having decided'.

καταβάντος ἐπ' αὐτὸ τοῦτο 'and having come down to the arena for this very purpose'. Or καταβάντος may refer to his coming down from Makedonia to Elis [cp. p. 69, l. 19 καταβήσομαι εἰς Ἰωνίην].

15. οἱ ἀντιθευσόμενοι 'those who would compete with him'. ἔξεργον 'tried to exclude', 'objected to him'.

18. ἐκρίθη i.e. by the Agonothetae.

ἀγωνιζόμενος στάδιον *cognate accusative* 'entering as a competitor in the long-race'.

19. συνεξέπιπτε τῷ πρώτῳ 'was decided to be equal to the first'; that is, he ran a dead-heat with the winner. συνεξέπιπτε appears to refer to the decision of the judges, 'he was decided to be equal to'.— The verb συνεκπίπτειν refers primarily to the voting pebbles falling from the urn, then to the votes (γνῶμαι) which those pebbles indicate (1, 206; 8, 49), then to the persons voting (8, 123), and finally, as here, to the persons voted for.

CHAPTER XXIII.

21. Μεγάβαζος δὲ resuming from c. 15.

24. τὴν...αἰτήσας ἔτυχε δωρεὴν μισθὸν 'the present which he had successfully asked for as a gift in reward for'. Both μισθὸν and δωρεὴν are in apposition to τὴν sc. Μύρκινον. Some MSS. have μισθὸν δωρεήν, which might be translated 'which he had successfully asked as a gift in reward for'.

2. ἐκ, see p. 6, l. 11.

4. κοῖόν τι 'what folly have you committed!'

6. ἴδη an epic word for 'a wood' (1, 110; 7, 111), whence Mt

Ida. The abundance of timber fit for ship-building (ναυπηγήσιμος) in this district is noticed by Thucydides (4, 108).

7. μέταλλα, see p. 9, l. 7.

9. προστάτεω ἐπιλαβόμενοι 'now that they have got a champion'. For προστάτεω see App. C. I. 4.

14. περιλάβῃς 'got him into your power'. Cp. 8, 106 ὡς δὲ ἄρα πανοικίῃ μιν περιέλαβε.

ποιέειν hortative infinitive for imperative.

CHAPTER XXIV.

18. μετὰ δὲ, p. 8, l. 9.

23. ἐπινοέω γάρ. For γάρ anticipating result cp. p. 10, l. 20.

24. ἵνα...ὑπερθέωμαι 'that I may communicate them to you'. [τίθημι, aor. subj. m. θῶμαι for θέωμαι, Epic θείομαι.] Cp. 1, 107 ὑπερθέμενος τοῖσι ὀνειροπόλοισι τὸ ἐνύπνιον.

26. μέγα ποιεύμενος 'regarding it as a great thing', for ποιέεσθαι in this sense cp. 9, 5 δεινὸν ποιησάμενοι. It is very frequent in Herodotos. Sometimes the plural is used, as 1, 119 μεγάλα ποιησάμενος.

2. σέ the subject of ἰδεῖν 'that you should see and come to speech with me'.

5. τά...ἀμφότερα...τὰ ἐμά 'both which qualities in you I can, in regard to my interests, bear witness to from personal knowledge'.

CHAPTER XXV.

12. ὕπαρχον...Σαρδίων. Sardis, after the fall of the Lydian kingdom, became the chief seat of the Persian government of Western Asia, which was divided into two Satrapies (3, 90): the ὕπαρχος of Sardis seems to have possessed a special character, superior to the ordinary Satraps, and to have been more definitely a military officer, see 6, 42.

13. ἅμα ἀγόμενος 'taking with him in his train', notice the middle compared with c. 23 Μεγάβαζος ἄγων τοὺς Παίονας.

14. στρατηγὸν...τῶν παραθαλασσίων ἀνδρῶν 'commander of the troops on the sea-coast', apparently on the European coasts of the Hellespont and the Euxine—not the Asiatic, see c. 30. It is not clear, however, whether Otanes was in any sense under the authority of Artaphernes.

17. ἐπὶ χρήμασι 'for a bribe'.
18. ἀνθρωπηΐην sc. δοράν 'human skin'. σπαδίξας (σπάω, σπαδίζω) 'having drawn off'.
20. ἐς...ἐδίκαζε 'on which Sisamnes used to sit for the administration of justice'.

CHAPTER XXVI.

25. διάδοχος...Μεγαβάζῳ. We hear no more of Megabazus, who perhaps died at this time.

3. ἔτι τότε 'at that time still',—in spite, that is, of the Hellenic immigrations into the other islands and coast towns.

CHAPTER XXVII.

5. ἐκακώθησαν 'were worsted'.
7. τοῦ βασιλεύσαντος 'who had once been king'. He had been secretary to Polykrates (3, 123). Of his subsequent accession to power see 3, 142.
8. οὗτος...τελευτᾷ is parenthetical, and is supposed by many editors to have been a later insertion.
9. αἰτίη δὲ τούτου 'now the cause of Otanes thus acting was as follows'.

CHAPTER XXVIII.

15. μετὰ δὲ οὐ πολλὸν χρόνον 'and afterwards, for a short time there was a cessation of the troubles' etc. This phrase would answer to the facts very well if we may place the Skythian expedition in B.C. 508 and the outbreak of the Ionic Revolt in B.C. 504—3. But Grote (vol. 4, p. 205, c. XXXV.) would date the Skythian expedition in B.C. 515—14 and would translate the words by putting the comma after χρόνον, 'and soon after this there was a cessation of troubles'—i.e. the troubles just caused by Otanes. In that case ἦν ought to have been ἐγένετο. For μετὰ δὲ adverbial cp. p. 15 l. 15.
16. καὶ ἤρχετο 'and then troubles began', cp. 1, 61 μετὰ δὲ, οὐ πολλῷ λόγῳ εἰπεῖν, χρόνος διέφυ καὶ πάντα σφι ἐξηρτύετο ἐς τὴν κάτοδον. τὸ δεύτερον 'again', 'afresh'. Cp. 6, 31, 126.
17. τοῦτο μὲν...τοῦτο δὲ 'in the first place', 'in the second place', p. 18 l. 1.

19. αὐτή τε ἑωυτῆς...ἀκμάσασα 'at that period was both at the highest pitch of prosperity it ever attained'. Cp. 1, 203 ἡ Κασπίη...τῇ εὐρυτάτη ἐστὶ αὐτὴ ἑωυτῆς. ἀκμάσασα sc. ἦν.

20. καὶ δὴ καὶ p. 11, l. 15.

τῆς Ἰωνίης ἦν πρόσχημα 'was the ornament of Ionia', the most conspicuous town in Ionia. Thus Polybios (3, 15) calls Carthagena ὡσανεὶ πρόσχημα καὶ βασίλειον Καρχηδονίων ἐν τοῖς κατὰ τὴν Ἰβηρίαν τόποις. And Sophocles (Elect. 682) calls the Pythian games τὸ κλεινὸν Ἑλλάδος πρόσχημα.

21. ἐπὶ δύο γενεάς 'during two generations'. For ἐπὶ indicating extension of time, see ἐπὶ ἐξ ἡμέρας 6, 101. Cp. 9, 8; p. 61, l. 19.

22. νοσήσασα 'disordered', used for political disturbance also by Demosth. de Cor. § 45 αἱ δὲ πόλεις ἐνόσουν, τῶν μὲν ἐν τῷ πολιτεύεσθαι δωροδοκούντων κ.τ.λ.

Πάριοι κατήρτισαν 'reestablished them on a sound footing'. The Parians were called in as arbitrators from a confidence in their character. This was a practice not uncommon in Greece. Thus the Achaeans were called to settle the disputes of the cities of Magna Graecia in the fifth century, and again in the disputes between Sparta and Thebes after B.C. 371 [Polyb. 2, 39]. See also the case of the Cyreneans in 4, 161.

23. ἐκ πάντων Ἑλλήνων 'out of all Greece'.

CHAPTER XXIX.

1. ὥρεον γὰρ for the anticipatory γὰρ see p. 10, l. 20. οἰκοφθορημένους 'ruined in their estates' (οἶκοι), cp. 1, 196; 8, 142.

3. ὅκως...ἴδοιεν 'as often as they saw'. Cp. 1, 17; 8, 52; iterative optative Madv. § 133; p. 36, l. 21.

4. ἐν ἀνεστηκυίῃ τῇ χώρῃ 'in a district which had been laid waste'. ἀνεστηκυίῃ = ἀναστάτῳ γενομένῃ.

5. ἀπεγράφοντο 'caused to be entered in a list'; the actual clerks ἀπέγραφον, see 7, 100; 8, 135. Cp. p. 64, l. 28.

8. ἁλίην ποιησάμενοι 'having called an assembly'. This word was used for a popular assembly in various parts of Greece, especially among the Dorians, as in Elis [Polyb. 4, 73]. Herodotos uses it of the Thebans c. 79, and of the Spartans 7, 134. It survived in Athens in the title of the judges ἡλιασταί, and their court ἡλιαία, as representing the assembly. For ἀπέδεξαν with infin. cp. p. 65, l. 2.

9. νέμειν 'to govern'. For the middle, see p. 52, l. 7.

10. **δοκέειν γάρ...σφετέρων** cp. Aeschines in Timarch. § 153 ἀποβλέπων πῶς τὸν καθ' ἡμέραν βίον ζῇ ὁ κρινόμενος καὶ ὅντινα τρόπον διοικεῖ τὴν ἑαυτοῦ οἰκίαν, ὡς παραπλησίως αὐτὸν καὶ τὰ τῆς πόλεως διοικήσοντα.

12. **τούτων πείθεσθαι** 'to obey these'. The genitive on the analogy of ὑπακούειν. Cp. p. 19, l. 23; 1, 126; 6, 12.

CHAPTER XXX.

14. **νῦν** sums up and dismisses a subject. Cp. p. 21, l. 13.

15. **τότε δὲ** 'but on the occasion of which I am now speaking', referring back to c. 28 ἐκ Νάξου τε καὶ Μιλήτου Ἴωσι κ.τ.λ.

16. **ἔφυγον** 'were banished', the aorist indicates the single fact, ἔφευγον would be 'were in banishment'. Cp. 6, 9 οἵ...ἔφευγον ἐς Μήδους.

17. **τῶν παχέων** 'the rich', cp. 6, 91; 7, 156; Arist. Vesp. 288 καὶ γὰρ ἀνὴρ παχὺς ἥκει τῶν προδόντων τἀπὶ Θράκης.

18. **ἐπίτροπος** 'deputy governor'.

21. **κατεῖχε** see c. 24.

23. **ξεῖνοι...Ἱστιαίῳ** that is, Histiaeos was their proxenus, p. 19, l. 17. **πρὶν** = πρότερον cp. 8, 37; 9, 109.

25. **ἐδέοντο...εἴ κως** a compressed sentence 'they begged him, if by any means he could give them succour, and so they might be restored, to do so'. Cp. 6, 52 βουλομένην δὲ εἴ κως ἀμφότεροι γενοίατο βασιλέες. 9, 14 θέλων εἴ κως τούτους πρῶτον ἕλοι.

26. For **κατέλθοιεν** of restoration from exile see 6, 107 and Aristoph. Ranae 1165 φεύγων δ' ἀνὴρ ἥκει τε καὶ κατέρχεται.

17 1. **ὡς...ἄρξει** 'he would be lord of Naxos'. After verbs *declarandi et sentiendi* ὡς with the future indicative is commonly used, more rarely the optative. Madv. § 159 R. 3.

4. **φερέγγυος** 'to be depended on for', 'capable' [lit. 'carrying a pledge'] a poetical word. Cp. 7, 49 λιμὴν τοσοῦτος...ὅστις φερέγγυος ἔσται διασῶσαι τὰς νέας.

6. **ὀκτακισχιλίην ἀσπίδα** 'eight thousand hoplites'. The singular is on the analogy of ἵππος χιλίη 7, 41. The ἀσπίς is a noun of multitude in this sense. Cp. Xen. Anab. 1, 7, 10 ἀσπὶς μυρία καὶ τετρακοσία.

7. **πλοῖα μακρά** 'ships of war', including apparently triremes and others. But πλοῖα is almost always used of vessels of inferior size to

triremes. In Thucyd. 1, 14 μακρὰ πλοῖα are opposed to τριήρεις and πεντηκόντοροι: and of the 31 instances in Thucydides of this word only twice is it so employed as to include triremes. In Herod. 6, 25 we have ναῦς μακραί opposed to ἱππαγωγὰ πλοῖα.

11. τῶν ἐπιθαλασσίων...Ἀσίη 'the people living on the coast of Asia'. Those on the European coast were under Otanes, see c. 25.

15. προσέθεσαν 'enjoined', cp. 3, 62 διεπρήξαο τό τοι προσέθηκα πρῆγμα.

18. ἐπιφανέωσι ἐς. For the pregnant use of ἐς cp. παρεῖναι ἐς 6, 1, 24.

20. ὡς=οὕτω p. 22, l. 27.

CHAPTER XXXI.

24. ὡς Νάξος εἴη...ἔνι. For the variation of mood in two cognate clauses [ἔνι=ἔνεστι] see on p. 6, l. 27.

25. καλή τε καὶ ἀγαθή 'both beautiful and productive'.

28. κατάγων see p. 55, l. 15. τοὺς φυγάδας ἐξ αὐτῆς=τοὺς φυγόντας.

1. τοῦτο μέν...τοῦτο δέ p. 26, l. 12.

2. ἀναισιμωμάτων 'the expenses'. ἀναισιμόω=ἀναλίσκω is common in Herodotos; but ἀναισίμωμα appears not to occur elsewhere.

4. νήσους 'island Greece', for the omission of the article when speaking of the islands collectively as opposed to the continent, see 3, 96; 9, 3; and cp. νησιῶται 6, 49; 8, 46.

5. τὰς ἐκ ταύτης ἠρτημένας 'which are dependent on it'. That Naxos exercised any right of sovereignty over the other islands is not known. If it did, it was probably of an informal kind.

8. εὐπετέως...Εὔβοίη 'you will have great facilities for attacking Euboea', that is by a voyage through the Cyclades. Thus in B.C. 490 Datis and Artaphernes hesitated to proceed to Euboea until they had secured Naxos, 6, 26.

12. ἐς οἶκον τὸν βασιλέος i.e. 'to the king', οἶκος βασιλέος 'the royal house' stands by an intelligible idiom for the king himself. Cp. 6, 9.

15. δέει...γίνεσθαι 'but we must get the king's assent to this movement'.

CHAPTER XXXII.

19. **ἐς Σοῦσα.** It was three months journey from the coast to Susa, see c. 50, but the Persian ἄγγαροι would no doubt do the journey in somewhat less.

21. **παρεσκευάσατο** 'he caused to be prepared'. Observe the force of the middle. See on p. 16, l. 5 ἀπεγράφοντο.

26. **εἰ δὴ ἀληθής γέ ἐστι ὁ λόγος** 'if, indeed, there is any truth in the story'. Thucydides represents Pausanias as asking for one of the king's own daughters (1, 128); but that his request was granted is not stated elsewhere, and it may very well have been a scandalous anecdote sent home among many more to his disfavour from the Greek fleet, in which he had made himself so unpopular.

ἡρμόσατο 'betrothed to himself', not 'married', cp. p. 27, l. 14 and 6, 65.

28. **σχών** 'having conceived a desire'.

CHAPTER XXXIII.

5. **πρόφασιν** 'professedly', elsewhere with preposition, see 1, 29; 4, 145. Cp. χάριν, p. 64, l. 21.

8. **καὶ οὐ γὰρ ἔδεε** 'but, as it was not destined that the Naxians should be ruined by this expedition'. For the anticipatory γάρ see p. 2, l. 17. For ἔδεε of fate or destiny cp. 6, 64, 105; 9, 109 τῇ δὲ κακῶς γὰρ ἔδεε πανοικίῃ γενέσθαι. p. 57, l. 24.

9. **συνηνείχθη γενέσθαι**, cp. 6, 86 ὁκοῖον μέντοι τι ἐν τῇ Σπάρτῃ συνηνείχθη γενέσθαι περὶ παρακαταθήκης.

11. **ἐπὶ...Μυνδίης** 'on board a ship of Myndos' (in Karia).

δεινόν τι ποιησάμενος 'greatly indignant', 8, 15; 9, 5, 53.

14. **δῆσαι διὰ θαλαμίης διελόντας τῆς νεός** 'to tie in an oar-hole of the ship so that he projected half way out'. The word διελόντας 'having divided him' is explained by the next sentence, 'arranging that his head should be outside, his body inside the ship'. The mode of tying the man also accounts for διά, he is to be put *through* the oar-hole.

κατὰ τοῦτο 'on this account', cp. p. 2, l. 18; p. 22, l. 10. 6, 1 κατὰ κοῖόν τι 'on what ground?' Thus Schweigh. takes it, and I think rightly. Baehr, Stein and Abicht however interpret it to mean 'thus', explained by the following clause. Stein compares c. 16 οἰκεῦσι δὲ τοιοῦτον τρόπον, κρατέων κ.τ.λ. But here there is nothing else for the participle to explain but τοιοῦτον τρόπον, whereas in our passage the participle ποιεῦντας would naturally enough explain δῆσαι διελόντας, and κατὰ τοῦτο thus interpreted is a mere incumbrance to the sentence.

17. ξεῖνόν οἱ 'his guest-friend'. Individuals are ξεῖνοι to each other, πρόξεινοι to states.

18. παραιτέετο τὸν Πέρσην 'he tried to induce the Persian to let him off'. 3, 132 τούτους βασιλέα παραιτησάμενος ἐρρύσατο. 6, 24 παραιτησάμενος βασιλέα ἐς Σικελίην ἀπίκετο.

21. ἐσπέρχετο 'was enraged with', 1, 32 Κροῖσος δὲ σπερχθεὶς εἶπε. It is a poetical word and generally used in the sense of 'haste', as in 3, 72 ἐπειδὴ ὥρα σπερχόμενον Δαρεῖον (λέγει)...ἐπείτε ἡμέας συνταχύνειν ἀναγκάζεις κ.τ.λ. But the two notions often combine as in the English 'hasty'; cp. Callim. Del. 158 Ἶρις...σπερχομένη μάλα πολλὸν ἀπέτραπεν· αἱ δ' ὑφ' ὁμοκλῆς Πασσυδίῃ σοβέοντο.

22. σοὶ δὲ καὶ τούτοισι...ἐστι; 'what have you got to do with such affairs as these?' For a speech introduced by δέ cp. 8, 142.

23. ἐμέο πείθεσθαι 'to obey me'. For the genitive following πείθεσθαι see p. 16, l. 13.

24. τί πολλὰ πρήσσεις; 'why do you interfere?' 'why do you act the busybody?' Hence πολυπράγμων, πολυπραγμοσύνη, cp. Arist. Ran. 228 εἰκότως γ', ὦ πολλὰ πράττων.

26. πλοίῳ 'in a small vessel',—not a trireme or war-ship. This distinction is always observed by Thucydides; see on πλοῖα μακρά p. 17, l. 7.

28. πρήγματα 'troubles', 'danger', 6, 40; 7, 147.

CHAPTER XXXIV.

1. οὐδὲν πάντως p. 37, l. 26.

3. ἐσηνείκαντο...τεῖχος 'they at once transported the moveables in the country farms within the walls of the town'. The first step in anticipation of a hostile occupation of the country. Cp. Thucyd. 1, 14 οἱ δὲ Ἀθηναῖοι ἀκούσαντες ἀνεπείθοντό τε καὶ ἐσεκομίζοντο ἐκ τῶν ἀγρῶν παῖδας καὶ γυναῖκας καὶ τὴν ἄλλην κατασκευήν.

5. ἐσάξαντο (σάττω) 'supplied themselves plentifully with', 'made large stores of', cp. 3, 7 Πέρσαι σάξαντες τὴν ἐσβολὴν ὕδατι. Elsewhere Herodotos uses the word to mean 'to equip' with armour, see 7, 62, 70, 73.

6. παρεσκευάδατο 'had made their preparations' i.e. when the enemy arrived. For the form see App. D. II. (a).

8. πρὸς πεφραγμένους προσεφέροντο 'found them already entrenched when they arrived'.

11. προσαναισίμωτο 'had been expended besides'. For the Ionic word ἀναισιμόω see 6, 41. Herodotos uses it where an Attic writer would use ἀναλίσκω. See p. 18, l. 2.

τοῦ πλεῦνός τε ἐδέετο ἡ πολιορκίη 'and the siege required always more', opp. to πολλά. Cp. 4, 43 περήσας δὲ θάλασσαν πολλὴν ἐν πολλοῖσι μησί, ἐπείτε τοῦ πλεῦνος αἰεὶ ἔδεε, ἀποστρέψας ἀπέπλωε ἐς Αἴγυπτον.

12. τοῖσι φυγάσι 'for the banished Naxians'. These walls would enable them to annoy their countrymen, and protect themselves.

CHAPTER XXXV.

15. τὴν ὑπόσχεσιν c. 31.

16. ἅμα...τε p. 59, l. 5.

17. ἀπαιτεομένη the demand made on him to refund the expenses of the expedition.

19. Μεγαβάτῃ διαβεβλημένος 'because he had been rendered an object of suspicion to Megabates'. Cp. 6, 64 Κλεομένεϊ διεβλήθη. 9, 116 Ξέρξεα διεβάλετο 'he aroused the suspicions and anger of Xerxes'. For another meaning of this verb see p. 62, l. 21.

19. ἐδόκεε 'he expected', followed by future infinitive on the analogy of other verbs of expecting, promising and threatening, cp. p. 17, l. 13; p. 21, l. 11.

21. συνέπιπτε 'it happened contemporaneously', cp. p. 21, l. 14; 8, 11 συνέπιπτε ὥστε ὁμοῦ σφέων γενέσθαι τὴν κατάστασιν.

26. ὥστε = ὡς or ἅτε, p. 49, l. 13; 6, 44; 9, 37; 8, 118. φυλασσομενέων. The guards posted on the great roads through Asia are mentioned again in 1, 125. Stein quotes Nehemiah 2, 7 'If it please the king, let letters be given me to the governors beyond the river, that they may convey me over till I come into Judah'.

21 1. κεφαλὴν ἔστιξε. Gellius (Noct. 17, 9) says that the slave's head was shaved on the pretence of medical treatment for sore eyes. Polyaenos (Strat. 1, 24) gives the words used Ἱστιαῖος Μιλήσιος ἐν Πέρσαις διάγων παρὰ Δαρείῳ βασιλεῖ βουλόμενος Ἰωνίαν ἀποστῆσαι γράμματα πέμπειν οὐ θαρρῶν διὰ τοὺς φύλακας τῶν ὁδῶν οἰκέτην πιστὸν ἀποξύρας τὰς τρίχας στίγματα ἐνεγράψατο τῇ κεφαλῇ "Ἱστιαῖος Ἀρισταγόρᾳ· Ἰωνίαν ἀπόστησον". καὶ τοῖς στίγμασι ἐπέθρεψε τὰς τρίχας.

5. κατιδίσθαι ἐς 'to look carefully at'. The middle, common in Herodotos (see 6, 61), is rare in Attic prose.

7. συμφορὴν ποιεύμενος μεγάλην 'regarding as a great grievance', 'much chafing at', p. 3, l. 12.

10. μετήσεσθαι fut. passive. So also the imperf. 1, 12 οὐ γὰρ μετίετο ὁ Γύγης. Histiaeos seems not to have been aware that he was an object of suspicion to Darius, and expected that in case of any revolutionary movement in Ionia the king would look to him as the most trustworthy person to put it down.

CHAPTER XXXVI.

13. νῦν p. 16, l. 14.

14. συνέπιπτε p. 20, l. 21.

15. τοῦ αὐτοῦ χρόνου 'about the same time', 'within the same period'; less definite than the dative. 2, 47 Σελήνῃ δὲ καὶ Διονύσῳ μούνοισι τοῦ αὐτοῦ χρόνου, τῇ αὐτῇ πανσελήνῳ, τοὺς ὗς θύσαντες κ.τ.λ.

18. γνώμην...ἐξεφέροντο 'gave an unanimous opinion'. Herodotos does not use precisely this phrase elsewhere. In 3, 80, 81 we have ἐσφέρειν γνώμην and ἀποδείκνυσθαι γνώμην. In 1, 207; 2, 120 etc. ἀποφαίνεσθαι γνώμην. And in the line above we have ἐκφήνας γνώμην. Such variety of phrase is characteristic of Herodotos' style.

19. ὁ λογοποιός 'the writer of histories'. Herodotos always gives him this title, see 2, 143; infr. p. 77, l. 18, which he also applies to the fabulist Aesop, 2, 134 (in 6, 137 he simply calls him ὁ Ἡγησάνδρου). Suidas calls him ἱστοριογράφος: Arrian (2, 16, 5; 5, 6, 5) calls him also λογοποιός, and Plutarch Lycurg. 20 calls him ὁ σοφιστής.

21. καταλέγων 'recounting', 'giving a list of', a word specially used when a number of things are mentioned, see c. 52.

23. δεύτερα opp. to πρῶτα μέν. The δέ which should belong to it is put at the beginning of the clause ἔπειτε δέ, but it was often omitted in such expressions. Cp. πρῶτον μέν followed by ἔπειτα Demosth. de Cor. § 1; μάλιστα μέν followed by ἔπειτα id. § 267. Madv. G. Gr. § 188 R. 5. ποιέειν ὅκως p. 70, l. 21.

24. ναυκρατέες τῆς θαλάσσης 'to take care to be masters at sea'. In 6, 9 ναυκρατέες without this genitive. In p. 44, l. 13 the same idea is conveyed by θαλασσοκράτορες.

25. ἔφη λέγων cp. p. 29, l. 2; 3, 156 νῦν τε, ἔφη λέγων, ἐγὼ ὑμῖν, ὦ Βαβυλώνιοι, ἥκω μέγιστον ἀγαθόν. 9, 2 ἔφασαν λέγοντες. In all of which

the phrase is used in introducing a continuation of a speech,—'he went on to say'. Cp. p. 30, l. 8.

ἐνορᾶν ἐσόμενον τοῦτο 'he declared therefore in his speech that he could see no other way by which this should be brought to pass'. 1, 140 ἐνορέω γὰρ ὑμῖν οὐκ οἴουσί τε ἐσομένοισι...πολεμέων Ξέρξῃ. Cp. 1, 123; 3, 53.

28. τὰ Κροῖσος...ἀνέθηκε see 1, 46 and Geographical Index s.v. *Branchidae*.

22

1. πολλὰς...ἐλπίδας p. 21, l. 9. ἐπικρατήσειν 'that they would become masters of the sea', p. 21, l. 24.

2. τοὺς πολεμίους...συλήσειν. What Hekataeos anticipated, that the Persians would take the treasures of Branchidae if the Ionians did not, seems to have come to pass, see 6, 19; and a second temple was pillaged after the return of Xerxes from Greece.

3. χρήματα...μεγάλα. Besides the rich offerings dedicated in such temples, they were used as places of safe deposit for money and valuables, like a modern bank.

4. ἐν τῷ πρώτῳ τῶν λόγων 'in my first book', see 1, 50; 1, 92.

5. οὐκ ἐνίκα ἡ γνώμη 'did not prevail', 'was not carried'. Sometimes the verb is used impersonally, 6, 101 ἐνίκα 'it was decided', cp. 8, 8. Sometimes the phrase is νικᾶν γνώμην 1, 61.

6. ὅμως sc. in spite of his arguments and advice.

7. τὸ στρατόπεδον 'the fleet' as at p. 72, l. 8, and in 8, 10 fin., and often. τὸ ἀπὸ τῆς Νάξου p. 20, l. 13.

8. συλλαμβάνειν πειρᾶσθαι 'to try to arrest'. For the double construction of πειρᾶσθαι with infinitive or participle, see on 6, 5; 8, 142; 9, 31. For συλλαμβάνειν cp. 6, 26; 6, 50 βουλόμενος συλλαβεῖν τῶν Αἰγινητέων τοὺς αἰτιωτάτους.

CHAPTER XXXVII.

10. κατ' αὐτὸ τοῦτο 'for this very purpose' p. 19, l. 14. p. 12, l. 14 ἐπ' αὐτὸ τοῦτο.

11—15. Ὀλίατον...συχνούς. These men are got hold of as being in the interests of the Persian king, and being likely to keep their respective states quiet; and also for the immediate purpose of putting the fleet of ships at the command of the revolting Ionians.

15. οὕτω δή when this was done, sometimes οὕτω, p. 31, l. 14. ἐκ τοῦ ἐμφανέος, 7, 205 ἀπερέουσι ἐκ τοῦ ἐμφανέος τὴν συμμαχίην. p. 62, l. 19 ἐκ τοῦ φανεροῦ.

17. λόγῳ 'professedly'. Aristagoras, though thus ceasing nominally to be in the position of tyrannus of Miletos (as deputy of Histiaeos) seems really to have retained under the name of Strategos his authority there: see p. 63, l. 27, where he still calls himself tyrant of Miletos, and c. 99, where he stays in Miletos to resist the Persian attack—στρατηγοὺς δὲ ἄλλους ἀπέδεξε Μιλησίων εἶναι, as though he still had supreme power.

18—19. ὡς ἄν...συναπισταίατο 'in order that they might (as in that case they would) willingly join him in the revolt'. For ὡς ἄν with optative (properly modal ὡς = ὅπως, and ἄν belonging to the verb) where another eventuality is implied, see 9, 22 ὡς ἄν...ἀνελοίατο, id. 51 ὡς ἄν μὴ ἰδοίατο. Cp. p. 64, l. 14. Goodwin, *M. and T.* § 351.

20. τοὺς μὲν ἐξελαύνων...ἐξεδίδου. For a participle and indicative thus coupled by μέν and δέ, see 8.

τοὺς δ' ἔλαβε. τοὺς is a relative, referring to the τούτους. For δέ with the apodosis (τούτους δέ) see p. 1, l. 9.

22. φίλα...πόλισι 'wishing to gratify the cities', cp. 2, 152 φίλα τοῖσι Ἴωσι ποιέεται.

24. εἴη opt. of indefinite frequency, p. 16, l. 3.

CHAPTER XXXVIII.

26. κατέλευσαν 'stoned to death', the usual mode of killing a man in a time of popular excitement, cp. 9, 4.

τὸν σφέτερον αὐτῶν sc. τύραννον, cp. p. 64, l. 3; Thucyd. 1, 5, 1 κέρδους τοῦ σφετέρου αὐτῶν ἕνεκα.

27. ὡς δέ = οὕτω δέ, p. 17, l. 20; 6, 14 ὡς δὲ καὶ οἱ πλεῦνες τῶν Ἰώνων ἐποίευν τὰ αὐτὰ ταῦτα.

3. στρατηγοὺς officers combining military and civil functions. The appointment of these Strategi, popularly elected, seems to have been a sort of compromise between the necessity of having some single commander and representative of each state and the odious name of Tyrannus. The title and office was in later times revived in the yearly Strategi of the Achaean and Aetolian Leagues, and in other Greek States.

5. ἀπόστολος ἐγίνετο 'set out on a mission', lit. 'became an ambassador', 1, 21 ὁ μὲν δὴ ἀπόστολος ἐς τὴν Μίλητον ἦν.

ἔδεε...συμμαχίης...ἐξευρεθῆναι 'it was necessary for him to find up some strong body of allies', lit. 'he stood in need of a strong alliance to be found up'. St. quotes 3, 36 καὶ πάλαι ἐς σὲ προφάσιός τευ ἐδεόμην ἐπιλαβέσθαι.

CHAPTER XXXIX.

8. οὐκέτι. See 1, 67 where some incidents in the reign of Anaxandrides are recorded.

10. κατὰ γένος 'in right of birth', i.e. as the eldest son of Anaxandrides. Cp. Hom. Il. 3, 215 γένει ὕστερος 'younger'.

11. ἀδελφεῆς ἑωυτοῦ θυγατέρα. For marriage of uncle and niece see 6, 71; 7, 239. Lysias Orat. 32 § 4.

12. καταθυμίης 'to his mind', 'beloved', cp. 9, 111 αὐτή τέ μοι κατὰ νόον τυγχάνει κάρτα ἐοῦσα.

13. οἱ ἔφοροι. For the Ephors see Biographical and Historical Index.

16. γένος τὸ Εὐρυσθένεος. That is, the elder family of the Heraklid kings. See 8, 131 and Biographical Index s.v. Herakleidae.

17. ἔξεο (ἐξίημι) 'divorce'.

20. οὐ καλῶς συμβουλεύειν. And yet the Spartan view of the sacredness of marriage must have been strangely different from the view in modern times if the Lycurgean principles were carried out. See Plut. Lycurg. 15.

22. ἐσαγαγέσθαι *ducere uxorem*, cp. 6, 63 οὕτω μὲν δὴ τὴν τρίτην ἐσηγάγετο γυναῖκα. The idea of the verb is 'to bring into one's house', **οὐδὲ** corresponding to τε in l. 20. Cp. 9, 41 συμβάλλειν τε τὴν ταχίστην μηδὲ περιορᾶν.

CHAPTER XL.

24. προσέφερον...τάδε 'made the following suggestion' p. 17, l. 3.

25. περιεχόμενον 'concerned for', 'attached to', cp. 3, 53 περιεχόμενος τοῦ νεηνίεω. Once with infin., 9, 57 περιείχετο αὐτοῦ μένοντας μὴ ἐκλιπεῖν τὴν τάξιν.

τῆς ἔχεις γυναικός. For this common attraction of the relative, and the place of the antecedent in the relative clause (assimilation), see Goodw. § 154.

26. ταῦτα...τούτοισι are emphatic, 'this at least which we are about to propose'.

27. ἀλλοῖον sc. κακόν. This euphemistic use of the word seems rare. L. and Sc. quote Diog. Laert. 4, 44; and a somewhat similar use in one of the προοίμια attributed to Demosthenes (Dem. 1142). ἄλλος and ἕτερος are more often used in this sense (Demosth. de Cor. 212. Lysias 12 § 48).

4. **ἐσάγαγε.** It does not seem easy to give any reason for the use of the active here instead of the middle as at p. 23 l. 22, and Van Herwerden has suggested *ἐσαγάγεο*. Perhaps, as it appears that Anaxandridas did not take his new wife into his old home, the Ephors contemplated some difference from ordinary marriage which would account for Herodotos putting into their mouths a word slightly differing from the ordinary expression. Such subtle distinctions are not unusual in careful Greek.

5. **μετὰ δέ** adverbial p. 15 l. 15.
6. **διξάς** App. A. 1 (6).
7. **οὐδαμῶς Σπαρτιητικά** neither in Sparta nor in other parts of Greece was bigamy lawful or practised. The half-Hellenic kings of Macedonia seem to have assumed the privilege, at any rate in later times. See Pausan. 3, 3, 7 Ἀναξανδρίδης Λακεδαιμονίων μόνος γυναῖκάς τε δύο ἅμα ἔσχε καὶ οἰκίας δύο ᾤκησε. That the Spartan kings at times assumed more than the common licence in their matrimonial affairs is shewn by the story of king Ariston in 6, 61, who however does not venture to have two wives at the same time, but divorces one to marry the other.

CHAPTER XLI.

8. **ἡ ἐσύστερον ἐπελθοῦσα γυνή** 'the additional wife who entered his family the later of the two'. The force of the ἐπί is almost that of intrusion into the place of another. Thus Medea says of her husband's second wife (Eurip. Med. 694) γυναῖκ' ἐφ' ἡμῖν δεσπότιν δόμων ἔχει. And Alcestis says to her husband when she is about to die (Eur. Alc. 305) καὶ μὴ 'πιγήμῃς τοῖσδε μητρυιὰν τέκνοις.

9—10. **αὕτη τε...καὶ ἡ προτέρη.** For τε and καί thus used to express close connexion in time, cp. 8, 83; 9, 55. **ἔπεδρον βασιλέα** 'heir to the royalty', lit. 'a king in reserve', like the ἔφεδρος in a contest waiting to take up the struggle with the successful combatant. Pindar N. 4, 96 μαλακὰ μὲν φρονέων ἐσλοῖς | τραχὺς δὲ παλιγκότοις ἔφεδρος. Arist. Ran. 791 of Sophocles' behaviour to Aeschylos

> ὅτε δὴ κατῆλθε, κἀνέβαλε τὴν δεξιὰν
> κἀκεῖνος ὑπεχώρησεν αὐτῷ τοῦ θρόνου.
> νυνὶ δ' ἔμελλεν, ὡς ἔφη Κλειδημίδης
> ἔφεδρος καθεδεῖσθαι· κἂν μὲν Αἰσχύλος κρατῇ
> ἕξειν κατὰ χώραν· εἰ δὲ μή, περὶ τῆς τέχνης
> διαγωνιεῖσθ' ἔφασκε πρός γ' Εὐριπίδην.

11. κῶς p. 66, l. 9.

12. χρησαμένη 'experienced', generally in a bad sense, cp. 8, 20 συμφορῇ χρᾶσθαι. But συντυχίῃ expresses a (fortunate) conjuncture of circumstances and time, cp. the use of συνηνείχθη p. 19, l. 9; συμπίπτειν and συνέβη (8, 15; Thucyd. 5, 15). ἔχουσαν sc. ἐν γαστρί, cp. 3, 32. ἀληθέϊ λόγῳ = ἀληθῶς, cp. 1. 120 οἱ ἀληθέϊ λόγῳ βασιλῆες.

14. ἄλλως 'vainly', 'without good grounds'.

15. ὑποβαλέσθαι 'to adopt a supposititious child'. Arist. Thesmoph. 340 εἰ...παιδίον ὑποβαλλομένης κατεῖπέ τις, id. 407 εἶεν, γυνή τις ὑποβαλέσθαι βούλεται | ἀποροῦσα παίδων. δεινὰ ποιεύντων. More often the middle is used in this expression (see p. 19 l. 20), but for the active see 2, 121; 3, 14.

16. τοῦ χρόνου συντάμνοντος 'when the time (for the child's birth) drew near'. There seems no other example of this use of συντάμνειν (Ionic for συντέμνειν) although in 7, 123 it is used intransitively, ὁ δὲ ναυτικὸς στρατὸς ὁ Ξέρξεω συντάμνων (sc. τὴν ὁδὸν) ἀπ' Ἀμπέλου ἄκρης. ὑπ' ἀπιστίης 'from distrust', 'suspiciously'. Cp. 1, 24, 68; 6, 107 ὑπὸ βίης.

17. ἐφύλαξαν p. 6, l. 14.

23. τὸ δεύτερον 'a second time' p. 15, l. 16.

CHAPTER XLII.

24. ἦν τε οὐ φρενήρης ἀκρομανής τε 'so far from being of sound mind was absolutely verging on madness'. For φρενήρης [φρήν, ἀρ- 'fit'] opposed to 'insane' cp. 3, 25 ἐμμανὴς ἐὼν καὶ οὐ φρενήρης. 3, 35; 9, 55. ἀκρομανής does not occur elsewhere. Its sense seems to be 'verging on' 'on the brink of madness'; what Herodotos elsewhere calls ὑπόμαργος 3, 29, 145; 6, 75 κατελθόντα [Κλεομενέα] αὐτίκα ὑπέλαβε μανιὰς νοῦσος, ἐόντα καὶ πρότερον ὑπομαργότερον. Cp. ἀκράχολος 'quick to anger', ἀκροθώραξ 'slightly drunk'. For τε οὐ...τε cp. p. 5, l. 17.

26. εὖ τε ἠπίστατο σχήσων 'and he quite expected', 'he fully believed that he should have the royal office himself on the ground of his gallant character'. Herodotos frequently uses ἐπίσταμαι in this sense, see 8, 5, 25, 80; but elsewhere with an infinitive, not participle. κατ' ἀνδραγαθίην, cp. p. 23, l. 10.

27. ὥστε, see p. 20, l. 26.

2. **χρεόμενοι τῷ νόμῳ** 'following the established law', i.e. of the succession of the eldest son.

4. **δεινὸν ποιεύμενος** 'indignant' p. 24, l. 15.

5. **αἰτήσας λεὼν Σπαρτιήτας** 'having demanded a body of men of the Spartans' [Baehr and Stein restore the form λεών, λεῷ here and in 2, 124 for the MS. forms which vary between λαόν, ληόν, λαῷ, ληῷ, on the ground that these latter are due to some scribe who adopted the Ionic forms in analogy with νηός (νεώς) κάλος (ως) λαγός (ως), whereas Herodotos always uses λεω- in composition, and the form λεών is given in the MSS. in 2, 129; 1, 22; 8, 136]. **ἦγε ἐς ἀποικίην** 'led them off to found a colony'.

6. **οὔτε τῷ...χρησάμενος** 'without having either consulted the oracle at Delphi'. It was it seems an invariable custom to consult an oracle before leading out a colony, see the case of Thyrii (Diodor. Sic. 12, 9) and cp. Cicero de Divin. 2 § 3 *quam vero Graecia coloniam misit in Aeoliam, Ioniam, Asiam, Siciliam, Italiam, sine Pythio aut Dodonaeo aut Hammonis oraculo?* The Spartans were specially accustomed to consult the oracle at Delphi on all public occasions, whence two Pythii lived with each of the kings, whose duty it was to communicate frequently with Delphi. See 6, 57; Xenoph. R. L. 15; Cic. de div. 1, 95.

7. **ἐς ἥντινα...ἴῃ** 'to what country he was to go', for this deliberative subjunctive, cp. 6, 35 ἐπειρησόμενος τὸ χρηστήριον εἰ ποιέῃ τὰ περ...προσδέοντο. 6, 86 ἐπειρωτέοντα τὸ χρηστήριον εἰ ὅρκῳ τὰ χρήματα ληΐσηται.

8. **τῶν νομιζομένων** 'any of the usual observances'. Chief of these was the starting from the Prytaneium of the parent state, taking fire from the ἑστία which was to light that on the ἑστία of the new town, see 1, 146 ἀπὸ τοῦ πρυτανηΐου τοῦ Ἀθηναίων ὁρμηθέντες. It was also customary to take priests from the parent town. Schol. in Thucyd. 1, 25. Hermann *Polit. Antiq.* § 74.

9. **τὰ πλοῖα** 'his transports'. **κατηγέοντο...οἱ** 'acted as his guides'. Cp. 6, 102 ἐς τοῦτό σφι κατηγέετο Ἱππίης ὁ Πεισιστράτου.

10. **Θηραῖοι.** Thera was a Spartan colony 4, 147, and as connected with Cyrene (4, 150—159) its inhabitants naturally directed him to Libya.

11. **παρὰ ποταμόν** 'on the banks of a river', an important thing in Africa. The river was also called Cinyps [mod. *Wadi Quasam*] 4, 175, 198.

CHAPTER XLIII.

15. ἐκ τῶν Λαΐου χρησμῶν 'in consequence of the oracles of Laius', such as were also current under the names of Bakis (8, 20, 77; 9, 44) and Musaeos (9, 43). Or it may refer to certain oracles obtained at the temple of the Furies of Laius and Oedipus at Sparta mentioned in 4, 149, although we know nothing of that temple as the seat of an oracle.

19. εἰ αἱρέει 'whether he should succeed in taking'. The present is used for the future for the sake of vividness. 'Am I taking?' for 'shall I take?' See 6, 53 τάδε δὲ κατὰ τὰ λεγόμενα ὑπ' Ἑλλήνων ἐγὼ γράφω. ib. 86 ἀποδιδόντες ποιέετε ὅσια. 6, 82 μαθεῖν δὲ αὐτὸς οὕτω τὴν ἀτρεκείην ὅτι οὐκ αἱρέει τὸ Ἄργος. 3, 155 αἱρέομεν Βαβυλῶνα.

21. παρὰ τὴν Ἰταλίην 'along the Italian coast': that is, he crossed to the Iapygian promontory and then coasted westward to Metapontum where Italy began, and thence southwards. The name Italy in the 5th century B.C. meant the southern part of the peninsula below a line stretching from Metapontum (Thucyd. 7, 33, 4 Μεταπόντιον τῆς Ἰταλίας) to Paestum, the Iapygian peninsula (Calabria and part of Apulia) being excluded. Thus in 6, 2 Thucydides speaks of the Sikeli crossing from 'Italy' to Sicily, being driven out by the Opicae, and in 6, 4, 5 of Cyme being in Opikia. North of Opikia (which included Latium, Dionys. Hal. 1, 72) was Tyrrhenia.

CHAPTER XLIV.

22. τὸν χρόνον τοῦτον B.C. 510.

26. σφίσι τιμωρῆσαι 'to assist them'. τιμωρεῖν τινι = (1) 'to assist a man', (2) 'to avenge a man'. 2, 100 τιμωρέουσα ἀδελφεῷ τὸν Αἰγύπτιοι ἀπέκτειναν. But τιμωρεῖσθαί τινα 'to exact vengeance on a man', 6, 135 βουλόμενοί μιν ἀντὶ τούτων τιμωρήσασθαι. τυχεῖν δεηθέντας 'that they succeeded in their request'.

27. δή 'accordingly, as they say'.

28. συνελεῖν 'joined them in taking' p. 26, 11.

4. μάντιν Ἠλεῖον 'a seer from Elis'. That is a professional seer of a mantic family, the Iamidae, who was in the service of the Tyrant of Sybaris. See Historical Index, s.v. Iamidae.

καὶ τοῦτον 'and even he'.

7. θυομένῳ ἐπὶ Κρότωνα 'when he was sacrificing with a view to an attack upon Kroton'. So with the dative 9, 10 θυομένῳ οἱ ἐπὶ τῷ Πέρσῃ 'with a view to the Persian', with the idea of getting the help of heaven against the Persian. The middle θύεσθαι is always used by Herodotos with the meaning of 'sacrificing for oneself for an object'. 9, 62 ἐγίνετο θυομένοισι τὰ σφάγια χρηστά. 7, 169 ἐθύοντό τε καὶ ἐπικαλέοντο τόν τε Βορῆν καὶ τὴν Ὠρειθυίην. οὐ προεχώρεε χρηστά 'did not turn out favourable': χρηστὰ is proleptic 'so as to be good'. προχωρεῖν 'to succeed' p. 36, l. 8.

CHAPTER XLV.

10. παρὰ τὸν ξηρὸν Κρᾶθιν 'by the dry bed of the Krathis'. The river descending from high ground through flat alluvial plains is subject to changes of its course unless artificial means are taken to dam it up and prevent inundations. The Krotonians after conquering Sybaris broke down the dams that the river might flood the site of the city of Sybaris: hence certain buildings which once stood on its banks would, if they remained, be near the 'dry course'.

12. τοῦτο δὲ 'in the second place', generally preceded by τοῦτο μὲν p. 18, l. 1. For the omission of the first τοῦτο cp. 8, 60 πρὸς μὲν τῷ Ἰσθμῷ συμβάλλων ἐν πελάγεϊ...ναυμαχήσεις...τοῦτο δὲ ἀπολέεις Σαλαμῖνα.

14. ὅτι παρὰ τὰ μεμαντευμένα 'that it was while acting contrary to the oracle that he perished'. The oracle had told him to go to Eryx and found Herakleia. Something must have happened, they argued, to account for his death before he had done so,—for the oracle must be held true. His death shows that he was acting contrary to the oracle, which he would have been doing in attacking us instead of going on to Sicily; and therefore our story offers a satisfactory explanation of an undoubted fact.

20. ἐς ἐμὲ Herodotos went to Thyrii, founded to take the place of Sybaris, in B.C. 443; and his residence in the neighbourhood explains the particularity of his account here. ἐνέμοντο, p. 62, l. 7.

21. Δωριέϊ δὲ καὶ τοῖσι...ἀπογόνοισι οὐδέν. But the probability is that Dorieus left no descendants. If he had left a son he would have succeeded Kleomenes before his younger brother Leonidas. A Euryanax s. of Dorieus is mentioned in 9, 10, 53, 55, and it has been argued that the same Dorieus is meant, and that he had forfeited the right of his son

to succeed by his residence abroad, or that Euryanax was illegitimate. It seems more probable on the whole that another Dorieus is meant; for the Spartans were strict as to the law of succession, and no such law as to forfeiture of a son's right by his father's foreign residence is known. That there should be no record of possessions bestowed on Dorieus for his services to Kroton would be accounted for by his having fallen in battle.

CHAPTER XLVI.

1. παντὶ στόλῳ 'in full force', 'with all their ships'. The definite article is omitted in this phrase, which technical or adverbial, is the naval equivalent to πανστρατιῇ.

3. ὑπό τε Φοινίκων καὶ Ἐγεσταίων 'by the Carthaginians and Segesteans'. The Phoenikians of Carthage were already the most powerful naval state in the West, and were beginning their encroachments in Sicily, which led to her contests with Syracuse (B.C. 480. Her. 7, 166) and finally to her struggle with Rome. It was their desire of retaining their hold in the western Mediterranean that caused them to join with the Tyrrhenians (B.C. 557) in resisting a settlement of exiled Phokaeans in Corsica [Her. 1, 165—166]; and similar motives caused them now to resist this Lakedaemonian colony in Sicily.

6. Μινώην Herakleia Minoa or Makara.

7. συνηλευθέρου 'and he joined in helping to free'.

8. μετὰ δὲ p. 15, l. 15; p. 24, l. 5.

11. ἐπὶ...βωμόν. A temple of Zeus Agoraios existed in several Greek cities, especially Dorian towns, as in Sparta (Paus. 3, 11, 9). The βωμός is probably the great altar outside the temple.

CHAPTER XLVII.

14. ἁρμοσάμενος p. 18, l. 27.

15. ψευσθεὶς τοῦ γάμου, cf. 9, 61 ψευσθῆναι τῆς ἐλπίδος.

17. οἰκήτῃ...δαπάνῃ 'in a trireme of his own and with men hired at his own expense'. Cp. 8, 17 Ἀθηναίων Κλεινίης (ἠρίστευσεν) ὁ Ἀλκιβιάδεω, ὃς δαπάνην οἰκηΐην παρεχόμενος ἐστρατεύετο ἀνδράσι τε διηκοσίοισι καὶ οἰκήτῃ νηΐ. Rich men seem to have often thus equipped themselves with the means of enterprise and independence. See the case of Alkibiades, Thucyd. 6, 61, 6.

21. ἡρώιον 'a chapel of a hero' or 'deified man'. A small temple-shaped erection on the summit of the mound which covered his body. See on 8, 39; 9, 25. The action of the state in adopting as a hero a stranger who had done good service to them is like that of the people of Amphipolis to Brasidas (Thucyd. 5, 11), and of the people of the Chersonese to the elder Miltiades (6, 38), see also c. 67. θυσίῃσι αὐτὸν ἱλάσκονται 'propitiate him with sacrifices'. The worship paid to the heroes was technically expressed by the word ἐναγίζειν 'to remove pollution': the Manes of the dead were supposed to exercise a baneful influence and to require propitiation.

CHAPTER XLVIII.

26. τινα πολλόν 'very long', cp. p. 19, l. 11. Kleomenes died in B.C. 491.

27. ἄπαις 'without a son' p. 40, l. 10. 7, 205 ἀποθανόντος Κλεομένεος ἀπαιδος ἔρσενος γόνου.

CHAPTER XLIX.

1. δ' ὦν 'be that as it may', resuming the story from c. 38.

4. χάλκεον πίνακα 'a brazen tablet'. This seems to be the earliest mention of a map which we possess, unless we may reckon the shield of Achilles as such, Il. 18, 483 ἐν μὲν γαῖαν ἔτευξ', ἐν δ' οὐρανὸν, ἐν δὲ θάλασσαν. Aristagoras probably got it from Hekataeos. An earlier Milesian philosopher, Anaximander, was said to have first invented terrestrial maps—μεθ' ὃν Ἑκαταῖος ὁ Μιλήσιος ἀνὴρ πολυπλανὴς διηκρίβωσεν ὥστε θαωμασθῆναι τὸ πρᾶγμα, Agathem. 1, 1. See Bunbury, *Ancient Geography* Vol. I., p. 122.

γῆς ἁπάσης περίοδος 'a circular chart of the whole earth'. Arist. N. 206 αὕτη δέ σοι γῆς περίοδος πάσης· ὁρᾷς; αἴδε μὲν Ἀθῆναι.

5. θάλασσά τε...πάντες 'and every sea and all rivers'. 'Every sea' means the Mediterranean, the Pontus, Arabian gulf etc. The Ocean would surround the whole. Il. 21, 195 οὐδὲ βαθυρρείταο μέγα σθένος Ὠκεανοῖο, ἐξ οὗπερ πάντες ποταμοὶ καὶ πᾶσα θάλασσα. See 4, 8, 36; though Herod. thought this a fable [2, 23].

9. τὰ κατήκοντα 'the actual state of things', with the idea of their being critical. 8, 19 ἐπὶ τοῖς κατήκουσι πρήγμασι, ib. 40 ἐπὶ καὶ τοῖς κατήκουσι.

11. τῶν λοιπῶν depends on ὑμῖν μέγιστον 'and of all other Greeks the greatest pain and reproach to you'.

προέστατε 'ye are at the head of', 'are the leaders of'. The hegemony of Greece, once held by the Argives, was now universally accorded to the Spartans, as was shewn a few years later [B.C. 491] by the denunciation to them of the medizing of the Aeginetans, as if they formed the proper national tribunal. See 6, 49.

14. εὐπετέως...ἐστί 'and you may succeed in doing this with ease'. χωρέειν like προχωρέειν (p. 26, l. 5) means here 'to succeed' 'to go on prosperously', cp. 3, 42 χωρήσαντος δέ οἱ τούτου, p. 53 l. 7 καί σφι χωρήσειν τὰ βούλονται.

16. ἐς τὰ μέγιστα ἀνήκετε 'have reached the highest perfection'. 8, 111 ἐς τὰ μέγιστα (τῆς πενίης) ἀνήκοντες, 7, 13 φρενῶν γάρ ἐς τὰ ἐμωυτοῦ πρῶτα οὔ κω ἀνήκω.

17. ἡ μάχη 'their mode of fighting', including their fashion of arms. Cp. 1, 79 ἡ δὲ μάχη σφέων ἦν ἀπ' ἵππων, δούρατά τε ἐφόρεον μεγάλα. Thucyd. 3, 95, 4 μάχης τε ἐμπειρίᾳ τῆς ἐκείνων καὶ χωρίων. 4, 34, 2 ἀήθεσι τοιαύτης μάχης. Xenoph. Cyrop. 2, 1, 7 τὴν δὲ μάχην μοι λέξον ἑκάστων ἥτις ἐστί. Σχεδόν, ἔφη, πάντων ἡ αὐτή· τοξόται γάρ εἰσι καὶ ἀκοντισταὶ οἵ τ' ἐκείνων καὶ οἱ ἡμέτεροι.

18. αἰχμὴ βραχέα 'a short pike' or 'spear'. The superior length of the Greek spears gave them an advantage over the Persians at Thermopylae, where the latter were in great difficulties ἅτε ἐν στεινοπόρῳ τε χώρῳ μαχόμενοι καὶ δούρασι βραχυτέροισι χρώμενοι, 7, 211; cp. 7, 62. ἀναξυρίδας 'loose trousers', 7, 61, which, according to the Greek ideas, would be fatal to activity.

19. κυρβασίας 'turbans' 7, 64. See Arist. Av. 486—7 of the upright turban of the kings, διὰ ταῦτ' ἄρ' ἔχων καὶ νῦν ὥσπερ βασιλεὺς ὁ μέγας διαβάσκει | ἐπὶ τῆς κεφαλῆς τὴν κυρβασίαν τῶν ὀρνίθων μόνος ὀρθήν. He means that by wearing this linen head-dress, instead of the helmet of the Greek soldier, they will be exposed to slaughter the more easily.

21. νεμομένοισι p. 26, l. 18.

24. τὰ θυμῷ—ἔχοιτε 'which you may have if you do but make up your minds to desire them'.

25. ἀλλήλων ἐχόμενοι...φράσω 'in the order which I will relate', lit. 'coming next to each other as I will relate'. Cp. 21, 28 τούτων ἐχόμενοι, etc.

26. Ἰώνων τῶνδε sc. ἔχονται.

27. οἶδε deictic; he points to Lydia on the map. **χώρην ἀγαθήν.** The basins of the Hermos, Kayster, and Kaikos are very fertile. The Hermos brought down sands from which gold was obtained; and there was gold in some abundance in Mt Tmolos. **πολυαργυρώτατοι** 'most plentifully supplied with money'.

2. **ἔφη λέγων** p. 24, l. 25. 29

4. **πολυπροβατώτατοι** 'the richest in sheep'. "The high table lands of Phrygia are especially adapted to pasturage. Flocks and herds, even under the present miserable system of government, are numerous". (Rawl.)

7. **κατήκοντες...κέεται** 'extending down to this sea here (τῇδε pointing to it on the map) in which Kypros here (pointing) lies'.

9. **τὸν ἐπέτειον φόρον** 'the yearly tribute', according to the assessment of Dareios when he divided the empire into νομοί. Cp. 3, 90 ἀπὸ δὲ Κιλίκων ἵπποι τε λευκοὶ ἑξήκοντα καὶ τριηκόσιοι, ἑκάστης ἡμέρης εἷς γενόμενος, καὶ τάλαντα ἀργυρίου πεντακόσια.

13. **ἐν τῇ δή** 'in which finally stands this town of Susa'. The δή concludes the series and marks the arrival at the final point of attack, the royal residence of Susa.

15. **δίαιταν ποιέεται** 'ordinarily resides'. So 2, 68 ἐν ὕδατι δίαιταν ποιεύμενοι. The King seems to have divided the year between Ecbatana and Susa, with occasional 'progresses', and residences in other palaces at Persepolis and elsewhere.

16. **οἱ θησαυροί** 'the royal treasures'. 3, 96 τοῦτον τὸν φόρον θησαυρίζει ὁ βασιλεὺς τρόπῳ τοιῷδε· ἐς πίθους κεραμίνους τήξας καταχέει, πλήσας δὲ τὸ ἄγγος περιαιρέει τὸν κέραμον· ἐπεὰν δὲ δεηθῇ χρημάτων, κατακόπτει τοσοῦτο ὅσον ἂν ἑκάστοτε δέηται. Alexander found 50,000 talents of silver there (Arrian 3, 16).

17. **θαρσέοντες ἤδη...ἐρίζετε** 'you may at once without hesitation challenge Zeus to a rivalry in wealth'. ἤδη sums up previous statements and indicates the necessary and immediate consequence of them, cp. 6, 53 ἤδη τηνικαῦτα. 8, 100 ἤδη ὦν, ἐπειδὴ οὐ Πέρσαι τοι αἴτιοί εἰσι, ἐμοὶ πείθεο. Thus ἤδη is sometimes merely to be taken as adding emphasis to a statement, see 8, 106 ὦ πάντων ἀνδρῶν ἤδη μάλιστα ἀπ' ἔργων ἀνοσιωτάτων τὸν βίον κτησάμενε. Aeschin. in Ctes. § 52. The imperative expresses a certain future: just as the present indicative, see on p. 25, l. 24. For **πλούτου πέρι** 'as far as wealth is concerned' cp. p. 28, l. 17 ἀρετῆς πέρι. In both instances the substantive precedes the preposition for the sake of emphasis on the important word.

8—2

18. ἀλλὰ περὶ μὲν χώρης ἄρα οὐ πολλῆς, the μέν is answered by παρέχον δέ in l. 24: 'you must indeed in this case (ἄρα) put off wars 'for an insignificant and poor country and a paltry territory against 'Messenians who are your match, and against Arkadians and Argives, 'who have nothing of the nature of gold or silver, for which one may 'really feel some enthusiasm to encounter death in the field,—but when 'you have the opportunity to become masters of all Asia without 'difficulty will you prefer any other course?'

20. ἀναβάλλεσθαι 'to put off', as in l. 27. Yet Baehr and some others take it here to mean 'to undertake', comparing ἀναρριπτέειν κίνδυνον 7, 50; ἀναιρεῖσθαι πόλεμον 5, 36. The meaning would then be 'must you undertake wars against Arcadians etc. and yet not become masters of Asia when you have opportunity?' But the use of the same word in such different senses within a few lines, though perhaps not unexampled in Herodotos, is very harsh, and no other instance of this use of ἀναβάλλεσθαι seems to exist. ἀλλά seems to be used, as in the orators, to introduce a supposed objection; which is answered by παρέχον—αἱρήσεσθε, a rhetorical question taking the place of a definite statement.

21. ἰσοπαλέας cp. 1, 82 for the contests between Sparta and Argos for Thyrea, where of the 300 champions selected to fight on either side he says μαχομένων δὲ σφέων καὶ γενομένων ἰσοπαλέων ὑπελείποντο ἐξ ἀνδρῶν ἑξακοσίων τρεῖς.

22. χρυσοῦ ἐχόμενον οὐδὲν 'nothing of the nature of gold or silver', 'nothing that appertains to'. Cp. 8, 142 τὰ οἰκετέων ἐχόμενα. 1, 120 τὰ τῶν ὀνειράτων ἐχόμενα.

23. τῶν πέρι. See on l. 17; it is to be taken closely with προθυμίη 'the desire to obtain which'.

24. παρέχον = παρεόν, cp. p. 64, l. 3; 8, 8, 65; Thucyd. 1, 120, 5; 5, 14, 2. For the use of the absolute neuter participle see on 6, 72.

27. ἀναβάλλομαι...ὑποκρινέεσθαι 'I postpone my answer till the third day, when I will give it'. The future infinitive includes two ideas, 'I put off answering to the third day', and 'I will answer on the third day'. Cp. 6, 86 ταῦτα ὦν ὑμῖν ἀναβάλλομαι κυρώσειν ἐς τέταρτον μῆνα ἀπὸ τοῦδε. (The active ἀποκρίνειν 'to select' 'to distinguish' is used by Herodotos (1, 194; 8, 7 etc.), but for the middle ἀποκρίνεσθαι he seems always to use ὑποκρίνεσθαι, though in a few passages some MSS. have ἀποκ-.)

CHAPTER L.

1. ἐς τοσοῦτο ἤλασαν 'they got thus far'. Cp. 2, 124 ἐς πᾶσαν 30 κακότητα ἐλάσαι.

2. ἡ κυρίη p. 61 l. 2.

4. ὁκόσων ἡμερέων...βασιλέα 'how many days' journey it was from the Ionian coast to the King', i.e. from Ephesos to Susa.

6. διαβάλλων 'misleading him', 'taking him in', cp. p. 63, l. 10; p. 69, l. 21.

7. χρεών sc. ὄν 'whereas he ought'. Cp. παρέχον p. 29, l. 24.

τὸ ἐόν 'the truth' p. 69, l. 8. βουλόμενόν γε 'that is to say, if he wished'.

8. λέγει δ' ὦν...φάς 'he however told him in his answer'. For δέ in apodosis see p. 1, l. 9; p. 22, l. 20, but δ' ὦν is not so common. The passage quoted by Stein [3, 80 ἐλέχθησαν λόγοι ἄπιστοι μὲν ἐνίοισι Ἑλλήνων, ἐλέχθησαν δ' ὦν] is not exactly parallel. For λέγει φάς cp. p. 10, l. 2, 3; p. 21, l. 25.

9. τὴν ἄνοδον 'the journey up the country' to Susa. Cp. the contrary καταβαίνειν p. 69, l. 19. See also the use of ἀνάγειν 6, 30, 41; ἀναβαίνειν 6, 24. ὑπαρπάσας τὸν ἐπίλοιπον λόγον 'interrupting him and preventing him finishing his speech'. Cp. 9, 91 ὁ δὲ ὑπαρπάσας τὸν ἐπίλοιπον λόγον, εἴ τινα ὥρμητο λέγειν ὁ Ἡγησίστρατος.

12. πρὸ δύντος ἡλίου 'before sunset', notice the absence of the article in such conventional expressions. Cp. p. 27, l. 1.

13. εὐεπέα 'pleasing'. A rare word: of the two instances quoted by L. and Sc., in the Kyneget. of Xenophon 13, 16 the φωνὴ εὐεπής of the huntsman is opposed to the φωνὴ αἰσχρά of the demagogue; and in Antholog. 11, 24 the water of Helicon is called ὕδωρ εὐεπές, apparently meaning 'that which inspires poetry'.

CHAPTER LI.

16. ἱκετηρίην 'a suppliant's bough'. Cp. 7, 141 συνεβούλευέ σφι ἱκετηρίας λαβοῦσι δεύτερα αὖτις ἐλθόντας χρᾶσθαι τῷ χρηστηρίῳ ὡς ἱκέτας.

17. ἔσω ἅτε ἱκετεύων 'having made his way into the interior' i.e. to the hearth, as the sacred centre of the house. See Thucyd. 1, 136, 4 Themistocles τῆς γυναικὸς (Ἀδμήτου) ἱκέτης γενόμενος διδάσκεται ὑπ' αὐτῆς τὸν παῖδα σφῶν λαβὼν καθίζεσθαι ἐπὶ τὴν ἑστίαν.

19. προσεστήκεε γὰρ δή 'for by the side of Kleomenes there was standing his daughter'. δή here introduces a necessary explanation, and might be translated 'in fact' or 'I should tell you'.

23. μηδὲ ἐπισχεῖν 'and not to refrain' from speaking. 7, 139 οὐκ ἐπισχήσω. ἐνθαῦτα δή 'in these circumstances', 'thereupon', p. 5, l. 20.

26. ὑπερβάλλων 'continually raising his offer'. ἐς δ...ὑπεδίδεκτο 'until he had undertaken to pay 50 talents'. The sum was a large one (about 10,000£), and the Spartans, professedly forbidden the use of money, were notoriously open to bribery. Yet Kleomenes had shewn some virtue in this respect before (see 3, 148), and when accused of corruption in his Argive expedition was acquitted by the Ephors (6, 82).

4. οὐδέ οἱ ἐξεγένετο 'nor had he the opportunity'.

ἐπὶ πλέον ἔτι 'any further', 'at greater length'; without ἐπί in 6, 42: for ἐπί with the idea of extent of time cp. p. 73, l. 23 χρόνον ἐπὶ πλεῖστον.

5. τῆς ἀνόδου p. 30, l. 9.

CHAPTER LII.

7. ἀμφί for περί, p. 10, l. 25. σταθμοί 'stations', round which grew towns belonging especially to the King. See 2, 152 βασιλήϊοι σταθμοί. 6, 119 ἐν σταθμῷ ἑαυτοῦ.

8. καταλύσιες 'inns' or 'places of rest', elsewhere called καταγωγαί l. 25, cp. 1, 181 καταγωγὴ καὶ θῶκοι ἀμπαυστήριοι.

10. σταθμοί here used for 'day's journeys', properly, as above, the 'stations' at the end of each day. The average day's journey is 5 parasangs; the parasang (the distance a mule or camel can walk in an hour) being reckoned as 30 stades or $3\frac{3}{4}$ miles, see 6, 42. The $94\frac{1}{2}$ parasangs in 20 days through Lydia and Phrygia make the day's journey slightly below the average.

12. ἐκδέκεται 'meets the traveller next', i.e. has then to be crossed. 4, 39 ἡ ἀπὸ ταύτης ἐκδεκομένη Ἀσσυρίη.

13. ἐπ' ᾧ πύλαι τε ἔπεισι...καὶ φυλακτήριον 'near which there is a pass which one must necessarily traverse before crossing the River, and there is a strong fort at the River itself'.

15. ἐπ' αὐτῷ sc. τῷ ποταμῷ. The editors mostly seem to take πύλαι as meaning literally 'gates' to the bridge over the River or to some

road leading to the bridge. But I agree with Stein in translating it 'Pass', in something of the same sense as it frequently occurs in other connexions,—Thermopylae, Kilikian pylae, Syrian pylae (Amanides);— whether the pass was wholly natural or partly artificial is another thing, but it is evidently separate from the φυλακτήριον on the river itself. 'Gate' as a term for a pass over a hill or mountain still exists in various parts of England. For οὕτω 'only after doing so' cp. p. 22, l. 15.

19. διξὰς πύλας 'two narrow passes'. Herodotos extends the frontier of Kilikia so far to the north of the line marked by other writers, and of that known in later times, that it is not easy to conceive where he places these πύλαι. He appears to mean two narrow points in the descent from the Anti-Taurus (the northern spur of Taurus) into what was afterwards a part of Kappadokia, which admitted of being blocked and defended.

21. ὁδὸν ποιευμένῳ sc. πορευομένῳ, see on p. 3, l. 12.

23. οὖρος δὲ Κιλικίης...Εὐφρήτης. This again conceives of Kilikia as containing the eastern part of what is usually marked as Kappadokia. The frontier of Kilikia is not the Euphrates either lower down, the district afterwards called Kommagene lying between.

24. νηυσιπέρητος 'that has to be crossed in boats', i.e. that is not fordable, cp. 1, 189.

25. σταθμοὶ καταγωγέων 'stations with inns', an explanatory genitive: 'stations consisting of places of rest'.

27. ἐκ δὲ ταύτης [τῆς Ἀρμενίης]. The later geography must again be modified to suit this description, and Armenia must be conceived as including part of what is elsewhere called Assyria. [Stein transferred the clause to this place from following τριηκοσίας p. 32, l. 10. The words καὶ τριήκοντα...ἑκατόν were first inserted by de la Barre. Bekker had marked the lacuna. The change and addition help greatly to clear up a serious difficulty and confusion.]

3. τέσσερες. The four rivers are (1) Tigris, (2) the Greater Zab [Zabatus] called also Lycus, (3) the Lesser Zab [called also Kapros], (4) the Gyndes which has been variously identified with the Mendeli, the Diyálah and others. These three last flow into the Tigris: the Greater Zab about 20 miles below Nineveh, the Lesser 60 miles further down still.

9. τὸν Κῦρος διέλαβε 'which Kyros once dispersed into 360 canals'. See 1, 189, 190 where Kyros on his march to Babylon is

said to have punished the river Gyndes for drowning one of the sacred white horses by draining it off into 180 trenches or canals on either bank. Immense irrigation works exist in connexion with more than one of the rivers which have been identified with the Gyndes,—some of immemorial antiquity. If Kyros was the originator of any of them, it seems more probable that he was so after his conquest of Babylon with the view of developing the country. Yet the example of Xerxes both in undertaking great engineering works before a campaign, and in the scourging of the Hellespont, may cause some hesitation in too confidently rejecting the story in Herodotos either as to the time or the motive of the work.

14. **οὗτοι οἱ πάντες—ἐς Σοῦσα ἀναβαίνοντι.** The reckoning as it here appears in the emended text agrees with Herodotos' totals:

From Sardis to the Halys	20	σταθμοί	94½	παρασάγγαι
„ Halys through Kappadokia	28	„	104	„
„ Frontiers of Kilikia to Euphrates	3	„	15½	„
„ Euphrates through Armenia to Matiene	15	„	56½	„
„ *Matiene to Kissia*	[34]	„	[137]	„
„ Kissia to Susa on the Choaspes	11	„	42½	„
	111		450	

If we take the reckoning of 5 parasangs for each day's journey as given in the next chapter, the whole time will be ninety days: a certain number of these σταθμοί therefore are not necessarily places at which a halt for the night was to be made, marking the end of the day's march, but places for temporary rest or refreshment. [If the text is not filled up by de la Barre's conjecture the totals obtained from adding the detailed statements come to 81 σταθμοί and 313 to 333 parasangs,—a discrepancy however which is not unusual in the calculations of Herodotos, see on 8, 48.] Bunbury, *Ancient Geogr.* I. p. 250—4.

CHAPTER LIII.

19. **δύναται τριήκοντα στάδια.** This statement is made also in 2, 6; 5, 42. Others however reckoned the parasang as 40 stadia [Strabo 11, 754]. The measure was originally one of time, i.e. the

distance that a mule or camel could walk in an hour; and it is evident that this must have varied considerably according to the nature of the country, roads, and animals. It is not extraordinary therefore that different people should have calculated it differently. When it became a conventional measure of distance known to the Greeks it seems to have been usually reckoned as Herodotos does. According to Strabo the *Stadium* = 625 feet; but Polybios reckoned it as 600 feet (34, 12).

20. τὰ βασιλήϊα τὰ Μεμνόνια in Susa, 'Shushan the Palace' of the prophets. See Biogr. Index s.v. *Memnon*.

24. ἀναισιμοῦνται Ionic for ἀναλίσκονται. Cp. 2, 31 τοσοῦτοι μῆνες εὑρίσκονται ἀναισιμούμενοι ἐξ Ἐλεφαντίνης πορευομένῳ ἐς τοὺς Αὐτομόλους. ἀπαρτί 'exactly', 2, 158 στάδιοι χίλιοι ἀπαρτί.

CHAPTER LIV.

25. τῷ Μιλησίῳ Ἀρισταγόρῃ. Dative of the agent with pluperfect passive εἴρητο.

27. ἄνοδον p. 39, l. 9.

29. τὴν ἐξ Ἐφέσου. The road up the country began at Ephesos, see 8, 103 where Xerxes sends his children under care of Artemisia thither.

31. θαλάσσης Ἑλληνικῆς i.e. the Aegean Sea.

1. μέχρι Σούσων. From Sardis to Susa is 450 parasangs or 30 × 450 = 13500 stades; add 540 stades from Ephesos to Sardis, total is 14040.

5. ἡ τρίμηνος ὁδός. The three months' journey mentioned by Aristagoras to Kleomenes, p. 30, l. 9.

CHAPTER LV.

9. Ἱππίεω τοῦ τυράννου. Thucydides (6, 54—5) says that there was a common notion that Hipparchos was the elder, and that Hippias became Tyrannus at his death, but that he had made careful enquiries and ascertained this not to be the case. Here Herodotos evidently takes Hippias to be ruling, and whatever power Hipparchos had to have been subordinate to that of the elder. ἰδόντα ὄψιν ἐνυπνίου 'after he had been warned in a dream', i.e. of his danger. Lit. 'when he had seen the vision of a dream'. Cp. 7, 47 εἴ τοι ἡ ὄψις τοῦ ἐνυπνίου μὴ ἐναργὴς οὕτω ἐφάνη κτλ.

10. **τῷ ἑαυτοῦ πάθεϊ**, bracketed by Stein, omitted by Abicht. If it stands it must depend on the notion of 'likeness', conveyed by ἐναργεστάτην.

11. **τὰ ἀνέκαθεν** 'originally', cp. 6, 125, 128 καὶ τὸ ἀνέκαθεν τοῖσι ἐν Κορίνθῳ Κυψελίδῃσι ἦν προσήκων.

13. **οὐδὲν ἔσσον**. Thucydides (6, 54, 5) asserts that the rule of the Peisistratidae had been mild and equitable until the murder of Hipparchos in B.C. 514, and that after that event greater severity was exercised. 6, 59, 2 τοῖς δ' Ἀθηναίοις χαλεπωτέρα μετὰ τοῦτο ἡ τυραννὶς κατέστη, καὶ ὁ Ἱππίας διὰ φόβου ἤδη μᾶλλον ὢν τῶν τε πολιτῶν πολλοὺς ἔκτεινε, καὶ πρὸς τὰ ἔξω ἅμα διεσκοπεῖτο εἴ ποθεν ἀσφάλειάν τινα ὁρῴη μεταβολῆς γενομένης ὑπάρχουσάν οἱ. **ἐπ' ἔτεα τέσσερα** B.C. 514—510. For ἐπί see p. 15, l. 21.

CHAPTER LVI.

15. **ἐν τῇ προτέρῃ...Παναθηναίων**. Thucydides explains that the conspirators waited for the Great Panathenaea, because on the day of that feast alone it was possible for a citizen to enter Athens with arms without rousing suspicion [6, 56, 2], see on 6, 35. The Panathenaea was celebrated towards the end of July, part of the ceremony being a grand procession in which all citizens might take part. The genitive **τῶν Παναθηναίων** is governed by the comparative word προτέρῃ. Cp. Polyb. 2, 43, 6 τῷ προτέρῳ ἔτει τῆς ἥττης. Herod. 1, 168 πρότερος τούτων. 3, 47 θώρηκα ἐλῄσαντο τῷ προτέρῳ ἔτει ἢ τὸν κρατῆρα οἱ Σάμιοι.

17. **αἰνίσσεσθαι τὰ ἔπεα** 'spoke these riddling verses'. ἔπος is used specially of such prophetic or oracular sayings, cp. 1, 13 τούτου τοῦ ἔπεος λόγον οὐδένα ἐποιεῦντο. 7, 143 εἰ ἐς Ἀθηναίους εἶχε τὸ ἔπος εἰρημένον ἐόντως, referring to the oracle ὦ θείη Σαλαμὶς κτλ.

18. **τλῆθι λέων...**

Thou as a lion endure with enduring soul the hard burden.
No one whose deeds are unjust shall escape the vengeance of heaven.

The 'lion' is often used as an emblem of a dangerous or tyrannical citizen. See p. 56, l. 20; 6, 131 where the mother of Perikles is said to have dreamed λέοντα τεκεῖν, and compare Aristophanes Ran. 1432 (of Alkibiades) and a comic oracle in Equit. 1037.

20. **φανερὸς...ὀνειροπόλοισι** 'he submitted them, without making any secret of so doing, to the interpreters of dreams'. Cp. 7, 18 τότε

ἀποσπεύδων φανερὸς ἦν. The influence of dreams on the minds of the Greeks is frequently illustrated in the Tragedians, and the interpretation of these was a regular part of the mantic art, as everywhere in the East. See 1, 128; 7, 13—17.

21. μετὰ δὲ, adverbial p. 15, l. 15. ἀπειπάμενος τὴν ὄψιν 'having repudiated the vision', i.e. either (1) 'said that he had not seen it', which would be the best antithesis to φανερὸς ἦν ὑπερτιθέμενος, or (2) 'said that he did not regard or care for it', that he 'dismissed it from his mind'. In 1, 59 ἀπείπασθαι τὸν παῖδα = 'to repudiate the child'. 7, 14 ἀπείπασθαι τὴν στρατηλασίην 'to abandon the expedition'.

22. ἔπεμπε τὴν πομπήν 'he proceeded to join the procession'. Cp. Thucyd. 6, 56, 2 τῶν πολιτῶν τοὺς τὴν πομπὴν πέμψαντας. Aristoph. Eccl. 757 οὔ τι μὴ | Ἱέρωνι τῷ κήρυκι πομπὴν πέμπετε;

ἐν τῇ δὴ τελευτᾷ 'in the course of which it was that he was slain'. Thucydides (6, 57) says that Hippias was engaged in marshalling the procession in the Kerameikos (διεκόσμει ὡς ἕκαστα ἐχρῆν τῆς πομπῆς προϊέναι), and the conspirators fearing that they were betrayed by one of their own number did not venture to attack him there; but meeting Hipparchos near the Leokorion, an heroon in another part of the Keramikos inside the walls, they killed him, while also engaged in marshalling a part of the procession [τὴν Παναθηναϊκὴν πομπὴν διακοσμοῦντι Thucyd. 1, 20, 3].

CHAPTER LVII.

25. τὴν ἀρχήν 'originally'. Usually without the article, but see 4, 28 τὸν χειμῶνα τοῦτον οὐκ ἀνέχονται τὴν ἀρχήν.

ἀναπυνθανόμενος 'by making (fresh) enquiries'. So ἀνάπυστα in 6, 64; 9, 109.

26. τῶν σὺν Κάδμῳ ἀπικομένων. For the Phoenikian colony brought into Boeotia by Kadmos, see 2, 49, and Biographical Index s.vv. *Kadmos* and *Phoenikians*.

2. τῆς χώρης ταύτης a topographical genitive, p. 37, l. 13, 'and occupied in this country the portion belonging to Tanagra which they had obtained as their allotment'. 4, 145 μοῖράν τε τιμέων μετέχοντες καὶ τῆς γῆς ἀπολαχόντες. For the fact cp. Thucyd. 1, 12, 3 Βοιωτοί...ἐξ Ἄρνης ἀναστάντες ὑπὸ Θεσσαλῶν τὴν νῦν μὲν Βοιωτίαν πρότερον δὲ Καδμηΐδα γῆν καλουμένην ᾤκισαν.

Ταναγρικήν. Tanagraeans were in later times called Gephyraeans [Strabo 9, 404 καλοῦνται δὲ καὶ Γεφυραῖοι οἱ Ταναγραῖοι].

5. ἐτράποντο ἐπ' Ἀθηνέων 'turned their steps towards Athens', p. 35, l. 18.

6. ἐπὶ ῥητοῖσι 'on definite conditions', that is, not making them simply citizens with all the rights which that status implied, but admitting them to certain defined parts of the citizen rights. Such imperfect citizenship was always known to Athenian law, as for instance in the case of the Metoeki, Isoteles, and citizens who had lost certain rights by partial ἀτιμία. An admission however, on such terms, of a people *en bloc* is not otherwise known in Athenian history. When in aftertimes the Plataeans were admitted they seem to have obtained full citizenship.

7. πολλῶν τέων καὶ οὐκ ἀξιαπηγήτων...ἔργεσθαι 'having enjoined that they should be excluded from certain privileges, numerous but not important'. For this disjunctive use of καὶ cp. Thucyd. 7, 42, 2 οὐδὲν ἧσσον ἴσον καὶ παραπλήσιον. 80, 3 ἥμισυ μάλιστα καὶ πλέον. In these cases καὶ must be translated 'but' where there is a negative, 'or' where there is not. Stein quotes Pausanias 1, 9, 3 Ἀθηναῖοι ὑπ' αὐτοῦ παθόντες εὖ πολλά τε καὶ οὐκ ἄξια ἀπηγήσεως. The things from which the Gephyraei were excluded were probably certain religious rites, for in religion they kept separate, see c. 61. It may have been on this ground that Harmodios' sister was denied her part in the Panathenaic procession. Thucyd. 6, 56, 1.

CHAPTER LVIII.

9. οἱ σὺν Κάδμῳ ἀπικόμενοι. The name Kadmos means 'the Eastern', and the early settlement of Phoenikians in Boeotia is supposed by some to be attested (1) by the survival of the name Kadmeia for the acropolis of Thebes, (2) by the worship of the Kabiroi 'great Gods', and (3) by the survival of certain Semitic words in the Theban dialect, especially ἐλιεὺς 'god' (Hesych.). See Taylor *The Alphabet* vol. 2 pp. 19—22. Herod. 2, 44, 49; 4, 147.

12. γράμματα. The earliest known Ionic writing is that on the colossal statues at Abu Simbel in Egypt, in the 7th century B.C. 'They prove that at the close of the 7th century B C. the Ionian Greeks were in possession of a well-developed alphabet of considerable antiquity which agreed in all essential points with the Greek alphabet in its final form'. Taylor vol. 2 p. 18. It remains to see whether the next remark of Herodotos, that the Greeks derived their letters from the Phoenikians varying the shapes and direction to suit the variation

		Thera.	Abu-Simbel.	For-mello.	Ancient Semitic.	
1	α	A	A		⨯ ⨯	Aleph
2	β		B		9 9	Beth
3	γ	⌐ ⌐ ⌐	⌐ ⌐		⌐	Gimel
4	δ	▷	▷		◁ ◁◁	Daleth
5	ε	⋷	⋷ ⋷		⋷	He
6	F (digamma)			F	Y	Vau
7	ζ			⨯	‡ I	Zayin
8	η	日	日		日 日	Cheth
9	θ	⊗ ⊕	⊗		⊕	Teth
10	ι	⌇ ⌇	I		ʔ Z	Yod
20	κ	Ik K	K		⅄ У	Kaph
30	λ	⌐	∧		L 6	Lamed
40	μ	M M	M		M У	Mem
50	ν	M	NN		⅄ ⅄	Nun
60	ξ	KM			⟊ ⟊ ⟊	Samekh
70	o	o	o		o o	Ayin
80	π	⌐	⌐ ⌐		⌐	Pe
90	⌐ (san)			M	⊢ ⊢	Tsade
100	ϙ (koppa)	φ Q	Q	Q	φ φ	Q'oph
200	ρ	ᴘ ᴘ	ᴘ D		ᴅ ᴅ	Resh
300	σ	M	⌇ξ	⌇	W W	Shin
400	τ	T	T		⊺⊺ X	Tau
	υ	Y μ	Y Y V			
	φ	⌐ 日	φ			
	χ	φ 日 K 日	⨯ X			
	ψ	M	ψ			
	ω	⊙				

of the languages, can be justified by existing letters on the earliest monuments. The earliest settlements of the Phoenikians were on the island of Thera, and the most ancient inscriptions found there furnish us with an alphabet which may be called Helleno-Phoenikian or Kadmeian. If we contrast this 1st with the Semitic Alphabet, and 2nd with that obtained from Abu-Simbel, we shall be able to see for ourselves (Taylor *Alphabet* vol. 2 p. 59. Roberts *Epigraphy* p. 5).

The table on the previous page shews that the first 19 letters α—τ of the later Greek alphabet are closely connected with the Semitic; and the original presence of Ϝ (vau) ⋔ (san) Ϙ (koppa) is indicated by the fact that the letters ϛ and the following, ρ and the following, retained the numerical value which they had before Ϝ ⋔ Ϙ went out of use as alphabetical characters. These are given in their right places in what is called the Formello alphabet, an alphabet on a vase found at Formello near Veii in 1882 [Taylor 2 p. 73—4]. Ϙ and ⋔ survived as numerical or other marks, see Arist. Nub. 23, 122. The last 5 letters υ φ χ ψ ω are subsequent introductions. For the history of Υ(υ) see Roberts p. 7. The aspirates φ χ and the double letter ψ, represented in the Theraean inscriptions by ΠΗ, ϘΗ or ΚΗ, Μ, appear in the Abu-Simbel inscriptions nearly in their subsequent forms. Ω is represented in Thera by ⊙ and does not appear in the Ionian alphabet in any inscription of which the date is certain before about B.C. 520.

15. τὸν ῥυθμὸν 'the shape and direction', properly 'the movement' or 'ordered motion', cp. our phrase 'a flowing hand'. Xenophon (Mem. 3, 10, 10) uses it of the shape of a breastplate, meaning 'right shape' or 'proportion', so as to fit the body. Here besides the shape, the change to writing first to βουστροφηδόν, and then from left to right, instead of the reverse, is indicated.

16. περιοίκεον...Ἴωνες. The traditional date of the first Hellenic settlements is about 1200 B.C. For reasons for thinking this not far wrong see Taylor 2, p. 22. In speaking of the Ionians as being nearest to them Herodotos seems to refer to the early settlements of Phoenikians in Kypros and Rhodes, from which they traded with Asia Minor and the Islands, and taught the Hellenes not only their alphabet but also their weights and measures and the art of mining (6, 47).

20. ἐφάτισαν...κεκλῆσθαι 'they called them', lit. 'they denominated them so that they were called'. Cp. p. 40 l. 31 τὴν ἐπωνυμίην ποιεύμενοι κεκλῆσθαι Αἰγιαλέας.

ἐφάτισαν is a poetical word for εἶπον.

ὥσπερ...ἔφερε 'as was indeed only fair considering that the Phoenikians introduced them'. ἔφερε 'suggested' or 'demanded'. Cp. 7, 137 τὸ δίκαιον οὕτω ἔφερε. The verb is used to convey the idea of 'tendency' in whatever shape, cp. 3, 133; 4, 90; 6, 42, 110; 9, 120.

21. **Φοινικήϊα.** We are able to confirm this statement of Herodotos by an inscription found in the neighbourhood of Teos [in Ionia] presenting a form of execration, of which the last sentence is ὃς ἂν τὰς στήλας ἐν ᾗσιν ἡπαρὴ γέγραπται, ἢ κατάξει ἢ φοινικήϊα ἐκκόψε(ι) ἢ ἀφανέας ποιήσει, κε(ῖ)νον ἀπόλλυσθαι καὶ αὐτὸν καὶ γένος. Circ. B.C. 475. C. I. G. 3044. Bauer p. 317, Roberts p. 170.

22. **τὰς βίβλους διφθέρας καλέουσι** 'they call their writing material skins', i.e. before the Greeks had obtained 'biblos' from Egypt they used 'skins' or, as it was afterwards called, parchment. Herodotos means that even after they had come to use biblos they called it 'skin'. This and the following sentence shew that Varro was wrong in saying that the use of skins for this purpose was *invented* by Eumenes II. k. of Pergamos (B.C. 197—159), though it seems true that, the supply of biblos from Egypt having by that time ceased or fallen short, he reintroduced the use of skins, from which circumstance the material came to be called 'parchment' (Pergamense). For the biblos of the Nile see 2, 92; 2, 38. The Greeks early became acquainted with Egypt and its learning, king Psammetichos (7th cent. B.C.) having had a large number of Hellenic mercenaries in his service (2, 154).

CHAPTER LIX.

26. **Καδμήϊα γράμματα** i.e. letters of the shape of those introduced by Kadmos from Phoenikia. The following reduced facsimiles (from Roberts' *Epigraphy* p. 24) of archaic inscriptions from Thera represent probably very nearly what Herodotos means by 'Kadmeian letters'.

1. IGA 440.   ΜΑΜΞΞΗ   Ἑ[ρ]μᾶς?

2. IGA 441.   ΜΟΜΟΨΨΔϞΞΨ   Κερδύνομος.

3. IGA 442.   ΟΨΒϞΟΤϞϞ   Κριτοφύλου.

4. IGA 443.  Φίλαιος.

5. IGA 444.   Θαρ(ρ)υμάχ[α].

The iota afterwards represented by a straight line is here crooked, and the aspirate φ is represented by ΠΗ. The fifth vowel υ has already made its appearance: but Σ is still in the form M, and the words are written from right to left.

1. τῇσι Βοιωτῶν i.e. Thebes in Boeotia as opposed to Thebes in Egypt.

2. τὰ πολλά 'in most respects'.

4. ἐὼν ἀπό 'on his return from', 'being here from', for παρεών. Thus in the opposite sense ὁ ἀπόστολος ἐς τὴν Μίλητον ἦν 'had arrived at Miletos'. Stein proposes to read θεῷ for ἐών and to take ἀπὸ Τηλεβοάων as 'from the spoil of the Teleboans'. For this meaning of ἀνέθηκεν ἀπό there is ample authority; but if ἐών is retained, we cannot take the words in this way.

5. ἡλικίην 'in age' l. 12. ἂν εἴη 'probably is', a less positive assertion than would be conveyed by the indicative. See 8, 136 τάχα δ' ἂν καὶ τὰ χρηστήρια ταῦτά οἱ προλέγοι 'and perhaps this was the meaning of the oracles'.

κατὰ Λάϊον τὸν Λαβδάκου 'in the time of Laïos son of Labdakos'. It is idle in the case of such references to heroic times to pretend to fix dates. Laïos father of Oedipus would be conceived by Herodotos as living at some time previous to the Trojan war, say before the 12th century B.C.

CHAPTER LX.

7. ἐν ἑξαμέτρῳ τόνῳ 'in hexameter verse'. Cp. 1, 174 ἐν τριμέτρῳ τόνῳ. It is curious that Herodotos should notice as to the 2nd and 3rd inscription that they are hexameters, and should not make the same observation as to the first. It might perhaps be explained if the word

θεῷ were written (as Stein supposes) instead of ἑών. The line would then be

'Ἀμφιτρύων μ' ἀνέθηκεν θεῷ ἀπὸ Τηλεβοάων

and Herodotos may have regarded ἀνέθηκεν θεῷ as depriving the line of metre. The ν ἐφελκυστικὸν we know to be found in ancient Attic inscriptions in defiance of metre. See Meisterhans *Gramm. der att. Inschrif.* p. 89.

Φουφαγόρας μ' ἀνέθηκεν Διὸς γλαυκώπιδι Φούρῃ.
Σῆμα τόδε Κύλων παίδοιν ἐπέθηκεν θανόντοιν.

9. **τείν** = σοι ethic dative.
10. **ἂν εἴη** l. 5.
11. **ἄλλος.** There was the statue of a Skaios at Olympia, a conqueror in boxing also, a native of Samos. Pausan. 6, 13, 5.

CHAPTER LXI.

15. **μουναρχέων** 'when sole ruler', a less presumptuous title than τύραννος or βασιλεύς.
16. **ἐπὶ τούτου...Ἀργείων** 'it was during the reign of this Laodamas that the Kadmeians were driven out by the Argives: referring to the expedition of the Epigoni, ten years after the 'Seven against Thebes'. For ἐξανιστέαται ὑπὸ cp. p. 34, l. 5.
18. **τράπονται** p. 34, l. 5.
19. **ὑπὸ Βοιωτῶν ἀναχωρέουσι** 'were made to retire by the Boeotians'. Cp. the construction of φεύγειν, 4, 125 ὁρέοντες τοὺς ὁμούρους φεύγοντας ὑπὸ Σκυθέων. See p. 16, l. 16.
21. **τῶν οὐδὲν...Ἀθηναίοισι** 'with which the other Athenians have nothing to do'. **μέτα** = μέτεστι.

ἄλλα τε...ὄργια the construction goes on from ἱρά ἐστι in l. 20 'among others which are separated from the rest of the national worship are the temple and rites of Demeter Achaia'. According to the ancient explanation 'Demeter Achaia' meant 'mourning Demeter' (ἄχος), that is, Demeter mourning for the loss of her daughter.

CHAPTER LXII.

24. **δὴ** resuming the thread of the story from c. 55.
2. **ἤια λέξων** 'I was proceeding to say'. Cp. 4, 82 ἀναβήσομαι δὲ ἐς τὸν κατ' ἀρχὰς ἤια λέξων λόγον.

4. ἐμπικραινομένου 'growing embittered with'. Cp. 6, 123 ἐξηγρίωσαν τοὺς ὑπολοίπους Πεισιστρατιδέων. Thucyd. 6, 59, 1 τοῖς δὲ Ἀθηναίοις χαλεπωτέρα ἤδη μετὰ τοῦτο ἡ τυραννὶς κατέστη.

6. φεύγοντες Πεισιστρατίδας 'being in exile at the bidding of the Peisistratids'. 6, 123 οἵτινες ἔφευγον τὸν πάντα χρόνον τοὺς τυράννους. Notice the plural used for the family and dynasty, though Hippias was sole tyrannus.

8. κατὰ τὸ ἰσχυρόν 'by force'. Cp. 1, 76 ἐπειρῶντο κατὰ τὸ ἰσχυρὸν ἀλλήλων. **προεχώρεε** p. 26, l. 7.

κάτοδος 'restoration', so κατάγων p. 17, l. 28.

προσέπταιον μεγάλως 'kept failing most disastrously'. The imperfect shews that more than one attempt had been made. For προσπταίω cp. 6, 45 ἅτε τῷ τε πεζῷ προσπταίσας πρὸς τοὺς Βρύγους καὶ τῷ ναυτικῷ μεγάλως περὶ Ἄθων.

10. Λειψύδριον...τειχίσαντες. In fortifying this small place on the skirts of Mt. Parnes, from which to harry the country and annoy the Peisistratids in Athens, the Alkmaeonidae were following a frequent custom in ancient warfare, and one which in the case of Athens was tried with great effect by the Spartans in B.C. 414 when they seized Dekelea.

11. ἐνθαῦτα 'thereupon', p. 45, l. 20.

12, 13. παρ' Ἀμφικτυόνων...μισθοῦνται 'took a contract from the Amphiktyons for the temple'. The Amphiktyonic council had special charge of the Delphic Temple.

13. τὸν νῦν ἐόντα. The temple burnt in B.C. 548 by an accident (2, 180; Paus. 10, 5) was the fourth which had existed on the same site. The new temple was to cost 75 talents, a quarter of which was to be supplied by the Delphians and the rest by subscription from all parts of the world. The architect was Spintharus of Corinth. The Alkmaeonids contracted to build the temple of the limestone which could be got in the near neighbourhood, but voluntarily built the Pronaos of the much more costly marble of Paros without extra charge. This temple had probably been completed long before Herodotos wrote. Pindar writing about B.C. 490 speaks of it, and its liberal Athenian contractors, as though it were then finished, Pyth. 7, 9 πάσαισι γὰρ πολίεσσι λόγος ὁμιλεῖ Ἐρεχθέος ἀστῶν, Ἄπολλον, οἳ τεὸν γε δόμον Πυθῶνι δίᾳ θαητὸν ἔτευξαν, 'In all cities is there talk of the citizens of Erechtheus, O Apollo, who made thy temple at holy Pytho a wonder to see'. The object of the Alkmaeonidae in this liberality, beyond a pious wish to promote the honour of the god, seems to have been to pose before the Hellenic world as promoters of Delphi as the religious centre of Greece as against Delos, which the Peisistratidae favoured. It was in fact as promoters of a central-Greece rather than an Island-Greece policy. There seems even to have been a rumour that the Peisistratidae had instigated the burning of the last temple. See Professor Middleton in the *Journal of Hellenic Studies* Oct. 1888 p. 287 sqq.

17. συγκειμένου σφι 'whereas they had agreed'.

πωρίνου λίθου. Pliny (N. H. 36, § 132) says that the stone called *porus* is white and hard like Parian marble, but less heavy (*minus ponderosus*), that is, that it is less compact in texture. It was used he says also (ib. § 53) for polishing the marble.

18. τὰ ἔμπροσθε, the Pronaos, but whether the whole Pronaos is meant, or only the columns in it, seems doubtful. Professor Middleton thinks that it means the columns only of the main front, perhaps including the two of the Pronaos. It does not mean that the walls were faced with marble; such work being only known later.

CHAPTER LXIII.

20. κατήμενοι ἀνέπειθον 'took up their residence at Delphi and continued to bribe the Pythia'. For ἀναπείθειν in this sense, see 6, 66, 123; 7, 33. The spread of this report at the time seems more appropriate to the Spartans, see p. 54, l. 21. But Herodotos is speaking apparently of the account current later, when the Athenians would wish to shew that the Spartans, both in helping to drive out the Peisistratidae and in endeavouring to restore them, had been acting without real authority from the god.

21. ὅκως ἔλθοιεν 'as often as any Spartans came'. For this frequentative use of the optative, see p. 16, l. 3 ὅκως ἴδοιεν. 8, 91 ὅκως δέ τινες τοὺς Ἀθηναίους διαφύγοιεν φερόμενοι ἐσέπιπτον ἐς τοὺς Αἰγινήτας. 6, 31, 61. G. § 213, 3.

22. εἴτε ἰδίῳ...χρησόμενοι 'to consult the oracle on private or public business', lit. 'on a private or public mission', p. 55, l. 3. So 6, 39 κοινῷ στόλῳ συλλυπηθησόμενοι. προφέρειν...ἐλευθεροῦν 'brought up the subject of liberating Athens', i.e. the Pythia reproached them with not doing it, or reminded them that they ought to do it. So in 4, 151 χρεομένοισι δὲ τοῖσι Θηραίοισι προέφερε ἡ Πυθίη τὴν ἐς Λιβύην ἀποικίην 'on the Theraeans consulting the oracle (on the subject of a

blight in Thera) the Pythia brought up the colony to Libya',—which had been ordered previously, i.e. she reproached them with not having done it.

24. **πρόφαντον ἐγίνετο** (=προεφαίνετο) 'upon this warning of the oracle being again and again repeated'. The word is again used of the warning of an oracle in 9, 93 πρόφαντά σφι ἔν τε Δωδώνῃ καὶ ἐν Δελφοῖσι ἐγίνετο. Cp. 7, 37 εἴρετο τὸ θέλοι προφαίνειν τὸ φάσμα. It was frequently the habit of the oracle when consulted on one matter to give answers referring to another. See for instances of this 4, 151, 155; 9, 33.

27. **ὅμως...μάλιστα** 'in spite of the fact that they were united with them in the closest bonds of friendship'.

ξείνους, observe that προξείνους is not used here to express the relationship of the Peisistratidae with Sparta. πρόξενος is a private person so connected with the state; the Peisistratidae are the ruling family at Athens and represent the state.

[The MSS. have ξεινίους which Stein retains, as did Gaisford. On the other hand Baehr, Abicht, Holder write ξείνους after Schaeffer, which is found in the corresponding passage p. 54, l. 21 and in Plutarch Malign. Her. c. 23. Stein cps. φίλος and φίλιος, but ξείνιος does not appear to be so used elsewhere.]

28. **πρεσβύτερα ἐποιεῦντο** 'they regarded as more important'. So Thucyd. 4, 61 πρεσβύτατον νομίζειν, cp. the Latin *antiquior*. For the sentiment cp. 9, 7 περὶ πλείστου δ' ἦγον τὰ τοῦ θεοῦ πορσύνειν.

29. **πλοίοισι** 'in transports'. The Spartans seem to have already possessed war-ships at this time, for in 3, 56 we are told of an expedition against Polycrates (B.C. 525); but at the Persian war of B.C. 480 they only supplied 10 as compared with 126 of the Athenians, 40 of the Korinthians and 12 of the Sikyonians (8, 2); they therefore naturally attacked Athens by land in preference, though they came by sea to avoid complications with Korinth and Megara.

30. **προσσχὼν ἐς Φάληρον** 'having put in at Phalerum', at that time the regular harbour of Athens. The Peiraeus, that is the bay on the western side of the promontory, did not come into general use until about the time of Perikles. For προσσχεῖν ἐς cp. 6, 99 προσίσχον πρὸς τὰς νήσους. ib. 119 ὡς προσέσχον ἐς τὴν Ἀσίην πλέοντες. The dative is also used, 4, 156 προσίσχειν τῇ γῇ.

31. **ἐπεκαλέοντο...ἐπικουρίην** 'they sent and asked for auxiliaries from Thessaly'. The alliance between Athens and Thessaly continued

for many years after this, and does not appear to have been closely connected with any personal feeling for the Peisistratidae (Thucyd. 1, 102, 107). ἐπικουρίην = ἐπικούρους, p. 47, l. 26.

3. **κοινῇ γνώμῃ χρεώμενοι** 'acting unanimously', 'with united action', cp. κοινῷ τε λόγῳ καὶ κοινῷ στόλῳ p. 55, l. 3. Thessaly was divided nominally into four districts,—Thessaliotis, Pelasgiotis, Histiaeotis, Phthiotis. Politically each town was supposed to be independent, but they practically fell into groups in which the towns of Larissa, Pharsalos, Krannon and Pherae exercised supremacy. The whole country in certain circumstances acted under a military commander called a Tagus; but it was usually with great difficulty that such united action could be secured, or even a Tagus appointed. At this time the most powerful families in Thessaly were the Aleuadae of Larissa and the Skopadae of Krannon; and in speaking of Thessaly acting 'in combination' Herodotos appears to mean that these two were in harmony. Grote 2 p. 282.

χιλίην ἵππον 'a body of 1000 cavalry'. Thessalian horses and cavalry were long famous, see 7, 28, 29; Thucyd. 1, 111; Polyb. 4. 8. The military class consisted mostly of the wealthy, the inferiors or *penestae*, who would form the infantry, appear to have been an agricultural or pastoral people who never became eminent as soldiers.

4. **τὸν βασιλέα τὸν σφέτερον.** There was no *basileus* of all Thessaly, as far as we know. By calling Kineas 'king of Thessaly', Herodotos may either mean that he was what was locally called the 'tagus',—a word peculiar to Thessaly and not used either by Herodotos or Thucydides,—or he may mean that he was one who had the title of *basileus* in his own town: just as, in 7, 6 he calls the Aleuadae Θεσσαλίης βασιλέες. I believe that on this occasion Kineas was *Tagus*, which Herodotos translates by the more generally understood word βασιλεύς. **Κονιαῖον.** No town of *Konium* is known in Thessaly. If the reading is to stand it must be supposed that Kineas came from Κόνιον or Κονιούπολις in Phrygia and had settled in Thessaly. Others have changed the word to Γοννᾶιον 'of Gonni', a town just N. of the pass of Tempe; or Κυτιναῖον 'of Kytina', another town of Thessaly mentioned by Steph. Byz.

6. **κείραντες** 'having cleared', i.e. by cutting down trees and other obstructions. Cp. 9, 15 ἔκειρε τοὺς χώρους. See also 6, 75; 8, 65. **τῶν Φαληρέων τὸ πεδίον** 'the plain of Phalerum', lit. 'of the Phalereans' i.e. the inhabitants of the deme Phalerum. By the 'plain

of the Phalereans' Herodotos means the open tract of country extending inland from the modern chapel of St George, through which the road to Athens went.

7. ἱππάσιμον 'suitable for cavalry', which the greater part of Attica was not, cp. 9, 14 οὔτε ἱππασίμη ἡ χώρη ἦν ἡ Ἀττική.

11. κατέρξαν 'forced them down (to the shore) to take refuge in their ships'. The word is used especially of 'pressing hard upon' an enemy, see 6, 102; though in this latter passage it may perhaps be taken intransitively 'pressing on'. δή summing up a previous narrative.

12. οὕτω ἀπήλλαξε 'fared as I have described', cp. 1, 16 ἀπὸ μὲν τούτων οὐκ ὡς ἤθελε ἀπήλλαξε ἀλλὰ προσπταίσας μεγάλως.

13. ταφαί 'a tomb', in this sense always in the plural in Herodotos, see 2, 170; 3, 10. It is used in Attic prose only for the funeral ceremonies, except perhaps in Aeschines in Ctes. § 236 τὰς δημοσίας ταφὰς ἀνελεῖν. And so in poetry, Soph. Aj. 1090, 1109.

τῆς Ἀττικῆς, topographical genitive 'in Attica', p. 34, l. 2.

14. τοῦ Ἡρακλείου...Κυνοσάργεϊ. The sacred enclosure of Herakles in Kynosarges contained a gymnasium, frequented by youths of parents who were not both Athenians, see 6, 116, Plutarch Them. 1. Alopekae was to the N.E. of Athens; the Spartans must therefore have penetrated some considerable way into the country.

CHAPTER LXIV.

14. μετὰ δέ, adverbial, p. 15, l. 15 'and on a subsequent occasion', i.e. in B.C. 510.

16. στρατηγὸν...ἀποδέξαντες 'having appointed as general of the expedition king Kleomenes'. The Spartan kings had absolute command in war when with the army (6, 56); but it appears that the government or Gerusia had the power of determining whether either of them, and which of them, should go on any particular expedition.

20. προσέμιξε. Herodotos does not state where this engagement took place: but as the Spartan force came by land it was probably in the plain of Athens itself, between the city and Eleusis, a district not suitable for cavalry, as Mardonius saw: cp. 9, 13. [For a discussion on a different account of what is supposed to be meant for this action by Andocides de myst. § 106 see Grote 4 p. 50 note.]

22. ὡς εἶχον ἰθύς 'as straight as they could', i.e. without going

back to Athens for baggage etc. Cp. 6, 17 ὁ δὲ ἰθέως ὡς εἶχε ἔπλωε ἐς Φοινίκην. ἐπὶ Θεσσαλίης 'in the direction of Thessaly'.

23. ἐς τὸ ἄστυ 'into the town', as distinguished from the Akropolis, cp. the capture of Athens by Xerxes in B.C. 480, see 8, 51. It seems plain that the ἄστυ was not fortified, or at least not with any wall which was defensible. The 'Pelasgic wall' mentioned in l. 25 defended the N. side of the Akropolis and apparently included also a space at the foot, which afterwards retained the name of τὸ Πελασγικόν (Thucyd. 2, 16): and though in describing the building of the town walls after the Persian invasion Thucydides (1, 90—93) speaks of it as a restoration (ἀνακοδομεῖν), and says that only small portions of the ancient ring wall (περιβόλου βραχέα) remained; yet it seems doubtful whether by this he means anything more than the Pelasgic fortification of the Akropolis, to which the original city had been almost entirely confined. Grote 4 p. 49.

24. τοῖσι βουλομένοισι i.e. the Alkmaeonids and their partisans.

25. τῷ Πελασγικῷ τείχεϊ, see Geographical Index, s.v. Pelasgi.

CHAPTER LXV.

26. οὐδέν τι πάντως ἂν ἐξεῖλον 'would certainly not have taken'. p. 20, l. 1. For ἐξεῖλον cp. p. 8, l. 5.

27. For οὔτε...τε cp. 6, 9; 16, 30.

28. ἐπέδρην ποιήσασθαι 'to make a prolonged siege'. Cp. 1, 17 ὥστε ἐπέδρης μὴ εἶναι ἔργον τῇ στρατιῇ.

31. νῦν δὲ 'but as it actually turned out'. συντυχίη, p. 24, l. 12. ἐπεγένετο 'supervened'.

1. ὑπεκτιθέμενοι 'while in the act of being secretly conveyed out of the country'. οἱ παῖδες According to Thucydides (6, 55, 1) of the three brothers Hippias, Hipparchos and Thessalos, only the first had children. He had five by his wife Myrrhina. Still there may have been νόθοι, and others belonging to female members of the family.

4. συνετετάρακτο, notice the force of the tense 'were at once completely upset'.

παρέστησαν...ἐκ τῆς Ἀττικῆς 'they gave in—on condition of the surrender of their children—to any terms the Athenians chose, which were that they should quit Attica within five days'. ἐπὶ μισθῷ τοῖσι τέκνοισι lit. 'on the terms of their children as the price', cp. 1, 160 ἐξέδοσαν δὲ οἱ Χῖοι ἐπὶ τῷ Ἀταρνεΐ μισθῷ. ἐπ' οἷσι...ὥστε The latter word is equivalent to ἐπ' ᾧτε. Cp. 8, 4 πείθουσι Θεμιστοκλέα ἐπὶ μισθῷ τριήκοντα ταλάντοις, ἐπ' ᾧ τε καταμείναντες πρὸ τῆς Εὐβοίης ποιήσονται τὴν ναυμαχίην. Thucyd. 4, 37 παραδοῦναι σφᾶς αὐτοὺς Ἀθηναίοις ὥστε βουλεῦσαι ὅ τι ἂν ἐκείνοις δοκῇ. For παρέστησαν cp. 3, 13 πολιορκεύμενοι χρόνῳ παρέστησαν. 6, 99 παρέστησαν ἐς τῶν Περσέων τὴν γνώμην. μετὰ δὲ, p. 37, l. 14.

7. ἄρξαντες...τριήκοντα 'after having reigned over the Athenians 36 years'. The tyrannis of Peisistratos began in B.C. 560 and the expulsion of Hippias took place in B.C. 510; but of these 50 years Peisistratos was in exile for about 15 [1, 59—64]: Herodotos in reckoning the number of years which the dynasty lasted only counts those during which Peisistratos actually reigned. Aristotle (Pol. 5, 12) reckons 35 years.

9. ἀνέκαθεν 'originally', a word Herodotos often uses in regard to pedigrees, see 6, 53; 6, 125; 6, 128.

10. ἐκ τῶν αὐτῶν...καὶ οἱ ἀμφὶ Κόδρον 'being sprung from the same ancestors as the families of Kodros and Melanthos'. He uses the phrase οἱ ἀμφὶ Κόδρον κ.τ.λ. because he is thinking of a whole race, not simply of Kodros and his father Melanthos. In later Greek the phrase is used sometimes as a mere periphrasis for the name. τῶν αὐτῶν καὶ 'the same as', cp. 6, 92 ἐπεκαλέοντο τοὺς αὐτοὺς καὶ πρότερον. 8, 45 τὠυτὸ πλήρωμα παρείχοντο καὶ ἐπ' Ἀρτεμισίῳ.

11. ἐπήλυδες 'immigrants', opposed to αὐτόχθονες 4, 197; 8, 73. Melanthos expelled from Pylos took refuge in Athens. See *Biographical Index*.

12. ἐπὶ τούτου 'on this ground', i.e. of his descent from Nestor, one of whose sons was called Peisistratos; Hom. Odyss. 3, 400, 415 etc. For ἐπί with genitive of the thing which is the basis of action see Demosth. de Cor. §§ 22, 210, 226 ἐπ' ἀληθείας, ἐπ' αὐτῶν τῶν ἔργων, ἐπὶ τῶν νόμων, ἐπὶ μαρτυρίας κ.τ.λ. Cp. 2, 57 δοκέουσι κληθῆναι πρὸς Δωδωναίων ἐπὶ τοῦδε αἱ γυναῖκες διότι βάρβαροι ἦσαν. ἀπεμνημόνευσε θέσθαι 'remembered to name him', almost equivalent to 'named him in remembrance'. For θέσθαι οὔνομα cp. Arist. Nub. 65—7 ἐγὼ δὲ τοῦ πάππου ἐτιθέμην Φειδωνίδην. p. 58, l. 10.

14. ἐπὶ τοῦ...ἐπωνυμίην 'intentionally naming him after Nestor's son Peisistratos'. So 4, 184 ἐπὶ τούτου τοῦ οὔρεος οἱ ἄνθρωποι οὗτοι ἐπώνυμοι ἐγένοντο. 7, 40 Νισαῖοι δὲ καλέονται ἵπποι ἐπὶ τοῦδε. Cp. p. 26, l. 10.

16. ὅσα ἔρξαν (ἔρδω) ἢ ἔπαθον 'what they achieved or endured which is in any way memorable'. Stein quotes Odyss. 8, 490 ὅσσ' ἔρξαν τ' ἔπαθον τε καὶ ὅσσ' ἐμόγησαν Ἀχαιοί.

CHAPTER LXVI.

22. ἐγίνοντο μέζονες 'began to grow more powerful'. Though Herodotos (cp. c. 78) seems to put forward the increasing greatness of Athens as the *consequence* of the revolution, and not merely as coinciding with it in point of time; yet his own words certainly imply that the upward tendency in her fortunes had begun before; and we know that Peisistratos commenced on a large scale the erection of public buildings in Athens, which, being so greatly extended afterwards in the time of Perikles, made Athens the admiration of the ancient world. He also promoted literature and collected a library; took measures for supplying Athens with water; and created a fund for the support of citizens disabled in war. All these things speak of growing wealth, and not of harassed industries or hampered enterprise. Mr Grote (4 p. 400) supposes that it was only when the democratic revolution had freed and encouraged private enterprise that the mineral wealth of Laurium began to be fully developed. But this is a conjecture founded on very slight indications; and it seems incredible that such a source of wealth should have been neglected or discouraged by the Peisistratids, if there had been any signs of its being successfully worked. The more natural account of the revolution seems to be that it was quite as much the consequence as the cause of the growing prosperity of the town. As wealthy and successful men were more likely than others to excite the jealousy of a tyrannus, the more numerous they became the more certain was it that they would eventually expel him; and the revolution therefore, as so often happened, though it in fact favoured the democracy, was at first not a popular but an aristocratic one. People looking back, however, would be inclined to confound its causes with its consequences.

23. ἀνὴρ Ἀλκμεωνίδης 'of the Alkmaeonid family'. His father was Megakles son of Alkmaeon. See *Historical Index*.

24. ὅσπερ δὴ λόγον ἔχει 'who is the man that has the reputation of having bribed the Pythia'. Cp. 9, 74 διξοὺς λόγους λεγομένους ἔχει and 9, 78 ὅκως λόγος σε ἔχῃ μέζων. 9, 84 ἔχει τινὰ φάτιν θάψαι Μαρδόνιον, but in 8, 94 φάτις ἔχει τούτους. For ἀναπεῖσαι see p. 36, l. 20.

Plutarch de Mal., c. 23, remarks on this sentence as an attempt on the part of Herodotos to disparage the glory of the revolution.

26. τὰ ἀνέκαθεν 'his origin', l. 9.

27. θύουσι δὲ...Καρίῳ 'but the family offer sacrifice to Zeus Karios'. Herodotos means that the family maintain a tradition of Karian origin. The Karians were at one time widely spread in Island Greece [1, 171; Thucyd. 1, 8], and it is not at all unlikely that some of them had settled in Attica. Plutarch (de Mal. 23) protests against the insinuation of a Karian origin of Isagoras, apparently as being a roundabout way of supporting an Alkmaeonid.

39 1. τὸν δῆμον προσεταιρίζεται 'took into partnership', 'identified the interests of the commons with his own'. Mr Grote supposes that the ground of Kleisthenes' quarrel with Isagoras was the proposal to bring in a reform such as is described in the next sentence; but the words of Herodotos seem evidently to imply that the difference between the two statesmen was in the first instance caused by an ordinary rivalry for power and influence, and that Kleisthenes adopted democratic measures (to which he was very likely already predisposed) as a means of strengthening his own position. Not that Herodotos regards this as in any way discreditable; it is on the contrary meant to exalt the patriotism of Kleisthenes.

μετὰ δὲ p. 15, l. 15; p. 13, l. 18. This redivision, then, was not the original measure shewing his alliance with the demos; but one adopted in consequence of it.

2. τετραφύλους...Ὅπλητος. The four Ionic tribes, the Geleontes, Aegikoreis, Argadeis, and Hopletes, are as usual referred for their names to supposed ancestors, in this case to four sons of Ion. It seems indubitable however that they represented classes or castes originally connected with the employments of the families or phratries of which they were composed. Whether they were equal politically, or whether the military tribe or Hopletes had, as it naturally might, some exclusive privileges, is a difficult problem, which has never been satisfactorily solved. And probably under the Peisistratids it did not much matter; as all political rights were merged under a central government which was practically autocratic, though administered more or less in accordance with the laws and under the established forms. But outside these tribes there had grown up a large population, originally perhaps resident aliens, liberated slaves, or even actual slaves, who though not nominally freed had been living apart from their

masters exercising trades and professions,—and these were now included in the ten tribes which were to embrace the whole free population of Attica.

[The derivation and meaning of the names of the four Ionic tribes are still somewhat obscure, the Αἰγικορεῖς 'goatmen' (κορεύς = κορός) were no doubt pastoral; the Ἀργαδεῖς (ἀργὸν = ἔργον) agricultural; of Ὅπλητες two theories are held (1) that the word is equivalent to ὁπλῖται which would indicate a military class; (2) that it is connected with ὅπλον 'a tool', and means 'craftsmen', δημιουργοί, as opposed to agriculturalists and pastoral folk; of Γελέοντες no certain account has been given. Some MSS. have Τελέοντος, but the Teian and Kyzikene inscriptions (C. I. G. 3078, 3664, 3665) show that the right form is Γελέοντες, and some have connected it with γῆ, as though it indicated the agricultural class and Ἀργαδεῖς the mechanical; but if the Ἀργαδεῖς are the agriculturalists and the Ὅπλητες the military class, it would seem that Γελέοντες ought rather to be a priestly caste.]

4. **ἀπαλλάξας τὰς ἐπωνυμίας** 'having got rid of these traditional designations'. ἐπωνυμία is a name given after some one or some thing. The transitive use of ἀπαλλάσσειν is somewhat rare in prose (see 6, 61).

5. **ἐξευρὼν ἑτέρων** 'and having hit upon designations drawn from other (heroes) who were connected with the country, except in the case of Ajax'. The ten Kleisthenic tribes were called after the following heroes, *Hippothoon* s. of Poseidon, *Antiochus* s. of Herakles, *Ajax*, *Leôs*, *Erechtheus*, *Aegeus* father of Theseus, *Oeneus* s. of Pandion, *Akamas* s. of Theseus, *Kekrops*, and *Pandion*: the names being Ἱπποθωντίς, Ἀντιοχίς, Αἰαντίς, Λεοντίς, Ἐρεχθηίς, Οἰνηίς, Ἀκαμαντίς, Κεκροπίς, Πανδιονίς (Paus. 1, 5, 2).

6. **τοῦτον δέ.** Ajax was a national hero of Salamis. According to tradition his sons Eurysakes and Philaeas migrated to Attica. At any rate Salamis had become politically united to Attica some sixty years before this; and the naming an Attic tribe after Ajax was a way of recognising and confirming this fact. See 8, 64.

7. **ξεῖνον**, see on p. 36, l. 27.

CHAPTER LXVII.

8. **ταῦτα δέ** 'now, in so acting': for ταῦτα ποιέων, cp. 9, 34 ταῦτα δὲ λέγων οὗτος ἐμιμέετο Μελάμποδα, ὡς εἰκάσαι.

δοκέειν ἐμοί, p. 41, l. 4. Sometimes with ὡς, see 6, 95 ὡς ἐμοὶ δοκέειν.

11—14. τοῦτο μέν...τοῦτο δέ 'in the first place', 'in the second place', p. 18, l. 1.

11. ῥαψῳδοὺς ἔπαυσε...ἀγωνίζεσθαι 'he put a stop to competitions of the reciters'. The rhapsodes, lit. 'singers of stitched songs', would sometimes recite their own compositions, but more often passages from Homer; and it was to the extracts from Homer recited by them that Kleisthenes is here represented as objecting.

> "The public recitation of the Homeric poems by Rhapsodes can be traced back to about 600 B.C., and was doubtless in use from a considerably earlier time. It is found at Sicyon in Peloponnesus,—at Syracuse,—at Delos,—at Chios,—at Cyprus,—and at Athens. This shows how widely the Homeric poems were diffused, from an early date, throughout the Greek world, among Dorians and Ionians alike. At Athens there was a special ordinance prescribing that Homer be recited (ῥαψῳδεῖσθαι) at the festival of the Great Panathenaea, once in every four years. This law was probably as old as 600—500 B.C. It was further provided that the competing rhapsodes at the Panathenaea should recite consecutive parts of Homer, instead of choosing their passages at random". Professor Jebb, *Homer*, p. 77.

In the 'Homeric Poems' Stein and Abicht understand the lost Θηβαΐς and Ἐπίγονοι to be included, on the ground that Argos and the Argives do not play so conspicuous a rôle in the Iliad and Odyssey as to explain this measure of Kleisthenes; and they quote the first line of the Thebaïs [preserved by the scholiast on Sophokl. Oed. C. 380] Ἄργος ἄειδε, θεά, πολυδίψιον ἔνθεν ἄνακτες. Still it may be said that, as Ἀργεῖοι in the Iliad is used as equivalent to the whole Greek army, and the king of Argos and Mycenae is the undoubted chief of the whole expedition, a sufficient prominence seems to be given to the Argives to provoke the prohibition.

13. τὰ πολλὰ πάντα ὑμνέαται 'are for the most part the exclusive theme'. Cp. 1, 203 ἔθνεα...ἔχει ὁ Καύκασος, τὰ πολλὰ πάντα ἀπ' ὕλης ἀγρίης ζώοντα, 'living exclusively on what the wild forest produces'.

14. ἡρώϊον γάρ. For γάρ introducing an explanatory sentence before the statement of the action explained see p. 2, l. 17. The ἡρώϊον means here a chapel built over the hero's tomb. See 9, 25; 6, 69.

16. τοῦτον sc. Ἄδρηστον. This king of Argos, who led the attack on Thebes, was worshipped as a hero at other towns also. The meaning of Kleisthenes' desire to expel him is that he wished to prohibit the worship paid at the shrine of a Dorian hero, his own family being Achaean, and his supremacy representing an anti-Doric movement in Sikyon.

18. **εἰ ἐκβάλλῃ**. For this deliberative subjunctive, see on p. 25, l. 7; 6, 35, 86.

20. **ἐκεῖνον** sc. Κλεισθένεα. Herodotos is not, as he generally does, giving the exact words of the oracle.

λευστῆρα. It seems doubtful whether this word is to be regarded as active or passive,—'one who deserves to be stoned' i.e. 'a traitor' (see c. 38 and 9, 5), or 'one who stones', i.e. 'a murderer'; Suidas gives the former, Hesychius the latter explanation. Casaubon wished to read λῃστῆρα 'a robber'. I am inclined to the first explanation as most appropriate. The Editors quote Cicero pro dom. sua, c. 5 *percussor lapidator, fur depopulator*, but the word there has a definite reference to a form of mob riot which had become common in Rome, and is not used as a general term for an assassin or rioter. Note that the Pythia was generally under Spartan influence, and was not likely to support an attack upon Dorians.

21. **τοῦτό γε οὐ παρεδίδου** 'refused him *this* permission'. The γε emphasises the contrast of τοῦτο (i.e. the expulsion of Adrastos) with the following μηχανήν.

22. **αὐτός** 'of his own accord'. The suppression of the worship of Adrastos was to involve the actual removal of his ἡρῷον it seems. Kleisthenes calculates that if he introduced a rival cult, that of Adrastos would be deserted, and the priests and others interested in the maintenance of his worship would abandon it, and even wish for the removal of the Heroum to some other town. In fact, as the oracle forbade its forcible removal, Adrastos was to be 'disestablished and disendowed' with the hope that his cultus (dear to the Dorians) would die a natural death before the endowed and protected worship of Melanippos. The motive of this, as of the change in the names of the tribes mentioned immediately afterwards, was to emphasise the separation of Sikyon from the Argive confederacy. The Dorian settlers had come from Argos, and the non-Dorian tribe of Kleisthenes being now in the ascendant this movement was possible. It was part of a general movement in Peloponnesus which was leaving Argos isolated, its old supremacy passing to Sparta.

27. **ἐν αὐτῷ τῷ πρυτανηΐῳ** 'in the precincts of the very court house', i.e. in the most sacred place in the town, where the city hearth ('Εστία) was burning. For the πρυτανήϊον as the official building, cp. 7, 197, λήϊτον καλέουσι τὸ πρυτανήϊον οἱ Ἀχαιοί. 6, 38. **μιν** i.e. his heroum or chapel.

40 1. ἐν τῷ ἰσχυροτάτῳ 'in the most secure place'. In apposition to ἐν αὐτῷ τῷ πρυτανηίῳ, the Prytaneium apparently being on the higher ledge of the plateau on which Sikyon was built.

8. ἡ γὰρ χώρη...αὕτη The territory of Sikyon was small, consisting of the valley of the Asopos, and had formerly been under the king of Korinth (Polybos).

10. ἄπαις 'without male offspring'. Cp. p. 27, l. 27.

12. πρός 'in addition'. πρός is adverbial, cp. p. 11, l. 13. τὰ πάθεα αὐτοῦ...ἐγέραιρον 'they used to celebrate his sufferings and death with tragic choruses', i.e. with the dances and lyric songs usually employed in the worship of Dionysos, which developed into the Tragic drama.

15. ἀπέδωκε 'restored', as though the honours paid to Adrastos had been wrongfully taken from the god.

τὴν δὲ ἄλλην θυσίην 'but the rest of the rite', the θυσίας τε καὶ ὁρτὰς of ll. 5—6.

CHAPTER LXVIII.

16. οἱ dative of the agent with pluperf. passive. See p. 32, l. 24.

17. ἵνα δὴ μὴ αἱ αὐταὶ ἔωσι 'that they might not be the same at Sikyon as at Argos'. The δή shows that the purpose is that in the mind of the subject of the sentence, not the motive assigned by the writer, cp. 6, 41. For the *dramatic* subjunctive ἔωσι after a verb in an historic tense (μετέβαλε), see 6, 30, 100, Goodwin, *Moods and Tenses*, p. 70.

19. ἔνθα 'wherein', i.e. in his assignment of the new names.

20. ἐπί p. 38, l. 12.

21. αὐτὰ τὰ τελευταῖα 'merely the terminations'. Cp. p. 50, l. 17; 6, 134 αὐτοὶ Πάριοι 'the Parians alone'.

πλὴν τῆς ἑωυτοῦ φυλῆς. His own tribe was non-Dorian (i.e. probably Achaean), and by giving it the name of the 'ruling tribe' (Ἀρχέλαοι) he was asserting the pre-eminence of the old Sikyonians over the Dorian immigrants.

24. ἕτεροι δέ, that is the Dorian inhabitants. Their three tribes are renamed after 'a boar', 'an ass', and 'a pig'. "The extreme bitterness of such an insult can only be appreciated when we fancy to ourselves the reverence with which the tribes in a Grecian city regarded the hero from whom their name was borrowed". Grote 3, p. 33.

27. **μετέπειτεν.** Sixty years after the death of Kleisthenes would indicate the period after the Persian wars, when the power of Argos was much diminished, and there would be no reason for the maintenance of an offensive distinction meant to mark resistance to it, and likely to give umbrage also to the Dorians of Sparta.

28. **λόγον σφίσι δόντες** 'having come to a conference with each other', 'having consulted with each other'. 1, 97 συνελέχθησαν οἱ Μῆδοι ἐς τὠυτὸ καὶ ἐδίδοσαν σφίσι λόγον. 8, 9 λόγον σφίσι ἐδίδοσαν. 6, 86 ἐμεωυτῷ λόγους ἐδίδουν. ib. 138 λόγον ἑωυτοῖσι (= ἀλλήλοις) ἐδίδοσαν. σφίσι = ἑωυτοῖσι = ἀλλήλοις, p. 44, l. 18.

29. **τετάρτους...προσέθεντο** 'and a fourth tribe they adopted'. This was the concession of the Dorians; the Archelai were not simply to be merged in the three tribes, but were to retain their separate existence, only under another name.

30. **ἐπὶ...Αἰγιαλέος.** The old designations of the three Dorian tribes [Δωριέες τριχάϊκες Odyss. 19, 177] were restored—Hylleis, Pamphyli, and Dymanteis [from Hyllos, son of Herakles, and Dymas and Pamphylos sons of the Dorian king Aegineios],—and the non-Dorian inhabitants made a concession, dropping the presumptuous title of Archelai, which involved a claim of superiority, and assuming another taken from a son of Adrastos (also killed at Thebes), whose worship was probably restored to something of its old preeminence.

CHAPTER LXIX.

2. **ὁ δὲ δή**, resuming the thread from c. 66.

3. **θυγατριδέος**, being son of his daughter Agariste, see 6, 131. ἐπὶ τούτου, p. 38, l. 12.

4. **δοκέειν ἐμοί**, p. 39, l. 8.

καὶ οὗτος, i.e. as well as the Dorians. Though he was an Achaean by descent, and not a Dorian, he despised the Ionians. For the disrepute of the Ionians in Greece cp. 1, 143 οἱ μέν νυν ἄλλοι Ἴωνες καὶ οἱ Ἀθηναῖοι ἔφυγον τὸ οὔνομα οὐ βουλόμενοι Ἴωνες κεκλῆσθαι· ἀλλὰ καὶ νῦν φαίνονταί μοι οἱ πολλοὶ αὐτῶν ἐπαισχύνεσθαι τῷ οὐνόματι.

7. **πρότερον ἀπωσμένον** 'formerly kept at a distance', i.e. from civic honours and privileges. This may be explained in two ways: (1) as referring to the Solonian arrangement of τιμήματα, which confined the Archonship and other offices to men of a certain amount of rateable property, (2) to the inhabitants of Attica, who being outside

the four Ionic tribes (c. 66) had no civic privileges at all. It is hard to decide whether we are to take ἀπωσμένον as referring to the general fact of the demos being kept out of these privileges, or to the policy of Kleisthenes himself before he adopted the democratical side. I think the former is the truer way, if the reading is right. See notes on text.

8. πρὸς τὴν ἑωυτοῦ μοῖραν προσεθήκατο 'attached to his own party'.

10. δέκα τε δὴ φυλάρχους 'and accordingly (δή) he appointed ten phylarchs', ten heads of tribes instead of the three φυλοβασιλεῖς of the original three tribes. Herodotos is not using φυλάρχους in the technical sense of later times, in which φύλαρχοι were the officers of the cavalry, but as a general word for the 'heads of tribes'.

δέκα δὲ καὶ τοὺς δήμους κατένεμε ἐς τὰς φυλάς 'and he made a tenfold division of the demes also among the tribes'. If these words meant, as at first sight they seem to do,—'ten to each tribe', it would follow that the number of demes was 100, whereas they were at least 170 in the 3rd cent. B.C. Accordingly various expedients have been adopted. Grote originally followed Wachsmuth in joining δέκα with φυλάς, which is intolerable; but in subsequent editions he followed a suggestion to join δέκα closely with κατένεμε, as I have done, which perhaps admits of the inequality of the number of demes in each tribe, though it is far from satisfactory [cp. 7, 121 τρεῖς μοίρας ὁ Ξέρξης δασάμενος πάντα τὸν πεζὸν στρατόν]. Another expedient is to strike out δέκα δέ from the text. A last method, the simplest, is to admit that Herodotos *does* say that there were 100 demes, and to suppose their number to have been gradually increased. The demes were not the creation of Kleisthenes, but existed long before (see for instance 1, 60), though it is possible that Kleisthenes may have introduced some modification in their boundaries and arrangement.

11, 12. ἦν τε...ἀντιστασιωτέων 'and when he had secured the adhesion of the demos he was far superior to his political opponents'. 1, 67 κατύπερθε τῷ πολέμῳ Τεγεητέων γενέσθαι.

CHAPTER LXX.

13. ἐν τῷ μέρεϊ 'in his turn'. 7, 212 κατὰ ἔθνεα κεκοσμημένοι ἐν μέρεϊ ἐμάχοντο.

14. ἐπικαλέεται 'he invoked the aid of Kleomenes the Lakedaemonian',—an early instance of the fatal vice inherent in all the small

autonomous states of Greece,—the beaten politician looks out for foreign aid.

17. **εἶχε αἰτίη** 'laboured under an imputation'. See on λόγον ἔχει p. 38, l. 24, and cp. 6, 115.

19. **ἐξέβαλλε** 'endeavoured to secure the expulsion of'. That he was not at once obeyed is shewn by the fact mentioned in the next chapter, that Kleisthenes retired voluntarily.

20. **τοὺς ἐναγέας ἐπιλέγων** 'adding as a description "those under a curse"'. Thus at the beginning of the Peloponnesian war the Spartans endeavoured to secure the expulsion of Perikles on the same ground [Thucyd. 1, 126], that is, of the curse incurred by the execution of the Kylonian conspirators. See Biographical Index, *s. v.* Kylon.

23. **εἶχον αἰτίην** 'laboured under the imputation', see on p. 38, l. 4 and cp. εἶχε αἰτίη in l. 17. **τοῦ φόνου τούτου** 'this murder', i. e. of the Kylonian partisans. **αὐτός** sc. Kleisthenes.

CHAPTER LXXI.

2. **ἦν Κύλων.** The attempt of Kylon to seize the tyranny at Athens has been variously assigned to B.C. 620 and 612. From Thucydides 1, 126 it is shewn to have been a year of the Olympic games; and from Plutarch, Sol. 12, we learn that one of the Archons was Megakles.

Ὀλυμπιονίκης, he had won the long race, the δίαυλος, Pausan. 1, 28, 1.

3. **ἐπὶ τυραννίδι ἐκόμησε** 'he assumed high airs with a view to absolute power', 'he had the audacity to aim at tyranny'. ἐπί with dat. sometimes expresses the end or object of action, so 4, 164 ἀπέστειλέ τινας ἐπὶ διαφθορῇ. Thuc. 1, 126 κατέλαβε τὴν ἀκρόπολιν ὡς ἐπὶ τυραννίδι. κομᾶν 'to wear the hair long', and then 'to give oneself airs', 'to be haughty'. Cp. Arist. Vesp. 130 ἐπὶ τῷ κομᾷς καὶ κομψὸς εἶναι προσποιεῖ; It perhaps rose from the idea of the dandies imitating the Spartans.

4. **ἑταιρηίην** 'an association', 'a band of friends'.

6. **πρὸς τὤγαλμα,** the statue of Athenè Polias which was in part of the building called as a whole the Erechtheium. Cp. Aeschyl. Eum. 80 ἵζου παλαιὸν ἄγκαθεν λαβὼν βρέτας.

οἱ πρυτάνιες τῶν ναυκράρων 'the heads of the naucraries who at that time had the management of Athens'. The name of the division here alluded to is ναυκραρία, for which Herod. uses οἱ ναύκραροι, properly 'the members of the naucraries'.

The naucraria was a division of the Attic people, for financial purposes, older than the time of Solon, and lasting till the reforms of Kleisthenes, when it was superseded by a division founded on the demes. There were 12 naucraries to each of the four tribes, and the head of each naucrary (πρύτανις τῶν ναυκράρων) performed functions analogous to those afterwards performed by the demarchs or heads of the 174 demes. From Pollux (8, 108) and Photius (s.v. ναυκραρία) it has been held that the naucraria continued to exist after the arrangement of the demes by Kleisthenes for certain specific purposes, their number being raised to 50 (5 for each of the ten tribes); which Mr Grote doubts on the ground of the improbability of the division founded on the fifth of a tribe being retained by the side of one founded on a third (τριττύς). The word itself is held by most to be equivalent to ναύκληρος 'ship-master', each ναυκληρία furnishing one ship and two horsemen to the state. It would thus bear some analogy in origin to that of our 'hundred', i.e. a district furnishing 100 men to the county levy or fyrd. Others however wish to derive it from ναίω and to explain it to mean *householders* (*assidui*). Grote, 4, p. 68.

As to the actual statement of Herodotos there is another difficulty. Thucydides (1, 126, 8) says that the whole business of reducing the Kylonian conspirators was left to the nine Archons, adding, τότε δὲ τὰ πολλὰ τῶν πολιτικῶν οἱ ἐννέα ἄρχοντες ἔπρασσον. This is confirmed by Plutarch (Solon c. 12) who says that those who thus negotiated with the men in sanctuary were Μεγακλῆς ὁ ἄρχων καὶ οἱ συνάρχοντες αὐτοῦ. Harpokration (s.v. ναυκραρικὰ) gets out of the difficulty by explaining that in this passage Herodotos uses ναύκραροι as equivalent to ἄρχοντες. But if so, what does οἱ πρυτάνιες mean? Stein accuses Herodotos of two errors, (1) of speaking of ναύκραροι before the time of Solon, and (2) of assigning to them the direction of public affairs (their office being local and definite). But his assertion that the division into naucraries was the work of Solon is not very fully supported by the passage of Aristotle quoted by Photius (lex. s.v. ναυκραρία); and for the latter part of his statement Herodotos and Thucydides may perhaps be reconciled, by supposing that the 48 naucrari, the nine archons, and the four phylarchs formed a council for administering public business. The actual destruction of the conspirators may have been directed by the archons, as the executive, but they may have been able to lay the blame afterwards on the Prytanies of the naucrari, as forming the majority of the council [Herod. says ἔνεμον, Thucyd. ἔπρασσον]; and Herodotos, who seems to have taken some of his facts in Athenian history from the Alkmaeonids (see 6, 121—4), may have had this version of the occurrence given him as the tradition of their family. This is not certain, but it seems better than to suppose Herodotos to have made a wilful misstatement, or an egregious blunder.

8. **ὑπεγγύους πλὴν θανάτου** 'liable to everything short of death', i.e. on the sole condition that their lives should be spared. A man is ὑπέγγυος who has given a pledge and so is liable to certain consequences. It is a poetical word, see Aeschyl. Choeph. 38 κριταὶ δὲ τῶνδ᾽ ὀνειράτων θεόθεν ἔλακον ὑπέγγυοι. Eurip. Hec. 1029 τὸ γὰρ ὑπέγγυον δίκᾳ καὶ θεοῖσιν. Cp. Thucyd. 4, 54, 2 ξυνέβησαν πρὸς Νικίαν...'Ἀθηναίοις ἐπιτρέψαι περὶ σφῶν αὐτῶν πλὴν θανάτου.

9. **αἰτίη ἔχει**, see on p. 38, l. 4.

CHAPTER LXXII.

11. **ἐξέβαλλε** 'tried to expel them', 'demanded their expulsion', p. 4, l. 19.

13. **ὑπεξέσχε** 'secretly withdrew', 6, 74 Κλεομένεα δεῖμα ἔλαβε Σπαρτιητέων καὶ ὑπεξέσχε ἐς Θεσσαλίην. **αὐτὸς** 'of his own accord', or 'for his own part', i.e. as opposed to those who stayed and were expelled by Kleomenes. **μετὰ δὲ** p. 15, l. 15.

παρῆν ἐς, see on p. 6, l. 5; p. 38, l. 24.

15. **ἀγηλατέει** 'expels as polluted' (ἄγος, ἐλαύνειν). Thucydides (1, 126, 13) says ἤλασαν μὲν οὖν καὶ οἱ Ἀθηναῖοι τοὺς ἐναγεῖς τούτους, ἤλασε δὲ καὶ Κλεομένης ὁ Λακεδαιμόνιος ὕστερον μετὰ Ἀθηναίων στασιαζόντων, τούς τε ζῶντας ἐλαύνοντες καὶ τῶν τεθνεώτων τὰ ὀστᾶ ἀνελόντες ἐξέβαλον. There had therefore, it seems, been before this some act of banishment past against the Alkmaeonidae.

ἐπίστια 'families',—those who sit at the same hearth (ἱστίη), p. 43, l. 15. The word is not used in this sense elsewhere; it is employed here apparently with a special view of the family as being united in religion and sharing therefore in the same pollution. ἱστίαι is used for 'families' in 1, 176.

17. **τὴν βουλήν**. The recently established council of 500 constituted by Kleisthenes, 50 from each of ten tribes, in the place of the old 400 of Solon, 100 from each of the four tribes.

καταλύειν ἐπειρᾶτο, for the construction see p. 55, l. 1.

τριηκοσίοισι...ἐνεχείριζε 'and he tried to put the offices in the hands of the 300 partisans of Isagoras'. That is, he endeavoured to limit the right of holding office to the old Eupatrid families, and even of them to such as had attached themselves to Isagoras. It was a movement analogous, allowing for the difference in the circumstances of the time, to the endeavour subsequently made by the Four-hundred and the Thirty to restrict political rights to a definite number of citizens.

22. τὰ αὐτὰ φρονήσαντες. Cp. p. 2, l. 15.

25. ἡ φήμη 'the well-known omen', Arist. Av. 720 φήμη γ' ὑμῖν ὄρνις ἐστί. See p. 20, l. 21 for this use of the definite article referring to something not before stated but well known.

43 2. ἤϊε 'was in the act of entering'. τῆς θεοῦ, the shrine of Athenè Polias, which formed part of the building called the Erechtheium. See p. 42, l. 6. The priestess of this shrine is mentioned again in 8, 41.

4. ἀμεῖψαι 'to cross', 'to pass',—a use confined elsewhere to poetry. See Soph. Phil. 1262; Eurip. El. 750.

7. Ἀχαιός. The Heraclid family reigning in Sparta claimed to have been royal before the coming of the Dorians, when the Peloponnese was still Argive or Achaean. δή 'accordingly'.

8. κληδόνι οὐδὲν χρεώμενος 'paying no heed to the warning', 'not availing himself of it'. κληδών is used especially of such prophetic warning conveyed by a word. Cp. 9, 91, 101. Kleomenes is again represented as showing contempt for religion in 6, 81. For χρεώμενος cp. 8, 21 οὐδὲν τοῖσι ἔπεσι χρησαμένοισι...παρῆν σφι συμφορῇ χρᾶσθαι.

τότε πάλιν 'on this occasion as before', referring to the unsuccessful attempt of the Spartans before to take the Peisistratids when entrenched on the Akropolis, c. 65. The repulse of Kleomenes and the Lakedaemonians seems to have been remembered with triumph for a long time. See Aristoph. Lys. 271 οὐ μὰ τὴν Δήμητρ' ἐμοῦ ζῶντος ἐγχανοῦνται· | ἐπεὶ οὐδὲ Κλεομένης, ὃς αὐτὴν κατέσχε πρῶτος, | ἀπῆλθεν ἀψάλακτος, ἀλλ' | ὅμως Λακωνικὸν πνέων | ᾤχετο θὤπλα παραδοὺς ἐμοί, | σμικρὸν ἔχων πάνυ τριβώνιον, πεινῶν, ῥυπῶν, ἀπαράτιλτος | ἐξ ἐτῶν ἄλουτος.

9. ἐξέπιπτε 'was driven out'. 6, 121 ὅκως Πεισίστρατος ἐκπέσοι ἐκ τῶν Ἀθηνέων.

10. κατέδησαν τὴν ἐπὶ θανάτῳ 'threw them into prison under sentence of death'. Cp. 3, 119 ἔδησαν τὴν ἐπὶ θανάτῳ. 8, 37 ἔδησαν ἐπὶ θανάτῳ. Xen. Mem. 4, 4, 3 ἐπὶ θανάτῳ ἀγαγεῖν τινα. Some cognate substantive such as δέσιν or ζημίαν is to be understood.

11. χειρῶν τε καὶ λήματος 'both of strength and courage'. Cp. 9, 62 λήματι καὶ ῥώμῃ. Herodotos is referring to the victories of

Timesitheos in the pancratium, at the Olympic and Pythian games. Pausan. 6, 8, 6.

CHAPTER LXXIII.

17. **συμμαχίην...Πέρσας.** This is the first instance of an attempt on the part of an Hellenic state to invoke the interference of Persia in Greek affairs. If the attempt of Kleomenes was in the archonship of Isagoras (B.C. 508), this message to Persia may perhaps be looked upon as having been sent in the following year B.C. 507.

18, 19. **ἠπιστέατο...ἐκπεπολεμῶσθαι** 'for they knew that the Lakedaemonians had been rendered thoroughly hostile to them'. Cp. 3, 66 ἵνα οἱ ἐκπολεμωθῇ πᾶν τὸ Περσικόν. [If πρός is kept in the text the verb must be taken impersonally,—'that a certainty of war with the Lakedaemonians and Kleomenes had been created for themselves'.]

21. **Σαρδίων ὕπαρχος,** p. 14, l. 12.

22. **τίνες ἐόντες...κῇ γῆς,** cp. p. 6, l. 27. [Stein reads κοῦ here as in c. 13. But cp. p. 2, l. 10 τῶν ταύτῃ οἰκημένων.]

24. **ἀπεκορύφου** 'answered shortly', lit. 'brought to a point'. A rare word, and not found again in this sense, for which the Attics would use κεφαλαιόω (Thucyd. 6, 91). Polybios (3, 48, 6) uses it of two rivers which bring a piece of land 'to a point' at their fork. Stein refers to the Pindaric use of κορυφαί and κορυφή λόγων (Olymp. 7, 68; Pyth. 3, 80) which seem to mean 'the full sense' or 'meaning of words'.

25. **γῆν τε καὶ ὕδωρ,** p. 9, l. 4.

26. **ὁ δὲ...συνετίθετο** 'in that case he (Artaphernes) offered to make an alliance with him'. For δέ in apodosis, p. 1, l. 8; p. 22, l. 20.

27. **ἐπὶ σφέων αὐτῶν βαλόμενοι** 'after considering it by themselves', 'on their own responsibility'. Cp. p. 69, l. 4. 3, 75 ὠφείλετε ἐπ' ὑμῶν αὐτῶν βαλλόμενοι ποιέειν ταῦτα. Ib. 155 ἐπ' ἐμεωυτοῦ βαλόμενος ἔπρηξα. 4, 160 ἐπ' ἑωυτῶν βαλλόμενοι ἔκτισαν τὴν πόλιν. Cp. 8, 109. With the genitive ἐπί often indicates exclusive connexion separate from all else. Cp. 9, 17 ἐπ' ἑωυτῶν ἵζεσθαι. Ib. 38 εἶχον γὰρ καὶ οὗτοι ἐπ' ἑωυτῶν μάντιν.

2. **αἰτίας...εἶχον,** see on p. 41, l. 17.

44

CHAPTER LXXIV.

3. **ἐπιστάμενος** 'considering', 'believing'. See on p. 24, l. 26.

5. ἐς τό 'for what purpose'. Thus τό is used for τί or ὅ τι *quid*, 8, 40; 9, 54, and ὅς for τίς, 9, 71.

9. δή in continuation, 'accordingly'.

10. ἀπὸ συνθήματος 'acting in concert', 'according to an agreement'.

11. τοὺς ἐσχάτους τῆς Ἀττικῆς, that is, on the frontier between Attica and Boeotia, high up on the range of Kithaeron.

12. ἐπὶ τὰ ἕτερα 'on the other side', i.e. on the East.

ἐσίνοντο ἐπιόντες χώρους 'they attacked and damaged the lands', the cultivated enclosures, farms, vineyards, oliveyards and the like. Cp. 9, 15 τῶν Θηβαίων ἔκειρε τοὺς χώρους.

13. ἀμφιβολίῃ ἐχόμενοι 'though attacked on both sides at once'. A single use of the word in this literal sense. Thucyd. (2, 76, 3; 4, 32, 3; 4, 36, 3) uses the adjective ἀμφίβολος for persons thus exposed to double attack: and the neuter,—δέοι...προχωροῦντας εἴσω διπλάσιόν τε πόνον ἔχειν καὶ ἐν ἀμφιβόλῳ μᾶλλον γίγνεσθαι.

14. ἐσύστερον ἔμελλον...ποιήσεσθαι 'they had to put off their vengeance upon the Boeotians and Chalkidians to a future opportunity'. ἐσύστερον is the emphatic word. ἔμελλον indicates a necessary result of surrounding circumstances. Cp. 8, 45 ἐπὶ τοῖσι κατήκουσι βουλὴν ἔμελλον ποιήσεσθαι 'they had to reconsider their plans in view of the circumstances that had occurred'. μνήμην ποιήσεσθαι is almost equivalent to μνησικακεῖν. 'I'll remember you' is a common form of vulgar threat in English.

16. ἀντία ἔθεντο τὰ ὅπλα 'pitched their camp opposite them'. Cp. 9, 52 ἀπικόμενοι ἔθεντο πρὸ τοῦ ἱροῦ τὰ ὅπλα. The Greeks did not entrench a camp as a matter of course wherever they halted, as the Romans did; nor, when they did so, did they do it so systematically or strongly. θέσθαι τὰ ὅπλα 'to pile arms' therefore was a natural phrase for them to use, where the Romans would have said *munire castra*. See Polyb. VI. c. 42.

CHAPTER LXXV.

17. μελλόντων δὲ συνάψειν τὰ στρατόπεδα, a variation of the phrase in 6, 108 μελλόντων δὲ συνάπτειν μάχην. Cp. 4, 80 μελλόντων δὲ αὐτέων συνάψειν. 1, 18 οὗτος ὁ τὸν πόλεμον ἦν συνάψας.

18. σφίσι αὐτοῖσι...λόγον, p. 40, l. 28 'having come to the conclusion after mutual discussion'.

20. μετὰ δέ p. 15, l. 15.

22. **συνεξαγαγών...Λακεδαίμονος** 'who had been in joint command of the army from Sparta'. For Demaratos' subsequent opposition to Kleomenes and its results, see 6, 50, 51, 61, 65—7.

25. **μὴ ἐξεῖναι...ἀμφοτέρους.** The law apparently only forbade the presence of both kings with the army together. But in practice it seems that they were rarely both absent from Sparta at the same time. See Müller's *Dorians*, I. p. 108. Xenoph. Hellen. 5, 3, 10 where the Phliasians are said not to have expected to be attacked by Agesilaus, because the other king Agesipolis was out of Sparta (B.C. 381). Both kings go to Aegina later on (6, 72), but there was a special reason for that. See on 9, 10.

2. **παραλυομένου...τοῦ ἑτέρου** sc. *τῆς στρατηγίης* 'and since one of **45** these kings was relieved of the command'. So 6, 94 Μαρδόνιον μὲν φλαύρως πρήξαντα τῷ στόλῳ παραλύει τῆς στρατηγίης. So καταλύει 6, 43.

καταλείπεσθαι dependent on νόμος ἐτέθη.

3. **τῶν Τυνδαριδέων τὸν ἕτερον**, that is, one of the images of the Tyndaridae (the Dioskuri), consisting it is said of two blocks of wood joined by two spars, which accompanied the kings on an expedition. The custom of taking such images or symbols of Heroes on a military expedition is exemplified again in the sending for the images of the Aeacidae before Salamis (8, 64, 83). Cp. p. 47, l. 25.

4. **ἐπίκλητοι** 'in answer to an invocation', 'as allies'. Cp. 8, 64 εὐξάμενοι γὰρ πᾶσι τοῖσι θεοῖσι αὐτόθεν μὲν ἐκ Σαλαμῖνος Αἴαντά τε καὶ Τελαμῶνα ἐπεκαλέοντο.

CHAPTER LXXVI.

9. **τέταρτον...ἀπικόμενοι** 'now this was the fourth time that Dorians had invaded Attica'. The nominative participle may perhaps be looked upon as referring back to the subject of οἴχοντο in l. 8, 'they departed after having made what was the fourth invasion'. For a nominative participle of similarly doubtful construction see 8, 49 ἐπιλέγοντες κ.τ.λ.

10. **ἐπὶ πολέμῳ** 'hostilely', 'as enemies'.

11. **ἐπ᾽ ἀγαθῷ τοῦ πλήθεος** 'for the benefit of the democracy'. See cc. 62—5.

12. **Μέγαρα κατοίκισαν** 'founded Megara'. Pausanias (1, 39, 4) says that Megara existed before. This no doubt was the case, and yet when the Dorians separated the Megarid from Attica they put a Dorian colony in Megara and thus refounded the town. **οὗτος...ὀρθῶς ἄν**

καλέοιτο 'this may be correctly described as the expedition in the reign of Kodros'. Abicht however inserts πρῶτος before ἂν καλέοιτο 'this expedition in the reign of Kodros may be correctly described as the first'.

CHAPTER LXXVII.

20. ἐνταῦτα 'thereupon', p. 36, l. 11.
22. ἐπὶ τὸν Εὔριπον 'as far as the Euripus'.
25. δή, p. 43, l. 7.
26. πολλῷ ἐκράτησαν, p. 2, l. 3.

46 1. τῆς δὲ αὐτῆς...ἡμέρης 'and in the course of this same day'. Genitive of the time within which.

4. κληρούχους, cp. 6, 100. This is the first that we hear of cleruchs, men to whom allotments of land were given in a conquered country, without ceasing to be citizens of their own State, as colonists (ἄποικοι) did. Probably it is the first instance of this arrangement. The cleruchs appear to have paid some rent to the state for their holdings, their names being engraved on pillars in the Stoa Basileios. In B.C. 427 a similar measure was carried out in regard to Lesbos (Thucyd. 3, 50, 3); and so elsewhere.

5. ἐπὶ τῶν ἱπποβοτέων τῇ χώρῃ 'in the land belonging to the nobles'. The Hippobotae (men who keep horses), like the knights at Athens, formed the wealthy class of Chalkis. See on 6, 35; and Demosth. de Cor. § 320, where a wealthy man is called ἱπποτρόφος. Aelian (V. H. 6, 1) says that the district in which their property lay was called Hippobotos. It seems likely that this was a name assigned in later time. The plain in which the lands mostly lay was called Lelantum. Grote, 3, p. 168.

6. οἱ παχέες 'the rich men', p. 16, l. 17.

9. δίμνεως ἀποτιμησάμενοι 'have assessed their ransom at two minae a head'. This (about £8) appears to have been at the time the usual rate of ransom in the Peloponnese but not in all parts of Greece, see on 6, 79. The word ἀποτιμᾶσθαι seems to be more than τιμᾶσθαι, and to indicate that there had been some bargaining or dispute on the subject, and that they let the men go after '*finally* assessing the ransom at two minae'. Cp. the distinction between πειρᾶσθαι and ἀποπειρᾶσθαι. This would be explained by supposing that the customary ransom in this part of Greece was one mina (τὸ μνᾶς λυτροῦσθαι, Aristot. Eth. 5, 10), and that the Euboean prisoners resisted the doubling of the sum.

10. ἀνεκρέμασαν...ἀκρόπολιν. Such memorials of historical events were generally preserved in this way. Cp. 9, 121 where the Athenian fleet is said to take home the grapples of Xerxes' bridge, ὡς ἀναθήσοντες ἐς τὰ ἱρά. Notice the use of ἐς in both passages. Cp. p. 6, l. 5.

12. ἐκ τειχέων, that is, the Pelasgic wall on the N. side of the Akropolis. περιπεφλευσμένων...Μήδου. For the burning of the sacred buildings on the Akropolis in B.C. 480 see 8, 53.

13. ἀντίον τοῦ μεγάρου...τετραμμένου 'opposite the chapel which faces to the West'. By this Herod. appears to mean the N. W. transept of the Erechtheium which projected from the main building towards the N. wall of the Akropolis. He calls it μέγαρον 'a shrine' i.e. of Athene Polias.

14. τὴν δεκάτην, the usual tithe from spoil and the like devoted to religious or commemorative purposes. See 9, 80.

16. τὰ προπύλαια. The gateway of Pentelic marble which existed in the time of Herodotos was begun in B.C. 437 on the foundations of the earlier gateway which he must have seen, on the west side of the Akropolis where the steep path ascends from the dip between it and the Areopagus.

18. ἔθνεα Βοιωτῶν. The writer of the epigram is said to have been Simonides of Keos. A piece of marble has been found on the Akropolis which apparently contains a fragment of this epigram. C. I. A. 334.

20. ἔσβεσαν ὕβριν. Cp. 8, 77 δῖα Δίκη σβέσσει κρατερὸν Κόρον, ὕβριος υἱόν. Heraklit. fr. 16 ὕβριν χρὴ σβεννύειν μᾶλλον ἢ πυρκαϊήν. The ὕβρις of the enemy is generally mentioned in such epigrams, cp. Dem. de Cor. 289

Οἵδε πάτρας ἕνεκα σφετέρας εἰς δῆριν ἔθεντο
ὅπλα, καὶ ἀντιπάλων ὕβριν ἀπεσκέδασαν.

21. τῶν 'from whom', i.e. 'from the ransom of whom': dependent on δεκάτην.

CHAPTER LXXVIII.

22. νῦν 'then', referring back to his previous statement in c. 66.

23. ἰσηγορίη 'equality', lit. 'equal right of speech'. Polyb. (2, 38, 6, cp. 6, 9, 4) joins ἰσηγορία and παρρησία as the necessary components of δημοκρατία ἀληθινή.

24. εἰ καὶ 'since'. Cp. 9, 68 δηλοῖ τέ μοι, ὅτι πάντα τὰ πρήγματα τῶν βαρβάρων ἤρτητο ἐκ Περσέων, εἰ καὶ τότε οὗτοι...ἔφευγον.

26. **τὰ πολέμια**, in c. 66 he had admitted that Athens was important before the downfall of the tyrants, which could hardly have been if the Athenians had always got the worst of it in war (τὰ πολέμια). Herodotos is expressing the feeling of his day as to tyranni; but whatever evils were connected with them, and they were many, it does not seem probable or indeed true that weakness in war was one of them.

27. **κατεχόμενοι**, cp. p. 54, l. 13.

28. **ἠθελοκάκεον** 'used to play the coward deliberately',—'did less than they could on purpose'. Cf. 6, 15 ἀποδεικνύμενοί τε ἔργα λαμπρὰ καὶ οὐκ ἐθελοκακέοντες.

47 1. **αὐτὸς ἕκαστος ἑωυτῷ**. Perhaps this rather expresses what ought to be the result of democratic liberty than what is actually so always.

2. **κατεργάζεσθαι** 'to carry work out thoroughly'.

CHAPTER LXXIX.

6. **ἐς πολύφημον δὲ ἐξενείκαντας** 'have referred it to the many-voiced', i.e. to the people. Baehr quotes Odyss. 2, 150 ἀλλ' ὅτε δὴ μέσσην ἀγορὴν πολύφημον ἱκέσθην, and Hesych. ἐκκλησίαν ἐν ᾗ πολλαὶ φῆμαι καὶ κλήδονες εἰσί.

7. **τῶν ἄγχιστα δέεσθαι** 'to ask (help) of those nearest to them'.

9. **ἀλίην**. Cp. p. 16, l. 8.

10. **ἀκούσαντες τούτων** 'when they had been told of these things'. If there is any distinction between ἀκούειν with accus. and genitive rei in Herodotos (cp. ἀκούσας ταῦτα, 2, 115 and p. 17, l. 14; Κροῖσος δὲ τούτων ἀκούσας, 1, 45) it seems that the former is used when the actual words heard are given, the latter when a whole account is more vaguely referred to. See Clyde § 72 f., Demosth. de Cor. § 9.

15. **ἀλλὰ μᾶλλον...χρηστήριον** 'nay, be sure the meaning of the oracle is something else than this'. Cp. 6, 85 ὅκως ἐξ ὑστέρης μή τι ὑμῖν...πανώλεθρον κακὸν ἐς τὴν χώρην ἐσβάλωσι. Some word like ὁρᾶτε must be understood before μή. Madv. § 124, Rem. 1.

CHAPTER LXXX.

16. **ἐπιλεγομένων**, cp. p. 17, l. 1. **δή κοτε** *tandem:*, 'at length'. **μαθών** 'having guessed the meaning', rather than as Rawl. 'having been informed of the debate'.

17. **τὸ ἐθέλει λέγειν**, cp. 4, 131 Πέρσας ἐκέλευε, εἰ σοφοί εἰσι, γνῶναι τὸ ἐθέλει λέγειν τὰ δῶρα. For **τό** see on p. 44, l. 5.

21. τιμωρητήρων (=τιμωρῶν) 'avengers', a word not apparently occurring elsewhere.

καὶ οὐ γάρ, p. 2, l. 17; p. 49, l. 13.

23. ἐπικαλεόμενοι 'inviting them', 8, 64 ἐπικαλέσασθαι τοὺς Αἰακίδας συμμάχους.

25. ἐπικουρίην p. 37, l. 1. τοὺς Αἰακίδας the actual images of the Aeakidae, see on p. 45, l. 3.

συμπέμπειν ἔφασαν 'said that they would send', or 'agreed to send them'. ἔφασαν amounts to a verb of promising, after which the present infinitive is sometimes used. G. § 203 Note 2.

CHAPTER LXXXI.

26. πειρησαμένων, sc. τῶν Ἀθηναίων understood from the next clause. Cp. 1, 76 ἐπειρῶντο κατὰ τὸ ἰσχυρὸν ἀλλήλων. 4, 80 τί δεῖ πειρηθῆναι ἀλλήλων.

1. κατὰ τὴν συμμαχίην 'in reliance on the support'.

2. τρηχέως περιεφθέντων 'having suffered severely at the hands of the Athenians'. 8, 18 τρηχέως δὲ περιεφθέντες καὶ οὐκ ἥκιστα Ἀθηναῖοι.

5. εὐδαιμονίῃ, referring to the commercial wealth and greatness of Aegina.

6. ἐχούσης ἐς 'directed towards', 'referring to'. 6, 2 ταῦτα ἐς τὴν ἀπόστασιν ἔχοντα εἶπε. ib. 77 ἐς τοῦτο τὸ πρῆγμα εἶχε τὸ χρηστήριον.

7. ἀκήρυκτον 'not formally proclaimed by a herald'. It was a series of plundering descents upon the Attic coasts; which their naval superiority enabled them to make.

8. ἐπικειμένων...Βοιωτοῖσι 'for while they (the Athenians) were engaged in attacking Boeotia'. Cp. 6, 49 ποιήσασι ταῦτα ἰθέως Ἀθηναῖοι ἐπικέατο.

9—10. κατὰ μὲν ἔσυραν...κατὰ δὲ 'thoroughly pillaged Phalerum, and not less so many townships along the rest of the sea-board', cp. 9, 15 κατὰ μὲν ἔλευσαν αὐτοῦ τὴν γυναῖκα, κατὰ δὲ τὰ τέκνα. 8, 99 ἀπὸ μὲν ἔθανεν ὁ στρατηγὸς...ἀπὸ δὲ ἄλλοι πολλοί. τῆς ἄλλης παραλίης, topographical genitive, p. 37, l. 13.

12. ἐσίνοντο 'they were inflicting great damage on'. [St. reads with some MSS. ἐσικνέοντο *pungebant*.]

CHAPTER LXXXII.

13. **ἡ προοφειλομένη** 'the grudge which the Aeginetans owed the Athenians'. So Thucyd. I, 32, 1 εὐεργεσία προοφειλομένη. The phrase, like our own, arises from the peculiarly Greek idea that to return evil for evil was as much an act of justice as good for good: Isocr. ad Dem. 26 ὁμοίως αἰσχρὸν νόμιζε τῶν ἐχθρῶν νικᾶσθαι ταῖς κακοποιίαις καὶ τῶν φίλων ἡττᾶσθαι ταῖς εὐεργεσίαις. Plato Rep. 332 ὀφείλεται παρά γε τοῦ ἐχθροῦ τῷ ἐχθρῷ ὅπερ καὶ προσήκει κακόν τι.

15. **ἀνεδίδου** 'was producing'. They sent at the end of a bad harvest or after more than one lean season. A failure of crops was a frequent subject on which to consult the oracle. Cp. 9, 93.

19. **ἄμεινον συνοίσεσθαι** 'things would turn out better for them', cp. 4, 156 Θηραίοισι συνεφέρετο παλιγκότως.

20. **ποιέωνται**, the dubitative subjunctive in spite of the historical tense ἐπειρώτεον, on the dramatic principle so common in Greek of using the tense which the speaker would have used. They would say ποιώμεθα 'are we to make?' p. 51, l. 7.

21. **οὐδέτερα τούτων** 'neither of these things', i.e. neither to make it of bronze nor of marble, p. 33, l. 19.

23. **ἐλαίην** 'olive', not specifying any number. But it appears from p. 49, l. 4 that more than one tree was used. **ταμέσθαι**, *middle* 'to have cut up', cp. 1, 186 ἐτάμνετο (Σεμίραμις) τοὺς λίθους 'Semiramis had the stones cut'. The actual workman would be said ταμεῖν, cp. 6, 46 ναυπηγεύμενοι 'having ships built'.

24. **ἱροτάτας.** The legend was that Athene produced the olive on the Akropolis in answer to the challenge of Poseidon who produced the horse; and that from this sacred tree (8, 55) others throughout Attica were propagated (μεμορημέναι, μορίαι), which were also sacred and the property of the state. The legend may possibly account for the statement which Herodotos makes in the next sentence, though guarding himself by the cautious λέγεται, that at one time the olives of Attica were the only ones in the world. Rawlinson quotes Deuteron. VII. 11; VIII. 8, to show that the olive had been cultivated in the East: still it may have been rare in the countries known to the Greeks within the period in which tradition might survive. In Sophocl. O. T. 694 it is said not to be known in Asia or the Peloponnese, and to have been first planted at Kolonos, pointing no doubt to a similar tradition.

26. **ἐπὶ τοισίδε...ἐπ' ᾧ** 'on the following terms...namely on condi-

tion that'. Cp. 7, 154 ἐρρύσαντο δὲ οὗτοι ἐπὶ τοῖσδε καταλλάξαντες, ἐπ' ᾧτε 'Ιπποκράτεϊ Καμάριναν Συρηκοσίους παραδοῦναι.

1. **ἀπάξουσι** 'they should bring and pay'. The word used for those paying φόρος or tribute. See 3, 89 τοῖσι μὲν αὐτῶν ἀργύριον ἀπαγινέουσι εἴρητο Βαβυλώνιον σταθμὸν τάλαντον ἀπαγινέειν.

τῇ 'Αθηναίῃ τε τῇ πολιάδι...'Ερεχθεῖ, that is, to the patron goddess and the mythical founder and first king of the Attic race, who both had shrines in the same building, the Erechtheum. These ἱρά would in fact constitute a kind of tribute to Athens, and an acknowledgement of some dependence however vague.

4. **ποιησάμενοι** 'having caused to be made', see p. 48, l. 23; p. 52, l. 14 and 6, 48 ναῦς μακρὰς ποιέεσθαι. So also **ἱδρύσαντο** 'had them set up'.

CHAPTER LXXXIII.

7. **'Επιδαυρίων ἤκουον** 'used to be obedient to the Epidaurians', i.e. as their mother-city, in a greater degree than was customary in such cases. See 8, 46.

8. **τά τε ἄλλα καὶ...διαβαίνοντες** 'in other ways and especially in the fact that they crossed to have their disputes settled by trial in Epidauros'. Cp. 2, 92 οἱ δὲ...τοῖσι μὲν αὐτοῖσι νόμοισι χρέονται, τοῖσι καὶ οἱ ἄλλοι Αἰγύπτιοι καὶ τὰ ἄλλα καὶ γυναικὶ μιῇ ἕκαστος αὐτῶν συνοικέει. To use the law courts of another state was the most complete acknowledgement of dependence. It was the attempt of the Athenians to make her subject allies do so which caused some of the most frequent expressions of discontent. [Xenoph.] Rep. Ath. 1 § 16. Arist. Ach. 505.

9. **ἐδίδοσαν καὶ ἐλάμβανον...ἀλλήλων** p. 56, l. 3.

10. **τὸ δὲ ἀπὸ τοῦδε** 'in after times'. **νέας—χρησάμενοι.** The rise of Aegina to wealth and commercial importance may be traced to the 8th cent. B.C., its supremacy at sea was secured considerably before B.C. 500. Cp. p. 48, l. 5.

11. **ἀγνωμοσύνῃ χρησάμενοι** 'and being obstinately defiant'. Cp. 6, 10 ἀγνωμοσύνῃ διεχρέοντο. There is an idea of arrogance and short-sighted obstinacy conveyed by the word, see 9, 3.

13. **ὥστε δὴ** 'as you might expect from their being masters of the sea'. For ὥστε = ὡς or ἅτε see 9, 37, 70. p. 20, l. 26.

καὶ δὴ καὶ p. 11, l. 15.

15. **ὑπαιρέονται**, historical present with verbs in coordinate clauses

in aorist, cp. 6, 4 ὁ δέ Ἕρμιππος πρὸς τοὺς μὲν ἀπεπέμφθη οὐ διδοῖ, φέρων δὲ ἐνεχείρισε τὰ βιβλία Ἀρταφέρνεϊ.

16. **τῆς σφετέρης χώρης**, topographical genitive, p. 37, l. 13; p. 48, l. 10. For the pregnant *ἐς* in **ἱδρύσαντο ἐς** 'took them into the centre of their island and there set them up', cp. p. 6, l. 5.

18. **τῆς πόλιος** i.e. Aegina.

19. **χοροῖσι γυναικηΐοισι κερτόμοισι** 'with choruses of women singing abusive songs'. Similar customs prevailed at the Eleusinian festivals and the Thesmophoria. Suidas (s.v. τὰ ἐκ τῶν ἁμαξῶν σκώμματα) ἐπὶ τῆς ἁμάξης ὀχούμεναι αἱ γυναῖκες αἱ τῶν Ἀθηναίων, ἐπὰν εἰς τὰ Ἐλευσίνια ἐβάδιζον εἰς τὰ μεγάλα μυστήρια, ἐλοιδόρουν ἀλλήλας ἐν τῇ ὁδῷ· τοῦτο γὰρ ἦν ἔθος αὐταῖς.

21. **ἑκατέρῃ τῶν δαιμόνων**, a separate chorus for each of the goddesses Damia and Auxesis.

κακῶς ἠγόρευον = ἐλοιδόρουν.

23. **ἦσαν** 'used to be', i.e. when they had the images.

24. **ἄρρητοι ἱρουργίαι**, *mysteria*.

CHAPTER LXXXIV.

27. **οὐκ ἐπετέλεον** 'ceased paying the tribute'.

28. **ἐμήνιον** 'expressed their anger with'. It is a word very rare except in Herodotos (see 7, 229; 9, 7). Euripides uses it once, Rhes. 494. Aeschylus has the middle μηνίεσθαι, Eum. 101; Suppl. 263.

ἀπέφαινον λόγῳ 'tried to prove by argument', cp. p. 61, l. 21. 1, 129 Ἀστυάγης δέ μιν ἀπέφαινε τῷ λόγῳ σκαιότατόν τε καὶ ἀδικώτατον ἐόντα πάντων ἀνθρώπων.

30. **ἐπιτελέειν** 'they continued to pay'. The infinitive takes the place of an imperfect indicative. Cp. λέγειν 6, 117.

31. **ἐπεὶ δὲ ἐστερῆσθαι** 'but since they had been deprived'. The infinitive in oratio obliqua is preserved in subordinate clauses, cp. 6, 137 ἐπείτε γὰρ ἰδεῖν. 8, 111 ἐπεὶ Ἀνδρίους γε εἶναι γεωπείνας. **ἀποφέρειν** = ἀπάγειν l. 1.

2. **πρὸς ταῦτα** 'wherefore', p. 23, l. 23.

4. **Ἀθηναίοισι...οὐδὲν πρῆγμα** 'that they had nothing to do with the Athenians'. Dem. de Cor. § 283 διομνύμενος μηδὲν εἶναι σοὶ καὶ Φιλίππῳ.

CHAPTER LXXXV.

6. **ἀποσταλῆναι...τούτους** 'now the Athenians, on their part, say that after this demand the body of citizens was sent on board a single trireme, who being sent by the state etc.'

The meaning of τούτους is not very clear. It must, I suppose, apply to some body of men whose mission to Aegina Herodotos considered to be notorious; but for οὗτος where we commonly use 'the' see 3, 155 οὐκ ἔστι οὗτος ὡνήρ, ὅτι μὴ σύ, τῷ ἐστι δύναμις. Abicht reads τριακοσίους, as though Herod. had written τ᾽ οὕς, and the scribe mistook it for τούτους. The ordinary number of men on a trireme was 200 (7, 184; 8, 17). For Madvig's ingenious reconstruction of the sentence, see notes on the text.

τριήρεϊ μιῇ. At this early period the Athenians were poorly supplied with ships of war, and in the course of the Aeginetan war had to borrow triremes from the Korinthians (6, 89).

7. **ἀπὸ τοῦ κοινοῦ** 'on a mission from the state', 'on the authority of the state'. Cp. 8, 135 ἕπεσθαι οἱ τῶν ἀστῶν αἱρετοὺς ἄνδρας τρεῖς ἀπὸ τοῦ κοινοῦ κ.τ.λ.

10. **ἵνα...ἀνακομίσωνται** 'that they might take them back home again', might *recover* them as belonging to Athens.

οὐ δυναμένους, the relative sentence is here abandoned, and the construction recurs to the main verb λέγουσι l. 5.

14. **ὑπὸ τούτων** 'by these portents'. **ἀλλοφρονῆσαι** 'went distracted', more commonly παραφρονῆσαι.

15. **κτείνειν**, imperf. p. 49, l. 30, 'began killing each other'.

16. **ἐς ὅ** 'until', p. 57, l. 22. In this phrase the aspirated form of the relative is used by Herodotos. App. C. II. 2, note 1.

17. **αὐτὸν** 'alone', p. 40, l. 21.

CHAPTER LXXXVI.

20. **καὶ εἰ...νέες** 'even if it had been the case (as it was not) that they had no ships of their own'. They mean that even supposing they had no means of beating back a trireme at sea, they would have been strong enough to resist the few men who could have landed from it.

21. **ἀπαμύνασθαι ἄν** 'they would have easily repulsed'. The aorist infinitive takes the place of the aorist indicative and retains the ἄν. See on 6, 50 ἅμα γὰρ ἂν συλλαμβάνειν. G. § 211.

25. **κατὰ τοῦτο** 'on this ground', p. 2, l. 18.

26. οἷόν τι καὶ ἐποίησαν 'what they actually did'. 3, 16 βουλόμενος ποιῆσαι τὰ δὴ καὶ ἐποίησε.

29. τραπέσθαι πρὸς τὰ ἀγάλματα 'turned their attention to the images', i.e. at once proceeded to attempt to remove the images; p. 5, l. 20; p. 7, l. 20.

51 1. οὕτω δή 'under these circumstances', i.e. when these efforts failed. See 6, 36; 8, 94; 9, 15, and frequently throughout.

4. ἄλλῳ δέ τεῳ 'but perhaps someone else may believe it'. 4, 42 ἔλεγον ἐμοὶ μὲν οὐ πιστά, ἄλλῳ δὲ δή τεῳ κ.τ.λ.

5. τὸν ἀπὸ τούτου χρόνον 'ever after'. Cp. p. 49, l. 10. Kneeling statues were not unknown; for there was one of Eilethuia in this attitude at Tegea, Pausan. 8, 48, 5.

7. τοὺς Ἀθηναίους 'as to the Athenians'.

9. τούς τε δὴ Ἀθηναίους 'and no sooner had the Athenians landed in Aegina, than the Argives were on the spot to assist them'. τε...καὶ mark simultaneousness. Cp. 8, 83 ἠώς τε δὴ διέφαινε καὶ προηγόρευε. See also 6, 138; 9, 55; so also καὶ...καὶ 9, 57.

Αἰγιναίην, sc. νῆσον cp. 8, 90.

10. βοηθέοντας σφίσι 'to help them (the Aeginetans'). The reading σφι would refer to the Athenians, and in this hostile sense βοηθεῖν is always followed by ἐπί τινα. [The text should be altered to σφίσι].

13. ὑποταμομένους τὸ ἀπὸ τῶν νεῶν 'having cut them off from their ships'. τὸ ἀπὸ τῶν νεῶν is a substantive, 'the road in the direction of their ships'. Cp. 8, 76 τὸ ἀπ' ἑσπέρης κέρας 'the westward wing'.

CHAPTER LXXXVII.

16. τάδε 'what I have just recorded', for the more usual ταῦτα in this sense, as τοῦδε for τούτου p. 49, l. 10.

17. ἕνα μοῦνον, p. 50, l. 16.

22. κομισθεὶς ἄρα, a statement in direct oration is suddenly introduced in the middle of a long oratio obliqua.

24. δεινόν τι ποιησαμένας, p. 19, l. 11. A similar act of violence is that of the women at Salamis 9, 5.

27. τῇσι περόνῃσι 'with their brooches', which had long pins catching into the hooked end of the circular part. For their use in inflicting wounds cp. Soph. O. T. 1269; Eurip. Hec. 1152; Phoen. 60.

τῶν ἱματίων 'of their tunics', woollen Doric tunics, which were sleeveless and were fastened on both shoulders by a brooch. ἱμάτιον here is not used in the technical sense of 'upper garment', but for the tunic or chiton, for the Doric virgins used only one garment. Cf. Eur. Hec. 928 μονόπεπλος Δωρὶς ὡς κόρα, which was more of the nature of the ἱμάτιον than the χιτών. See Müll. *Dorians*, vol. 2 p. 274 sqq.

28. ὅκῃ, St. reads ὅκου, cp. p. 43, l. 22.

4. ἐς τὴν Ἰάδα ' to the Ionic dress'. The Ionic linen tunic (χιτών) 52 had sleeves and therefore did not require a brooch. The Doric tunic again was short; the Ionic reached to the feet.

6. μετέβαλον 'they forced the women to change'.

7. ἵνα δή ' in order that, as the men intended, they might not use brooches'. For δή with the final conjunction see p. 40, l. 17. For the subj. χρέωνται after historical tense, cp. p. 48, l. 20.

CHAPTER LXXXVIII.

8. ἀληθέϊ λόγῳ χρεωμένοισι 'to be precisely accurate', 1, 14 ἀληθέϊ δὲ λόγῳ χρεωμένῳ οὐ Κορινθίων τοῦ δημοσίου ἐστὶν ὁ θησαυρός.

10. Κάειρα 'Karian'. This feminine of Κάρ occurs in 1, 146; Hom. Il. 4, 142 Μῃονὶς ἠὲ Κάειρα. Elsewhere Herod. uses Καρίη (γλῶσσα 8, 135). The assertion that the dress which was called Ionian was in reality Karian is a good illustration of the remark of Thucydides [1, 8] that at one time the Karians were the prevailing inhabitants in the Islands. That some of them even penetrated to continental Greece we have seen was probable c. 66.

12. τοῖσι δὲ...νόμον εἶναι. The sentence has no construction as it stands. Either some word like ἔδοξε has dropped out, or we must understand λέγεται from c. 87, '(and it is said) that the Argives and Aeginetans on this account also caused the following to be a law besides in their own respective countries'. Abicht brackets καί before πρὸς ταῦτα, and ἔτι.

14. ἡμιολίας 'half as large again'. ποιέεσθαι 'to get made for them', p. 49, l. 4.

16. περόνας μάλιστα...τὰς γυναῖκας 'that their women should offer brooches in preference to any thing else in the temple of these goddesses'.

17. μήτε κέραμον. The Attic pottery work was of ancient date. Hence the district in Athens called Kerameicos; and the tradition that brick-making was first invented by Euryalos and Hyperbios at Athens.

Pliny, N. H. 7, § 194. This measure of the Argives and Aeginetans was what in our day would be called a boycott of an enemy's industry.

18. ἀλλ' ἐκ...πίνειν 'but that it should be a law for the future there to drink from home-made cups'.

20. ἐκ τότε 'from this (distant) period'. Cp. μέχρι δεῦρο, εἰς ὁπότε, μέχρι πόρρω and the like. [This is the reading of S. (the Sancroft MSS.), the others have ἔκ τε τόσου. Ab. and St. read ἐκ τίσου.]

21. ἐφόρεον 'used to wear'. See on 6, 61.

CHAPTER LXXXIX.

24. κατά = κατὰ τά. p. 5, l. 19; 8, 89.

25. τότε δή 'accordingly on this occasion', referring to the narrative in c. 82; the intervening cc. 83—88 being a parenthetical account of the reasons which the Aeginetans had for anger with Athens. προθύμως join with ἐβοήθεον.

1. δή 'as I have said'. p. 41, l. 2.

4. ἐπισχόντας, the whole sentence down to καταστρέψεσθαι is an oratio obliqua depending on μαντήϊον, which includes the idea of the direction conveyed by the oracle. ἀπὸ ἀδικίου 'from doing trespass on the Aeginetans',—a rare word for ἀδικίας, which survived in legal language: a δίκη ἀδικίου is mentioned by Harpocration; cp. Plut. Pericl. 32 εἴτε κλοπῆς καὶ δώρων εἴτε ἀδικίου βούλοιτό τις ὀνομάζειν τὴν δίωξιν.

6. ἀποδέξαντας 'having dedicated', 'presented', p. 39, l. 27. Cp. 8, 35 ὅκως βασιλέϊ Ξέρξῃ ἀποδέξαιεν τὰ χρήματα.

7. χωρήσειν, p. 28, l. 15.

10. ποιήσειν sc. κακά 'inflict'.

12. τῷ μὲν Αἰακῷ τέμενος...ἐπὶ τῆς ἀγορῆς ἵδρυται. This temenos (in the *old* Agora between the Odeon and Areopagus) was called τὸ Αἰακεῖον, οὗ φασὶ Αἰακὸν οἰκῆσαι Ἀθήνῃσι (Hesych.).

15. ἀνάρσια 'acts of hostility'. 9, 37.

CHAPTER XC.

17. πρῆγμα 'trouble'.

18. τὰ ἐκ τῶν Ἀλκμαιωνιδέων...μεμηχανημένα, p. 36, ll. 11, 12.

21. συμφορὴν ἐποιεῦντο διπλόην 'they regarded it as a double grievance', 'they were annoyed in two respects'. p. 3, l. 12.

22. ξείνους, p. 36, l. 27.
ἐκ τῆς ἐκείνων sc. χώρης 'from their (the Peisistratids') country'.
24. ἐφαίνετο 'was being manifested'.
2. ἐξ Ἀθηναίων 'at the hands of the Athenians', p. 6, l. 11. The 54 evils to be inflicted on the Spartans according to the oracle were, it appears, to come from the demos. The Spartans therefore felt that they had made a mistake in driving out their friends, who, like other dynasties, were more occupied in preserving their own position than in attacking outsiders. See Thucyd. 1, 17, 1.
7. ἐν τῷ ἱρῷ i.e. in the Erechtheium, see cc. 72, 82.

CHAPTER XCI.

13. κατεχόμενον, p. 46, l. 27.
14. μαθόντες δέ, summing up and repeating the whole previous sentence. Cp. p. 73, l. 21: for δέ cp. p. 1, l. 9; p. 22, l. 21. τούτων ἕκαστα, p. 7, l. 2.
16. ἐς τὸ καταφεύγουσι, p. 38, l. 7.
18. ἀγγέλους = πρέσβεις 'ambassadors', 'representatives'. 1, 36, 69.
21. κιβδήλοισι 'spurious'. Cp. 1, 66 χρησμῷ κιβδήλῳ πίσυνοι, ib. 75 ἀπικομένου χρησμοῦ κιβδήλου.
22. ἀναδεκομένους...Ἀθήνας, this seems like a great and wilful exaggeration.
25. ἀχαρίστῳ, p. 53, ll. 23—4.
27. δόξαν δὲ φύσας 'but having become proud', lit. 'having grown pride'. So (8, 104) πώγωνα φύειν 'to grow a beard'. Cf. Soph. Oed. K. 804 φύσας φρένας. Elektr. 1463 μηδὲ πρὸς βίαν φύσῃ φρένας.
28. ὥστε = ὡς. The reference in regard to the Boeotians and Chalkidians is to the events mentioned in c. 77.
30. τις καὶ ἄλλος, used when a vague reference is purposely employed, of a minatory character, which will be well understood by the hearers, cp. 9, 45. Here the persons especially meant are the Korinthians and perhaps the Spartans themselves.
ἐκμαθήσεται ἁμαρτών 'will learn that he has erred', i.e. in not accepting the present proposals of the Spartans. Some have taken it to mean 'will learn if he offends them' (i.e. the Athenians). ἐπείτε 'since', p. 9, l. 25; p. 23, l. 17.

31. πειρησόμεθα...ἀκεόμενοι 'we will try to remedy our mistake'. For the construction of πειρᾶσθαι see 6, 5; 8, 142.

4. κοινῷ στόλῳ, p. 36, l. 22; p. 37, l. 3.

CHAPTER XCII.

7. οὐκ ἐνεδέκετο, notice the tense, 'did not show any disposition to accept the proposal'.

8. ἡσυχίην ἦγον 'kept silence', cp. 7, 150; p. 57, l. 2.

§ 1.

10. ἦ δή 'surely!'. ὅ τε οὐρανὸς...οὐρανοῦ. An amplification of a common proverb to express utter confusion and the most unexpected disasters. Cf. Lucian, Prom. 192 διὰ τοῦτο ἐχρῆν τὸ τοῦ λόγου τῇ γῇ τὸν οὐρανὸν ἀναμεμῖχθαι. Ter. Haut. 719 *quid si redeo ad illos qui aiunt 'quid si nunc caelum ruat'?* Livy, 4, 3 *caelum atque terras miscere*. Juv. 6, 28 *mare caelo confundere.* The reversal of the order of nature compared with that in morals is also expressed by Eurip. Med. 409 ἄνω ποταμῶν ἱερῶν χωροῦσι παγαί | καὶ δίκα καὶ πάντα πάλιν στρέφεται. Cp. also Verg. Aen. 1, 133; 12, 204; Juv. 2, 25; Ovid, Tr. 1. 8, 5.

12. νομὸν ἐν θαλάσσῃ ἕξουσι 'shall have their habitation in the sea', p. 66, l. 7.

13. ὅτε γε *siquidem* 'when, as it seems is now the case'.

14. ἰσοκρατίας, cp. ἰσηγορίη, p. 46, l. 24.

15. κατάγειν 'to restore', p. 17, l. 28.

τοῦ sc. χρήματος 'a thing than which'. Cp. p. 60, l. 16 τοιοῦτο μέν ἐστι ὑμῖν ἡ τυραννίς. St. quotes Soph. O. T. 541 τυραννίδα | θηρᾶν δ πλήθει χρήμασίν θ' ἁλίσκεται.

18. ὥστε, epexegetic of τοῦτό γε, p. 68, l. 1.

20. οὕτω 'when you have done that'. δίζησθε. A verb almost entirely confined to non-Attic poetry and to Herodotos, who often uses it. It is found however once in a chorus of Aeschylos (Suppl. 800).

21. νῦν δέ 'but as it is'.

φυλάσσοντες...μὴ γενέσθαι 'guarding with the utmost rigor against its establishment in Sparta'. The participle has here a negative sense, and is therefore followed by μή. Madv. § 210.

23. παραχρᾶσθε ἐς τοὺς συμμάχους. This is generally explained to mean 'ye are behaving carelessly or contemptuously towards your allies'. And this seems to be the meaning of παραχρᾶσθαι elsewhere in

Herod., the παρά having the same sense as in πάρεργον. See 1, 108; 2, 141; 8, 20. Cp. 4, 159 οὐ πεπειρημένοι πρότερον οἱ Αἰγύπτιοι Ἑλλήνων καὶ παραχρεόμενοι διεφθάρησαν. But in all these passages the verb is transitive with an object expressed or understood. Here alone it is used absolutely, and may perhaps only mean 'you are acting wrongly', *inique agitis*, as Stein takes it.

24. ἔατε = ἦτε, App. D. IV. (d). So we have ἔα (2, 19), ἔας (1, 187).

κατά περ, p. 52, l. 24.

25. συμβαλέσθαι 'to bring forward in debate'. 8, 61 οὕτω ἐκέλευε γνώμας συμβάλλεσθαι.

§ 2.

1. πόλιος κατάστασις 'a political settlement', 'a constitution'. **56** Plat. Rep. 426 C ἡ κατάστασις τῆς πόλιος. So 2, 173 κατάστασις πρηγμάτων 'an arrangement of business'.

2. οὗτοι sc. οἱ ὀλίγαρχοι.

3. ἔνεμον, p. 42, l. 7.

ἐδίδοσαν δὲ καὶ ἤγοντο, p. 49, l. 8, 'gave their daughters and took wives'—i.e. had *conubium*.

6. γάρ, anticipatory, p. 2, l. 17 and Index.

8. τὰ ἀνέκαθεν, p. 33, l. 11.

10. περὶ γόνου, a common subject upon which to consult the oracle, see 9, 33.

11. ἐσιόντα...ἰθέως 'and immediately on his entering', i.e. the μέγαρον. The address is made more impressive by the Pythia speaking at once without waiting for question.

13—15.
No man, Eëtion, honours thee though worthy of honour!
Labda conceives and will bear—a rock leaping down on the rulers.
For upon them it will fall, and Korinth thereby shall be chastened.

13, 14. Notice the play on words in the Oracle, Ἠε-τίων, and ὀλοοίτροχος 'rolling stone', alluding to Πέτρη the deme of Eetion. [The derivation of ὀλοοίτροχος is uncertain: it has been connected with εἴλω *volvo*, and ὅλος, and is written also ὀλοίτροχος or ὀλοίτροχος, see 8, 52.]

15. δικαιώσει = κολάσει, 1, 100; 3, 29.

17. τὸ μὲν πρότερον...Κόρινθον 'the oracle which had on a former occasion been given in reference to Korinth'. Sosikles speaks of it as though well known to his hearers.

18. **φέρον ἐς τὠυτό** 'to the same effect', 'of the same tendency'. Cp. *ἔχειν ἐς* p. 48, l. 6; 6, 42 *ἐς νεῖκος φέρον* 'hostile'.

19. **τὠυτὸ καί** 'the same as', cp. p. 38, l. 10.

20—23.
High on its rocky eyrie an eagle is breeding: a lion
Ravening and strong it shall bear, that the knees of many shall loosen.
Look to it well, men of Korinth, who by the fountain Peirene
Dwell, and the beetling brow of the craggy Akro-Korinthos.

20. **λέοντα**, see n. on p. 33, l. 18. 6, 131. Aristoph. Equit. 1037. There seems another play on Eetion's name in *ἀετός*.

23. **ὀφρυόεντα**. This, like the phrase ὑπὸ γούνατα λύσει, is Homeric; but it was commonly applied, according to Strabo, p. 482, to Korinth on account of the broken and rocky nature of its surrounding soil. The allusion is here to the lofty Akro-Korinthos, on which was the fountain Peirene.

§ 3.

2. **εἶχον ἐν ἡσυχίῃ** 'they said nothing', p. 55, l. 8.

3. **ὡς...τάχιστα** 'as soon as'.

10. **ἄρα** 'as it appeared', p. 77, l. 13.

12. **προσουδίσαι** 'to dash it on the ground'.

14. **καὶ τόν** = καὶ τοῦτον.

15. **ἴσχει ἀποκτεῖναι**, 'prevented him from killing the child'. Generally with μή p. 65, l. 13; and with μὴ οὐ after negative, 9, 12 οὐ δυνατοί αὐτὴν ἴσχειν εἰσὶ μὴ οὐκ ἐξιέναι.

20. **ἀλλήλων ἅπτοντο** 'began chiding each other'. Cp. 6, 69 τῇ δέ σευ μάλιστα καταπτονται οἱ ἐχθροί.

22. **ἐς ὃ δή** 'until at length', p. 50, l. 16.

χρόνου ἐγγινομένου 'some time elapsing', 'after a while', 1, 190 χρόνου ἐγγιγνομένου συχνοῦ.

§ 4.

24. **ἔδεε** 'it was fated', p. 29, l. 8.

25. **ἀναβλαστεῖν** 'should spring up', 3, 62 οὐ μή τί τοι ἔκ γε ἐκείνου νεώτερον ἀναβλάστῃ. Cp. 7, 176. The simple βλαστάνειν is a favourite word with Sophokles (of whose language there is so frequent a trace in Herodotos), but the compound ἀναβλαστάνειν is rare in other writers, and does not seem to occur in early Attic.

28. **ἐς τό**, relative, 'in what seemed to her the place least likely to be guessed'.

2. μέλλοιεν 'they were certain to', for the construction of this **58** verb with fut. infinitive, see on 8, 2.

τὰ δὴ καὶ 'which in fact actually happened'. See p. 50, l. 26.

5. τὰ ἐκεῖνοι ἐνετείλαντο, the behaviour of these men is more naturally accounted for if we suppose them not to have been members of the oligarchic families (p. 57, l. 4 σφέων αὐτῶν), but, as Nicolas of Damascus (fr. 56) tells the story, men of the guard (ὑπασπισταί).

§ 5.

9. ἐπωνυμίην, see on p. 39, l. 4. It is used here adverbially, 'by way of calling him after the chest'. Cp. 1, 14 ὑπὸ τῶν Δελφῶν καλέεται Γυγάδας ἐπὶ τοῦ ἀναθέντος ἐπωνυμίην. This box of cedar wood and adorned with figures in ivory and gold was said to be preserved in the Heraeum at Olympia. Paus. 5, 17, 2.

10. οὔνομα ἐτέθη, p. 38, l. 13.

11. ἀμφιδέξιον 'ambiguous', 'two-edged' (Eurip. Hippol. 780), that cuts both ways.

14—16.
Goodly the fate of the man who into my temple descendeth
Kypselos, son of Eëtion, the lord of glorious Korinth,
Lord—himself and his sons, but not the sons of his children.

15. Ἠετίδης, the proper patronymic of Ἠετίων is Ἠετιωνίδης, accordingly the word has been variously altered to Αἰακίδης and Αἰετίδης (see p. 56, l. 20). But Stein shows that for metrical reasons similar changes are made, e.g. of Δευκαλίων, Δευκαλίδης (Il. 12, 117), Ἀνθεμίων, Ἀνθεμίδης (Il. 4, 488).

16. παῖδες παίδων. Eëtion was succeeded by his son Periander, who left no children and was succeeded by a relative Psammetichos s. of Gorgias or Gordias (Aristot. Pol. v. 12). [Nicolas of Damascus (fr. 58) says that Psammetichos succeeded to Korkyra, and that Periander was succeeded in Korinth by another Kypselos, brother of Psammetichos.]

18. τοιοῦτος, Aristotle l.c. seems to imply on the other hand that Kypselos ruled mildly, Κύψελος δημαγωγὸς ἦν καὶ κατὰ τὴν ἀρχὴν διετέλεσεν ἀδορυφόρητος ('without a body-guard'). Nicolas fr. 56 Κύψελος δὲ Κορίνθου πράως ἦρχεν οὔτε δορυφόρους ἔχων οὔτ' ἀποθύμιος ὢν Κορινθίοις.

§ 6.

21. τριήκοντα, Kypselos reigned 30 years, Periander 44, Psammetichos 3½. Aristot. l.c.

22. **διαπλέξαντος εὖ** 'having completed in prosperity', a metaphor from weaving [4, 67 τὴν φιλύρην διαπλέκων]. Pind. Nem. 7, 99 βίοτον ἁρμόσας ἥβᾳ λιπαρῷ τε γήραϊ διαπλέκοις εὐδαίμον' ἐόντα. Cp. 4, 205 εὖ τὴν ζόην κατέπλεξε. 8, 83 καταπλέξας τὴν ῥῆσιν.

1. **ὅντινα τρόπον...τῶν πρηγμάτων**, see p. 47, l. 17. ἄν belongs to ἐπιτροπεύοι.

5. **ἅμα τε διεξήϊε...καὶ ἐκόλουε αἰεὶ** are the correlative clauses. Cp. p. 20, l. 16.

6. **ἀναποδίζων** 'questioning him again'. Aesch. in Ctes. § 192 πολλάκις ἀνεπόδιζον τὸν γραμματέα καὶ ἐκέλευον πάλιν ἀναγιγνώσκειν τοὺς νόμους. Pollux 2, 196 ἀναποδιζόμενα τὰ πάλιν ἐξεταζόμενα. In 4, 116 ἀνεπόδισε ἑωυτὸν appears to mean 'went back upon himself', 'contradicted himself'.

7. **καὶ ἐκόλουε αἰεὶ, ὅκως...ὑπερέχοντα** 'and he kept knocking off the ears of corn whenever he saw any one standing out above the rest'. For **κολούειν** cp. 7, 10 § 5 φιλέει ὁ θεὸς τὰ ὑπερέχοντα κολούειν. For **ὅκως** frequentative see p. 36, l. 21. A similar tale found its way into Roman legends, see Livy 1, 54. According to Aristotle (Pol. 3, 8) Thrasybulus sent the message and Periander gave the answer in this way.

10. **ὑποθέμενος ἔπος οὐδὲν** 'without having made any suggestion', or, 'without having added any remark'. 1, 156 Κροῖσος ταῦτά οἱ ὑπετίθετο.

14. **θωυμάζειν τε αὐτοῦ** 'and he wondered at him' (Periander). θωυμάζειν is often followed by the genitive of the person whose conduct creates the wonder, the actual thing wondered at being in the accusative or expressed by a clause, e.g. Plat. Apol. 1, 4 μάλιστα δὲ αὐτῶν ἐν ἐθαύμασα τῶν πολλῶν ὧν ἐψεύσαντο.

16. **σινάμωρον** 'destructive of' (σίνομαι), from which Herod. has the verb σιναμωρέειν (1, 152; 8, 35).

17. **πρὸς Θρασυβούλου** 'done by Thrasybulus'.

§ 7.

18. **νόῳ σχὼν** 'having grasped'. The phrase νόῳ ἔχειν is usually employed by Herod. to mean 'to intend', see 6, 44; 8, 7, 8; 9, 11, 52. Here it is equivalent to νόῳ λαβὼν p. 54, l. 11.

20. **ἐνθαῦτα δὴ** 'thereupon', 'it was in these circumstances that'. p. 30, l. 23; p. 36, l. 11; p. 45, l. 20. **πᾶσαν κακότητα** 'utter wickedness', *summam malitiam*.

21. **ὅσα** sc. κακά.

26. ἐπὶ τὸ νεκυομαντήϊον 'to the oracle where the dead are consulted'. The spirits of the dead were called up and consulted, as in the case of Saul and the witch of Endor; cp. Plut. Cim. c. 6. Pausan. 9, 30, 6 ἄλλοις δὲ εἰρημένον ἐστι ὡς προαποθανούσης οἱ ('Ορφεῖ) τῆς γυναικὸς ἐπὶ τὸ Ἄορνον δι' αὐτὴν τὸ ἐν τῇ Θεσπρωτίδι ἀφίκετο· εἶναι γὰρ πάλαι νεκυομαντεῖον αὐτόθι· νομίζοντα δέ οἱ ἕπεσθαι τῆς Εὐριδίκης τὴν ψυχήν κ.τ.λ.

παρακαταθήκης πέρι ξεινικῆς 'about a deposit entrusted to him by some friend', which he had apparently mislaid. For a consultation of an oracle in regard to such a trust cp. the case in 6, 86.

1. οὐ κατακαυθέντων 'because they had not been burnt'. It is curious that clothes should be buried with an urn after a body had been burnt. Baehr thinks that the story is an exaggerated version of what Periander did, who only obliged the women solemnly to mourn Melissa, and burn some of their clothes on a funeral pile.

16. τοιοῦτο...τυραννίς, see on p. 55, l. 15.

18. θῶυμα μέγα εἶχε, cp. 8, 135 ἐν θώυματι ἔχεσθαι ἀκούοντας.

21. ἐπικαλεόμενοι ὑμῖν. Cp. 3, 65 θεοὺς τοὺς βασιληίους ἐπικαλέων ὑμῖν.

22. οὐκ ὦν παύσεσθε 'if you will not desist', a vivid future in the place of the usual protasis, and an imperative for the apodosis. Cp. 4, 118 οὐκ ὦν ποιήσετε ταῦτα· ἡμεῖς μὲν πιεζόμενοι ἢ ἐκλείψομεν τὴν χώρην ἢ μένοντες ὁμολογίῃ χρησόμεθα. The converse is more common, i.e. the imperative for a protasis, and the future in the apodosis, as Hom. Il. 23, 71 θάπτε με ὅττι τάχιστα, πύλας Ἀΐδαο περήσω. Plato Crit. 48 ἀντίλεγε, καί σοι πείσομαι. Donald. Gr. Gr. § 520.

23. κατάγοντες, p. 17, l. 28.

CHAPTER XCIII.

27. ἐπικαλέσας, cp. l. 21 ἐπικαλεόμενος. There seems very little difference, if any, in the meaning of the two words; both imply invoking the gods as an appeal to the person indicated by the dative.

1. ἡμέραι αἱ κύριαι 'the days appointed' (by fate). Cp. p. 30, l. 2.

2. τοὺς χρησμούς, those kept in the Erechtheium. See c. 90.

4. εἶχον ἐν ἡσυχίῃ, p. 57, l. 2.

6. φωνὴν ῥήξας 'breaking silence'. 2, 2 ἥντινα φωνὴν ῥήξουσι πρώτην. Cp. Lat. *rumpere vocem* (Verg. Aen. 2, 129).

αἱρέετο 'expressed his preference for'.

8. **μηδὲν νεώτερον** 'anything revolutionary', or simply 'any violence', p. 10, l. 19. **περὶ πόλιν Ἑλλάδα**, cp. Ἑλλὰς γλῶσσα 6, 98; 9, 16.

CHAPTER XCIV.

10. **ἐδίδου** 'offered to give'.

12. **αἱρέετο** 'was willing to accept', notice the imperfect as compared with the aorist (εἷλε) immediately afterwards.

15. **νόθος**, a boy born of a foreign mother was νόθος, even though his parents were married. See Plutarch Them. c. 1.

19. **χρόνον ἐπὶ συχνὸν** 'during a considerable period', cp. 9, 8 ἐπὶ δέκα ἡμέρας. 9, 62 χρόνον ἐπὶ πολλόν. p. 15, l. 21.

21. **λόγῳ**, p. 49, l. 28.

22. **οὐδὲν μᾶλλον...ἢ οὐ** 'no more share than themselves and the rest'. The latter negative cannot be used in the English equivalent, any more than the double comparative (πλουσιώτερος ἢ σοφώτερος) used in Greek in both clauses; similarly the Greek idiom admits of a negative in both. Cp. 4, 118 ἥκει γὰρ ὁ Πέρσης οὐδέν τι μᾶλλον ἐπ' ἡμέας ἢ οὐ καὶ ἐπ' ὑμέας.

23. **συνεπρήξαντο** 'joined in exacting vengeance for'. 7, 169 συνεξεπρήξαντο αὐτῷ τὸν ἐν Καμίκῳ θάνατον γενόμενον. The plural **ἁρπαγάς** is poetical.

CHAPTER XCV.

28. **φεύγων ἐκφεύγει** 'joining in the flight effected his escape'. Cp. 4, 23 ὃς ἂν φεύγων καταφύγῃ. 6, 30 ἀνήχθη ἀγόμενος. See also p. 24, l. 25; p. 29, l. 2. **τὰ ὅπλα**, shield and spear which he had thrown away to facilitate his flight.

1. **ἀνεκρέμασαν**, p. 46, l. 10.

2. **ἐν μέλεϊ ποιήσας** 'having related in an ode'. What looks like the beginning of this Ode is given in Strabo XIII. 1, 38, but it is so corrupt as not to be worth quoting. It was perhaps in imitation of this ode that Horace commemorated his own disaster at Philippi, where he fled *relicta non bene parmula* (Odes 2, 7, 9; 3, 4, 26).

3. **ἐπιτιθεῖ** 'he posted it to Mytilene', the verb seems to mean 'he gave it (to some letter-carrier) to take'. Cp. 3, 42 γράφει ἐς βιβλίον πάντα, γράψας δὲ ἐς Αἴγυπτον ἐπέθηκε.

5. **κατήλλαξε Περίανδρος.** That Periander should have been selected as an arbitrator in the quarrel shows some confidence in his character. The reputation of a tyrannus fared generally very ill in all literature, and we must be on our guard against taking all the abuse as well-grounded.

7. **ὧδε** 'on the following terms', 'by a decision to the following effect'.

νέμεσθαι, p. 26, l. 20, 'should possess'.

CHAPTER XCVI.

10. **πᾶν χρῆμα ἐκίνεε** 'began doing all he possibly could', 'began moving heaven and earth'.

15. **οὐκ ἐῶντες** 'dissuading', 'protesting against the Persians giving credit to the exiles from Athens'.

16. **ἐκέλευε...Ἱππίην.** It was the policy of the Persian court at present to support absolute government in the Greek States; when that policy was reversed, Artaphernes was recalled. See 6, 43.

18. **οὐκ ὦν δή...Ἀθηναῖοι** 'the Athenians however absolutely refused to admit the proposal'. **οὐκ ὦν,** p. 60, l. 22.

19. **ἐδέδοκτο** 'the resolution was at once come to'. **ἐκ τοῦ φανεροῦ,** cp. p. 22, l. 15.

CHAPTER XCVII.

21. **διαβεβλημένοισι** 'rendered hostile', 'embittered with the Persians', not as at p. 20, l. 18, 'rendered objects of suspicion to' (in spite of Schweighäuser). Cp. Thucyd. 8, 83, 1 οἱ δὲ Πελοποννήσιοι... καὶ πρότερον τῷ Τισσαφέρνει ἀπιστοῦντες, πολλῷ δὴ μᾶλλον ἔτι διεβέβληντο. id. 8, 81, 2 ἵνα...οἱ πολέμιοι τῷ Τισσαφέρνει ὡς μάλιστα διαβάλλοιντο.

25. **τῶν λοιπέων** i.e. of all besides Sparta.

2. **ταὐτὰ τὰ...Σπάρτῃ.** See c. 49.

4. **ἀσπίδα,** the Persian archers had γέρρα at Plataea, long wickerwork shields, but they were not used like Greek shields, i.e. held in the hand during a personal encounter, but stuck in the ground for a fence, behind which the archers shot. See 9, 61. **νομίζουσι** 'habitually employ'.

7. **ἄποικοι.** The tradition that the Ionian settlers in Miletos

(which was inhabited by Karians before) had gone from Athens, led by Neleus son of Kodros, is referred to again in 9, 97.

10. **διαβάλλειν** 'to delude', p. 30, l. 6; p. 69, l. 21.

12. **τρεῖs μυριάδαs**. It is not easy to feel sure that the number of full Athenian citizens at this time would be as great as 30,000, which would imply free inhabitants numbering not less than 120,000. In 8, 65 in the case of the *τρισμύριοι* who are said to be attending the ceremonies at Eleusis, the word perhaps stands vaguely for any large number. However in Thucyd. 2, 13, 6 the number actually on duty is said to be 29,000 (B.C. 431) which would indicate a still larger number of capable citizens; and in Aristoph. Eccl. 1132 we have *πολιτῶν πλεῖον ὄντων ἢ τρισμυρίων* which may be again a vague expression for a larger number. Still the recurrence of this number seems to indicate that it was regarded roughly as the number of the citizens.

15. **ἀποδέξαντες...εἶναι**, p. 14, l. 21.

17. **ἀρχὴ κακῶν**. Cobet from Homer Il. 5, 62 *ὅs καὶ Ἀλεξάνδρῳ τεκτήνατο νῆας ἐίσας | ἀρχεκάκους, αἳ πᾶσι κακὸν Τρώεσσι γένοντο*, and Plut. Malign. 24 *ἀρχεκάκους τολμήσας προσειπεῖν*, would read here *ἀρχέκακοι*. Anyhow we must be careful to translate '*a* beginning of evils', not '*the* beginning', for the Ionian Hellenes were already at feud with and had suffered from the Persians.

CHAPTER XCVIII.

21. **τούτου εἵνεκεν** sc. to benefit the Ionians.

23. **ἐπὶ τοὺs Παίοναs...γενομένους**, see cc. 12—15.

25. **ἐπ' ἑωυτῶν** 'to themselves', i.e. unmixed with native Phrygians. For *ἐπί* with genitive indicating connexion with a thing or person as distinct from all else cp. 9, 17, 38; 8, 32. Thucyd. 2, 63, 3 *ἐπὶ σφῶν αὐτῶν αὐτόνομοι οἰκεῖν*. Cp. p. 68, l. 4.

27. **ὁ Μιλήτου τύραννος**. See on p. 22, l. 17. It is surprising that Aristagoras after professing to have laid down his supreme power should be here made to describe himself as 'tyrannus', although he no doubt retained the reality of power, and Herodotos still calls him by the title. p. 28, l. 2.

3. **παρέχει = ἔξεστι**. Cp. p. 29, l. 24.

4. **τὸ ἀπὸ τούτου**, p. 49, l. 10.

6. **ἀσπαστὸν ἐποιήσαντο** 'regarded it as welcome', p. 36, l. 28.

7. ἀπεδίδρησκον 'began to make their escape'. The word usually employed for runaway slaves, for the Paeonians are now servants of the great king.

14. ὅκως ἄν...ἀπέλθοιεν 'in order that the Paeonians should quit the island and return'. Cp. ὡς ἂν p. 22, l. 18. See on 9, 51. The ὅκως is properly modal, 'they send a demand of such a kind that, if they obeyed it, the Paeonians would quit the island'. See Goodw. *M. and T.* (ed. 1889) § 350. Herod. 1, 9; 2, 126; 3, 44.

CHAPTER XCIX.

21. οὐ τὴν Ἀθηναίων χάριν 'not for the sake of the Athenians'. For the article in this adverbial phrase, cp. Soph. Phil. 1413 τὴν σὴν ἥκω χάριν.

24. τὸν πρὸς Χαλκιδέας πόλεμον. This war was of ancient and uncertain date (about the 8th century B.C.), and is noticed by Thucydides (1, 15) as the earliest conspicuous instance in which other Greeks ranged themselves respectively on one side or the other in a contest between two powerful towns. The importance of Eretria and Chalkis was naval and commercial, and naturally at this early time the other portions of Hellas affected are the Islands and the Ionians, both Samos and Miletos being powerful naval states.

26. οὗτοι ὦν, repeating the subject after the parentheses. οὗτοι are the Athenians and Eretrians.

28. ἐποιέετο 'set about despatching'. For the force of the middle, see p. 16, l. 5. Ἀρισταγόρης repeats the subject again from l. 19.

αὐτὸς μὲν δὴ 'the truth is, he did not go on the expedition himself'. The reason apparently was that the Persian forces were already threatening, if not actually besieging Miletos on the land side (Plut. Malign. 24).

2. ἀπέδεξε εἶναι, p. 63, l. 15.

CHAPTER C.

5. πλοῖα 'transports'.

7. ποιεύμενοι...ἡγεμόνας 'adopting as leaders', 'following the lead of'.

11. τὴν ἀκρόπολιν. The akropolis of Sardis, only to be ascended by one very precipitous path (1, 84), was a high isolated rock, and was

regarded as all but impregnable by the means of attack then in use; it was therefore an important place for the Ionians to seize as commanding all Asia Minor. ἐρρύετο 'was defending'.

CHAPTER CI.

13. **τὸ δὲ μὴ ληλατῆσαι...ἔσχε τόδε** 'but what prevented them from plundering the city though they took it was this'. For construction see on p. 57, l. 15. Ab. quotes Thucyd. 3, 1 καὶ τὸν πλεῖστον ὅμιλον τῶν ψιλῶν εἶργον τὸ μὴ τὰ ἐγγὺς τῆς πόλεως κακουργεῖν.

18. **ἐπενέμετο** 'spread itself over', lit. 'pastured upon'. Polyb. 14, 5, 7 τό τε γὰρ πῦρ ταχέως ἐπενέμετο καὶ περιελάμβανε πάντας τοὺς τόπους.

20. **ὥστε** = ὡς or ἅτε, p. 20, l. 26; p. 49, l. 13.

21. **τὰ περιέσχατα** 'the suburbs'. Cp. 1, 86 τῆς πυρῆς ἤδη ἀμμένης καίεσθαι τὰ περιέσχατα.

23. **ψῆγμα χρυσοῦ** 'gold dust'. If this gold dust was ever found in the deposit of the Pactolus, it had ceased to be so when Strabo wrote, i.e. about 20 B.C.

CHAPTER CII.

3. **ἐν δὲ αὐτῇσι** 'and among them'. Herodotos particularises the temple of Kybebe, first because it was large and famous, and secondly because it was not actually in the town, and might therefore have escaped.

4. **τὸ σκηπτόμενοι**, see 6, 101 οἱ δὲ ἐσελθόντες ἐς τὴν πόλιν (Eretria) τοῦτο μὲν τὰ ἱρὰ συλήσαντες ἐνέπρησαν, ἀποτινύμενοι τῶν ἐν Σάρδισι κατακαυθέντων ἱρῶν, τοῦτο δὲ... For other instances of such destruction see 8, 31. Subsequently Mardonios offered to restore those that belonged to the Athenians, at any rate, if they would accept his terms. 8, 140.

7. **νομούς**, p. 55, l. 12.

9. **κως** 'as it happened', p. 24, l. 11.

10. **κατὰ στίβον** 'on their track'. Cp. κατὰ πόδας p. 64, l. 11.

11. **ἐν Ἐφέσῳ** must mean in the territory of Ephesos, hardly in the town itself.

15. **στεφανηφόρους ἀγῶνας** 'victories in the games in which the prizes were wreaths'. Cp. Aesch. in Ctes. § 174 εἰς τὰ Ὀλύμπια ἢ εἰς ἄλλον τινὰ τῶν στεφανιτῶν ἀγώνων. The winners in the four great

games were thus crowned (ἆθλα δὲ τῶν κότινος, μῆλα, σέλινα, πίτυς). The victors were often also rewarded richly by their own states, who felt themselves honoured by their success, but such rewards had nothing to do with the prizes actually given (Dem. Lept. § 141). For ἀναραιρηκότα cp. 9, 33 ἀναιρησόμενος γυμνικοὺς ἀγῶνας. 6, 70 Ὀλυμπιάδα ἀνελόμενος τεθρίππῳ.

16. πολλὰ αἰνεθέντα 'much' or 'often praised', that is, in some of the epinikian odes of Simonides.

17. ἀνὰ τὰς πόλιας 'into their several cities'.

CHAPTER CIII.

19. μετὰ δέ, p. 15, l. 15.

21. πολλά 'urgently'. So 9, 91 πολλὸς ἦν λισσόμενος. 3, 46 ἔλεγον πολλὰ ὡς κάρτα δεόμενος.

22. τιμωρήσειν 'assist', cp. 1, 141 τιμωρέειν τοῖς Ἴωσι. 7, 169 τιμωρέουσι τῇ Ἑλλάδι.

23. οὕτω γάρ σφι ὑπῆρχε is explained by the next clause, γὰρ being, as often, anticipatory, see p. 2, l. 17. 'They had so committed themselves by their acts of hostility towards the king, that they (in spite of their loss of allies) prepared to go on with the war'. ὑπῆρχε means 'there was to their (dis)credit', 'they had such acts of violence already committed to start from'. So in 7, 11 τὰ ὑπαργμένα ἐξ ἐκείνων means 'the deeds already committed by them'.

25. ἐσκευάζοντο 'they proceeded with their preparations'.

1. ἐς τὸν Ἑλλήσποντον in its widest sense, including the Propontis and Bosporus (St.). 67

2. ταύτῃ 'in that direction'.

3. ἐκπλώσαντές τε ἔξω τὸν Ἑλλήσποντον 'and having sailed back out of the Hellespont'. ἔξω 'in an outward direction' is a repetition of the ἐκ in ἐκπλώσαντες, which governs the accusative, as ἐξῆλθον τὴν Περσίδα γῆν (7, 29). Cp. l. 17. 7, 58 ὁ δὲ ναυτικὸς ἔξω τὸν Ἑλλήσποντον πλώων... Apoll. Rhod. 2, 646 ἀλλ' ὅτε πέτρας Πληγάδας ἐξέπλωμεν.

CHAPTER CIV.

10. οὗτοι sc. οἱ Κύπριοι.

15. ἐπικείμενος 'pressing him hard', p. 48, l. 8.

16. ἐνῆγε 'tried to induce him', p. 54, l. 1. ἐνθαῦτα, p. 36, l. 11.

17. ἐξελθόντα, see above, l. 3.

20—22. ἀνέπειθε...ἀνέπεισε, the imperfect of the attempt, the aorist of the successful act, see on 6, 5.

CHAPTER CV.

68 1. τῆς συλλογῆς, the collection of forces, i.e. of the Athenians, Eretrians, and Ionians. ὥστε, p. 55, l. 18. συνυφανθῆναι 'devised', 'woven together', cp. Hom. Od. 13, 303 ἵνα τοι σὺν μῆτιν ὑφαίνω.

3. Ἰώνων......ποιησάμενον 'without taking any account of the Ionians'. Cp. 9, 7 καὶ δὴ λόγον οὐδένα τῶν Ἀθηναίων ποιέεσθε. The aorist is used because it is not meant to express the king's attitude generally, but his action at the moment. He did not show any interest in the question of the Ionians, but at once asked questions about the Athenians.

4. οὐ καταπροΐξονται 'that they would not finally escape with impunity'. Cp. 3, 156 οὐ γὰρ ἐμέ γε ὧδε λωβησάμενος καταπροΐξεται. So also 3, 36; 7, 17. [This future is the only tense in use. Veitch supposes a present προΐσσομαι. In Attic it is only found in comedy. See Arist. Eq. 435; Nub. 1240; Vesp. 1366, 1396; Thesm. 566. Its origin is doubtful. It ought perhaps to be written καταπροΐξεται without the signs of diaeresis. See Rutherford, *New Phrynichus*, p. 254.]

8. μιν i.e. the arrow. The king shoots the arrow into the air, for the Persian religion personified the heaven as their supreme deity, τὸν κύκλον πάντα τοῦ οὐρανοῦ Δία καλέοντες 1, 131.

ὦ Ζεῦ. The Greeks represent the supreme god of all religions by Ζεύς. The Persian name was Ormuzd.

9. ἐκγενέσθαι 'may it be my lot', 'grant me'. Cp. Hom. Odyss. 17, 354 Ζεῦ ἄνα, Τηλέμαχόν μοι ἐν ἀνδράσιν ὄλβιον εἶναι, καὶ οἱ πάντα γένοιθ' ὅσσα φρεσὶν ᾗσι μενοινᾷ. Aesch. S. c. Th. 253 θεοὶ πολῖται, μή με δουλείας τυχεῖν. Goodw. *M. and T.*, § 785 (ed. 1889).

11. ἐς τρὶς, cp. 1, 86.

CHAPTER CVI.

14. κατεῖχε, c. 24.

16. νεώτερα, p. 10, l. 19.

23. ἐξ ὑστέρης, cp. 6, 85 ὅκως ἐξ ὑστέρης μή τι ..κακὸν ἐς τὴν χώρην ἐσβάλωσι. Cp. ἐκ νέης, p. 73, l. 26. σεωυτὸν ἐν αἰτίῃ σχῇς 'lest you

get into trouble', 'lest you find yourself blamed'. Cp. 8, 99 Μαρδόνιον ἐν αἰτίῃ τιθέντες.

25. **κοῖον ἐφθέγξαο** Homeric. ποῖόν σε ἔπος φύγεν ἕρκος ὀδόντων.

26. **ἀνασχήσειν** 'to happen'. Cp. 7, 14 τάδε τοι ἐξ αὐτέων ἀνασχήσειν.

27. **ἐπιδιζήμενος** 'seeking more', i.e. than I have got at present. For this meaning of δίζησθαι, see p. 55, l. 20. In 1, 95 ἐπιδίζηται means to 'inquire', or 'examine further'.

1. **πάρα**=πάρεστι, p. 35, l. 21. **πάντων...ἀξιεῦμαι** 'and am counted worthy by you to listen to all your counsels', i.e. I am admitted to your confidence. For **ἀξιεῦμαι** cp. 9, 111 μέγα ποιεῦμαι ἀξιεύμενος θυγατρὸς τῆς σῆς.

4. **ἐπ' ἑωυτοῦ βαλλόμενον** 'on his own account', 'by himself', i.e. without consultation with me. Cp. p. 63, l. 25; p. 43, l. 28. 3, 155; 4, 168. The meaning of βάλλεσθαι in this phrase is to 'turn over in the mind'. Cp. 8, 68 τόδε ἐς θυμὸν βάλευ.

5. **ἀρχὴν δὲ...οὐδὲ ἐνδέκομαι** 'but to begin with I don't even admit the story'. This is the proper meaning of ἀρχήν, but sometimes it may be translated 'at all', as in 1, 193 τὰ γὰρ ἄλλα δένδρεα οὐδὲ πειρᾶται ἀρχὴν φέρειν. Sometimes Herod. uses the definite article, 4, 28 τὸν χειμῶνα τοῦτον οὐκ ἀνέχονται τὴν ἀρχήν. It is generally used in a negative sentence, but occasionally without a negative, as in 1, 9; 8, 132.

6. **ὅκως**=ὡς, p. 53, l. 14.

7. **ἄρα** 'really', 'after all', p. 77, l. 13.

8. **τὸ ἐόν**, p. 30, l. 7.

10. **ἀνάσπαστον**, p. 5, l. 23.

12. **ἄν...ὑπεκίνησε** 'would have stirred', intransitive, and of a *slight* movement, as in Arist. Ran. 664 σκόπει νυν ἢν μ' ὑποκινήσαντ' ἴδῃς 'flinch'.

14. **ἵνα...καταρτίσω** 'that I may restore all these things to their old order'. Cp. p. 15, l. 23. ἐκεῖνα πάντα sc. πράγματα.

16. **ἐγχειρίθετον** 'into your hands', an ἅπαξ λεγόμενον, but we have had ἐγχειρίζειν p. 42, l. 18.

18. **μὴ πρότερον ἐκδύσεσθαι...κιθῶνα** 'that I will not put off the tunic in which I shall descend to Ionia, until I have made Sardinia, the greatest of islands, tributary to you'. Cp. 8, 120 καὶ ὡς αὐτοὶ λέγουσι Ἀβδηρῖται...πρῶτον Ξέρξης ἐλύσατο τὴν ζώνην φεύγων ἐξ Ἀθηνέων ὀπίσω.

19. For **καταβήσομαι** see on p. 30, l. 9. For **νῆσον μεγίστην** cp. 1, 170 Σαρδώ...νήσων ἁπασέων μεγίστην νεμομένους.

Colonization in the west—in Sicily, Italy, and Sardinia,—was the El Dorado of the Greeks, and reports of the wealth and size of Sardinia made it a favourite subject of speculation. See c. 124.

CHAPTER CVII.

21. διέβαλε, p. 30, l. 6; p. 63, l. 10. The aorist seems to me better than the imperfect, which is written by some, 'he succeeded in deceiving'. See on p. 67, l. 21.

22. ἐπεάν...ποιήσῃ 'as soon as he had accomplished'.

CHAPTER CVIII.

28. μεμετιμένος 'having been let go'. Cp. 6, 1 (=μεθειμένος).

ἐπὶ θάλασσαν i.e. to the maritime district of the Ionians, and the Islands; as in l. 9.

70   1. πολιορκέοντι, see c. 104.

4. ἐς, see p. 6, l. 5.

6. οὐκ ἐς μακρὴν βουλευσάμενοι 'without long deliberation', 'promptly'. Cp. 2, 121, § 1 τοὺς δὲ παῖδας αὐτοῦ οὐκ ἐς μακρὴν ἔργου ἔχεσθαι.

8. παρῆσαν ἐς 'arrived at', cp. p. 42, l. 14.

10. τὴν ἄκρην the promontory on the N. W. of Kypros, Anthol. Pal. 7, 738 κληῖδες πόντου καὶ ἐσχατιαὶ Σαλαμῖνος (Baehr).

CHAPTER CIX.

12. οἱ τύραννοι τῆς Κύπρου, that is, the Tyrants of the nine towns in Kypros, Salamis, Kition, Amathus, Kurion, Marion, Soloi, Lapēthos, Keryneia, Chytros. See 7, 90.

15. προσφέρεσθαι 'to be opposed to', 'to face', cp. p. 20, l. 8.

17. διαπειρᾶσθαι 'to attack', as πειρᾶσθαι p. 47, l. 26. 1, 68 ὅκως πειρῷατο ἀλλήλων. The compound is only a strengthened form 'to test thoroughly', 6, 128. ὥρη 'time', cp. 3, 85 ὥρη μηχανᾶσθαι καὶ μὴ ἀναβάλλεσθαι.

18. ἐκβάντας, the participle is attracted into the accusative case by the infinitive τάσσεσθαι. Cp. 6, 22 τοῖσί τι ἔχουσι...ἐδόκεε...ἐς ἀποικίην ἐκπλώειν μηδὲ μένοντας δουλεύειν. ib. 103 αὐτῷ φεύγοντι συνέβη Ὀλυμπιάδα ἀνελέσθαι...καὶ ταύτην τὴν νίκην ἀνελόμενόν μιν... ἐξενείκασθαι...

21. ποιέειν...ὅκως...ἔσται 'to secure the freedom of Kypros'. The future indicative in a consecutive clause introduced by ὅκως, 'act in such a way that Kypros shall be free'. Cp. 7, 18 ποίεε δὲ οὕτω ὅκως τῶν σῶν ἐνδεήσει μηδέν. 1, 8 ποίεε ὅκως ἐκείνην θηήσεαι γυμνήν. Goodw., *M. and T.* § 578 (ed. 1889).

22. τὸ κατ' ὑμέας 'as far as in you lies', 7, 158.

24. τὸ κοινὸν τῶν Ἰώνων 'the community of the Ionians',—this community was originally only a union for religious purposes though the ideas of political and religious union were not sharply separated in these times, but the Ionian states were now for a time acting in what was really political union, see 6, 10—12. The expression is used for a state as τὸ κοινὸν τῶν Σαμίων 6, 14; Σπαρτιητέων τὸ κοινὸν 6, 50, 58.

28. πειρησόμεθα εἶναι, p. 42, l. 17. χρηστοί 'brave'.

CHAPTER CX.

3. μετὰ δέ, p. 15, l. 15.
4. οἱ βασιλέες, p. 70, l. 13.
7. ἀπολέξαντες τὸ ἄριστον sc. τοῦ στρατοῦ 'having selected the flower of their army'.

CHAPTER CXI.

10. ἤλαυνε 'was riding'. See on 6, 62.
12. γάρ, p. 2, l. 17.
13. Κάρ a Karian mercenary. The Karians were universally employed in this way; and the explanation that follows, that he was also a man of courage, is a commentary on the low estimation proverbially attaching to Karians. See Biographical Index, s.v. *Karian*.

καὶ ἄλλως 'and in other respects', 'and besides', cp. 1, 60 γυνὴ... μέγαθος ἀπὸ τεσσέρων πηχέων ἀπολείπουσα τρεῖς δακτύλους καὶ ἄλλως εὐειδής. p. 4, l. 6.

14. λήματος, p. 43, l. 12.
16. κατεργάζεσθαι 'fights', 'tries to destroy' (his enemy).
18. φυλάξας 'having waited for', p. 71, l. 18; p. 6, l. 4.
19. ὁ ὀπέων 'the attendant', 'the squire', see 9, 50. Thus in the Iliad 8, 263 Meriones is squire (ὀπάων) to Idomeneus.
20, 21. καὶ...καὶ 'both or either'.

καὶ πάντως 'and, in a word, whatever you order me to do'.

27. **ὑπ' ἀξιόχρεω**, proverbial, cp. Arist. Ran. 735
χρῆσθε τοῖς χρηστοῖσιν αὖθις· καὶ κατωρθώσασι γὰρ
εὔλογον· κἄν τι σφαλῆτ', ἐξ ἀξίου γοῦν τοῦ ξύλου
ἤν τι πάσχητε, πάσχειν τοῖς σοφοῖς δοκήσετε.

Baehr quotes Verg. Aen. 10, 830 *hoc tamen infelix miseram solabere mortem: Aeneae magni dextra cadis.*

1. **τὰς μηχανὰς** 'his tricks'.

CHAPTER CXII.

6. **ἄκροι** 'eminent', 'supremely good'. Cp. 6, 122 ἀνὴρ ἄκρος ἐλευθερῶν τὴν πατρίδα. p. 77, l. 8.

8. **συνῆλθον...συμπεσόντα ἐμάχοντο.** The plural verb with the neuter noun which implies living persons. Cp. 4, 149 οὐ γὰρ ὑπέμειναν τὰ τέκνα. Thucyd. 7, 58. Hadley *Gr. Gr.* § 604.

12. **κατὰ** = καθ' ἅ, p. 5, l. 19.

15. **δρεπάνῳ** 'with a reaping-hook': a weapon which the Karians seem to have generally used. In the fleet of Xerxes they carry δρέπανα καὶ ἐγχειρίδια (7, 93) Stein.

17. **αὐτοῦ ταύτῃ** 'on the spot', so αὐτοῦ τῇδε p. 10, l. 17.

CHAPTER CXIII.

19. **τύραννος**, as in p. 70, l. 13; but βασιλεὺς p. 67, l. 11; p. 71, l. 5. **προδιδοῖ** 'plays the traitor', 'deserts', without an object as in 6, 15 ὁρέοντες τοὺς πολλοὺς τῶν συμμάχων προδιδόντας. 3, 45 ἦν ἄρα προδιδῶσι οὗτοι πρὸς τοὺς κατιόντας.

23. **ἐποίεον**, see l. 8.

24. **κατυπέρτεροι**, cp. 1, 67 κατυπέρτεροι τῷ πολέμῳ ἐγεγόνεσαν.

26. **καὶ δὴ καί**, p. 11, l. 15; p. 15, l. 20; p. 40, l. 12.

2. **τὸν Σόλων...αἴνεσε** 'whom Solon the Athenian, when he visited Kypros, praised in a poem above all tyrants'. According to the story in Plutarch (Sol. 26) in the course of his ten years' travel, after settling the constitution of Athens, Solon visited Kypros from Egypt, and there being received with special kindness by Philokypros, he advised him to remove his town from its unfavourable position to a better, and himself assisted in the new arrangement. He addressed the king in Elegiacs.

νῦν δὲ σὺ μὲν Σολίοισι πολὺν χρόνον ἐνθάδ' ἀνάσσων
τήνδε πόλιν ναίοις καὶ γένος ὑμέτερον·

αὐτὰρ ἐμὲ ξὺν νηὶ θοῇ κλεινῆς ἀπὸ νήσου
ἀσκηθῆ πέμποι Κύπρις ἰοστέφανος·
οἰκισμῷ δ' ἐπὶ τῷδε χάριν καὶ κῦδος ὀπάζοι
ἐσθλὸν καὶ νόστον πατρίδ' ἐς ἡμετέρην.

CHAPTER CXIV.

6. **ἐπολιόρκησε**, see c. 104.
7. **ἀνεκρέμασαν** 'hung it on a gibbet above the gates'. Compare the treatment of the body of Leonidas 7, 238; and of Polycrates 3, 125.
11. **γὰρ**, p. 2, l. 17.
12. **θύειν ὡς ἥρωϊ**, see on p. 27, l. 21.
13. **ἄμεινον συνοίσεσθαι**, p. 48, l. 19.

CHAPTER CXV.

15. **καὶ τὸ μέχρι ἐμεῦ** 'even up to my time'. Cp. 6, 119 οἳ καὶ μέχρι ἐμέο εἶχον τὴν χώρην ταύτην. Cp. p. 52, l. 21.
21. **αὐτίκα οἱ μαθόντες Ἴωνες ταῦτα**, the subject repeated after a long intermediate sentence, as at p. 54, l. 14.
23. **χρόνον ἐπὶ πλεῖστον**, p. 15, l. 21.

CHAPTER CXVI.

26. **ἐκ νέης** 'afresh', cp. ἐξ ὑστέρης p. 68, l. 23.
4. **ἐσαράξαντες** 'having driven them into their ships', cp. 4, 128 οἱ δὲ Σκύθαι ἐσαράξαντες τὴν ἵππον (ἐς τὸν πεζόν).
6. **ἐπιδιελόμενοι** 'having distributed among themselves', i.e. each undertaking the reduction of certain cities.

CHAPTER CXVII.

10. **ἐπ' ἡμέρης ἑκάστην αἱρέε** 'he took each within the space of a day'. With the genitive of the time within which ἐπὶ generally has some proper name such as ἐπὶ Κύρου βασιλεύοντος and the like, or a word which by itself is not temporal as ἐπὶ τοῦ προτέρου πολέμου (Thucyd. 6, 6). Still it is different from ἐπ' ἡμέρῃ ἑκάστῃ in p. 32, l. 24, where a daily journey (lasting the whole day) is being described; here the prominent point is that the action was a day's work and no more. Stein however reads ἡμέρῃ.

CHAPTER CXVIII.

15. **καί κως** 'and by some means or another'.

16. **πρὶν ἤ** "For πρὶν the poets, Herodot., and sometimes Attic prose writers, use πρὶν ἤ". Madv. 167 R. For πρότερον πρὶν ἤ cp. 9, 93 οὐ πρότερόν τε παύσεσθαι τιμωρέοντες ἐκείνῳ πρὶν ἢ δίκας δῶσι.

21. **ἄλλαι τε...ἐμοί** 'and among many plans suggested there, there was one which appears to me quite excellent, namely that of Pixodarus'.

24. **ἡ γνώμη ἔφερε** 'his opinion was to the effect that', followed by a sentence with infinitive, as in 3, 133; 4, 90; 6, 42; 8, 100. Cp. p. 77, l. 19.

26. **οὕτω** 'when so situated', p. 31, l. 14.

28. **ἔτι ἀμείνονες τῆς φύσιος** 'still braver than they naturally would be': equivalent to ἀμείνονες ἑωυτῶν. See on p. 71, l. 13. And cp. 7, 103 παρὰ τὴν ἑωυτῶν φύσιν ἀμείνονες.

75 1. **ἐνίκα** See on p. 22, l. 5. **ἀλλὰ τοῖσι Πέρσῃσι...γίνεσθαι** sc. ἐνίκα 'but they resolved that the Persians should have the Maeander on their rear'.

3. **δηλαδή** 'because as they put it', intimating that the reason was not in the writer's opinion a good one. Cp. 6, 39; 4, 135. δή = δῆθεν.

5. **ἐσπίπτοντες** 'because they would be driven into the river'. Here, as in ἐκπίπτειν p. 43, l. 9, πίπτειν is equivalent to the passive of βάλλειν.

CHAPTER CXIX.

9. **ἐπὶ χρόνον πολλὸν**, p. 73, l. 23.

12. **κατειλήθησαν** 'were crowded into the temple of Zeus in Labranda'. Cp. 1, 176 κατειληθέντες ἐς τὸ τεῖχος [κατειλεῖν 'to roll up', 'to crowd together']. 8, 170 ἐν ὀλίγῳ χώρῳ...πολλαὶ μυριάδες κατειλημέναι.

15. **Διὶ στρατίῳ**, the Ζεὺς Κάριος of c. 66. **θυσίας ἀνάγουσι**, cp. 6, 111 μεγάλας ἀνάγοντες θυσίας.

18. **ἄμεινον πρήξουσι** 'they would be best off', cf. ἄμεινον συνοίσεσθαι p. 73, l. 13.

CHAPTER CXX.

21. **ἐνθαῦτα δὲ** 'and in these circumstances', p. 36, l. 11.

22. **οἱ δὲ**, cp. for this repetition of the subject, p. 20, l. 27.

23. **ἀρτέοντο** 'began making their preparations', cp. 8, 97 ἀρτέετο ἐς πόλεμον.

24. ἐπὶ πλεῦν ἢ πρότερον 'even longer than before', see l. 8 ἐμαχέσαντο ἐπὶ χρόνον πολλόν. Others join with ἐσσώθησαν 'were beaten to a greater extent than before', cp. p. 31, l. 4.

25. πεσόντων...ἐπλήγησαν 'and while all the allies lost a large number the Milesians suffered most severely'. τῶν πάντων is a partitive genitive depending on πολλῶν. Abicht compares 1, 76 πεσόντων ἀμφοτέρων πολλῶν. Notice the absence of definite article with Μιλήσιοι. See p. 49, l. 7.

26. ἐπλήγησαν, cp. 8, 130 ἅτε δὲ μεγάλως πληγέντες οὐ προῇϊσαν ἀνωτέρω. So a defeat is called a τρῶμα p. 76, l. 1; 4, 160; 6, 132.

CHAPTER CXXI.

1. μετὰ δὲ, adverbial, p. 66, l. 19. τοῦτο τὸ τρῶμα ἀνέλαβον 76 'they retrieved this disaster'. Cp. 7, 231.

2. ἀνεμαχέσαντο 'rallied', 'renewed the war', cp. 8, 109 νενικημένους ἀναμάχεσθαί τε καὶ ἀναλαμβάνειν τὴν προτέρην κακότητα.

4. ἐλόχησαν τὴν...ὁδόν 'they beleaguered the road near Pedasos'. Elsewhere λοχᾶν takes accus. of person or thing laid in wait for, 6, 138, ἐλόχησαν τὰς Ἀθηναίων γυναῖκας. Here it amounts to 'they watched the road in ambush'. For ἐν 'near' cp. p. 73, l. 16.

CHAPTER CXXII.

14. ἐξελών, p. 37, l. 26.
16. ἐπὶ Καρίης 'was marching towards Karia'.
20. αἱρέων 'while engaged in subduing'.

CHAPTER CXXIII.

2. ὁ Σαρδίων ὕπαρχος, p. 14, l. 12. 77

CHAPTER CXXIV.

7. γάρ, anticipatory, p. 56, l. 6.
8. οὐκ ἄκρος 'not good', 'far from eminent in courage', cp. p. 72, l. 6. ἐγκερασάμενος 'embroiled', 'thrown into excitement and confusion', a metaphor from cooking or mixing drugs.
10. πρὸς δὲ, adverbial as in p. 11, l. 13; p. 40, l. 12.

11. **πρὸς ταῦτα δὴ ὦν**, 'it was for these reasons therefore', i.e. his cowardice, and his view of the insuperable power of the king.

13. **κρησφύγετον** 'a place of refuge', see 8, 51; 9, 15, 96. The origin of the word is uncertain: it used to be explained as a place of refuge from the Kretan (Κρής). **ὕπαρχον εἶναι** = ὑπάρχειν 'should be ready', a solitary instance of the word. For ὑπόρχειν see p. 66, l. 24. **ἦν ἄρα** 'if after all', p. 69, l. 7.

16. **ἐτείχεε** 'was engaged in fortifying', i.e. when he was summoned to Dareios. The imperfect indicates that the work was left incomplete.

CHAPTER CXXV.

18. **λογοποιοῦ**, see on p. 21, l. 19.

19. **στέλλειν** intransitive as in 4, 147. **ἔφερε ἡ γνώμη**, p. 74, l. 24.

20. **ἡσυχίην ἄγειν** 'to keep quiet', 'to make no movement', 2, 45 τέως μὲν ἡσυχίην ἔχειν ἐπεὶ δὲ κ.τ.λ. In another sense in p. 57, l. 2. There is properly a difference between ἡσυχίην ἄγειν and ἡσυχίην ἔχειν, the former being voluntary, the latter rather that which is allowed.

21. **ἔπειτα δὲ** 'and after doing that', i.e. after fortifying Leros, and waiting awhile.

22. **κατελεύσεσθαι**, p. 16, l. 26.

CHAPTER CXXVI.

1. **ἡ πλείστη γνώμη** 'the prevailing feeling'. Cp. 1, 120 ταύτῃ πλεῖστος γνώμην. 7, 220 ταύτῃ καὶ μᾶλλον τῇ γνώμῃ πλεῖστός εἰμι.

2. **ἀπάγειν** 'to depart', used intransitively like ἀπαίρειν. The full phrase perhaps would be ἀπάγειν τὸν στρατόν.

6. **ἀπόλλυται**, historic present. Herodotos is anticipating the course of his History in order to give at once the end of Aristagoras, who appears from Thucyd. 4, 102, 2 to have fallen in B.C. 497, while endeavouring to make a settlement in a town of the Edonians, on the site of which Amphipolis afterward stood.

7. **περικατήμενος καὶ βουλομένων** 'whilst besieging a town, and though the Thracian garrison were willing to abandon it if terms were granted them'. For such a combination of participles referring to different persons, see p. 34, ll. 17—19.

HISTORICAL AND GEOGRAPHICAL INDEX.

ABYDOS, C. 117.

In Mysia on the Asiatic coast of the Hellespont opposite Sestos, a colony from Miletos [Thucyd. 8, 61], whence probably its participation in the revolt.

ACHAIAN, C. 72.

The inhabitants of Argolis, Lakonia, and Messenia were called Achaioi in Homer. When expelled by the Dorians they retreated to the Northern district of the Peloponnese, which thus retained their name. By claiming to be an Achaian Kleomenes means that his family the Herakleidae (q. v.) belonged to the race which ruled in Lakonia before the coming of the Dorians.

ACHAIAN DEMETER, see *Demeter Achaia*.

ACHAIMENIDAE, C. 32.

The family of which the kings of Persia were descended [1, 125; 3, 65]. The pedigree of Xerxes is traced by himself, as being 9th in descent from Achaemenes [7, 11].

ACHERON, C. 92 § 7.

A river of Epeiros in the district Thesprotia (Mod. *Gurla*) flowing into the bay called γλυκὺς λιμήν *Port Fanári* [Thucyd. 1, 46, 5]. Like other rivers of the same name it was thought to be connected with the lower regions. Pausanias believed that it and the neighbouring river Kokytos were those from which Homer named the infernal rivers [Paus. 1, 17, 5].

ACHILLEIUM, C. 94.

A city near Sigeium in the Troad, probably built and fortified by the people of Mytilene to annoy the Athenian colonists of Sigeium. It got its name from the fact of its including the tumulus which was believed to be the tomb of Achilles. One report was that it was built from the stones of Troy [Strab. 13, 1, 39].

ADRASTOS, cc. 67—8.

Adrastos son of Talaos, king of Argos and Sikyon [Il. 2, 572], led the seven heroes in the attack upon Thebes. Aeschyl. [S. c. Th. 50]. He was worshipped as a hero at Sikyon, at Megara [Paus. 1, 43, 1], and in Attika [Paus. 1, 30, 4]. His death (τὰ πάθεα αὐτοῦ) gave rise to a proverbial saying Ἀδράστεια νέμεσις, of great prosperity followed by disaster. Adrastos died at Megara after the second expedition against Thebes, in grief for the loss of his son Aegialeos (q. v.) [Paus. 1, 43, 1].

ADRIA, c. 9.

The Adriatic Sea, mod. *Gulf of Venice*. According to Herodotos the Phokaeans were the first Greeks who navigated it [1, 163].

AEAKOS, c. 89.

AEAKIDAE, cc. 80, 81.

Aeakos was said to be son of Zeus by the nymph Aegina, whose reputation for justice on earth caused him to be made one of the judges in the nether world. The Aeakidae his descendants were the national heroes of Thessaly, Aegina, and Salamis [6, 35; 8, 64, 84]: they were Peleus, Achilles, Telamon Ajax and Teukros.

AEGIALEOS, AEGIALEIS, c. 68.

Aegialeos was a son of Adrastos by Amphithea daughter of Pronax [Apoll. 1, 6, 13]; he was one of the Epigoni who joined in the second attack on Thebes [id. 3, 7, 2] and was killed there [Paus. 1, 43, 1]. The people of Sikyon named a tribe Aegialeis after him in honour of his father, and as a sort of compromise for the old worship of that hero, which had been got rid of as a symbol of the Dorian supremacy in Sikyon.

AEGIKORES, c. 66.

A son of Ion, from whom one of the four Ionic tribes at Athens was supposed to be named. The Aegikores according to Plutarch [Solon 23] were the pastoral folk τοὺς ἐπὶ νομαῖς καὶ προβατείαις διατρίβοντας: while Euripides (Ion 1581) makes Athene declare that they are named from her Aegis,

$$\text{ἐμῆς τ' ἀπ' αἰγίδος}$$
$$\text{ἓν φῦλον ἕξουσ' Αἰγικορῆς.}$$

AEGINA, cc. 80, 84, 87.

AEGINETANS, cc. 80—89.

The Aeginetans were a Dorian colony from Epidauros [8, 46]. The causes of their enmity with Athens are given in this book [cc. 81, 82], though in all probability these circumstances were only a few out of many acts of provocation and retaliation which occurred between the two states arising from commercial jealousy : and the Athenians gladly seized the opportunity soon afterwards of denouncing the Aeginetans to

Sparta for giving earth and water to the Persian king [6, 49—50, 87—93]. The war which these occurrences brought about was renewed in B.C. 489 after Marathon, and was the cause of the rise in the Athenian naval power which took place then [7, 144]. Aegina became subject to Athens in the time of Perikles, and its Dorian inhabitants were expelled in B.C. 431 and Attic settlers put in their places. The Spartans gave the banished Aeginetans lands in the district of Kynuria, whence they were restored to Aegina by Lysander in B.C. 405 [Thucyd. 2, 27; 7, 57; Xen. Hell. 2, 2, 5—9]. The island contains about 40 square miles, and is 12 miles from the coasts of Attica and Epidauros. It was early prosperous, and by B.C. 500 was the most powerful naval and commercial state in Greece.

AEOLIS, c. 123.

AEOLIANS, cc. 94, 122—123.

The district properly called Aeolis was afterwards included in Mysia, and was a strip of the coast of Asia Minor opposite Lesbos between the promontory of Lectum on the N. and the R. Hermos. The boundaries however are differently stated at different times; and the Aeolians who gave their name to it were widely spread over Greece, descended it was said from Aeolus the second son of Hellen. They had first made settlements in Thessaly; driven thence they settled partly in Boeotia, Aetolia, Lokris, Korinth, Elis and Messenia, Lesbos, the Troad and other parts of Asia Minor. They were generally seafaring folk, and sent out numerous colonies. Their most powerful settlement at this time was in Lesbos [see 6, 8, 28, 98]. Their antiquity is indicated by a tradition that they were once called Pelasgi [7, 96]; and they very early produced a poetical literature.

AGRIANIANS, c. 16.

A Thrakian tribe believed to have lived in the upper valley of the Strymon [Thucyd. 2, 96, 3]. As they resisted Megabazos, so they succeeded in resisting all other attempts to subject them, until they submitted to Alexander [Arrian 1, 5].

Aïas, c. 66.

Son of Telamon, and grandson of Aeakos (q. v.). One of the Attic tribes (Αἰαντίς) was named after him because he was the national Hero of Salamis, which had been united to Attica since about 560 B.C., while tradition also said that his two sons Eurysakes and Philaeos migrated to Athens, the latter giving his name to a deme (Philaïdae), Plut. Sol. 10. It was also thought wise to put back the connexion of Athens and Salamis to as remote a period as possible, and one of the arguments of Solon in proving the Athenian claim was to quote two verses of Homer to show that at the time of the Trojan war the two were closely united (Il. 2, 557—8):

> Αἴας δ' ἐκ Σαλαμῖνος ἄγε δυοκαίδεκα νῆας
> στῆσε δ' ἄγων ἵν' Ἀθηναίων ἵσταντο φάλαγγες.

ALEXANDER, cc. 17, 19—22.

Son of Amyntas I., king of Lower Makedonia, the chief cities of which were Edessa and Pella. We do not know the year in which he succeeded his father: but it was some time before B.C. 480, and, according to Justin 7, 4, very soon after the events mentioned in this book, i.e. between 506 and 500 B.C. His Greek descent [c. 22] which was admitted at Olympia is derived by Herodotos [8, 137; cp. Thucyd. 2, 99] from Temenos of Argos, whose grandson Perdikkas first established the dynasty. When Xerxes invaded Greece in B.C. 480 he was compelled to submit and serve in the king's army; but though he consented to carry a message to Athens advising the Athenians to accept the Persian terms [8, 140], he showed that he wished the success of the Greek arms at Plataea, by riding up to the Greek lines at night and warning them of the coming attack [9, 44]. The year of his death is uncertain: the last notice we have of him is in the year B.C. 463 [Plut. Kim. 14], and we know that his son succeeded before B.C. 432. From traditions as to the length of his reign he probably died about B.C. 454.

ALKAIOS, c. 95.

A poet of Mitylene, who is generally considered to have flourished about B.C. 611. We know little about his life, except that after joining in this war against the Athenians for the possession of Sigeium (B.C. 606) he and his brother Antimenidas joined Pittakos in overthrowing the tyrant Melanchros, and that when Pittakos became tyrant (B.C. 589) he and his party were exiled. He retired to Egypt, but after some time returned and was leniently treated by Pittakos. His works written in the Aeolic dialect, and consisting of Hymns, Stasiotika (political), Skolia (drinking songs) and Erotica (love songs) have perished, with the exception of fragments quoted in the works of Grammarians or others.

ALKMAIONIDAE, cc. 62, 67, 70—1, 90.

A large and powerful family in Athens taking their name from an ancestor Alkmaion [circ. B.C. 1100], and bearing in alternate generations the name of Alkmaion and Megakles. After their banishment and recall as narrated in this book [about B.C. 612], we find that they never became quite free from the disadvantages of the taint supposed to have been incurred by the execution of the Kylonian conspirators. Just as Kleisthenes is here [c. 70] calumniated on that ground, so was Perikles in B.C. 432 [Thucyd. 1, 126]. See also 6, 125, 127, 130.

ALOPEKAE, c. 63.

An Attic deme [Fox-town] lying to the N. East of the city of Athens. Near its side is the modern village of *Ampelokipi* on the Kephisia road, just before it divides, the left going to Pentelicon, the right to Marathon and Laurium. It was the birthplace of Aristeides and Sokrates.

AMORGES, c. 121.

A Persian general, of whom we know nothing except his death here recorded. He may perhaps have been connected with an Amorges, k. of the Sakae, who was captured by Kyros [Ctesias 72]. The name occurs in later times again [Thucyd. 8, 5, 5].

AMATHUS, c. 114.
AMATHUSIANS, cc. 104—5, 108, 114.

A very ancient Phoenikian city on the S. coast of Kypros, near the modern *Limasol*, and 35 miles W. of Kitium (*Larnaka*). It seems long to have retained traces of its Phoenikian origin, especially as to religion, cp. Steph. Byzant. πόλις Κύπρου ἀρχαιοτάτη, ἐν ᾗ Ἄδωνις Ὄσιρις ἐτιμᾶτο, ὃν Αἰγύπτιον ὄντα Κύπριοι καὶ Φοίνικες ἰδιοποιοῦνται. The Tyrian god Melcharth was also worshipped there; its territory was rich in corn and minerals.

AMPHION, c. 92, § 1.

One of the family of the Bakchiadae (q. v.) of Sikyon, and father of Labda.

AMPHITRYON, c. 59.

The father of Herakles. He was, according to the legend, son of Alkaios king of Troezen, but retired to Thebes to be purified from the pollution of an involuntary homicide. His expedition against the pirates called Teleboï or Taphians was to avenge the death of his wife Alkmene's brothers who had fallen in war with them. His tomb was shown at Thebes [Paus. 1, 41, 1].

AMYNTAS, cc. 17, 20, 94.

The sixth king of Makedonia (or, as others reckon, the ninth), and father of Alexander I. (q. v.). He was the son of Alketas [8, 139], and died probably before B.C. 500. See also *Gygaea*.

ANAXANDRIDAS, cc. 39—41, 61.

Son of Leon king of Sparta of the elder house [see s.v. *Herakleidae*]; he reigned about B.C. 560 to B.C. 520, and left four sons, Kleomenes by his second wife: Dorieus, Leonidas and Kleombrotos by his first [7, 205]. In his reign the Spartans at length got the better in their long war with Tegea [1, 67].

ANCHIMOLIOS, c. 63.

The Spartan commander in the first invasion of Attica for the purpose of expelling the Peisistratids. The Thessalian cavalry summoned by the latter, in fighting with which Anchimolios fell, are alluded to in Aristoph. Lysist. 1152.

ANDROS, c. 31.

The most Northern and, next to Naxos, the largest of the Cyclades, being 21 m. long by 8 m. broad. It was fertile, and rich in vines, though its inhabitants pleaded poverty when Themistokles demanded a contribution in B.C. 480 [8, 111].

ANTANDROS, c. 26.

A town on the coast of the Troad, at the head of the gulf of Adrymittium. It was a very ancient town, once apparently inhabited by Pelasgi (hence called Pelasgis 7, 42), or by Leleges [Strabo 12, 1, 51]; and was seized by the Kimmerii, those northern barbarians who in the 7th century B.C. overran Asia [1, 6]. It was then settled by Aeolians [Thucyd. 8, 108, 4].

ANTHEMUS, c. 94.

A city of Makedonia just N. of Chalkidike. The district to which it gave its name is mentioned by Thucydides [2, 99, 5] as one of those which the Makedonians had gradually absorbed, and retained up to his time.

ANTICHARES, c. 43.

A man of Eleon in Boeotia.

APOLLO, cc. 60—1. APOLLO ISMENIAS, c. 59.

The worship of Apollo, as the Sun-god, but especially as the God of prophecy was very widely spread in Greece: the two chief seats of it being Delos and Delphi. ISMENIAN APOLLO means the temple of Apollo at Thebes built on a hill at the foot of which flowed the river Ismenios [1, 52, 92; Pausan. 9, 10, 2].

ARCHELAOI, c. 68.

The name which Kleisthenes of Sikyon gave to the tribe to which he himself belonged,—meaning 'the ruling tribe' or 'rulers of the people'.

ARES, c. 7.

God of war. Herodotos translates by it the name of the Thrakian god of war, which is not known to us.

ARGADEIS, c. 66.

One of the four tribes at Athens before the reforms of Kleisthenes,— meaning probably 'work-men', though popularly supposed to be named from one of the sons of Ion.

ARGIVES, cc. 22, 49, 57, 61, 67—8, 86—8.

ARGOS, c. 67.

Argos in Homeric times was perhaps a name given to all the Peloponnese, and the Argeioi is used almost equally with Achaioi as a general appellation of the Greeks. The original inhabitants of Argolis (as known afterwards) were subdued by the invading Dorians, under whom it was still for a long time powerful. The enmity between it and Sparta, to which Aristagoras refers in c. 49, was caused by border disputes, and especially in regard to the possession of Kynuria or Thyreatis. About B.C. 547 the Spartans finally possessed themselves of this district, and gradually supplanted the Argives in their leading position. This national antipathy was intensified by the invasions of Kleomenes, about B.C. 510 [6, 75—6, 82—3]. In this book [cc. 67—8] we have a reference to the earlier state of things, when Argos was a formidable power in Peloponnese and accordingly is viewed with jealousy by Sikyon. But the Argives so much resented the superiority of Sparta, that they decidedly Medized in B.C. 480 [7, 150—2; 9, 12], and were always ready long afterwards to join any state that would combine against Sparta [Thucyd. 1, 102; 5, 44, 47].

ARISTAGORAS, cc. 30—8, 49—51, 54—5, 65, 97—9, 103, 105, 124, 126.

Son of Malpagoras, nephew and son-in-law of Histiaios tyrant of Miletos. His part in the Ionic revolt, and his efforts to rouse an Hellenic movement in its support, as well as his final failure and death are narrated in this book. After his retreat to Myrkinos he seems to have lived for some years, and to have been killed in B.C. 497 while endeavouring to establish a colony on the spot called the Nine-Ways where Amphipolis afterwards stood [Thucyd. 4, 102, 2]. Herodotos evidently regards him as deficient in courage and honesty, and as having started the revolt from selfish motives.

ARISTAGORAS, c. 37.

Son of Herakleides tyrant of Kyme; he was one of the Greek Princes who consulted as to the breaking of the bridge over the Ister, during the Skythian expedition of Dareios [4, 138].

ARISTOGEITON, c. 55.

One of the assassins of Hipparchos, who with the other assassin Harmodios, was a member of the family called Gephyraei, which had migrated to Attika from Eretria, or, as Herodotos asserts, from Phoenikia [cc. 57—8]. The immediate effect of the murder was to incite the survivor Hippias to increased severity, which contributed to his downfall; and though the account in Thucydides [6, 54—59] does not tend to exalt their characters and motives, their memory was held in the highest reverence by the Athenians as the authors of their freedom [6, 109].

ARISTOKYPROS, c. 113.

King or tyrannus (for Herodotos sometimes calls these Kyprian rulers βασιλεῖς and sometimes τύραννοι) of Soli in Kypros, and son of Philokypros (q. v.).

ARISTO, c. 75.

Fourteenth king of Sparta of the junior house (the Eurypontidae) whose reign falls about the middle of 6th century B.C. He was father of Demaratos (q. v.), and contemporary with Anaxandridas (q. v.). During his reign there were constant wars with Tegea [1, 67].

ARKADIANS, c. 49.

The Arkadians inhabited the mountainous district in the centre of the Peloponnese, in which they were able to resist the Dorians when they conquered the rest. They therefore remained more purely Pelasgic or Achaian, and in many respects were a peculiar race, sympathising with the subject races of Argos and Lakonia [6, 83] and living much apart. Their quarrels with the Spartans were chiefly caused by the constant wars between the latter and Tegea, which only ended by the final submission of Tegea and its consenting to form a close alliance with Sparta [1, 65; 9, 35].

ARMENIA, c. 52.
ARMENIANS, c. 49.

By Armenia Herodotos means Armenia Major,—the whole country between the Euphrates in the West and the Caspian sea in the East without defining its limits to the North and South,—but as the upper Tigris is said to be in Armenia he must conceive it as going at least as far to the S. as the Mt. Masius, thus including what is elsewhere reckoned as part of Assyria or Media; and it would not at the most go farther N. than the Kaukasos. It is a land of mountains and valleys suitable almost entirely to pastoral purposes.

ARTEMIS, c. 7.

Goddess of the chase, by which name Herodotos here represents the Thrakian Bendis. This name was used in Greece, and a shrine (Bendideion) to the goddess stood in Munychia. Dem. de Cor. 107, Plat. R. 328, Livy 38, 41.

ARTYBIOS, cc. 108, 110—2.

A Persian commander in the war in Kypros.

ASIA, cc. 12, 17, 50, 96—7, 119.

"In general terms it may be said the portion of Asia with which "Herodotos was acquainted did not amount to one third of the whole... "it was almost entirely confined to the Persian Empire, which as it "then existed, comprised the whole of Western Asia (with the excep- "tion of the Arabian peninsula) from the Erytheraean Sea to the "Caucasus and the Caspian, and from the shores of the Mediterranean "and the Euxine to the valley of the Indus" (Bunbury, *Ancient Geography*, vol. I. p. 218). Earlier still (Hom. Il. 2, 461) the term Asia was only applied to a district of Lydia; and after Herodotos it was sometimes confined to what we call Asia Minor, the latter name not being used till about A.D. 500.

ASOPOS, c. 80.

The river-god of the river Asopos in Boeotia, which rises in Mt. Kithaeron and flows eastward to the Euboean Sea. In the western part of its valley stood Thebes. Hence the legend that the nymph Thebè was daughter of Asopos. The further legend that the other daughter of Asopos was the nymph Aegina, who gave her name to the island, was either invented for the express purpose of founding a claim to union between Thebes and Aegina, or, existing before, was seized on as a convenient pretext for suggesting that union, which was really caused by a common jealousy of Athens. For the legend of the carrying off of Aegina by Zeus, and her settlement in the island then called Oenone, but afterwards Aegina, see Apollod. 3, 12, 6.

ASTAKOS, c. 67.

Father of Melanippos (q. v.), and other heroes engaged in the attack on Thebes,—Ismaros, Leades, and Amphidakos. Apoll. 3, 6, 8.

ASTER, c. 63.
A Spartan, father of Anchimolios (q.v.).

ATHENÈ KRATHIAS, cc. 45, 82.
Athenè whose temple was on the Krathis, the river on which Sybaris stood.

ATHENIAN, c. 69.

ATHENIANS, cc. 55, 57, 61—6, 70—4, 76, 78—9, 81—9, 90, 94—7, 99, 103, 105.

In this book we have scattered notices of Athens just at the point when she was beginning to develope her power. Thus the occupation of Sigeium by Peisistratos may be looked upon as the beginning of the foreign dominion of the city [c. 65]; and the constant wars with the Aeginetans not only eventually caused the efforts which made her the first naval state in Greece, but indicate that she was beginning to rival the commercial importance of that island. At the time treated of here she had but few war-ships [c. 85] and was reduced to borrow or hire them from Korinth [6, 89]; still even with that small equipment the Athenians were able to hold their own with some effect. Herodotos regards the expulsion of the Peisistratidae as marking a distinct period in the rise of her power and importance: but that power must have been on the increase for some time before; and Athens had long been looked upon as the leading Ionian state, and possibly the mother-city of all the Ionian settlements, though the Athenians were inclined to repudiate the name [1, 143]; and it was partly this connexion with Ionia, and partly the fact of the distinct position occupied by them as the second power in Greece, that prompted the application of Aristagoras.

ATHENS, cc. 54, 57, 61—6, 70—1, 82, 87, 91, 96—7.

ATTIC, cc. 87—8, 91.
Derived probably from ἀκτή headland or coastland. It is a peninsula about 50 miles long, 30 broad, and containing about 700 sq. miles. It had once been divided into a number of independent cantons, whose names in many cases survived in historical times in those of various demes. The political combination of these (συνοίκισμος) was uniformly attributed to Theseus. It lay out of the direct road from upper Greece to the Peloponnese, and was besides a rocky and unfruitful soil not tempting to invaders, hence its inhabitants had not changed within the memory of man, and the people regarded themselves as autochthonons [Thucyd. 1, 2; Herod. 1, 143]; and they were doubtless of very ancient standing; nor is there any trustworthy tradition of their first settlement or the first establishment of Athens.

ATTIKA, cc. 63—5, 74, 76, 81, 87, 89.

AUXESIA, c. 82.
Pausanias [2, 30, 3] says that he himself saw the statues of Auxesia and Damia (q.v.) at Epidauros, and offered sacrifice in the same man-

ner as to Demeter. This confirms the idea, naturally suggested by the name, that Auxesia represents the principle of natural growth, 'the goddess that giveth the increase'. There were statues of the same goddesses at Troezen, and the people there said that they were virgins who had come from Krete, with which island Troezen had very anciently had relations of commerce [Eurip. Hippol. 155—7]. Stein quotes Homer Hymn 4, 408 καρπὸν ἄεξε φερέσβιον ἀνθρώποισιν.

BAKCHIADAE, c. 92, § 1.

A family or clan at Korinth (as well as at Miletos, according to Hesychios) who for some time before the usurpation of Kypselos engrossed all power and offices in the state, including it appears the king-ship. According to Diodoros [vii. fr.] they were Herakleids, but changed their designation to Bakchiadae from Bakchis the fourth in descent from Aktes. Some few of the clan distinguished themselves in various ways; one seems to have been a constitutional philosopher, and was employed to draw up a constitution for Thebes [Arist. Pol. 2, 12]; and another, Eumelos, was said to be the author of an Epic on the history of Korinth [Paus. 2, 1, 1]. But the downfall of their supremacy was brought about apparently by an unpopularity gradually accumulated from the violence and licence which seem generally to have been the marks of close oligarchical corporations [Aelian V. H. 1, 19; Plutarch Narrat. Am. 2]. Kypselos was able to secure their downfall as usual by winning the favour of the people, especially by mild administration of the office of Polemarch, in which capacity he had control over the imprisonment of state-debtors. As usual too the Oracle of Delphi was appealed to, and even perhaps tampered with, to induce it to forbid certain of the Bakchiadae, who had consulted it, to return to Korinth, and to warn the people to regard Kypselos as their god-appointed deliverer. Thus the basileus Patrokleides was killed, the rest of the Bakchiadae banished, their goods confiscated, and many others who were unfriendly to the new regime induced to go out to found colonies [Nicol. Dam. fr. 56; Polyaen. 5, 31]. The bulk of the banished Bakchiadae retired to Sparta [Plutarch Lys. 1]; and of them Demaratos is said to have gone to reside at Tarquinii in Etruria, which he had often visited before for commercial purposes, and there to have become the father of Aruns and Lucumo, the latter of whom was to be afterwards king of Rome as Tarquinius the elder [Dionys. Hal. 3, 46—48].

BOEOTIA, c. 57.

BOEOTIAN, c. 59, 67.

BOEOTIANS, cc. 57, 61, 74, 77, 81, 89, 91.

Boeotia, the district immediately North of Attica, from which it is separated by the ranges of Kithaeron and Parnes, was a somewhat loose confederacy of at least nine towns, of which Thebes had for some time been far the most important. The Boeotians were an Aeolian people from Phthiotis in Thessaly [Thucyd. 1, 12], who being expelled by the Thessalians moved into Boeotia, where they found not only Pelasgi, but a colony of Phoenikians also, who had settled in Thebes. Their enmity to Athens, which appears to have been of long standing, was doubtless principally owing to border disputes, and the contest for the possession of such frontier towns as Oenoe, Hysiae, and Oropos; the difference of race and habits had also probably something to do with it.

BRANCHIDAE, c. 36.

Properly Branchidae is the name of a priestly caste which had charge of the temple and oracle of Apollo at Didyma, or Didymi, in Karia about 12 miles from Miletos [1, 46; 2, 159; Paus. 1, 16, 3]. It is also used for the place itself, as here [cp. 1, 92, 157; Diod. Sic. 19, 90]. It was the oracle used by all Ionians, was consulted and presented with rich offerings by Kroisos [1, 46, 92], and by Necos king of Egypt [2, 159]. The temple burnt and plundered at the end of this revolt [6, 19] was said to have been rebuilt, but again plundered and burnt by Xerxes [Strabo 14, 1, 5]. At some subsequent period the Milesians set to work to restore it, and on such a large scale, that it was never roofed; nor does it seem to have recovered its character as an oracle [Strabo 17, 1, 43]. The ruins which are now visible are of this last erection. The destruction by the Persians does not appear to have been very complete, for inscriptions still exist on the Sacred Way which seem to belong to the sixth century B.C. [see Roberts, *Epigraphy*, pp. 161—165].

BUBARES, c. 21.

A Persian, son of Megabazos, who married Gygaea daughter of Amyntas king of Makedonia. He was afterwards superintendent of the canal works at Athos [7, 22], and his son Amyntas was made lord of Alabanda in Phrygia by the king [8, 136].

BUTAKIDOS, c. 47.

A native of Kroton in Italy, father of Philip (q.v.).

BYZANTIUM, cc. 26, 103.

A colony of Megara on the site of the modern Constantinople, founded in B.C. 657 [4, 144]. After its capture by the Persians (c. 103) it remained in their hands until B.C. 478, when it was taken by Pausanias [Thucyd. 4, 78]. Its subsequent history is a troubled one. A member of the confederacy of Delos [B.C. 477—440], it revolted in B.C. 440 and again submitted; garrisoned by Spartans B.C. 411 it was recovered by Athens in B.C. 408. Surrendered again to Lysander B.C. 405, it was afterwards a constant source of quarrel between the Greeks and Makedonians, for it commanded the narrow straits through which the corn-ships must come that supplied Athens and other states; and Demosthenes exerted himself in B.C. 339 to unite it with Athens in resisting Philip. Its subsequent troubles were caused generally by the rivalry of Rhodes (B.C. 220) and the attacks of the Keltic tribes living in its neighbourhood, until it came under the power of Rome (about

B.C. 59), and was made a Roman province by Vespasian (about A.D. 74). After many vicissitudes in the struggle of various Emperors, and after suffering much especially under Severus, it was refounded by Constantine in A.D. 330. The key to its history is its geographical position which Polybios [4, 30] describes as on the seaward side the most advantageous in the world, while on the landward it is exactly the reverse.

CHALKIDIANS, cc. 74, 77, 91, 99.

The inhabitants of Chalkis in Euboea (Mod. *Egripo*) on the point of the coast where the Euripos is narrowest, and is now spanned by a bridge. It had long been a flourishing town, and was the Mother city of many colonies. Its rivalry with Eretria, and their frequent contests for the rich *Campus Lelantus* (τὸ Λελάντιον πεδίον) which lay between the two towns, occasioned a war which Thucydides notices as the most important in old times, as causing the other Greek states to take part on the one side or the other, much as they did later in the Peloponnesian war [Thucyd. 1, 15, 5]. It was said to have been originally a colony of Athens [Strabo 10, 1, 8], and probably frequent jealousies and quarrels now determined the Athenians to secure its submission by the measure described in c. 77.

CHAROPINOS, c. 99.

Brother of Aristagoras of Miletos.

CHERSIS, cc. 104, 113.

King of Salamis in Kypros, father of Gorgos and Onesilos.

CHIANS, 98.

An island off the coast of Asia Minor, separated from the peninsula of Erythrae by a strait, which at its narrowest is about 5 miles across. It is 32 miles long and 18 to 8 miles broad. It was celebrated for its wine and pottery, and was therefore wealthy [Thucyd. 8, 24—5]. It was seized by Histiaios after the fall of Miletos [6, 26], but was afterwards taken by the Persians and severely treated [6, 31]. After the Persian wars it was included in the confederacy of Delos, but revolted in B.C. 412 [Thucyd. 8, 14].

CHIOS, cc. 33—4, 98.

CHOASPES, cc. 49, 52.

A river in Susiana, rising in the Laristan Mountains and flowing into the Tigris, and on which Susa stood [1, 188]: its modern name is the *Kerkhah*; and it has sometimes been confused with the Eulaeus (mod. *Karùn*) which flows in an almost parallel course with it.

CHOEREATAE, c. 68.

Swine-folk (χοῖρος) a name given to a tribe at Korinth by Kleisthenes instead of the older Dorian name. It was looked upon as a bitter insult to the Dorians by this Achaian ruler; yet perhaps it may have been founded on the occupation of a number of the tribe, as were the ancient names of the Attic tribes.

DAMIA, cc. 82—3.

Damia is coupled with Auxesia (q. v.) as the goddesses of abundance, and perhaps they are mere local names for Demeter and Persephone, or rather personifications of some of the functions of these goddesses. The derivation of the word has been much disputed. Some have held that it is equivalent to Δημία [Dor. Δα-] 'the people's god'; others that it is Δᾶ—μαῖα Earth-mother (δᾶ=γῆ); others derive it from δαμ- [δαμάω] the goddess which 'subdues' the soil (*subigere*). Against the last is the quantity of the Latin *damium* and *damia*, the former of which, according to Festus, was the name of a sacrifice to the Bona Dea, the latter a name of the Bona Dea herself.

DARDANOS, c. 117.

A city of the Troad coterminous with Abydos [7, 43; Thucyd. 8, 104]; the two territories being divided by the stream Rhodios. There had been an older town of the same name at the foot of Mt. Ida. It was not a strong place in a military sense; and when the Romans became supreme in Asia Minor, after conquering Antiochos (B.C. 190), it was declared a free town on the ground of the descent of its inhabitants from Troy, and its foundation by king Dardanos. It was really however an Aeolian colony.

DAREIOS, cc. 1, 2, 11—14, 18, 23—5, 30, 32, 36—7, 65, 73, 96, 98, 103, 105—8, 116, 124.

Dareios son of Hystaspes was king of Persia from B.C. 521 to B.C. 485. He was of the royal Achaimenid stock [7, 11], and had served Kambyses in Egypt in B.C. 525 [3, 38]. On the death of that king he combined to put down the false Smerdis, and was made king [3, 70—88]. He organized the Empire which Kyros had founded, dividing it into 20 Satrapies with a fixed tribute and regular officers [3, 88—96]. His expedition in Skythia was partly for the security of his Northern frontiers, partly to give employment to the military class of his subjects [4, 85—144]. He had to cope with several great rebellions during his reign: at Babylon [3, 150—160]; in Ionia, the beginning of which is described in this book; and in Egypt [7, 1—5]: and while preparing to put down the latter he died. Dareios was a statesman as well as a soldier, and seems to have made honest and, in the main, successful efforts to rule his vast possessions with justice and clemency, and to the advantage of his subjects.

DAURISES, cc. 116—8, 121—2.

A Persian noble married to one of the daughters of Dareios.

DELPHI, cc. 42—3, 62—3, 67, 82, 89, 92.

DELPHIANS, c. 72.

The town of Delphi stood in a kind of natural amphitheatre to the

S. of the sloping foot of a precipitous two-headed cliff which terminates the range of Parnassos. It was very ancient, but it owed its whole importance to the Temple and Oracle of Apollo, which was frequented by people from all parts of the world. Its name in the Homeric poems is Pytho, and it was originally controlled by the inhabitants of Krissa; but as a town grew up round the temple the inhabitants claimed to manage it independently; and when Kirrha took the place of Krissa, this claim led to a sacred war which ended with the destruction of Kirrha by the order of the Amphiktyons (B.C. 525). From this time Delphi was a free town, but still had contests with the Phokian League as to the control of the Temple, a question which both Spartans and Athenians tried to settle by war in the way which suited themselves, the Spartans siding with the Delphians, the Athenians with the Phokian League [about B.C. 449, Thucyd. 1, 112]. See *Pythia*.

DEMARATOS, c. 75.

Son of Ariston, 14th king of the junior royal house of Sparta (the Eurypontidae). The rupture between him and Kleomenes mentioned in this chapter was followed by another in the matter of Aegina [6, 50]. Kleomenes determined to get rid of him, which he did by casting doubt on his legitimacy [6, 63—69]. He remained in Sparta for a time after his deposition, but stung by an insulting speech of Kleomenes he secretly left Sparta and escaped to the court of Dareios [6, 67—70]: and afterwards accompanied Xerxes in his invasion [7, 101—104, 209, 234—7].

DEMARMENOS, c. 41.

A Spartan, father of Prinetedas, and grandfather of the second wife of king Anaxandridas. Another son of his, Chilon the wise, whose daughter married Demaratos though already engaged to Leotychides, is mentioned in 6, 65.

DEMETER ACHAIA, c. 61.

For the worship of Demeter see 6, 91; 9, 57, 65, 69. For the Athenians the chief seat of her worship and the celebration of her mysteries, representing the secret operations of nature, was at Eleusis. But she had many temples in various parts of Greece, and usually in some solitary spot outside the town. The words DEMETER ACHAIA are generally taken to mean 'Demeter the mourner' [ἄχος], alluding to the myth of her mourning for her daughter Persephone, mystically representing the yearly return of gloom at the death of Nature in the winter. [The scholiast on Arist. Acharn. 708—9 derives the word from ἠχώ and refers it to the noise of cymbals and drums used in her worship.]

DIONYSOS, cc. 7, 67.

The god of wine, whose worship was believed to have been introduced into Greece from Asia, and even from India. The revels which accompanied that worship were held in many places; and the dance or song seem pretty generally to have formed a part in it. Thus the theatres in which they, as well as the Tragedies and Comedies which were developed from them, were performed, were sacred to Dionysos, and contained an altar of that god. In c. 7 Herodotos uses the Greek name for a Thrakian god of wine, whose local name was Sabazios. Herodotos also identifies him with Osiris in Egypt [2, 42, 144]; with Orotal in Arabia [3, 8]; and his orgies with those of Orpheus [2, 81]. For his worship in Thrace cp. 7, 111; and for the legend of his birth at Thebes, 2, 145—6; 3, 97.

DOBERES, c. 16.

A Paeonian tribe living to the N. of Mt. Pangaeum, in the neighbourhood of what was afterwards Philippi [7, 113].

DORIANS, cc. 68, 76.   DORIAN, a, c. 72.   DORIC, cc. 87, 88.

One of the three great divisions of the Hellenic race. They settled first in Northern Greece, where their name survived in Doris [8, 31], and then making their way into the Peloponnese conquered, and in part drove out, the Achaian inhabitants of Argolis, Lakonia, and Messene [1, 56; 8, 31, 73]. The myth derived them from Doros son of Hellen [1, 56].

DORIEUS, cc. 41—2, 44—8.

Son of king Anaxandridas, and brother of Leonidas and Kleombrotos. He was disgusted that, as the eldest son of his father by his first wife, he was not allowed to succeed in preference to Kleomenes the son by the (unlawful) second wife. His adventures are narrated in this book, and his death in Sicily referred to again in 7, 105. It seems doubtful whether he is meant in 9, 10 by 'Dorieus father of Euryanax', or whether another member of the royal family of the same name is intended.

DORISKOS, c. 98.

A plain in Thrakia on the west of the river Hebros (*Maritza*). The Persians afterwards built a town in it on the coast, which bore the same name [7, 25, 59, 105], but which never seems to have been large, and in after times survived only as a fort [Livy 31, 16].

DYMANATAE, c. 68.

The name of one of the three ancient Dorian tribes. It was supposed to be derived from Dyman one of the sons of Aegimios king of Doris. The other two were Hylleni and Pamphyli. These tribes are traceable in nearly every place where Dorians settled—Sikyon, Argos, Sparta, Epidauros, Aegina and elsewhere. They were divided into 10 phratries or *obae* each. See Müller's *Dorians*, vol. 2, p. 76—78.

DYSORUM, c. 17.

A mountain separating Paeonia from Makedonia, when Makedonia had been extended to the neighbourhood of the Strymon.

ECHEKRATES, c. 92, § 2.

Father of Eetion, the husband of Labda; a man of the township Petra (q.v.) in the Korinthian territory.

EDONIANS, c. 124.

A Thrakian tribe living between the Strymon and Axios. They founded the town of the Nine Ways ['Εννέα ὁδοί, 7, 114], and it was in his attack upon this, in order to occupy it with his own people, that Aristagoras fell. They successfully resisted an attempt of the Athenians about B.C. 465 to make a settlement near Datum, in the same district, for the purpose of working the mines [9, 75]; but they were eventually forced further east as the Makedonian power increased [Thucyd. 2, 99, 3].

EETION, c. 92, § 2.

Son of Echekrates (q.v.) and husband of Labda (q.v.), by whom he was father of Kypselos.

EGESTANS, cc. 46, 47.

The inhabitants of Egesta in the N.W. of Sicily, 34 miles N.W. of Panormos. The evidence of coins shows that the inhabitants called it Segesta, though the Greek writers all have the form Ἔγεστα. Their hostility to the Selinuntians was of old standing, at least as early as B.C. 590 [Diod. V. 9]; and it was continued in after years, as we know that in B.C. 416 it was an appeal from the people of Egesta to the Athenians against Selinos that formed the pretext for the famous Athenian expedition; they having already in B.C. 426 made an alliance with Athens [Thucyd. 6, 6]. It was plundered and depopulated by Agathokles in B.C. 307, and its name changed to Dikaeopolis [Diodor. 20, 71], though it afterwards assumed its old name again. The people imagined themselves to be descended from certain Trojan exiles. The modern town *Castell'a Mare* stands near its site.

ELEAN, c. 44.

A native of Elis, the north-western district of Peloponnesos; the city of Elis was said to have been established by a colony from Aetolia [8, 73].

ELEONIAN, c. 43.

A native of Eleon a village in the territory of Tanagra in Boeotia [Strabo 9, 5, 18].

ELEUSIS, cc. 74—6.

About 11 miles W. of Athens opposite Salamis. The road from the Peloponnese to Athens passed through it, and it was a natural place for an invading army to halt, as it commanded also a pass over the mountains to Boeotia. From it to Athens the road was called 'the Sacred Way', from the processions which yearly went to its famous temple of Demeter.

ENCHELEIS, c. 61.

A tribe in Illyria living on the coast above Epidamnos (Dyrrhachium). There was a legend that Kadmos had once assisted them against the other Illyrians, and then himself reigned over the Illyrians; and this tradition may point to some connexion between the two peoples which made it natural for the Kadmeians to seek safety among the Encheleans [Apollod. 3, 5, 4].

ENETI, c. 9.

The Veneti, a tribe living on the N. of the Adriatic. They were 'nearly allied', says Polybios [2, 17], 'to the Kelts, but using quite a different language'. The name is found also in Brittany, on the shores of the Baltic, and in Paphlagonia [Hom. Il. 2, 85]. They were known to the Greeks principally as exporters of amber, and as breeders and sellers of horses [see Eurip. Hipp. 231, 745, 1131].

EPHESIA, EPHESIANS, c. 100.

A town on the coast of Lydia at the mouth of the Kayster, whose harbour Panormos, once excellent, has now been silted up. It was one of the 12 Ionian towns [1, 142, 148], and eventually occupied so eminent a position among them that the yearly Ionian festival came to be called the Ephesia [Thucyd. 3, 104]; yet it seems not to have taken any part in the Ionic revolt. As it was the starting-point for the road to Sardis, it was doubtless restrained by the presence of a Persian guard, if not by considerations of interest. Moreover Ephesos and its dependency Kolophon were apparently always somewhat divided from the main Ionian body [1, 147].

EPHESOS, cc. 54, 100, 102.

EPHORS, the, cc. 39, 41.

The name of 5 magistrates at Sparta appointed originally by Lykurgos, according to Herodotos and Xenophon [1, 65; Xen. R. L. 8, § 3]. Müller holds that they were originally appointed only to inspect (ἐφορᾶν) the markets; but, whatever their original duties, they had become the most formidable power in Sparta, interfered with and even tried the kings [c. 39; 6, 82], sent out armies [9, 9], and even accompanied them [9, 76]. They were elected annually by the whole body of free citizens.

EPIDAURIANS, cc. 82—4.

A Dorian town on the coast of Argolis opposite Aegina, which was colonised from it [8, 46]. It was a prosperous town and in B.C. 480 sent ten war-ships to the united fleet at Artemisium [8, 1], as well as soldiers to the defence of the Isthmos [8, 72].

EPIDAUROS, cc. 82, 86.

ERECHTHEUS, c. 82.

A mythical king of Athens, and believed to be Earth-born [γηγενής

8, 55], or, as it was sometimes put, a son of 'Ατθίς an Earth-nymph. Cp. Hom. Il. 2, 546

οἱ δ' ἄρ' 'Αθήνας εἶχον, ἐϋκτίμενον πτολίεθρον,
δῆμον 'Ερεχθῆος μεγαλήτορος, ὅν ποτ' 'Αθήνη
θρέψε Διὸς θυγάτηρ—τέκε δὲ ζείδωρος ἄρουρα—
κὰδ δ' ἐν 'Αθήνῃς εἷσεν, ἑῷ ἐνὶ πίονι νηῷ.

To him were attributed the establishment of the worship of Athenè at Athens, the building of the temple of Athenè Polias, and the institution of the Panathenaic festival, and the change of the name from Κράναοι to 'Αθηναῖοι [8, 44].

ERETRIA, c. 57. ERETRIANS, cc. 99, 102.

The Eretrians inhabiting a town in Euboea nearly opposite Oropos were mostly Ionians [8, 46], and had long been an active commercial people, and rivals of Chalkis, in their wars with which town they had been aided by the Milesians. Their help given now in return to the revolted Ionians cost them dear; all of them who did not effect an escape into the centre of the island being carried off by Datis and Artaphernes in B.C. 490 and settled in a district near Susa [6, 101, 119]. The town however recovered sufficiently to contribute to the Greek fleet and army in B.C. 480—479 [8, 46; 9, 28].

ERXANDER, c. 37.

A man of Mytilene in Lesbos, father of Koes (q.v.), cp. 8, 97.

ERYX, c. 43. ERYKINIAN TERRITORY, c. 45.

A town and district in the extreme W. of Sicily, about 6 miles from Drepana. Its inhabitants were not Greeks [Thucyd. 6, 2], but a Sicilian tribe called Elymi. In the territory was Mt. Eryx [*Mte. S. Giuliano*] on which was a celebrated temple of Aphrodite. It was believed to have been founded by Aeneas [Verg. Aen. 5, 759], or according to others by Eryx, who contended with Herakles for it and was conquered [Diod. Sic. 4, 23].

ETEOKLES, c. 61.

Son of Oedipus and Iokaste, and joint ruler of Thebes with his brother Polyneikes. The latter after sundry quarrels took refuge with Adrastos (q.v.), who led the expedition of the Seven against Thebes. Eteokles and Polyneikes fell by each other's hands [Paus. 9, 5, 6].

EUALKIDAS, c. 102.

A man of Eretria, and a successful competitor in the games.

EUBOEA, c. 31.

The statement in the text that Euboea is 'as large and rich as Kypros' is not true; Kypros being rather more than twice as great as Euboea. It stretches from the Malian gulf about half-way down the coast of Attica, and is divided by the range of hills which, running down the centre, marks it out into three principal plains, that of Histiaia (Oreos) in the North, that between Chalkis and Eretria in the Western region (Lelantum), and that of Karystos in the South. The country people in the centre were a hardy race of mountain shepherds; and such towns as the island had were either Ionian colonies (as Eretria) or inhabited by the older race of Dryopians, or Thrakian immigrants from Abae.

EUELTHON, c. 104.

A king of Salamis in Kypros, who died somewhere about B.C. 530 [4, 162].

EUPHRATES, c. 52.

Herodotos conceives the Euphrates as bounding Kilikia and Armenia, which is giving Armenia a much greater extension than in subsequent times. It has a length of 1780 miles. Rising in the Taurus, and uniting with the Tigris at *Kurndh*, it discharges itself into the Persian Gulf near the town of *Basrah*. Before joining the Tigris it passes Babylon [1, 180], above which it was navigated in wicker boats or coracles covered with skins [1, 194]. Kyros is said to have crossed it by draining off a great deal of its water into a marsh [1, 191]. Cp. Polyb. 9, 43.

EURIPOS, c. 77.

The channel between Euboea and the mainland, which at its narrowest point opposite Chalkis was joined in B.C. 410 by a bridge, whence the modern name of Euboea,—Negropont [Egripo—Pont]. The current through this strait is exceedingly rapid and frequently changes. See Aeschin. in Ctes. § 90. Plato Phaedo, 901.

EUROPE, cc. 1, 12.

According to Herodotos Europe ended at the Kolchian Phasis (*Rioni*); though others looked upon the Tanais (*Don*) as the boundary to the N.E. [4, 45]. Its extremities to the N. and W. were unknown [3, 115—6].

EURYLEON, c. 46.

One of the followers of Dorieus in his expedition into Italy and Sicily.

EURYSTHENES, c. 39.

Son of Aristodemos, and fifth in descent from Herakles, with whom began the elder family of the kings of Sparta [6, 51, 52; 8, 131]. See *Herakleidae*.

GELEON, c. 66.

Mythical son of Ion, from whom the Attic tribe of Geleontes was supposed to be descended. For the form see note to the passage.

GEPHYRAEI, cc. 55, 57—8, 61—2.

Literally the 'People of the bridge', that is of Tanagra in Boeotia, which was once called Gephyra from the bridge over the Asopos [Steph. Byz.; Strabo, 9, 404]. The Phoenikian origin here ascribed to them by Herodotos is regarded by Plutarch [de Malign. 23] as a covert insult to Aristogeiton. Another theory as to the name is that which derives it from a deme Gephyreis [Γεφυρεῖς] on the road to Eleusis, so called from a bridge over the Kephisos.

GERGITHAE, c. 122.

A tribe in the Troad living in the hill-country S. of Lampsakos, between the Skamander and Granikos, whose chief town was Gergis. The country was famous for its vines. The name was also known in the territory of Kymae; but the Gergithae were believed to be a remnant of the Trojan people [Her. 7, 43; Strabo 13, 1, 19].

GETAE, cc. 3, 4.

A Thrakian tribe, near the Danube [4, 96]. The name in later times was used as equivalent to 'Dacians' [Dio Cass. 51, 22]. The similarity of the name, and of some of their customs, has induced some scholars to hold the theory that they are identical with the Goths. They were warlike and predatory long after this, as we know from Ovid in his exile at Tomi [Trist. 3, 1, 6].

GORGO, cc. 48, 51.

Daughter of Kleomenes, king of Sparta, who married her half-uncle Leonidas [7, 239]. She was praised by Plutarch as among the famous women and wives in Greece [Conjugal. praecept. 48]; and he attributes to her the famous retort to some one who said 'Your Spartan women are the only women who govern the men'. 'Yes, for we are the only women who bear men' [Lycurg. 14].

GORGOS, c. 104.

King of Salamis in Kypros.

GYGAEA, c. 21.

Sister of Alexander of Makedonia, and wife of the Persian Bubares, by whom she had a son Amyntas [8, 136].

GYGES, c. 121.

A Lydian, father of Myrsos [3, 122].

GYNDES, c. 52.

The river now called *Diyalah* (or *Diala*) which rises in the mountains of Matiene, and falls into the Tigris a little below Bagdad. See 1, 189, and Bunbury, *Ancient Geography*, vol. i. p. 253. It has however been identified by others with the *Kerkhah* and the *Mendeli*. See Smith's *Dict. of Ancient Geography*. The doubt has arisen from Herodotos in this passage seeming to place the river near the Choaspes and Susa.

HALYS, c. 52.

A river in Asia Minor, rising in the mountains of Armenia, which, after flowing southward through Pontos and Kappadokia, turns to the north and falls into the Euxine. In the last part of its course it is the boundary between Paphlagonia on the west, and Pontos and Galatia on the east. When the Lydian kingdom was flourishing, it formed the boundary between it and the Persian Empire. Thus it came to be considered as marking a great division between two great parts of Asia, —Asia *cis Halyn* [ἐντὸς Ἅλυος] and *trans Halyn* [1, 6, 28, 72].

HARMODIOS, c. 55.

One of the assassins of Hipparchos [6, 109, 122]. See *Aristogeiton*.

HEGESANDROS, c. 125.

Father of Hekataios (q.v.), a man of Miletos [6, 137].

HEGESISTRATROS, c. 94.

A natural son of Peisistratos by an Argive woman, whom his father made ruler of Sigeium. Nothing is known of his life or rule.

HEKATAIOS, cc. 36, 125—6.

A native of Miletos, son of Hegesandros, and of a family of wealth and distinction [2, 143]. He flourished about B.C. 520, and between that time and about B.C. 500 produced different works on history [γενεαλογίαι or ἱστορίαι], and on geography [περίοδος γῆς or περιήγησις]. He travelled in Egypt, and along the N. Coast of Africa, and probably more widely in Asia and Europe. For the extent and nature of his knowledge see Bunbury, *Ancient Geography*, vol. i. pp. 137—144. Herodotos knew and used his works, but denies some of his statements [4, 36].

HELEN, c. 94.

Wife of Menelaos of Sparta, and daughter of Tyndareus and Leda, whose abduction by Paris led to the Trojan war. For another legend as to her previous abduction into Attica by Pirithoos and Theseus, see 9, 73.

HELLAS, cc. 32, 49, 93.

HELLENES, cc. 20—3, 47, 58, 94, 97, 102.

HELLENIC DRESS (Women), c. 88.

The dress of Greek women consisted of a chiton and an outer garment answering to the men's himation and called ἐπίβλημα or ἀμπεχόνη or ἀμπεχόνιον. It is the chiton only that Herodotos alludes to in this chapter, and he distinguishes between the Doric i.e. woollen shift fastened on the shoulders by brooches, and the Ionic or long sleeved chiton of linen. See Becker's *Charicles*, pp. 421—7.

HELLENIC GODS, c. 49.

Herodotos uses Hellas and Hellenes in the widest sense, to include all united by common descent from Hellen, common language, and in the main common religion. He says that the inhabitants of Hellas were originally Pelasgi, who did not move much, and on whom the Hellenic immigrations were engrafted [1, 56].

HELLENIC SEA, the, c. 54.

The Aegean Sea, and the part of the Mediterranean which washes the shores of Greece.

HELLESPONTII, c. 1.

Not a national name; but applying generally to the people living in the various towns on the shores of the Hellespont.

HELLESPONTOS, cc. 13, 14, 23, 33, 91, 103, 117, 122.

The narrow strait (varying in breadth from 1 to 3 miles), now called the *Dardanelles*, between the Thrakian Chersonese and the coast of Asia. For the Greek colonies on its shores, see 6, 33. They had mostly been attracted there by the trade with the countries round the Black Sea [6, 26].

HERAEUM, c. 92, § 7.

Temple of Herè at Korinth, on the ascent to the Akropolis, built by a certain Bounos [Paus. 2, 4, 7].

HERAKLEIA, c. 43.

Herakleia Minoa on the S. coast of Sicily between Agrigentum and Selinus. The legend said that it was founded by Minos of Krete in a part of Sicily of which Herakles had taken possession after conquering the hero Eryx. It was believed to occupy a site formerly held by a town named Makara, and the probability is that the name Herakleia was given it when the place was taken by Euryleon. It became rapidly prosperous, but was destroyed by the Carthaginians about B.C. 450—400. It afterwards revived, and was of some importance in the 1st Punic war, but is now represented only by some insignificant ruins on the S. bank of the River Halykos (*Platani*).

HERAKLEIDAE, c. 43.

Descendants of Herakles. The received legend was that the family of Herakles, expelled from Argos by Eurystheus, returned with the Dorians living near Parnassos under Hyllos son of Herakles, and conquered Argolis, Lakonia, and Messene. The royal families of Sparta were believed to be Herakleids (though not Dorian, see c. 72), as was also the royal family of Lydia [1, 7; 7, 204; 9, 26]. The Spartan families were traced as follows [8, 131]:

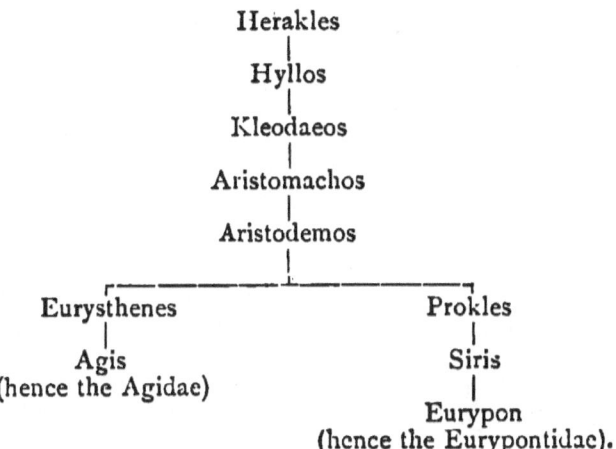

HERAKLEIDES,

(1) c. 37. Father of Aristagoras, ruler of Kymae.

(2) c. 121. Son of Ibanolis, ruler of Mylasa in Karia. For his brother Oliatos, see c. 37.

HERAKLEION, c. 63.

A temple and precinct of Herakles in Attica at Kynosarges (q.v.).

HERAKLES, c. 43.

Son of Zeus and Alkmena. For his widely spread worship see 2, 43—4; 4, 59. The part of the legend of Herakles here referred to is his conquests in the West, on his journey to and from Erytheia to fetch the oxen of Geryones. At Rhegium one of the oxen leapt into the sea and swam to Sicily, when Eryx, son of Poseidon, took it and put it in his own herd. Herakles followed, fought and killed Eryx, and then took possession of a large part of western Sicily [Apoll. 2, 5, 10].

HERMES, c. 7.

The messenger of Zeus, the god of the market-place and the rostrum. To him is ascribed the invention of useful arts and sciences, success in business, craft and subtlety. To what Thrakian god Herodotos here gives the name of Hermes is not known.

HERMOPHANTOS, c. 99.

A Milesian, one of the commanders of the Ionian expedition against Sardis.

HERMOS, c. 101.

The chief river of Lydia, south of which stood Sardis [1, 55], and into which the Paktolos, which ran through Sardis, falls. The district towards its mouth in which Kymae stood was called Hermopedion from it [Steph. Byz.].

HIPPARCHOS, cc. 55—6, 62.

Younger son of Peisistratos. His elder brother Hippias succeeded his father as tyrannos of Athens. There was a belief current soon after in Athens that he was the elder, and that Hippias only became tyrannos on his death. But Thucydides [6, 54—5] says that he had satisfied himself that this was not the case; Herodotos' words confirm this, for he never gives him the title of tyrannos. For his assassination, see *Aristogeiton*.

HIPPIAS, cc. 55, 62, 91—2, 94, 96.

The elder son of Peisistratos (q.v.). His expulsion took place in B.C. 510, four years after his brother Hipparchos' assassination, which embittered him with his subjects and induced him to many acts of severity [Thucyd. 6, 59]. His vain attempt to recover his power, and his retirement to Sigeium are narrated in this book. He afterwards went to the court of Dareios, and accompanied the Persian expedition beaten at Marathon in B.C. 490, to which spot he guided the enemy [6, 102, 107—9, 121], just as he had before landed there with his father [1, 62]. He was then an old man and seems to have died shortly afterwards; for no more is heard of his interference in Greek politics [Thucyd. 6, 59].

HIPPOKOON, c. 60.

Drove his brothers Tyndareus and Ikarion from Sparta, and was afterwards slain by Herakles [Apollod. 3, 10, 5].

HIPPOKRATES, c. 65.

Father of Peisistratos. He was a private citizen and was warned of the great future of his yet unborn son by a prodigy [1, 59].

HISTIAIOS, cc. 11, 24—5, 30, 35, 106—8, 123.

Son of Lysagoras, and tyrant of Miletos. He was one of the Greek tyrants who resisted the proposal to cut the bridge over the Ister, and so to prevent the retreat of Dareios from Skythia [4, 137—8]. For that service he was rewarded by the gift of Myrkinos and its territory in the land of the Edones. After the events narrated in this book, he came down to Ionia at the bidding of Dareios; and finding that Artaphernes was quite aware of his secret part in the revolt, and being refused admittance into Miletos, he went to Chios; and thence, after being imprisoned and released, to Byzantium [6, 1—5], where he supported himself by piracy and laying contributions on the corn-ships; and when he was strong enough he tried to punish the Chians by seizing the island [6, 26—7]. Next he attacked Thasos for the sake of its gold mines. Thence, in fear of the king's Phoenikian fleet, he went to Lesbos. Not finding sufficient provisions there, he crossed to the mainland, where he was captured and taken to Sardis. There Artaphernes, without waiting to refer to the king, crucified him [6, 28, 30].

GEOGRAPHICAL INDEX.

HOMER, c. 67.

Herodotos considers that Homer flourished 400 years before himself [2, 53]. He attributes to him or 'some earlier poet' the idea of a circumambient Ocean [2, 33]; and, in conjunction with Hesiod, the mythical lineage and inter-connexion of the gods [2, 53]. His quotations from Homer [see 2, 117; 4, 29; 7, 161] are not frequent, but in each case agree with the text of the Iliad and Odyssey as we now have them. The *Kypria* and *Epigoni* he does not believe to be by Homer [2, 117; 4, 32].

HOPLES, c. 66.

A son of Ion, from whom the Ionic tribe of Hopletes in Attica were supposed to have sprung. His daughter Meta was said to have married Aegeus, father of Theseus [Apollod. 3, 15, 6].

HYATAE, c. 68.

A name given in scorn to one of the Dorian tribes at Sikyon by Kleisthenes, lit. Pig-folk [ὗς].

HYLLEIS, c. 68.

One of the three Dorian tribes. See *Dymanatae*.

HYSIAE, c. 74.

A small border town on the N. slope of Kithairon, on the pass from Attica to Thebes [6, 108; 9, 15, 25].

HYSTASPES, c. 73.

Father of Artaphernes, and of Dareios (q.v.), son of Arsames [1, 209].

IAMIDAE, c. 44.

A family of Elis in which the mantic art was hereditary, descended from Iamos, reputed son of Apollo by a nymph Euadne [Pind. Olymp. 6, 30—5]. Their chief resort was Sparta where they had a tomb [9, 33; Pausan. 3, 12, 8]; but members of the family went to other places where a mantis was in request, as to the court of Polykrates of Samos [3, 132], and to Syrakuse [Pind. l.c.].

IATRAGORAS, c. 37.

An Ionian employed to seize the fleet lately employed by Artaphernes against Naxos.

IBANOLIS, cc. 37, 121.

A man of Mylasa in Karia, and father of Oliatos and Herakleides.

IDRIAS, c. 118.

A city and district in Karia. Stephanos Byz. says that it was formerly called Chrysaoris; and it is supposed that its site was afterwards occupied by the town of Stratonikeia, on the mouth of the river Marsyas [mod. *Eskihissar*], Leake, *Asia Minor* p. 229.

H. V. 14

ILIUM, territory of, c. 94, 122.

The territory which was believed to have formed the kingdom of Troy or Ilium, and which in the time of Herodotos was still called the Troad (Troas), forming a district of Mysia, and comprising the coast district on the Aegean from Cape Lektum to Abydos on the Hellespont [7, 42]; cp. 2, 118 ἡ Τευκρὶς γῆ.

IMBROS, c. 26.

An island off the Thrakian Chersonese, about 35 miles in circumference, mountainous and well wooded, with fertile valleys. Its Pelasgic inhabitants were afterwards replaced by, or amalgamated with Athenian colonists.

INDIANS, c. 3.

The knowledge of India possessed by Herodotos was confined to the Punjaub and valley of the Indus. These Indians were the people living furthest East of any known to him [4, 40]; beyond them was an unknown sandy desert [3, 98; 4, 40—4]. He knows also nothing of their habits, or of the produce of the country except cotton, gold and bamboos [3, 106]. Some of the tribes he says were extraordinarily barbarous [3, 98—101], but these were in all probability tribes living not in India, but on the frontiers. The Indians were partially subdued by Dareios and subjected to tribute [3, 98, 101; 4, 44]; and we find some of them serving in the great army of Xerxes [7, 65; 9, 31]. See Bunbury, *Ancient Geography*, vol. I. p. 226.

IOLKOS, c. 94.

A city of Magnesia at the bottom of the Pagasaean Gulf, and at the foot of Pelion; it was inhabited by Minyes, and from it the Argo was said to have started. It is called by Homer εὐρύχορος [Il. 2, 712] 'with fair wide territory'; but it lost importance in historical times, and was finally deserted on the foundation of Demetrias in B.C. 290.

ION, c. 66.

The mythical ancestor of the Ionians; he was said to be the son of Xuthos, third son of Hellen [7, 74; 8, 44].

IONIA, cc. 30, 31, 98, 106, 108, 115, 123.
IONIANS, cc. 28, 30, 49, 58, 97—109, 111, 115—7, 122—3.
IONIAN, c. 33. IONIC, c. 87.

Ionia was the maritime district of Asia Minor, extending from the River Hermos on the north to a short distance S. of Miletos. 'The 'region', says Herodotos, 'is the fairest in the whole world: for no 'other is so blessed as Ionia, either North or South or East or West of 'it. For elsewhere the climate is either too cold and damp, or else the 'heat and drought are oppressive' [1, 142]. Pausanias [7, 5, 2] also says that, 'The Ionians have the very best possible temperature of the seasons'. In this pleasant region the cities were colonized by the Ionians, and together with the islands of Samos and Chios established an Amphiktyony, or community for religious worship, the centre of which was the Panionium, or temple of Poseidon, on the promontory of Mykale; though for political purposes the states were independent. Ephesos and Miletos, the two principal cities, were believed to have been founded by the two sons of Kodros, king of Athens, Androkles and Neileos; and therefore Athens was regarded as in a sense the Metropolis or mother city of Ionia. But the Athenians and other Ionic states in Greece became ashamed of the title 'Ionian', and did their best to renounce it. The Asiatic cities on the other hand were proud of it, and they became to all intents and purposes 'Ionia'. The cities were Miletos, Myūs and Priene, *in Karia:* Ephesos, Kolophon, Lebedos, Teos, Klazomenae, Erythrae and Phokaea, *in Lydia:* the islands of *Samos* and *Chios*. They were not purely Ionic; for the Ionian settlers had intermarried with the original Karians, Lydians, and other inhabitants, and they did not all speak the same dialect; but the predominant element in them all was Ionian. By B.C. 528 all these towns had been reduced to subjection to Persia, by Harpagos the general of Kyros [1, 162—170]. The only member of the confederacy still remaining free was Samos, which under Polykrates for a time maintained great power and prosperity. But by B.C. 519 Samos too submitted to become tributary [3, 39—47; 54—6; 120—5]. It is the rising of these tributary states, beginning by the expulsion of the despots established by Persian influence, and its suppression, as related in the first part of this book, that served to bring about the collision between Persia and the continental Greeks.

ISAGORAS, cc. 66, 70, 72, 74.

Son of Tisander, and Archon Eponymos at Athens, B.C. 508 [Ol. 68, 1]. Almost all that we know of him is what Herodotos here tells us of his opposition to Kleisthenes. Plutarch [de Mal. 23] remarks that assigning him a Karian origin was meant as a sneer [εἰς Κᾶρας ὥσπερ εἰς κόρακας ἀποδιοπομπουμένου τὸν Ἰσάγοραν]. His forcible occupation of the Akropolis, in order to obtain absolute rule, involved some of his followers in condemnation and death, though he seems to have escaped himself [Paus. 6, 8, 6].

ISTER, cc. 9—10.

The Danube, which according to Herodotos, forms the northern boundary of that part of Europe known to the Greeks as partaking in any civilization. The countries now known as Hungary and Austria would at that time be much covered with vast forests. The river is said by Herodotos to rise in the country of the Kelts near the town Pyrene, (which seems to be a confusion for the Pyrenees, he being unacquainted with the Alps) and flowing through the whole of Europe to finally fall into the Euxine [2, 33; 4, 49]. See Bunbury, *Ancient Geography*, vol. I. p. 168.

ITALIA, c. 43.

By Italy Herodotos seems to mean what was afterwards Lucania, and especially the Greek colonies planted on its coast [see note ad loc.]. Calabria he calls Iapygia [3, 138; 4, 99] and it does not seem clear whether Tarentum is conceived as being in Italy proper [1, 24; 3, 138; 7, 170]. The most northerly Greek towns on the W. coast mentioned by him are Velia and Posidonium, the former of which is said to be in Oenotria [1, 167]. He seems to have known nothing of central Italy, but the Tyrrhenians on the N. of the Tiber are mentioned several times [1, 163, 166—7; 6, 17, 22]; and he seems to have some confused notion of the Kelts living north of Umbria, though he appears to place both further west than Italy, while he thinks that the 'Alps' is the name of a river [4, 49].

KADMEIANS, cc. 57, 61.   KADMEIAN LETTERS, c. 59.

KADMOS, c. 57—8.

According to the legend accepted by Herodotos, Kadmos (whose name means 'Eastern') was a Tyrian [2, 49], son of Agenor, who set out in search of Europa, and first landed in the island of Thera, where he left some of his Phoenikian companions [4, 147], and proceeded himself to Boeotia [2, 49], where he either founded or occupied Thebes, and was the father of Semele, Inoe and Agauè [2, 45; Paus. 9, 5, 2]. Thence he migrated to the Illyrians, where the grave of his wife Harmonia was shewn [Athen. xi. p. 462 B], and where their posterity reigned [c. 51; Pausan. 9, 15, 3; Strab. 7, 7, 8]. A spot was shewn on the Akropolis of Thebes where his house was said to have stood [Paus. 9, 12, 3], as well as the place where he sowed the dragon's teeth [Paus. 9, 10, 1]. There were many variations in this legend: one tradition, for instance, asserting that he came not from Phoenikia, but from Egypt [Paus. 9, 12, 2]. There is reason to think that the legend has behind it a real fact of a Phoenikian migration into Greece, or at least of the introduction of certain Phoenikian arts by the traders of that part of the world.

KAINEADES, c. 92, § 2.

Descendants of Kaineus, the family to which Eëtion (q.v.) belonged. Kaineus was said to be the son of Koronos, one of the Lapithae [Il. 1, 264; Paus. 5, 10, 8].

KALCHEDONIANS, c. 26 (or Chalkedon).

The inhabitants of Kalchedon (*Kadi-Kioi*), in Bithynia at the entrance of the Thrakian Bosporus, and opposite Byzantium, from which it is separated by about 1¾ miles [Polyb. 4, 39], with a territory extending along the Asiatic side of the Bosporus. It was a colony of Megara [Thucyd. 4, 75], and Megabazos remarked that the founders must have been blind not to have chosen the better site of Byzantium, which was founded 17 years later [4, 144]. [The coins that remain all have Καλχ. not Χαλκ., as have the best MSS. of Herodotos.]

KALLIAS, cc. 44—5.

A mantis of Elis, of the family of the Iamidae (q.v.).

KAMBYSES, cc. 25—6.

Son and successor of Kyros and Kassandane. He became king of Persia, according to the usual reckoning, B.C. 529 and died B.C. 521.

The chief event of his reign was his expedition into and conquest of Egypt [3, 1—25]. His undoubted madness was attributed by the Egyptians to his profaning the festival of their god Apis, and even wounding the god himself [3, 29—39]. But in spite of this his rule appears to have been popular with the subject countries, which he relieved of heavy taxation [3, 67]. During his absence a revolt was raised in Persia by two Magi, and a man named Smerdis (pretended to be his half-brother) was put up in his place. Kambyses heard of this when he had removed to Ekbatana in Syria, and was on the point of marching to suppress the revolt, when he was accidentally wounded by his own sword, and, after lingering for about 3 weeks, died from mortification of the wounded limb [3, 61—66].

KAPPADOKIA, c. 52. KAPPADOKIANS, c. 52.

The district between the Halys on the west, Armenia on the east, the Pontos on the north and the Tauros on the south. The limits however are not clearly defined by Herodotos, who counts part of the district north of the Tauros in Kilikia. The people are also called Syri or Syrii [1, 72], and in Makedonian times (i.e. after B.C. 330) it was divided into two kingdoms,—the southern, bordering on the Tauros, being called *the Kappadokia*, the northern 'Kappadokia on the Pontos', or simply 'Pontos'. Under the Persians these kingdoms were two Satrapies.

KARCHEDONII, c. 42.

The inhabitants of Karchedon (Carthage). The Carthaginians were the natural rivals and enemies of the Greeks and their extension in the West, especially in Sicily [7, 163]. They naturally therefore joined in ejecting Dorieus and his Greek followers, when trying to set up a Greek colony in Africa. This jealousy of Greek activity was utilised by the Great King in his own war on Greece [7, 165—7]. For their Phoenikian origin see 3, 19.

KARIA, cc. 103, 117, 122.
KARIANS, cc. 117—121. KARIAN, a, cc. 111—112.

The Karians, inhabiting a district in Asia Minor, between Ionia on the north and Lykia on the south, were according to Herodotos an ancient race of Leleges with a mixture of Dorian and Ionian settlers. They had once been widely spread in the Islands [1, 171; Thucyd. 1, 8], whence they had been forced back, according to tradition, by Minos of Krete. The country now called by their name had been subdued by Kroisos [1, 28] and then by the Persians under Harpagos [1, 174]. Though they are described in this book as winning some successes against the Persians in behalf of the Ionians, they submitted again after the fall of Miletos [6, 25].

KARIAN DRESS, c. 88.

The Karians were not regarded as Hellenic, though their language was largely mixed with Greek words [1, 171; Hom. Il. 2, 867; cp. 8, 135]; but that their dress should have come to be considered as the original Ionian dress is in accordance with what Herodotos says about their introduction of particular fashions in armour afterwards adopted by Hellenes.

KARIAN ZEUS, see *Zeus*.

KAUKASA, c. 33.

An unknown place on the coast of the Island of Chios.

KAUNOS, c. 103.

A town in the S. of Karia opposite Rhodes, the district being therefore called the Rhodian Peraea. The people looked upon themselves as immigrants from Krete, though Herodotos does not believe it. Their customs differed from those of other Karians, though their language was closely allied with Karian [1, 172]. It had been reduced into the power of the Persians by Harpagos [1, 176]. It was afterwards in possession of the Rhodians, though from time to time freed from them [Polyb. 30, 19; 31, 7].

KAYSTRIOS, c. 100.

The River, the mouth of which formed the harbour of Ephesos, flows down the valley between the Mt. Messogis and Tmolos. It is now called the *Little Mendere*, and the great amount of alluvial deposit brought down by it has turned what was once a harbour into a flat swamp, in continuation of what Homer called the Ἄσιος λειμών [Il. 2, 461; cp. Verg. G. 1, 383].

KEIAN, a, c. 102.

A native of the island of Keos (*Zea*), whose inhabitants were Ionians from Athens [8, 46]. See *Simonides*.

KELEAS, c. 46.

A Spartan, one of the companions of Dorieus in his expedition to Italy.

KILIKIA, cc. 52, 108. KILIKIANS, cc. 49, 52, 118.

In later times the northern frontier of Kilikia was Mt. Tauros, and the eastern Mt. Amanos, but Herodotos (c. 52) seems to extend it to the N. over the district otherwise called Kataonia, so as to be coterminous with Kappadokia, and to the E. up to the R. Euphrates. The inhabitants, called once Hypachaei [7, 91] were probably connected with the Phoenikians.

KINDYAN, c. 118.

A native of Kindys, a town in Karia, near Bargylia. See Polyb. 16, 12 'Among the people of Bargylia it is a common report widely believed that the statue of the Kindyan Artemis, though in the open air, is never touched by snow or rain'. The exact position of Kindys however is unknown.

GEOGRAPHICAL INDEX.   215

KINEAS, c. 63.

A king (or perhaps Tagus) in Thessaly, a native of the town Konium in Phrygia. For the doubt as to the name of the town and the position of Kineas, see note.

KINYPS, c. 42.

A river and town between the two Syrtes on the coast of Africa. The river is described by Herodotos [4, 175] as rising in a height called the Hill of the Graces (*Mt. Ghuriano*). It was in a district rich in corn [4, 198] and famous for goats with very beautiful hair [Verg. G. 3, 312].

KIOS, c. 122.

A city in Mysia (or according to later divisions in Bithynia) on the Kianaean Gulf (*Gulf of Mundamieh*), on a river of the same name. It was destroyed in B.C. 202 by Philip V. of Makedonia, and handed over to king Prusias, who refounded it and called it by his own name [Strabo 12, 4, 3; Polyb. 15, 21—23; Livy, 31, 31]. It was a colony from Miletos.

KISSIA, cc. 49, 52.

A district in Asia [mod. *Khuzistan*] of which the capital was Susa.

KLAZOMENAE, c. 123.

One of the Ionian cities in Lydia [1, 142], between Smyrna and Erythrae. It was really on an island or islands close to the mainland, from which the inhabitants had removed for security against the Persians [Paus. 7, 3, 8]. The Klazomenians were a prosperous and enterprising people; were engaged in trade with Egypt [2, 178]; endeavoured to colonize Abdera in Thrace [1, 168]; and in conjunction with the Milesians founded Kardia, the largest city on the Hellespontine Chersonese [Strabo, 7, § 51]. They had a treasure-deposit at Delphi [1, 51].

KLEISTHENES,

(1) cc. 67, 69.

The last tyrannos of Sikyon of a dynasty established by Orthagoras, which lasted 100 years, owing, says Aristotle (Pol. 5, 11), to the moderate and law-abiding character of the Sovereigns. His high reputation is shewn by his being selected by the Amphiktyons to command the joint army in the Sacred War [B.C. 595—585] in which Kirrha was destroyed [Paus. 10, 37, 7]. He died some time after B.C. 582. His famous device for selecting a husband for his daughter Agariste is described in 6, 126, 128—130.

(2) cc. 66—7, 69, 70, 72—3, 75.

Son of Megakles (son of Alkmaeon) and Agariste the daughter of Kleisthenes of Sikyon. For his reforms on the Solonian constitution at Athens, see notes to c. 66, and Grote, *History of Greece*, vol. IV. p. 56—68. The foundation of the reforms was the division of all into ten tribes, containing a certain number of demes, the demes being not necessarily contiguous, and often designedly remote. Hence came various arrangements founded on this tenfold division, as, the ten strategi with the taxiarchs and phylarchs, the council of 500, the 6000 Heliastic dikasts, and the 10 Apodektae or commissioners of the Exchequer. The upshot was that political rights of individual citizens were founded on the membership of a deme, which to a man of clear Attic birth depended on place of residence, and not on membership of a particular family or gens. Of Kleisthenes' life after his banishment and recall we know nothing.

KLEOMBROTOS, cc. 32, 41.

Son of Anaxandridas (q.v.), king of Sparta, and twin brother of Leonidas. When Leonidas fell at Thermopylae in B.C. 480, leaving an infant son Pleistarchos, Kleombrotos became his guardian, but dying between the autumn and spring of B.C. 480—479 was succeeded in that office by his own son Pausanias [8, 71; 9, 10].

KLEOMENES, cc. 39, 41—2, 48—53, 64, 70, 72—4, 76, 90, 97.

Son of Anaxandridas by his 2nd wife, and 16th king of Sparta of the elder line (Agidae) from B.C. 520 to B.C. 491. He was apparently always eccentric and finally became hopelessly insane and killed himself in a fit of madness, which was supposed to have been brought on by intemperance [6, 76]. Before the visit of Aristagoras he had led an invasion of Argos, and behaved in it with both impiety and cruelty [6, 76—83]. After the events in his life recorded in this book, we find him engaged in punishing Aegina for giving earth and water to the King's ambassadors [6, 49—51, 73]; deposing his colleague Demaratos [6, 61, 65—7]; and after a temporary exile restored to his kingdom, and dying by his own hand [6, 74—5].

KODROS, cc. 65, 76.

Kodros son of Melanthos was, according to the legend, the last king of Athens. He sacrificed himself for his country by disguising himself and provoking one of the Dorian invaders to kill him, whom an oracle had declared would conquer Athens 'if they spared her king'. —*Codrus pro patria non timidus mori* [Hor. Od. 3, 19, 2]. There was a statue of him at Athens, and the place where he met his death was shewn [Pausan. 1, 10, 1; 1, 19, 5]. His son Neileos was said to have been the founder of Miletos [9, 97].

KOES, cc. 11, 37—8.

Son of Exander of Mitylene. He commanded the Lesbian contingent in the army of Dareios in the invasion of Skythia, and with the other Greek princes was left in charge of the bridge across the Danube [4, 97]. In return for his good service he was made tyrant of Mitylene, and either because of the manner of his appointment, or from the way he exercised his power, seems to have excited the hatred of his people more than most tyranni.

KONIAEAN, c. 63.

See Kineas, and note on the passage. If it is to stand, it must be interpreted to mean of Konium or Ikonium in Phrygia, mod. *Koniyeh*.

KORESSOS, c. 100.

A town near Ephesos, probably on the coast, and apparently considered as a suburb of Ephesos [Paus. 5, 24, 8].

KORINTHOS, cc. 92—3.   KORINTHIAN, cc. 87, 92—3.

KORINTHIANS, cc. 75, 92.

The territory of Korinth was mountainous and rugged, separated from the Megarid by the range of Geraneia, and from Argolis by another range which is an extension of the Akrokorinthos and Mts. Oneia. Its importance arose from its position between two seas, and its commanding the road from Northern Greece to Peloponnesos. The inhabitants were chiefly Dorians; and, though we find them now on friendly terms with the Athenians, soon after the Persian wars the two peoples became estranged, and the Athenians were eager to minimise the service done by the Korinthian ships at Salamis [8, 94]. The city consisted of a lofty and secure citadel, the Akrokorinthos, and a town round its base enclosed by a wall, and two harbour towns, Lechaeum on the West, and Kenchreae on the East, the latter some eight miles from the chief town. Korinth was the mother city of many flourishing colonies, such as Syrakuse, Korkyra, Potidaea. Its early maritime greatness is attested by the fact that triremes were first built there [Thucyd. 1, 13].

KORONEIANS, c. 79.

The inhabitants of Koroneia, a town in Boeotia, on a hill near Mt. Helikon and looking over the Lake Kopais. The inhabitants had originally come from Thessaly near a town of the same name (in Phthiotis). In the plain at the foot of the hill was a temple of Athene Itonia at which the Panboeotia was held [Paus. 9, 34, 1].

KRATHIA, see *Athenè*.

KRATHIS, c. 45.

A considerable river in Bruttium, flowing into the gulf of Tarentum. Near it stood the city of Sybaris. It received its name from the Achaian founders of Sybaris after a stream in Achaia [1, 145].

KRESTONIANS, cc. 3, 5.

The inhabitants of Kreston or Krestonia, a town and district of Thrakia, or afterwards of Makedonia, south of Mygdonia. They were Pelasgians, and spoke a language which Herodotos supposed to be Pelasgic [1, 57; cp. Thucyd. 4, 108].

KROISOS, c. 36.

King of Lydia from B.C. 560 to B.C. 546. He conquered the Asiatic Greeks [1, 26], and attempted, though unsuccessfully, to do the same to the Islanders [1, 27], and was finally conquered and deposed by

Kyros, who however spared his life [1, 79—88, 155—7; 3, 34—6]. His presents to the temple of Branchidae here mentioned were among numerous offerings made to Greek oracles which he consulted at the time he was expecting the attack of Kyros [1, 46 sq.; 6, 37—8, 125].

KROTON, cc. 44, 47. KROTONIAT͟S, the, cc. 44—7.
KROTONIATIS, c. 45.

An Achaian colony in Bruttium, which, founded about B.C. 710, rapidly rose to great wealth and power, so that in the 6th century B.C. it was the most important place in Magna Graecia, with a city whose walls enclosed as much as 12 miles in circuit [Livy 24, 3]; could put an army of 130,000 men in the field; and had a territory stretching across the Bruttian peninsula from sea to sea, bounded on the N. by the river Hylias [Thucyd. 7, 35]. The cause of its quarrel with Sybaris is not known. The two towns were both Achaian colonies, and for a long time appear to have grown side by side in amity. But about the middle of the 6th century [B.C. 550—540] the philosopher Pythagoras settled there, and under his influence, or that of his followers, great political changes appear to have taken place, ending in an uprising of the populace and the burning of the Pythagorean clubs or schools. It was apparently during this period that the war with Sybaris took place, possibly promoted, as so often in Greek towns, by exiled politicians. Some time after this (according to the most likely chronology) the Krotoniats suffered a crushing defeat on the River Sagras at the hands of the Lokrians and Rhegians. At the time of the 2nd Punic war it was still a large and important town with a harbour much used, at any rate in the summer [Polyb. X. 1]. The Krotoniats were celebrated for their handsome appearance, and for their success in the great Greek games. A flourishing school of physicians existed there very early and long survived [3, 129—138].

KURION, c. 113.

A town in Kypros (mod. *Piscopia*), said to have been founded by Kureos son of Kinyras the Phoenikian conqueror of the Island. It was 16 miles from Amathūs (*Limasol*) and near the River Lykos.

KYBEBE, c. 102.

A dialectical form of Kybele [Κυβέλη] the great goddess of the Phrygians and Lydians, whose orgiastic worship was principally celebrated on mountains and in woods [4, 76; Anacreontea 11; Strabo x. 3, 15]. Her worship was passed on to the Ionians and other Greeks, and she was identified with Rhea, mother of the gods. The temple here referred to at Sardis was a short distance S. of the town in a small plain of the Paktolos. Leake, *Travels in Asia Minor*, p. 342.

Κυκλάδες αἱ, cc. 30, 31.

A general name for the group of Islands S. of Attika and Euboea which are ranged roughly in a circle (ἐν κύκλῳ) round Delos. The number reckoned in the group has differed at different times, and according to different geographers. The oldest reckoning was apparently 12, viz. Keos, Kythnos, Seriphos, Melos, Siphnos, Kimolos, Paros, Naxos, Syros, Mykonos, Tenos, Andros. This however does not count Delos itself and Rheneia; the latter is sometimes inserted instead of Melos. Most of them were colonized by Ionians, who had supplanted the original Karian inhabitants [Thucyd. 1, 4]. Herodotos uses νῆσοι and νησιῶται (without article) to represent 'Island Greece', as opposed to Continental Greece; and the inhabitants seem very early to have acquired characteristics and a prosperity of their own. Until the Ionic revolt they had remained free from the subjection to the Persians to which the Asiatic Ionians had submitted.

KYLON, c. 71.

An Athenian of high birth, and enjoying the prestige of a victory at the Olympic games, married a daughter of Theagenes tyrant of Megara. This connexion seems to have been the ultimate motive for an attempt to obtain for himself the position of tyrannus at Athens. Consulting the oracle at Delphi he was bidden seize the Akropolis 'at the chief feast of Zeus'. With help of Theagenes and his own partisans he seized the Akropolis at the time of the next Olympic festival. But he was told afterwards that by the 'chief feast of Zeus' the god meant the Diasia which was celebrated outside Athens. He was immediately beleaguered on the Akropolis, and after standing a siege for a long while until he and his men were on the point of starvation, Kylon and his brother managed to escape, while the rest sat down as suppliants at the altar of Athene Polias, but were afterwards put to death by Megakles the Archon [see *Alkmaeonids, Kleisthenes*]. Herodotos seems to infer that Kylon himself perished in this way, but other authorities say that he escaped. [See Thucyd. 1, 126; Plutarch Sol. 12; Pausan. 1, 28, 40; 7, 25; Suid. s.v. Κυλώνειον ἄγος.] Whether Kylon was a mere selfish conspirator, or a leader of a popular movement against the Eupatrids, does not seem certain. If he was a popular champion, he lost the popular confidence when he went to the length of a seizure of the Akropolis; and Thirlwall, with some probability, thinks that the employment of Megarian troops, lent by his father-in-law, turned the people against him.

KYMEANS, cc. 37—8. KYME, c. 123.

Kyme a city of Aeolis, also sometimes called Amazonia from a supposed foundress Kyme an Amazon, north of the Hermos near a place now called *Sanderli*. It was a very ancient town, and apparently prosperous, but was never of great importance in Greek history. It was sometimes called Kyme Phrikonis [1, 149]. In conjunction with the Chalkidians of Euboea it founded the colony of Cumae in Italy [Strabo 5, 4, 4].

KYNOSARGES, c. 63.

A precinct of Herakles and gymnasium outside Athens near the Dromeian gate on the road to Marathon [6, 116].

KYPROS, cc. 31, 108—9, 113, 115.
KYPRIANS, cc. 9, 104, 109, 110, 112, 115—16.

An island off the coast of Kilikia, 150 miles long with a maximum breadth of 40 miles. Its inhabitants were a mixed race. The earliest known were Phoenikians; but there were also settlers from Arabia, as well as Greek colonies from Salamis, Athens and Kythnos [7, 90]. The island, though consisting of a number of quasi-independent states, had been successively reduced to subjection by Amasis of Egypt [2, 182], the Persians [3, 19, 91], and after the attempt at freedom recounted in this book was again reduced to subjection. It was important as a naval station, and was freed from the Persian sway, for the greater part, in B.C. 479 [Thucyd. 1, 94]; but the Athenians in B.C. 450 made a less successful attempt to drive the Persians out [Thucyd. 1, 112]. It was completely Hellenized under the influence of Euagoras king of Salamis [about B.C. 404—374], but it fell under the Persian yoke again in the time of his successor. From B.C. 295 it was attached (after some vicissitudes) to the kingdom of Ptolemy of Egypt, and was in B.C. 58 annexed to the Roman province of Kilikia.

KYPSELOS, cc. 92, 95.

The founder of a dynasty (*Kypselidae*) which ruled in Korinth through three generations, from B.C. 655 to B.C. 581. He himself ruled 30 years [B.C. 655—625]. He was a popular ruler, and was able to dispense with a body guard [Arist. Pol. 5, 12]. His romantic birth and preservation are narrated in these chapters. The means by which he obtained the tyranny were as usual the ingratiating himself with the people, first by his private conduct in contrast with the licentious behaviour of the Bakchiadae (q.v.), and secondly his mild administration of his office of polemarch [Nic. Dam. Fr. 56].

KYRENE, c. 47.

An Hellenic colony in Africa (*Ghrennah*) founded by Dorians under Battos from Thera B.C. 631 (according to the best theory, 4, 150 sqq.). Situated about ten miles from the shore it is in one of the most beautiful and fruitful districts in the world [4, 199]; and the Greek settlers forming close relations with the original inhabitants [4, 170], the colony soon became a large and prosperous state, governed at this time by a dynasty descended from the founder [the Battiadae], which was superseded by a republic about B.C. 450. It was celebrated for having the second best Medical School, that of Kroton being the best [3, 131]. The Kyrenaeans submitted to give presents and even tribute to Kambyses [3, 131]; but they seem to have held their own against Aryandes, the commander of the expedition sent by Dareios [4, 203].

KYROS, c. 52.

The founder of the Medo-Persian Empire. For the story of his birth and preservation see 1, 107 sqq. He is there said to have been the son of Kambyses by Mandane, daughter of Astyages king of the Medes. About B.C. 560 he led down the Persians from the hill country, conquered the Medes, and dethroned Astyages. In B.C. 546 he conquered the Lydian kingdom; and in B.C. 538 took Babylon [1, 190]; and died B.C. 528, slain in a battle with queen Tomyris [1, 214].

LABDA, c. 92, § 2.

Daughter of Amphion, one of the Bakchiadae of Korinth, and mother of Eetion (q.v.). The name is said to be from Λ, because of the malformation of her feet.

LABDAKOS, c. 59.

Father of Laios, and grand-father of Oedipus. He was grandson of Kadmos, and for a time king of Thebes.

LAIOS, cc. 43, 59—60.

Son of Labdakos and father of Oedipus (q.v.). Slain at the 'Schiste Hodos' by his son, who did not know him [Paus. 9, 5, 2].

LAKEDAEMON, cc. 38, 63, 75, 96.
LAKEDAEMONIANS, cc. 42, 50, 63—5, 90—3.
LAKEDAEMONIAN, cc. 32, 70, 97.

Lakedaemon is used as a synonym for Sparta; but, though 'Lakedaemonians' is often used indifferently for 'Spartans', it is sometimes employed by Herodotos to distinguish the whole inhabitants of Lakonia from the Spartans properly so called, i.e. the citizens of Sparta [see for instances 6, 80; 9, 28]. The number of these last is said to be about this time, or soon after, 8000 men of military age [7, 234]. At this period the Spartan territory included Lakonia and Messene, though the original inhabitants of Messene were always inclined to break away. Their rising supremacy in Hellas is shewn by the appeal to them to punish the Aeginetans for Medizing [6, 49], and by their being selected first by Aristagoras as the state to appeal to for help in Ionia, with which Athens had stronger natural ties and greater community of interests.

LAMPONIUM, c. 26.

An Aeolian colony on the Troad opposite Lesbos, sometimes called also Lamponeia [Steph. Byz.].

LAMPSAKOS, c. 117.

A city of Mysia on the Hellespont, originally called Pityusa, colonised and renamed from Phokaea and Miletos. Its tyrant Hippokles had a son Aeantides married to a daughter of Peisistratos [Thucyd. 6, 59]. It had a good harbour and a territory rich in vines.

LAODAMAS, c. 61.

A king of Thebes, son of Eteokles (q.v.), during whose reign the Epigoni attacked Thebes, and conquered him on the river Glisas. Laodamas fled to Illyricum [Paus. 9, 5, 7].

LAPITHAE, c. 92 § 2.

Supposed to be descended from Lapithes a son of Apollo, and to live in the mountain regions of Thessaly; after their famous fight with the Centaurs at the wedding of their king Peirithoos they were subdued by Herakles.

LEIPSYDRION, c. 62.

A place in Attica, fortified by the Alkmaeonids and other exiles to secure a hold on Athens, and their own return. It was in the deme Paeonia (or Paeonidae) which was to the north of Athens. See Arist. Lys. 665. A *skolion* or drinking-song is preserved in Athen. 695 E on the fighting which took place there

$$αἴ αἴ Λειψύδριον προδωσέταιρον$$
$$οἴους ἄνδρας ἀπώλεσας, μάχεσθαι$$
$$ἀγαθούς τε καὶ εὐπατρίδας$$
$$οἳ τότ' ἔδειξαν οἵων$$
$$πατέρων ἔσαν.$$

This confirms the statement in the text that the Alkmaeonidae had suffered severely at this place.

LEMNOS, cc. 26, 27. LEMNIANS, c. 27.

An island lying between the promontory of Athos and the Hellespont, about 150 square miles in area. Its earliest known inhabitants are called Sinties, which perhaps means pirates (σίνομαι); it afterwards received the Pelasgi expelled from Athens [6, 140]. Later on it was captured by Miltiades [6, 140].

LEONIDAS, c. 41.

The third son of Anaxandridas II. by his original wife, afterwards king of Sparta from B.C. 491 to B.C. 480, when he fell at Thermopylae [7, 204—222]. He left a young son called Pleistarchos by his wife Gorgo (q.v.) daughter of Kleomenes.

LĔROS, c. 125.

One of the Sporades, still called *Lero*, 30 miles South-west of Miletos, of which it was a colony, and by which it was governed.

LESBIANS, cc. 26, 98.

The inhabitants of Lesbos, an island about 7 miles from the coast of Mysia. Its original six territories were now reduced to two, those of Methymna and Mytilene, the latter of which later on gave its name to the whole Island. The inhabitants were mostly Aeolians. It had never fallen under the Lydian kings, though it had submitted to the suzerainty of the Persian king for a while [1, 169], and we find Dareios nominating a tyrannos of Mytilene [c. 11].

LIBYA, cc. 42—3. LIBYANS, c. 42.

Africa, as known to Herodotos, was the Northern part of the continent bounded by the Great Desert, beyond which he knew of no inhabited country. He had visited Egypt and gone to Elephantine just below the First Cataract, and had been informed of the course of the Nile further up [2, 29]. He had also probably been as far Westward as Kyrene [2, 181]. He thought it smaller than Europe, and had heard of its being circumnavigated with the exception of the Isthmus of Suez by some Phoenikians [4, 42]. The Libyans, as opposed to the Egyptians, the Carthaginians, the Hellenic colonists in Kyrene and Naukratis, and the Aethiopians, consisted of numerous tribes, which Herodotos mentions in two great divisions. First, those nomad tribes which lived between the western frontier of Egypt and the lake Tritonis. Second, the tribes living between lake Tritonis and the Pillars of Herakles or even beyond. South of this was 'wild beast Libya' (ἡ θηριώδης Λιβύη), and South again of this was a ridge of sand (ὀφρύη ψάμμης) where some tribes (not nomadic) dwelt in Oases, round hills from which gush streams of salt water, and on which lie huge masses of rock-salt [4, 168—187, cp. 2, 32]. This threefold division of N. Africa answers roughly to Barbary, Biledulgerid (land of dates), the Great Sahara. Bunbury, *Ancient Geography*, vol. I. p. 275.

LIGYES, c. 9.

The Ligures, who gave their name to the N. Western district of Italy are conceived of by Herodotos as living in Gaul just above Marseilles; and they did occupy that district until some centuries afterwards [Polyb. 33, 7]. But though Gauls by residence they were not Kelts, as the other Gauls were, but a distinct race coming perhaps from Illyricum.

LYDIA, c. 51. LYDIAN, c. 31. LYDIANS, cc. 12, 49, 101—2.

Lydia was properly the district in Asia Minor separated from Mysia on the N. by the range of Temnos, and from Karia on the south by the Messogis Mts. or by the R. Maeander. In Homer [Il. 2, 865 etc.] the inhabitants of this country are called Meiones (Μῄονες), who appear to have been of Pelasgic origin. At some period before B.C. 700 these Meiones were conquered by the Lydi, whose place of origin is quite unknown, but who appear to have been connected ethnologically with the Karians. In the reign of Kroisos [B.C. 560—546], of the 3rd dynasty established by Gyges [1, 8—13], the kingdom of Lydia included all Asia Minor except Lykia and Kilikia. This kingdom was annexed to Persia by Kyros [B.C. 546], and by Dareios Lydia and Mysia were formed into a Satrapy, the seat of government being Sardis [3, 90]. Herodotos describes them as an active and warlike race [1, 7], the first to engage in commerce and coin money [1, 94], with institutions similar to the Greeks [1, 35, 74, 94]. Yet their blood relationship to the Karians was commemorated by a joint worship of the Karian Zeus [1, 171].

LYKARĒTOS, c. 27.

Made tyrant of Lemnos by the Persians. He was the brother of Maeandrios the secretary of Polykrates of Samos, who had been entrusted with the government of the Island and had then seized the royal power. Lykarētos, when his brother fell ill, had tried to secure the succession for himself by ruthlessly executing some of the opposite party. When his brother was expelled from Samos Lykarētos appears to have made his submission to the Persians, and was rewarded by being made tyrant of Lemnos, although another brother Charilaos, who was half insane, was allowed to commit an act of extreme violence against them [3. 142—146].

LYSAGORAS, c. 30.

Father of Histiaios of Miletos.

MAEANDER, cc. 118—9.

A river in Asia Minor rising near Kelenae in Phrygia [7, 26], and flowing at the foot of the Southern range of Messogis, in so winding a course that it has given a word to more than one language for anything tortuous. After receiving several important tributaries, especially the Lykos, it falls into the Ikarian Sea between Priene and Myus, on the opposite side of the deep bay or harbour to that on which Miletos stood.

MAEANDRIOS, c. 27.

A Samian, and secretary to Polykrates. When the latter went on his last fatal journey to Sardis, he left the government in the hands of Maeandrios; and when news came that Oroetes had arrested him and put him to death, Maeandrios attempted to establish a democracy in Samos, asking only for a moderate compensation for himself. But finding that he could not safely lay down his power he imprisoned some of his opponents, whom his brother Lykarētos murdered. On the interposition of the Persians he connived at some acts of violence against them by his brother Charilaos, and then took ship and sailed away [3, 142—146]. He first went to Sparta, where he attempted by a great display of wealth, which he brought with him, to excite the Spartan king Kleomenes to take his part. Kleomenes resisted the temptation and secured the dismissal of Maeandrios from Sparta; after which we hear no more of him [3, 148]. To the action of Maeandrios some were fond of tracing the Graeco-Persian wars [Ael. v. h. 12, 53]; and certainly the destruction of the Samian power and independence was the beginning of Persian supremacy in the Aegean.

MAKAE, c. 42.

A tribe in Libya, on the shore of the Greater Syrtis, who wore their hair in the shape of a crest, and had shields decorated with ostrich feathers [4, 175].

MAKEDONIA, c. 17. MAKEDONIANS, cc. 18, 20.
MAKEDONIAN, c. 94.

The Makedonia of Herodotos seems to mean what was called Lower Makedonia, which, originally consisting of the basin of the Axios, was being gradually extended eastward towards the Strymon, and south-eastward to the sea (the Thermaic gulf) by the energy of its sovereigns the Temenidae [see *Alexander*]. The capital was Edessa or Aegae, afterwards removed to Pella [Thucyd. 2, 99].

MANTYES, c. 12.

A Paeonian, one of the brothers who endeavoured by attracting the notice of Dareios to their sister to secure the sovereignty of their people.

MARSYAS, cc. 118—9.

A river in Karia, and tributary of the Maeander on its left bank (*Cheena Chi*).

MASSALIA, c. 9.

A colony of the Phokaeans founded circ. B.C. 600, the modern Marseilles. The Phokaeans were the first of the Ionian peoples to explore the Adriatic, the coast of Tuscany, and Spain [1, 163]; and, according to the story, on one of these voyages a Phokaean named Euxenos obtained the hand of Petta daughter of Nonnos king of the country near Marseilles, and founded the town [Aristot. in Athen. XIII. 576]; according to others the Phokaean leaders were Simon and Protis, and Protis married Kyptis daughter of Nonnos king of the Segobrii [Plut. Solon c. 2, Just. 4, 3]. This founding of a Greek centre of commerce in the west was unsuccessfully resisted by the Carthaginians [Thucyd. 1, 13, 8].

MATIENI, cc. 49, 52.

The exact position of the Matieni is not certain. They seem to be placed somewhere in Media Atropatene, or in Armenia, in the wider extension which Herodotos gives to that appellation [1, 72]. They are classed with the Paphlagonians in regard to their armour and general equipment in the army of Xerxes [7, 72]. The river Gyndes (q.v.) is said to rise in the Matienian Mountains i.e. the *Khurdish Hills* [1, 189].

MAUSŌLUS, c. 118.

A native of Kindys, and father of Pixodaros. He was probably an ancestor of the prince of Karia [about B.C. 370] whose tomb was the wonder of the world, and has given a word to modern languages.

MEDES, cc. 9, 77, 104, 109.

Herodotos often uses 'Medes', as in the last three of these chapters, as a general appellation of the Persian Empire, which in reality was Medo-Persian, besides containing many subject states of other nationalities. But sometimes he distinguishes them clearly. Thus in c. 9 he evidently means really the Medes, before the coming of the Persians. In 9, 68 he distinguishes them in regard to their excellence as soldiers, giving the palm to the Persians. And, as the Persians after the conquest of Kyros generally monopolised offices, he notes when Medes are employed [1, 62, 156; 6, 94; 7, 88]. The Medes were an Aryan people [7, 62] inhabiting, when first heard of, a district south of the Kaspian, now called Khorassan, whence they removed to the districts afterwards called Media, the capital of which was Ekbatana [*Hamadán*]. They became independent of the Assyrians about B.C. 635, but were afterwards conquered by Kyros about B.C. 559.

MEDIC DRESS, c. 9.

A long flowing robe, as opposed to the short tunic and leather trousers of the Persians [Xen. Kyrop. 8, 1, § 40. Rawl. vol. 1. p. 220]. Cp. 1, 71, 135. The Persians adopted the dress of the conquered Medes apparently, along with the turban or fez [Strabo 11, 13, 9].

MEGABATES, c. 32—3.

Nephew of Dareios, who commanded the Persian expedition against Naxos.

MEGABAZOS, cc. 1—2, 10, 12, 14—7, 23—6, 98.

One of the Seven who joined in slaying the usurping Magi, after the death of Kambyses [3, 70]. He advised the setting up of an oligarchy in place of the monarchy [3, 81]. When Dareios became king however he appears to have acquiesced, and to have been trusted by that king, who left him in command of the army of Europe, after the Skythian expedition, to reduce the cities on the Hellespont [4, 143—4]. All that we know of him besides is contained in this book.

MEGARA, c. 76.

A town and district lying between Attika and the Isthmus of Korinth. The town stood about a mile from its harbour Nisaea. The district was once counted as part of Attika, hence the ancients accounted for its not being mentioned in the list of towns by Homer. It was afterwards invaded by the Dorians, in the time of king Kodros it was said. At any rate at some time it was occupied by Dorians. In B.C. 455, owing to a quarrel with Korinth, the Megarians united themselves with the Athenians, who caused the long walls between it and Nisaea to be built; occupying at the same time its other harbour on the Korinthian gulf, Pegae [Thucyd. 1, 103]: but the Athenians had to surrender both at the 30 years truce B.C. 445. It was thus an outpost of Dorian power against Athens. The 'Megarian decree', whereby the Athenians tried to ruin it commercially, was alleged as one of the causes on the part of Sparta for beginning the Peloponnesian War [Thucyd. 1, 67, 159].

MEKISTEUS, c. 67.

Brother of Adrastos, slain while attacking Thebes by Melanippos, [Hom. Il. 2, 566; 23, 678; Paus. 1, 28, 7].

MELANIPPOS, c. 67.

A Theban, son of Astakos. Æschylus [s. c. Th. 414] calls him son of Agrios. His tomb was shewn at Thebes as one of the bravest of warriors [Paus. 9, 18, 1].

MELANIPPOS, c. 95.

A friend of the poet Alkaios.

MELANTHIOS, c. 97.

An Athenian, who commanded the fleet of 20 ships sent to aid the Ionians.

MELANTHOS, c. 65.

Father of Kodros, and son of Andropompos [1, 147].

MELISSA, c. 92, § 7.

Wife of Periander of Korinth, daughter of Prokles of Epidauros; according to Herodotos she was put to death by her husband [1, 50]. Her tomb was shewn outside Korinth in the time of Pausanias [2, 28, 8]. According to a story related by Pythaenetos, in his history of Aegina, Periander fell in love with her when he saw her serving wine to some labourers [Athenae. XIII. 569 f.].

MEMNON, cc. 53, 54.

Son of Tithonos and Eos [Aurora]. His father, according to the legend, reigned at Susa, though he is generally called king of Aethiopia, and led a combined army of Aethiopians and Susiani to the assistance of Priam, brother of his father [Od. 4, 189; 11, 522. Pausan. 10, 31, 7].

MENELAOS, c. 94.

King of Sparta, brother of Agamemnon, and husband of Helen.

MILESIA, c. 29. MILESIANS, cc. 11, 29, 30, 36, 38, 49, 106, 120.

MILESIAN, cc. 49—50, 54, 65, 97, 99, 105—6, 124.

MILETOS, cc. 11, 24, 28—30, 32—3, 35, 92, 98—9, 106, 124, 126.

Miletos, an Ionian city in Karia, stood on a peninsula on the South-west of the Latmian bay, opposite the mouth of the Maeander, which was at this time about ten miles distant. The deposits of the Maeander have now filled up the Latmian bay, and covered the ancient site of the city. It was formerly inhabited by Karians, whose women remained when their husbands and other male relations were massacred by the Ionians, who under their leader Neileus occupied the town [1, 146. Homer Il. 2, 867], though some authorities speak also of Leleges and Kretans as forming part of the inhabitants. Between the time of its settlement by Ionians and its capture by the Persians, in B.C. 494, it had risen, greatly owing to its favourable situation and excellent harbour, to a position of high prosperity and power, though frequently in the hands of tyrants [1, 20—2], and torn by violent civil strife [cc. 28—9]. It had offered a firm resistance to the encroachment of the Lydian kings, and had made a treaty on favourable terms with them [1, 17—22]; as also with Kyros [1, 143, 169]. After its fall at the end of the revolt [6, 18—21] it was restored on the defeat of the Persians at Mykale [B.C. 479], and joined the confederacy of Delos, but revolted from the Athenian supremacy in B.C. 445 [Thucyd. 1, 115], and maintained its independence for some time [Thucyd. 8, 25, 84]. It never however quite recovered its old position as the chief city of the Ionians.

MINOA, c. 46.
Sometimes called Herakleia, sometimes Herakleia Minoa. See *Herakleia*.

MOLPAGORAS, c. 30.
Father of Aristagoras (q.v.).

MYLASIAN, a, cc. 37, 121.
A native of Mylasa, a city of Karia (mod. *Melasso*), not far from Halikarnassos. In it was the temple of Ζεὺς Κάριος [1, 171], in which there was said to be a well connected with the sea (which was 10 miles away), as in the Akropolis of Athens [Pausan. 8, 10, 4].

MYNDIAN, c. 33.
Of Myndos, a town on the coast of Karia between Halikarnassos and Bargylia. It was a colony from the Dorians of Troezen, and had a good harbour and strong walls.

MYRKINOS, cc. 11, 23—4, 123, 126.
A town in the country of the Thrakian Edonians, given by Dareios to Histiaios. It was not a large or important place ['Ηδωνικὸν πολισμάτιον], and was afterwards included in the territory of Amphipolis, when that town was settled by the Athenians 34 years after the death of Aristagoras [Diodor. Sic. XII. c. 68]. It was yielded to Brasidas in B.C. 424 [Thucyd. 4, 107, 3], and a body of Myrkinian peltasts served in his army [id. 5, 6, 4], one of whom killed Kleon [id. 5, 10, 9]. It still existed in the time of Strabo, who counts it among the cities on the Strymonic gulf [7 fr. 33].

MYRSOS, c. 122.
A Lydian, son of Gyges, serving in the Persian army in Karia. He had before been employed by Oroetes to entrap Polykrates [3, 122].

MYSIA, c. 122.
Mysia in Asia Minor is made here to include the town of Kios [q.v.] as it is by Xenophon [Hell. 1, 4, 7]; and therefore extends to the shore of the Propontis and includes part of what was afterwards included in Bithynia. This was properly Mysia Minor. The southern part, bordering on Lydia, was Mysia Major. It had been conquered by Kroisos [1, 28], and afterwards included by Dareios in the 2nd Satrapy [3, 90]. The native Mysians, apart from the Hellenic colonies, were unwarlike and somewhat backward in the arts of war as well as peace [7, 74]; hence perhaps the proverb for unresisting prey τὴν Μυσίων λείαν Dem. de Cor. § 72.

MYTILENE, cc. 11, 37, 95. MYTILENIANS, cc. 38, 94.
The chief town of the island of Lesbos (q.v.), to which it afterwards gave its name. It had for some years been subject to the Persians [1, 169]. When Lesbos revolted from Athens in B.C. 427 the whole of the inhabitants were condemned to death; but the Athenians relented in

time and were content with ordering the death of the ringleaders, and turning the inhabitants who owned land into tenants paying rent to a number of Athenian Cleruchs [Thucyd. 3, 34—50]. It made terms with Makedonia in after-times; and though it suffered capture and plunder by the Romans for siding with Mithridates, it was afterwards treated honourably by them, and has remained to the present day on its original site.

MYŪS, c. 36.

A town in Karia, the smallest of the 12 Ionian cities [1, 142], on the left bank of the Maeander about 4 miles from its mouth. The inhabitants were eventually transferred to Miletos.

NAXOS, cc. 28, 30—1, 33—4, 36—7.

NAXIANS, cc. 30, 33.

The largest of the Cyclades [1, 64], and the wealthiest [c. 28]. It had been under the power of a tyrant called Lygdamis, who appears to have been assisted in seizing the tyranny by Peisistratos of Athens about B.C. 540 [1, 61—64; but see Aristotle fr. ap. Athenae. 348 A]. He appears to have been deposed about B.C. 525 by the Spartans, and from that time until the events mentioned in these chapters the government had been again in the hands of an oligarchy, which Lygdamis had put down, acting, as usual, as champion of the people [Aristot. Pol. 5,6].

NELEIDAE, c. 65.

Descendants of Nestor son of Neleus, and king of Pylos in Messenia. The family was said to have migrated to Athens at the invasion of the Dorians; and from them sprang the Paeonidae [see *Paeonia*] and the Alkmaeonidae (q.v.) [Paus. 2, 11, 9].

NESTOR, c. 65.

Son of Neleus and Chloris [Hom. Odyss. 11, 281—286]. He is the 'old man eloquent' of the Greek army at Troy [Il. 1, 247 ἡδυεπής. Il. 11, 637 ὁ γέρων]. His wife was Euridike [Odyss. 3, 452]. His sons are Peisistratos [Od. 3, 400], and Thrasymedes [Od. 3, 448].

ODOMANTI, c. 16.

A mountain tribe dwelling on the northern slopes of Mount Pangaeum, which shuts in the valley of the Strymon [7, 112].

OEDIPUS, c. 60.

Son of Laïos and Iokaste. The story of Oedipus (Swell-foot) was that an oracle declaring at his birth that he was destined to kill Laïos, his father had him exposed on Kithairon to perish, his feet being pierced with thongs. Being preserved by a shepherd of Polybos king of Korinth, he was brought up at Korinth. Afterwards when told by an oracle that he was to kill his father and marry his mother he left Korinth, believing Polybos to be his father. He met Laïos in a narrow road, and in a scuffle killed him, and proceeding to Thebes married Iokaste. Many years afterwards discovering what he had done he put out his eyes.

OENOË, c. 74.

A town on the slopes of Kithairon, just on the Attic side of the frontier of Attika and Boeotia. It lay on the road to Thebes, and was an Attic deme of the tribe Hippothoontis, near Eleutherae. The Athenians, at any rate afterwards, fortified it to protect the frontier [Thucyd. 2, 18, 19].

OIË, c. 83.

A town somewhere in the centre of the island of Aegina, but its exact position is not known.

OLYMPIA, c. 22. OLYMPIONIKAE, cc. 47, 71.

The valley of Olympia (*Andilalo*), three miles long and one broad, on the N. bank of the Alpheios on its junction with the R. Kladeos, was the scene of the Olympic games which took place every fifth year. There were innumerable statues, and many buildings: but the chief of all was the Olympieium, the temple and oracle of Olympian Zeus which stood in the S. Western portion of the Altis or sacred grove, which abutted on the Kladeos. The contests took place on the Stadium and Hippodrome; the former being in the Altis, the latter between it and the River Alpheios. The victors at these games, which were open to all persons of Hellenic descent [2, 160], were marked men, and sure usually to be popular and influential in their native towns [see 6, 70, 103, 125]. The Eleians had the management of the games [6, 127], and the only official prize was a wreath of olive [8, 26].

ONEATAE, c. 68.

A name given by Adrastos to one of the tribes at Sikyon ('Ass-folk').

ONESILOS, cc. 104—5, 108, 110—115.

King of Salamis in Kypros. His name appears to be a Grecised form of some Phoenikian name, and Amathos, the people of which worshipped him as a hero, was one of the most ancient of the Phoenikian settlements in the island.

ORBELOS, c. 16.

A Mt. in North-eastern Makedonia near Philippi and lake Prasias.

OTANES, cc. 25—6, 116, 123.

A Persian, son of Sisamnes.

PAEONIA, c. 62.

A deme in Attica, which appears to have got its name from the Paeonidae, one of the families descended from the Neleids of Pylos [Paus. 2, 18, 9]. It is distinguished by Harpocration from the better known Παιανιεῖς, though it belonged to the same tribe, the Leontis. See *Leipsydrion*.

PAEONIA, cc. 13, 24, 98. PAEONIANS, cc. 1, 12—15, 17, 23, 98.

A tribe claiming to be colonists from the Trojans, and living originally on both banks of the Axios [Il. 16, 287],

καὶ βάλε Πυραίχμην, ὃς Παίονας ἱπποκορυστὰς
ἤγαγεν ἐξ Ἀμυδῶνος ἀπ' Ἀξιοῦ εὐρυρέοντος.

Their name remained in a large tract of the centre of Upper and Lower Makedonia, but they seem to have been pushed gradually eastwards; and the Paeonians removed by Dareios were two small tribes apparently living near the Strymon, called the Siriopaeonians and Paeoplians [see 7, 113]. They seem not to have been connected in blood either with the Illyrians, or Makedonians, or Thrakes; and their tradition of descent from the Teukri points to some Asiatic origin.

PAEOPLAE, c. 15.

A tribe of Paeonians (q.v.).

PAESOS, c. 117.

A town on the European coast of the Hellespont, between Lampsakos and Parium, a colony from Miletos [Il. 5, 612].

PAKTŌLOS, c. 101.

A small river in Lydia flowing from Mt. Tmolos into the Hermos, which was said to carry down a considerable quantity of gold in its sands (mod. *Sarabat*).

PALLAS, c. 77. See *Athene*.

PAMPHYLIANS, c. 66.

The inhabitants of Pamphylia, a narrow tract of country bordering on the Mare Lykium, immediately west of Kilikia, and bounded on the north by Pisidia. Its chief towns were Perga and Attaleia.

PANATHENAEA, the, c. 55.

A yearly festival at Athens to celebrate the union of the 12 old cantons of Attika into one state (συνοικισμός). It was celebrated every year about the end of July, but every fourth year with special magnificence.

PANGAION, c. 16.

A range of mountains in Makedonia, stretching from the left bank to the east and inclosing the basin of the Strymon between itself and the sea (Strymonic Gulf). Mod. *Pirnari*. In it were gold and silver mines [7, 112].

PARIANS, cc. 28—30. PAROS, c. 31.

One of the larger of the Cyclades, 6 miles W. of Naxos, celebrated for its quarries of white marble. It is said to have been originally inhabited by Kretans and Arkadians, and afterwards to have been colonised by Ionians. The selection of the Parians as arbitrators in the civil disputes at Miletos is a strong testimony to the character of the inhabitants for honesty, which they are said still to enjoy. It is spoken of [c. 31] as depending on Naxos; but it does not seem that it ever formally lost its independence. One Parian ship is spoken of in 6, 133 as serving in the Persian fleet of B.C. 490, and the island was accordingly attacked by Miltiades in the following year for medising [6, 133—6]; and similarly in B.C. 480 the Parians held aloof from Salamis, and hastened afterwards to make their peace by paying the indemnity demanded by Themistokles [8, 67, 112]; it seems therefore that the object of the Parians was to be let alone as much as possible to exercise their trade, and not to incur the hostility of either party.

PARIAN MARBLE, C. 62.

Mt. Marpessa, which occupies the whole of the centre of the island of Paros, sloping down to a maritime plain round the coast had celebrated quarries of marble [*Marpessia cautes*, Verg. Aen. 6, 471], which was considered second only to the marble of Mt. Pentelikos. The finest kind was called λύγδος [Diod. Sic. 2, 52] or λυχνίτης.

PARIUM, C. 117.

A town in the Troad (Mysia), on the shore of the Propontis (mod. *Kamares*), a joint colony from Miletos, Erythrae and Paros. It had a harbour capable of taking in a considerable number of ships [Xen. Hell. 1, 1, 13].

PEDASOS, C. 121.

A town in Karia of uncertain site. It seems most probably to have been a few miles south of Mylasa. It was N. of Halikarnassos and more inland than that city. There was a temple of Athene in it, the priestess of which grew a beard when any evil was threatening [1, 175].

PEIRENE, C. 92, § 2.

A vaulted chamber in the Akrokorinthos on the S. E. of the summit, supplied with water from a natural spring, the sweetness and purity of whose water was widely celebrated. It was elaborately adorned with marble and niches for the water [Paus. 2, 3, 2].

PEISISTRATOS, CC. 55, 65, 71, 91, 54. PEISISTRATIDAE, CC. 62—3, 65, 70, 76, 90, 93.

Peisistratos, son of Hippokrates, and a relation on his mother's side of Solon, became tyrant of Athens in the usual way by taking the lead of the poorer classes against the two factions of the wealthier men which were led respectively by Lykurgos and Megakles. By pretending that his life had been attempted by his oligarchical enemies he obtained a grant of a body-guard, and thus was enabled to possess himself of absolute power. He was born about B.C. 612. His first usurpation took place in B.C. 560 and his death in B.C. 527. Of the 33 years between his usurpation and death he was only in actual possession of power for 17 years, being twice driven out by Megakles and the Alkmaeonidae, and twice restored [1, 59—63]. The dates of these two exiles are not certain; but we are told that the second lasted 10 years

[1, 62]. He made no changes in the laws, and ruled well and wisely [1, 59].

By the PEISISTRATIDAE is meant the sons of Peisistratos, and their families. Peisistratos left three legitimate sons, Hippias, Hipparchos, and Thessalos [Thucyd. 1. 20]. Of these Hippias succeeded his father, and Hipparchos was associated with him in some way not clearly defined. [See *Hipparchos, Hippias*.] The third son Thessalos never appears to have had any part in the government; and it is said he was a philosopher, an ardent admirer of equality, and lived as a private person in great repute at Athens [Diodor. Sic. x. fr.]. Hipparchos was assassinated in B.C. 514, and Hippias and all the family of the Peisistratidae expelled in B.C. 510. Peisistratos had during his lifetime secured possession of Sigeium, to which the people of Mitylene had long laid claim, and had placed his natural son Hegesistratos in command of it [5, 94—5]. The Peisistratidae accordingly retired thither.

PEITHAGORAS, c. 46.

Tyrant of Selinus in Sicily.

PELASGI, the, c. 26. THE PELASGIC WALL, c. 64.

The inhabitants of a great part of Greece before the coming of the Hellenes, to whom however they seem to have been allied. Their name survived in that of Pelasgic Zeus [Il. 16, 233] and Pelasgic Argos [Il. 2, 681; 24, 437], and in a tribe living near Larissa in Thessaly [Il. 2, 840, 843]. Herodotos mentions remnants of them at Kreston, Skylake, and Plakia (in Makedonia and Mysia), and says that their language was barbarous [1, 57] and that it was those of them that remained in Attika that got the credit of being Hellenes [2, 51]. We know nothing of their language except that Larissa and Argos are said to be Pelasgic for 'fortress' and 'plain'. They settled in rich plains and were great builders and reclaimers of land. Thucydides speaks of them as the prevailing race in Greece before the Hellenic name superseded them [1, 3, 2]; and asserts that some of them migrated to Etruria and returned afterwards to Chalkidike, as well as to Lemnos and Athens [5, 109, 3; cp. Pausan. 7, 2, 2]; though Pausanias was told that they came from Sicily [1, 28, 3]. A reminiscence of the Pelasgic building at Athens was the place called τὸ Πελασγικὸν beneath the Akropolis [Thucyd. 2, 16]. Their name was also connected with a part of Arkadia [Paus. 8, 1, 6] and with Pylos in Messenia [id. 4, 36, 1]. The 'Pelasgic wall' mentioned in c. 64 is the wall round the Akropolis [see 6, 136—7].

PELOPONNESOS, cc. 42, 74.

PELOPONNESIANS, cc. 74, 76.

At the time of the Homeric poems the Peloponnese seems to have been the most important centre of Greek life. In the catalogue of the ships 430 came from it, as compared with 302 from Central Greece, and 147 from the islands, and 280 from Northern Greece. It was not however known by that general name. In the Iliad, if it has any name, it is Argos [6, 152] or Ἀπίη 'distant land' [1, 269]; while in the Odyssey we have Ἄργος Ἀχαιϊκὸν apparently for it, as opposed to Pelasgic Argos [3, 251]; and 'Argos' at any rate includes Lakonia in Odyss. 4, 173. The name Peloponnese was believed to have arisen after the Dorian invasion from the wealth and power of Pelops son of Tantalos. Again Agamemnon king of Argos is the principal sovereign in the Greek army, which seems to indicate the preeminence of Argos, a preeminence which by the time that Herodotos treats of had passed to Sparta, though not without some remains of an Argive tradition. The Peloponnesians in Lakonia, Argos, Elis, Messenia were a mixed race. The Dorian invaders found ancient inhabitants there, Achaians, Epeians, and others, most of whom were reduced to subjection, and became either slaves or unenfranchised landholders paying rents to various Dorian lords. The resistance of the Messenians had been crushed in the two Messenian wars, though it afterwards broke out again, and the Spartan citizens were lords of Messenia. Argos and Elis however held aloof, and in these countries the Dorian conquerors seem to have coalesced more completely with the natives, and they remained distinct nationalities. The mountaineers of the central district, Arkadia, had been able to resist the Dorians and retained their ancient characteristics; while a number of the dispossessed Achaians retreated to the Northern district of the Peloponnese, which acquired their name.

PERDIKKAS, C. 22.

One of the three sons of Temenos of Argos, who fled first to the Illyrians, and afterwards to upper Makedonia. According to both Herodotos [8, 137] and Thucydides [2, 99; 5, 80] Perdikkas became the first king of Makedonia of the Temenid line, which lasted to Alexander III., son of Alexander the Great [i.e. to B.C. 311]. Other authorities however give two kings before him, Karanos and Koenos [see Clinton vol. 2 p. 221]. Amyntas and Alexander mentioned in this book are the 5th and 6th in descent from Perdikkas. The Hellenic descent of the Temenidae, admitted by Herodotos and Thucydides, and by the managers of the Olympic games on more than one occasion, is denied by Demosthenes [3 Phil. § 40].

PERIANDER, CC. 92, §§ 6, 7; 95.

Son of Kypselos, and tyrant of Korinth B.C. 625—585. He was reckoned by some among the seven wise men of Greece [Paus. 1, 23, 1; Plut. Sol. c. 12], and his reputation at any rate, as we see [c. 25], was sufficient to make him the man to be selected to arbitrate in disputes between states. Acts of cruelty and tyranny are recorded of him in 3, 48—53, and Nicolas Damasc. [fr. 57] says that he 'turned his royalty into tyranny by his cruelty and violence'. But what he proceeds to state would not strike a modern quite in the same light, 'He prevented his subjects from owning slaves and being idle, always finding some works for them to do. And if he saw any one sitting idle in the market-place he fined him, for fear he should be plotting against him'. He was warlike and enterprising, seems to have kept a hold on the Korinthian colony of Korkyra, and seized Epidauros from his father-in-law Prokles [3, 52]. Plutarch (de Malign. c. 24).

PERINTHOS, cc. 1, 2.

A town on the Thrakian coast of the Propontis, afterwards called Herakleia (mod. *Erekli*), a colony of Samos, founded about B.C. 599.

PERSIANS, cc. 2, 10, 15, 17—8, 20—1, 32, 34, 36, 73, 96—7, 101—2, 108—110, 112, 115, 118—9, 120—1.

PERSIAN, a, cc. 33, 116.

PERSIAN CUSTOM, cc. 12, 97, 108.

The Persians were brought into contact with the Greeks by the conquest of Lydia [B.C. 546] to which a great number of the Greek towns of Asia had been already subjected. Herodotos speaks generally of the Persian armies and kingdom under the name of 'Persians', and sometimes of 'Medes'; but he also sometimes distinguishes the two clearly [e.g. 9, 68], and strictly the Persians were the conquering race led down by Kyros from the Mts. about B.C. 549, who vanquished the Medes, Lydians and Babylonians, and thus united the chief Asiatic kingdoms into one Medo-Persian Empire; in which Persians occupied most of the important posts. See *Medes*.

PETRA, 92, § 2.

A village or township in the territory of Korinth,—perhaps on the Northern slopes of the Mts. separating Korinthia from Argolis.

PHALERUM, cc. 63, 81, 85.

At this time the regular harbour of Athens [6, 116], on the E. side of the bay which goes by its name, and somewhat nearer to the city than the Peiraeus harbour, which superseded it about a century later owing to its safer basin. The 'plain of Phalerum' means the flat piece of country about three miles in extent between it and the city.

PHILIPPOS, c. 47.

A native of Kroton in Italy, and son of Butakidas, who met Dorieus at Kyrene and joined his expedition into Italy. Like many Krotoniats [see *Kroton*] he was an Olympic victor.

PHILOKYPROS, c. 113.

King of Soli in Kypros, and father of Aristokypros (q.v.). The visit of Solon, and his advice to him to remove his town to a better site is narrated by Plutarch [Sol. 26], who says that he called the new town Soli in his honour, although accounts give it a much earlier origin, and describe it as an Athenian colony.

PHOENIKES, cc. 46, 57, 108—9, 112.

The Phoenikes in this book are spoken of in three connexions: (1) as living in Libya and interfering in Sicily i.e. Carthaginians [c. 46], (2) as coming into Greece with Kadmos [c. 57], see *Kadmeians*, (3) as supplying the Persian king with ships. The last refers to the main Phoenikian nation settled in the N. of Palestine, whither they had come from the shores of the Persian gulf [1, 1]. They were active sailors and traders throughout the Mediterranean, and were the chief supports of the Persian naval power [6, 14, 40—1; 7, 89; Thucyd. 1, 16, 100; 8, 46, 81]. Besides the introduction of letters into Greece attributed to them in this book, they had in early times commercial intercourse with the Ionians [3, 107], taught them mining [6, 47], and were ahead of them in engineering [7, 23, 34].

PHRYGIA, cc. 52, 98. PHRYGIANS, c. 49.

The central district of Asia Minor, a mountainous and well-watered country. The people inhabiting it were, it appears, connected in origin with certain Thrakian tribes. After their subjection to the Persians, following that to the Lydians, they gave up their old warlike habits and devoted themselves to agriculture [1, 28; 3, 90; 7, 73].

PIXODAROS, c. 118.

Son of Mausolus, a prince of Kindys in Karia.

POLYBOS, c. 67.

King of Korinth and Sikyon, in whose house the infant Oedipus was brought up [Apoll. 3, 5, 7].

POLYDOROS, c. 59.

Son of Kadmos and father of Laïos [Apoll. 3, 4, 2, 4].

PRASIAN LAKE, the, cc. 15—17.

Another name for the Kerkenitis, which is an enlargement of the R. Strymon, varying in size according to the time of year [τὸ λιμνῶδες τοῦ Στρυμόνος Thucyd. 5, 7].

PRINETADAS, c. 41.

A Spartan, father of the second wife of Anaxandridas.

PROPONTIS, c. 122.

The mod. *Sea of Marmora*, connected with the Pontos by the Bosporos, and with the Aegean by the Hellespont (*Dardanelles*). Herodotos gives an estimate of its breadth and length as 500 and 1400 stades respectively, which is not very wide of the mark, about 50 miles and 135 miles being nearly the true reckoning [8, 85].

PYLII, c. 65.

Inhabitants of Pylos in Messenia, on the promontory of Koryphasium on the N. of the bay now called *Bay of Navarino*. Its inhabitants emigrated to Kyllene and thence to Sicily at the end of the second Messenian war [B.C. 668], whence it was an uninhabited spot when Demosthenes raised a fortification there in B.C. 424 [Thucyd. 424]. In the Iliad it is the town of Nestor.

GEOGRAPHICAL INDEX. 237

PYTHAGORAS, c. 126.

A man left in charge of Miletos by Aristagoras when he departed for Myrkinos.

PYTHIA, the, cc. 43, 63, 65, 67, 79, 82, 90, 92.

The prophetess of the temple of Apollo at Delphi, so called from the ancient name of Delphi [Πυθώ]: a young girl, generally of the lower class, selected by certain families at Delphi. The replies which she gave from the tripod, set over a hole from which came some gas, were reduced to writing, apparently, by the priest [προφήτης] or by some 'poets' kept for the purpose at the temple [Strabo 9, 3, 5]. At the time of the greatest influence and importance of Delphi, there seem to have been two or three such priestesses. Instances of the priestess being tampered with or bribed are c. 63, 69 and 6, 66. So later on she was said φιλιππίζειν. Plut. Dem. 20; Cic. De Div. 2 § 118.

SALAMIS, cc. 104, 108, 115.

SALAMINIANS, cc. 104, 110, 113, 115.

A town on the E. coast of Kypros [mod. *Nicosia*], which was believed to have been founded by Teukros, from the Island of Salamis. It was a flourishing mercantile town, with considerable trade relations with Kyrene. The struggle for independence with Persia here recorded was renewed again in the 4th century by Evagoras and his son Nikokles; but it eventually came into the power of the Ptolemies and then of Rome, under whom it was much frequented by Jews, a rebellion of whom caused the destruction of the city, which was afterwards revived under another name, Constantia.

SAMIANS, cc. 99, 112.

The inhabitants of Samos, a considerable island off the coast of Karia. It had under Polykrates [B.C. 535—522] attained to considerable power; but during the disputes which followed his death the Persians had made it tributary, and established a tyrant there who would support their supremacy [3, 120—5]. The excellence of its navy created by Polykrates seems to have been shewn in this Ionian revolt [c. 112].

SARDIS, cc. 11—13, 23—4, 31, 52—4, 73, 96, 99, 100—3, 105—6, 108, 110, 122—3.

SARDIANS, c. 25.

The capital of Lydia (q.v.) situated on the slope of Mt. Tmolos, and on either bank of the Paktōlos. It seems to have been but slenderly furnished with defences, but its citadel was almost impregnable [cp. Polyb. 7, 15—17; 8, 17—23].

SARDO, cc. 106, 125.

Sardinia, which is here said to be the 'largest of all islands', is in fact larger than Sicily, and therefore the largest island known at this time. The report of its wealth and fertility had made its occupation a favourite speculation among the Greeks, and Bias is said to have advised the migration of the Ionians there after the first Persian conquest [1, 170]. Their information in regard to it was doubtless obtained through the Phoenikian merchants.

SELINUS, c. 46. SELINUNTIANS, c. 46.

A Greek colony from the Sicilian Megara (Megara Hyblaea) on S.W. coast of the island [Thucyd. 6, 4]. It was founded about B.C. 600, and in its turn founded Herakleia Minoa. It was early prosperous, and found itself in collision with the Carthaginians. It has been governed by an oligarchy, but was now under a despot called Peithagoras.

SIGEIUM, cc. 65, 91, 94—5.

The north western promontory of the Troad at the entrance of the Hellespont, and also a town and district near it, a colony—it was said—founded by Aeolians from Mytilene, who used in building their town the stones of ancient Troy. Early in its history the Athenians (about B.C. 606) sent an expedition under Phrynon to secure the town, in which they were opposed by the Mytileneans, and eventually the dispute was referred to Periander of Korinth, who decided in favour of the Athenians. Timaios asserted, though according to others falsely, that Periander had originally given help against the Athenians. At any rate it seems to have been regarded as the personal possession of the Peisistratidae, rather than of the Athenian State, and was governed by an illegitimate son of Peisistratos, Hegesistratos [Strab. 13, 1, 38—9].

SIGYNNAE, c. 9.

A tribe placed by Herodotos somewhere N. of the Danube. Other writers mention Sigynnae as living in Asia near the Euxine or Kaspian.

SIKELIA, cc. 43, 46.

Sicily had for a century and a half before this been a favourite place for Hellenic colonisation. The earliest colony was Naxos [*Tauromenium*] from Chalkis [B.C. 735]. Several circumstances made intervention in Sicily always possible. The Greek colonies quarrelled a great deal among themselves, and were also subject to raids from the native Sikeli or Sikani who lived in the centre, and had besides a common enemy in the Carthaginians, whose object it was to get complete control of the island for commercial purposes. The leading Greek state in resisting this was Syracuse [B.C. 734], and the consequent attempts of that town to secure its own supremacy and unite the Greeks against the Carthaginians, led to other quarrels.

SIKYON, c. 67. SIKYONIANS, cc. 67—8.
SIKYONIAN, a, c. 89.

A town in the N. of Peloponnese in the valley of the Asopos, on some flat table-land about two miles from the sea. Though this table-land is not of great elevation its sides are precipitous, so that it can be ascended by only two narrow passages. This served as the Akropolis, while there was a town at the foot of the hill, and a post-town on the coast. According to tradition Adrastos was its first king [Il. 2, 572]. It afterwards became subject to Argos or Mykenae [Paus. 2, 6, 6], shared in the fate of other cities in submitting to the Dorians, and after the conquest was again subject to Argos; but about B.C. 676 it became subject to a dynasty of kings who were not Dorians [see *Kleisthenes*], and whose object seems to have been to lower the commanding position of the Dorian families, and to raise those of the ancient inhabitants, as well as to break all ties that held Sikyon to Argos. This was the dynasty of the Orthagoridae. This policy was brought to a head by the last of the Orthagoridae, Kleisthenes, who died about B.C. 560. After the Dorian reaction mentioned in c. 68, the Sikyonians renewed their connexion with the Dorians in Sparta, instead of Argos, and for the remainder of this period are found acting under Spartan influence [6, 92; 8, 71; 9, 28]. Sikyon was afterwards an important member of the Achaian League [Polyb. 2, 43].

SIMONIDES, c. 102.

A famous poet born in the island of Keos; who lived from B.C. 556 to B.C. 469, and celebrated most of the great national triumphs of that period in epigrams and other poems. He was known in all Greek towns and states in Sicily as well as Greece, republics and monarchies alike, and was popular everywhere without entering into politics. His epigrams on the dead at Thermopylae are quoted in 7, 228. Besides such compositions he wrote Hymns, Parthenia, Dithyrambs, and Threni, as well as Epinikia or odes in honour of the victors at the games.

SIRIOPAEONIANS, c. 15.

A tribe of Paeonians (q.v.) living near Siris, a town which gives its name to a great plain N. of the Strymonic lake [see *Prasias*]. The name of the town is also written Serrhae [Σέρραι].

SIROMOS, c. 104.

A king of Salamis in Kypros, father of Chersis. The name is Phoenikian [= Hiram], though the family appears to have been Greek. There was perhaps a marriage with some Phoenikian woman.

SISAMNES, c. 25.

A Persian, father of Otanes (q.v.), executed and flayed by order of Kambyses for corruption as a judge. Another man of the same name is mentioned in 7, 66.

SISIMAKES, c. 121.

A Persian general killed in Karia.

SKAIOS, c. 60.

A boxer, supposed to be one of the sons of Hippokoon, who with his 12 sons was killed by Herakles [Apoll. 3, 10, 5].

SKAMANDER, c. 65.

A small river in the Troad, on which the town of Sigeium stood,—by the Gods called Xanthos [Hom. Il. 20, 74], although later writers describe two distinct rivers, the Xanthos and Skamander.

SKYLAX, c. 33.

A native of Myndos in Karia.

SKYTHAE, cc. 24, 27.

The inhabitants of the country N. of the Danube and the Euxine, including the Tauric Chersonese [*Crimea*], and extending to an unknown distance northwards. Dareios is referring to his expedition into their country [4, 98—141].

SOLIANS, cc. 110, 113.

Inhabitants of Soli in Kypros, on the North coast of the Island [see *Philokypros*], to which the inhabitants had removed from Aipeia, the city on the height [αἰπύς]. It was near the mod. village *Aligora* in a valley still called *Solea*.

SOSIKLES, cc. 92, § 1; 93.

A Korinthian, who spoke against giving assistance to restore the Peisistratids.

SPARTA, cc. 39, 48—50, 65, 75—6, 90, 92, 97.

SPARTANS, cc. 39, 41—2, 46, 50, 63, 71, 91.

The appeal to Sparta first for help to the revolted Ionians, is an indication of the position of supremacy by this time accorded to Sparta by public opinion in Greece; which is further illustrated by the appeal made to them in the case of Aegina [6, 49]. This seems to be due to the fighting power of its citizens, rather than to its prosperity in the ordinary sense of the term, or to the strength of its town; for Sparta was not fortified, nor were its public buildings splendid [Thucyd. 1, 10]. But the institutions attributed to Lykurgos had secured that its citizens [the ὁμοῖοι or peers numbering about 8000] should be trained soldiers, who should have no cares for mere maintenance, which was supplied by the Perioeki and Helots. Sparta, thus constituted, had become the leading power in Greece, and its sympathies were usually enlisted in the various states with the party opposed to a completely popular government. But the Spartan government had also very close relations with the oracle at Delphi [6, 67], and the influence which the Alkmaeonidae were able to bring to bear on the oracle seems to account for its unusual policy in helping to drive out the Peisistratidae. When the Spartans discovered that they had been deceived in that matter, they returned to the policy more congenial to them of supporting royalty,—though to the debased form of royalty known as 'tyranny' they were generally opposed. Although they refused to help the Ionians on the present occasion, they had in former times shewn that they looked upon the Island and Asiatic Greeks as of interest to them. They had, in answer to a former appeal from the Ionians, sent a message to Kyros bidding him harm no Greek state [1, 152]; and had undertaken an expedition against Polykrates of Samos to restore the citizens whom he had exiled [3, 39—56].

STESANOR, c. 113.

Tyrant of Kurion in Kypros. No reason is given for his treachery; but if his town was, as it is said, an Argive colony, it may help to account for it; for the Argives were always inclined to medize, and the same feeling may have had influence here [7, 148—152].

STRYMON, cc. 1, 13, 23, 98.

The modern *Struma* (or in Turkish *Karasu*) is a river which at this time formed the boundary between Makedonia and Thrake. It rises in Mt Skomios [8, 115] and flows into the Strymonic gulf, being navigable for a few miles above Amphipolis. Shortly before reaching Amphipolis it widens into the Prasian lake.

SUSA, cc. 24—5, 30, 35, 49, 52, 54, 117.

The capital of Susiana on the eastern bank of the Choaspes [*Kirkhah*], called in the Old Testament *Shushan* [Esther 1, 2]. It had been one of the principal residences since the time of Kyros [1, 188], though some attributed its foundation to Dareios. See *Memnon*.

SYBARIS, cc. 44. SYBARITES, cc. 44—5, 47.

SYBARITIC WAR, c. 45.

A colony of the Achaians and Troezenians in S. Italy between the rivers Krathis and Sybaris. It had become exceedingly powerful and wealthy, and the luxury of its citizens, which had become proverbial, was in marked contrast to the habits of its neighbour Kroton. The enmity of the two cities was brought to a crisis by the refusal of the Krotonians to deliver up the fugitive oligarchs driven from Sybaris when Telys became tyrant. The Sybarites proclaimed war, and were conquered, their city taken and destroyed, the river Krathis being turned over its ruins about B.C. 510, an event which marks the beginning of the decadence of Magna Graecia [Diod. Sic. 12, 9—10; cp. Her. 6, 21, 127].

SYENNĚSIS, c. 118.

A name, or title, of a line of kings of Kilikia [see 1, 74; Xen. Hell. 3, 1, 1; Diodor. Sic. 14, 20]. He seems to be again referred to in 7, 98.

TALAOS, c. 67.

An Argive, father of Adrastos (q.v.).

TANAGRAEANS, c. 69.

Inhabitants of Tanagra, a town in Boeotia on the left bank of the Asopos, on a round hill commanding the road from Oropos to Thebes [9, 15, 35, 43].

TELEBOANS, c. 59.

A people of Akarnania, identified by Strabo [10, 2, 14] with the Taphians. See also Steph. Byz. μοῖρα τῆς Ἀκαρνανίας, ἀπὸ Τηλεβόου, ἣ πρότερον Ταφίων ἐκαλεῖτο. They appear to have been a nation of pirates, like so many of the peoples on the West of Greece; and the legend of the expedition of Amphitryon no doubt refers to some effort to suppress their robberies [Strabo 10, 2, 20].

TELYS, cc. 44, 47.

Tyrant, or king, of Sybaris (q.v.). He had acquired his power in the usual way, by setting up as a leader of the populace against the aristocracy, and persuading them to banish 500 of the wealthiest citizens, who took refuge in Kroton. He then sent to demand the extradition of these exiles on the penalty of war. The Krotonians preferred war, and Sybaris was destroyed [Diod. Sic. 12, 9—10]. Another account however asserts that Telys was deposed before the war, and attributes the fall of the Sybarites to the cruelties in this revolution [Herakl. Pont. in Athenae. 521 E].

TERMEREAN, c. 37.

An inhabitant of Termera, a city in Karia, on the coast west of Halikarnassos [7, 98].

TEUKRI, cc. 13, 122.

The inhabitants of Troy and the Troad (q.v.). They perhaps consisted of two distinct races, the Teukri coming from Thrace,—whence the inverted idea of the Paeonians that they were descended from them,—and the other branch being natives of Phrygia. Their supposed survivors the Gergithae are mentioned again in 7, 43. Both may have been of Pelasgian origin, and the Phrygians themselves were said to have come from Europe originally [7, 73].

THEBE, c. 80.

A river-nymph, daughter of the Asopos, who gives her name to Thebes, properly the town growing round the Kadmeia [Paus. 2, 5, 2].

THEBES, cc. 59, 67. THEBANS, cc. 79, 81, 89.

Thebes, the chief city of Boeotia, was built round a hill in the valley of the Asopos. This hill which formed its Akropolis was called the Kadmeia, from the tradition of a Phoenikian settlement there under Kadmos (q.v.). Its importance in Boeotia was post-Homeric; in the Iliad the chief city of Boeotia is Orchomenos; yet the earliest legends belonging to Thebes are more numerous and more elaborate than those of any other town. The people were said to be an Aeolian tribe who migrated from Thessaly and ejected the Kadmeians [Thucyd. 1, 12]. The first known occasion on which Thebes and Athens became embroiled with each other is that alluded to in 6, 106; when about B.C. 519 (or as Mr Grote thinks after B.C. 510), the Athenians interfered in behalf of the Plataeans, who wished to be independent of Thebes.

[Thucydides (3, 68, 7) says that the destruction of Plataea in B.C. 427 was in the 93rd year of their alliance with Athens, i.e. the original alliance was in B.C. 520. See Grote 4, p. 94.]

THERA, c. 42.

The largest island of the Sporades, a group of Islands lying between the Cyclades and Krete. It was colonised by Spartans and Minyae, under the Spartan Theras, according to the received mythology, eight generations after it had first emerged from the sea [4, 147]. Before this colonisation it had been inhabited by Phoenikians. From it went Battos, the founder of Kyrene [4, 150—1]. It is a crescent-shaped island with a coast-line of 30 miles, but never more than three miles broad; it and the islands near it are full of signs of volcanic action.

THESPIANS, c. 79.

The inhabitants of Thespiae, in Boeotia, about eight miles W. of Thebes, with a harbour in the Korinthian Gulf called Kreusis.

THESPROTIANS, c. 92, § 7.

Thesprotia is the S. W. district of Epeiros, terminating at the Ambrakian Gulf, from the River Thyamis on the North, and bounded on the East by the territory of the Molossi, though the line of division seems to have varied at different times, the Thesprotian territory at one time being taken to include Dodona.

THESSALOS, c. 46.

A Spartan, a follower of Dorieus.

THESSALY, c. 63. THESSALIANS, c. 63.

Thessaly is the district between Makedonia on the N., Epeiros on the W., and Phthiotis on the S. It is a great alluvial plain, surrounded by mountains, and drained by one river system, that of the Peneios and its tributaries [7, 129]. Politically it was a somewhat loose confederation of free states; but there were certain families—such as the Aleuadae of Larissa and the Skopadae of Krannon—who seem to have had a sort of hereditary supremacy through large parts of the country, in which Larissa and Krannon, as well as Pharsalos and Pherae, were the centres of a kind of league. There was, at any rate in later times, an officer for the whole called a *tagos* [Xen. Hell. 6, 1, 6—8], whom Herodotos appears to mean here by the title βασιλεύς, who had the right of summoning a league army. Still Thessaly seldom acted as a united nation: the action of the Aleuadae in B C. 480 in inviting the Persians was not by any means shared in generally by the Thessalians [7, 6, 130, 172]. The Thessalian cavalry were famous, partly because the country was suited to horses [7, 196], and partly that the superior orders were all 'knights' i.e. serving on horseback, while the infantry were composed of the poor or subject populace (πενέσται). There had apparently long been a traditional amity between Athens and the Thessalians, perhaps—as Rawlinson suggests —from a common jealousy of Boeotia. Their most constant enemies however were the Phokians [7, 176; 8, 27—9].

THRAKIA, cc. 2, 14, 23, 126. THRAKIANS, 3, 8, 10, 126.

The district N. of Makedonia, bounded on the E. by the Euxine. Towards the N. W. the frontier between it and the Keltic tribes was undecided; but Herodotos regards the Danube as separating it from Skythia [4, 99]. When he says, 'The Thrakians are the most powerful people in the world, except of course the Indians' [c. 3], he is referring to their great numbers, as well as to their warlike character; and in various places he mentions 18 distinct tribes of them; but the conquests of Dareios [4, 93] and Megabazos [c. 2] seem only to include those tribes who lived on or near the coast.

THRASYBULOS, c. 92, § 6.

Tyrant of Miletos [about B.C. 636—0], during whose reign Alyattes king of Lydia for eleven years was warring against Miletos [1, 17—22]. Aristotle [Pol. 3, 13; 5, 10] represents Periander as the giver of the advice to Thrasybulos in the manner described by Herodotus, instead of Thrasybulos to Periander. Dionys. H. [4, 56] agrees with Herodotos.

TIGRIS, c. 52.

The river Tigris is formed by the union of several rivers flowing from Armenia and Matiene. It flows for 100 miles in a N. E. direction, then turning S., and finally to the S. E., joins the Euphrates at a place about 130 miles from the common mouth in the Persian Gulf. 'Herodotos was not only familiar with the two great streams of the Euphrates and Tigris, and knew that they both flowed from the Mts of Armenia, but he correctly describes several of the principal affluents of the latter stream.' Bunbury, *Ancient Geogr.* vol. I. p. 233.

TIMESITHEOS, c. 72.

A native of Delphi who won in the Pancratium, three times at the Pythian, and twice at the Olympic games [Pausan. 6, 8, 4—6].

TISANDER, c. 66.

Father of Isagoras (q.v.).

TMOLOS, c. 100—1.

A mountain in Lydia, at the Northern foot of which stood Sardis [1, 84, 93]. It was rich in metals, and grew celebrated vines [Eur. Bacch. 55, 64]. Euripides also calls it 'flowery', ἀνθεμώδης [Bacch. 462, cp. Anthol. 9, 645].

TRAUSI, cc. 3—4.

A Thrakian tribe, perhaps somewhere to the S. of Mt Rhodope (*Despoto Dagh*).

TROAS, cc. 26, 122. TROY, c. 13.

The Troad was a part of Mysia, comprising the coast district on the Aegean from Lektum on the S. to somewhere beyond Abydos on the Hellespont; and inland far enough to include Mt Ida. In earlier language it would include all the kingdom of Troy, and therefore a much wider tract. The site of TROY has always been a subject of dispute. About B.C. 700 a new town called Ilium was founded on the site of the modern mound of *Hissarlık* and was supposed to occupy the site of Troy. Others however fix that site on a hill called *Bali Dagh* above a village named *Bunárbashi*. See Jebb's *Homer* pp. 148—9.

TYDEUS, c. 67.
Son-in-law of Adrastos (q.v.), father of Diomede [Il. 5, 126].

TYMNES, c. 37.
Of Termera, father of Histiaios [7, 98].

TYNDARIDAE, c. 75.
Here means the figures of Kastor and Polydeukes, sons of Tyndareus and Leda [though, according to the legend, Polydeukes was son of Zeus, Kastor of Tyndareus]. Tyndareus was king of Lakonia, but surrendered his kingdom to his son-in-law Menelaos. A house at Sparta was shown as having been theirs [Paus. 3, 16, 3]. For the particular symbols of the twins here referred to, see note ad loc.

ZEUS, cc. 49, 105.
In the first of these chapters Zeus is mentioned as the Supreme deity of Greek theology, father of gods and men, of boundless power and wealth. In the second the name is the Greek rendering of the Persian Supreme God *Ormuzd*, cp. 1, 131; 2, 55. In inscriptions titles indicating every kind of nationality are assigned to Zeus,—Assyrius, Baeticus, Bursurius, Serapis, Nilus, Ammon, Capitolius, Cassius, Phrygius, etc. [see 6, 56].

Ζεὺς ἀγοραῖος, c. 46.
Zeus of the market-place, i.e. an altar of Zeus set up in the market-place at Selinus.

Ζεὺς Κάριος, c. 66.
The temple Zeus Karios was at Mylasa (q.v.) and was the common place of meeting and worship for all Karians, to which also Lydians and Mysians were admitted as being of kindred blood [1, 171. Strabo 14, 2, 23].

Ζεὺς στράτιος, c. 119.
Zeus the god of Armies was also an object of worship to the Karians. The temple was at Labranda at some distance from Mylasa, to which a paved road (a *via sacra*), near seven miles in length, led from the temple. The most distinguished of the citizens were appointed to the priesthoods in this temple for life [Strabo l.c.].

INDEX TO THE NOTES.

[*The references are by page and line.*]

Accusative (*by attraction*) *of participle with infinitive* 70, 18
ἄγαλμα 42, 6
ἄγγελοι 54, 18
ἄγεσθαι 8, 11; 14, 13
ἀγηλατέειν 42, 15
ἀγνωμοσύνη 49, 11
ἀγορεύειν 49, 21
ἄγχιστα, οἱ 47, 7
ἀγῶνες 66, 15
ἀγωνιζόμενος στάδιον 12, 18
ἀδίκιον 53, 5
ἀεθλεύειν 12, 14
ἀθανατίζειν 2, 22
αἰνίσσεσθαι 33, 17
αἱρέετο 61, 6
αἰτήσας ἔτυχε 12, 24
αἰτίη ἔχει τινα 41, 17; 42, 8; ἔχει τις αἰτίην 41, 23; 44, 2; ἐν αἰτίῃ τινα ἔχειν 68, 23
αἰχμῇ βραχέα 28, 18
ἀκεόμενοι 55, 1
ἀκήρυκτος 48, 7
ἀκούειν, τινων *or* τινα 47, 10; '*to obey*' 49, 7
ἀκρομανής 24, 25
ἀκρός 72, 6; 77, 8
ἀλγηδόνες ὀφθαλμῶν 10, 6
ἀληθέϊ λόγῳ 24, 12
ἀλίη 16, 18; 47, 9
τὰ δὲ ἄλλα καί 49, 8
ἀλλά, *introducing objection* 29, 20

ἀλλὰ γάρ 2, 17
ἀλλαφρονέειν 50, 14
ἀλλοῖος 23, 27
ἄλλως 4, 6; 71, 13; '*vainly*' 24, 14
alphabet, *the Greek* cc. 58—9
ἀμείβειν 43, 4
ἀμήχανον μή 2, 17
ἀμφί 10, 25; 31, 7; 38, 10
ἀμφιβολίη 44, 13
ἀμφιδέξιον 58, 11
ἀνά 66, 17
ἀναβάλλεσθαι 29, 20, 27
ἀναβλαστεῖν 57, 25
ἀνάγειν 75, 15
ἀναδιδόναι 48, 15
ἀναισιμοῦν 32, 23
ἀναισίμωμα 18, 2
ἀνακαίεσθαι 10, 21
ἀνακλίνειν 8, 21
ἀνακομίζεσθαι 50, 10
ἀνακρεμᾶν 46, 10; 62, 1; 73, 7
ἀναλαβεῖν 76, 1
ἀναμάχεσθαι 76, 1
ἀναξυρίδες 28, 18
ἀναπείθειν 38, 24; 67, 21
ἀναπλῆσαι 2, 27
ἀναποδίζειν 59, 6
ἀναπυνθάνεσθαι 33, 25
ἀναραιρηκώς 66, 15
ἀνάρσια 53, 15
ἀνάσπαστος 5, 23; 69, 10
ἀνατίθημι 21, 28

ἀναχωρέειν ὑπό 35, 19
ἀνέκαθεν 33, 11; 38, 9, 26; 56, 8
ἀνεστηκυίῃ τῇ χώρῃ, ἐν 16, 4
ἀνέχειν 68, 26
ἀνέχεσθαι 10, 24
ἀνήκειν 28, 17
ἀνθρωπηΐη δορά 14, 18
ἄνοδος 30, 9; 31, 5; 32, 26
ἀντία 44, 16
ἀντιθευσόμενοι 12, 15
ἀντιστασιῶται 41, 12
ἀξιαπήγητα 34, 7
ἀξιεῦμαι 69, 1
ἀξιόχρεω, ὑπὸ 71, 27
aorist, force of 6, 29; 67, 21
ἀπάγειν 49, 1; 78, 2
ἀπαθὴς κακῶν 10, 13
ἄπαις 27, 25; 40, 10
ἀπαλλάσσειν 37, 12
ἀπείπασθαι 33, 21
ἄπειρος 4, 12
ἀπὸ πολέμου 3, 22; δείπνου 9, 16; συνθήματος 44, 10; τοῦδε 49, 10; τὸν ἀπὸ τούτου χρόνον 51, 5; ἑὼν ἀπό 35, 4
ἀπό of source or agent 2, 4
ἀπογράφεσθαι 16, 5
ἀποδείκνυμι 'appoint' 14, 21; 16, 8; 37, 16; 63, 15; 65, 2; 'present' 39, 27; 53, 6
ἀποδιδόναι 40, 15
ἀποδιδράσκειν 64, 7
ἀποκορυφόω 43, 24
ἀπομνημονεύειν 38, 12
ἀποσημαίνειν 11, 2
ἀπόστολος 23, 5
ἀποτιμᾶσθαι 46, 9
ἀποφαίνειν 49, 28
ἀποφέρειν 49, 31
ἅπτεσθαι 57, 20
ἀπωσμένος 41, 7
ἄρα 57, 10; 69, 7; 77, 13
ἀργός 3, 21
ἄρδω 6, 16
τὸ ἄριστον 71, 7
ἁρμόζεσθαι 18, 26; 27, 12
ἁρπαγάς 61, 23
ἄρρητος 49, 24
ἀρχὴ κακῶν 63, 16

ἀρχῆθεν 10, 4
ἀρχήν adv. 69, 5
ἀρχήν, τήν 33, 25
ἄσπαστος 64, 6
ἀσπίς = ὁπλῖται 17, 6
ἄστυ 37, 23
Athenians, number of 63, 12
Attika, invasions of 45, 9
attraction, 23, 25
αὐτὴ ἑωυτῆς ἀκμάζειν 15, 19
αὐτὸ τοῦτο 1, 15; 7, 4; 12, 14; 22, 11
αὐτός sponte 39, 22; 42, 13; alone 40, 21; 50, 17
αὐτοῦ ταύτῃ 72, 17; τῇδε 10, 17

βάλλεσθαι ἐπὶ σφῶν αὐτῶν 43, 28; ἐπ' ἑωυτοῦ 69, 4
βασιλεύς (of Thessaly) 37, 4; applied to the same person as τύραννος 67, 11; 71, 5; cp. 70, 13
βίβλος 34, 22
βουλή 42, 17
βωμός 27, 11

γάρ anticipatory 2, 17; 10, 20; 13, 24; 16, 1; 19, 8; 39, 14; 66, 23; 73, 11; 77, 7
γεραίρειν 40, 12
γῆ καὶ ὕδωρ 9, 4; 43, 24
genitive of part affected 8, 17: topographical 34, 2; 37, 13; 48, 10; 49, 16: of time within which 46, 2: 74, 10: partitive 75, 25
γνώμη 21, 18; 22, 5; ἡ πλείστη γνώμη 78, 1
γνώμῃ κοινῇ χρεόμενοι 37, 1
γράμματα 34, 12, 26 (Καδμήϊα)

δάκτυλος (metric) 4, 18
dative of agent 32, 24; 40, 16
δέ in apodosis 1, 9; 22, 20; 54, 14
δ' ὦν 4, 26; 5, 7; 28, 1; in apodosis 30, 8
δέεσθαι εἰ κως 16, 25
δεῖ of destiny 19, 8; 57, 24; ἔδεε συμμαχίης ἐξευρεθῆναι 23, 6

INDEX TO THE NOTES.

δεκάτη 46, 16
δεύτερον, τό 15, 16; 24, 23; δεύτερα 21, 23
διαπειρᾶσθαι 70, 17
διαπίνειν 9, 17
διαπλέκειν 58, 22
διέποντες, οἱ 12, 12
δή resumptive 2, 4; 35, 24; 41, 2; 53, 1: *summing up* 5, 16; 29, 13: '*accordingly*' 25, 27; 43, 8; 44, 9; 45, 25: ὅσπερ δή 38, 24: ἵνα δή 40, 17; 51, 7; 52, 25: δηλαδή 75, 3
δημότης 5, 18
διαβάλλειν 30, 6; 63, 10; 69, 21
διαβεβλημένος 20, 19; 62, 22
δίαιταν 29, 15
διαλαμβάνειν 32, 9
διαπλέκειν 58, 22
δίγαμμα 34, 12
διδόναι καὶ ἄγεσθαι 6, 3; καὶ λαμβάνειν 49, 8
διελόντες 19, 14
διζῆσθαι 55, 20
δίκας δοῦναι καὶ λαβεῖν 49, 8
δίμνεως ἀποτιμήσασθαι 46, 9
διφθέραι 34, 22
δοκέειν ἐμοί 39, 8; 41, 4; δοκέειν '*to expect*' 20, 19
δόξαν φύσας 54, 27
δρέπανον 72, 15
dress, Ionic 52, 4
δύντος ἡλίου 30, 12
δύσριγα 5, 5

ἔατε = ἦτε 55, 23
ἐγγίγνεσθαι 57, 22
ἐγκεράννυμι 77, 8
ἐγχειρίζειν 42, 18
ἐγχειρίθετον 69, 16
ἐθέλει λέγειν 47, 17
ἐθελοκακέειν 46, 28
εἰ *with deliberative subjunctive* 39, 18: εἰ δή 18, 26: εἰ καί 46, 25
ἐκ *with genitive of agent* 6, 11; 11, 29; 13, 2; 53, 19; 54, 2: ἐκ προκλήσιος 1, 12; ἐκ τοῦ φανεροῦ 62, 19; ἐκ τοῦ ἐμφανέος 22, 15; ἐκ νέης 73, 26; ἐξ ὑστέρης 68, 23;

ἐκ τοῦ βραχίονος 6, 8; ἐκ τειχέων 46, 12; ἐκ τότε 52, 20; ἀρτᾶσθαι ἐκ 18, 5
ἐκβάλλειν 41, 19; 42, 11
ἐκγενέσθαι 68, 9
ἐκοέκομαι 31, 12
ἐκμαθήσεται ἁμαρτών 54, 30
ἐκπίπτειν 43, 9
ἐκπλώειν *with accus.* 67, 3
ἐκπολεμοῦσθαι 43, 18
ἐκφέρειν 47, 6; ἐκφέρεσθαι γνώμην 21, 18
ἐλαίη 48, 23
ἐλαύνειν 71, 10; ἐλαύνειν ἐς τοσοῦτο 30, 1
Ἑλλὰς πόλις 61, 8
ἐμπικραίνεσθαι 36, 4
ἔμπροσθεν, τά 36, 18
ἐμφανέος, ἐκ τοῦ 22, 15
ἐναγέες 41, 20
ἐνάγειν 67, 16
ἐνθαῦτα 36, 11; 45, 20; 67, 16
ἐνθαῦτα δή 30, 23; 59, 20; 75, 21
ἐνορᾶν 21, 25
ἐξαιρέειν 8, 5; 37, 26; 76, 14
ἐξάμετρος τόνος 35, 7
ἐξανίστασθαι ὑπό 34, 15; 35, 16
ἐξεργάζεσθαι 10, 24
ἐξευρεῖν 39, 5
ἐξίημι 23, 17
ἔξω 67, 3
ἐόν, τό 30, 7; 69, 8
ἐπέδρη 37, 28
ἔπεδρος 24, 9
ἐπελθεῖν 24, 8
ἐπήλυδες 38, 11
ἐπί *acc.* δύο γενεάς 15, 21; ἔτεα τέσσερα 33, 13; πλέον 31, 4; 75, 24; ὕδωρ 6, 7; χρόνον 61, 19; 73, 23; 75, 9; τὸν Εὔριπον 45, 22; τὴν θάλασσαν 69, 28; τὰ ἕτερα 44, 12
„ *gen.* ἑωυτῶν 63, 25; ἑωυτοῦ 69, 4; ἡμέρης 74, 10; Καρίης 76, 16; τοῦ 38, 14; τούτου 35, 16; 38, 12; 40, 12; 41, 3; σφῶν αὐτῶν βάλλεσθαι 43, 28; 69, 4
„ *dat.* μισθῷ 38, 4; πολέμῳ 45, 10; ῥητοῖσι 34, 6; τοισίδε 48, 26;

INDEX TO THE NOTES.

τυραννίδι 42, 11; τῇ χώρῃ 46, 5;
ἐπ' ᾧ 49, 1 : δέειν τὴν ἐπὶ θανάτῳ
43, 10;
ἐπιγίγνεσθαι 37, 31
ἐπιδαψιλεύεσθαι 11, 16
ἐπιδιαιρεῖσθαι 74, 6
ἐπιδιζήμενος 68, 27
ἐπιθαλάσσιοι 17, 11
ἐπικαλέειν 60, 27; ἐπικαλέεσθαι 1,
7; 36, 31; 41, 14; 47, 23; 60,
21
ἐπικεῖσθαι 48, 8
ἐπίκλητος 45, 4
ἐπικουρίη 37, 1; 47, 25
ἐπιλέγειν 3, 3; 41, 20; ἐπιλέγεσθαι
7, 12; 47, 16
ἐπιμελές 6, 10
ἐπινέμεσθαι 65, 18
ἐπιπίπτειν 7, 21
ἐπίστασθαι 44, 3; ἠπίστατο σχήσων
24, 26
ἐπίστια 42, 15
ἐπισχεῖν 30, 23
ἐπιτελέειν 2, 24; 49, 27
ἐπιτιθέναι 62, 2
ἐπίτροπος 16, 18
ἐπιχώριος 52, 18
ἐπωνυμίη 38, 15; 39, 4; 58, 9
ἔργον 2, 1
ἔρδειν καὶ παθεῖν 38, 16
ἐρίζειν 29, 17
ἐς *pregnant sense of* 3, 10; 6, 5;
14, 20; 17, 18; 42, 14; 70, 4:
ἐς ἐμέ 26, 16; ἐς μακρήν 70, 7;
ἐς ὅ 50, 16; 57, 22; ἐς τό 44, 5;
ἐς τρίς 68, 11; ἐς τὠυτὸ φέρειν
56, 18; χρηστήριον γενόμενον ἐς
Κόρινθον 56, 17; ἔχειν ἐς 48, 6;
κατανέμειν ἐς 41, 10
ἐσάγειν 24, 4; ἐσάγεσθαι 9, 20;
23, 22
ἐσαράσσειν 74, 4
ἐσηνείκαντο 20, 3
ἐσπίπτειν 75, 5
ἐσύστερον 44, 14
ἔσω 30, 17
ἑταιρηίη 42, 4
εὐδαιμονίη 48, 5
εὐεπής 30, 13

εὐεργεσία 5, 11
εὐπέτεια 10, 28
ἔφοροι 23, 13
ἔχειν ἐς 48, 6; νόῳ ἔχειν 59, 18;
ἔχει μὴ λεηλατέειν 65, 13; λόγον
ἔχει 38, 25
ἔχεσθαι 9, 6; 28, 25; οὐδὲν χρυσοῦ
ἐχόμενος 29, 22
ἔχθρη προσοφειλομένη 48, 13

future, vivid, as protasis 60, 20;
as imperative 11, 2

ἦ δή 55, 10
ἤδη 29, 17
ἤθεα, τά 7, 8
ἤια λέξων 36, 2
ἡλικίη εἶκε 10, 16; ἡλικίην 35, 5
ἡμεροῦσθαι 2, 10
ἡμιολίη 52, 14
ἡρῷον 27, 21; 39, 14
ἥρως 27, 19; 73, 12
ἡσυχίην ἄγειν 55, 8; 77. 20; ἐν
ἡσυχίῃ ἔχειν 57, 2; 61, 4

θαλαμίη 19, 14
θαλάσσῃ Ἑλληνικῇ 32, 31
θεραπηίη 11, 25
θέσθαι οὔνομα 38, 11; 58, 10; τὰ
ὅπλα 44, 16
θησαυροί 29, 16
θύεσθαι ἐπί τινα 26, 5
θύμῳ βούλεσθαι 28, 24
θυσίαι *to a hero* 27, 19
θῶυμα ἔχει τινας 60, 18
θωυμάζειν τινός 59, 14

ἰδέσθαι 5, 21
ἴδη 13, 6
ἰδίῳ στόλῳ 36, 22
ἰδόμενος 5, 21
ἱδρύσαντο 49, 5
ἰθύς 37, 22
ἱκετηρίη 30, 16
ἴκρια 8, 5
ἱμάτιον 51, 27
imperative for future 29, 17; *as
apodosis* 60, 22
imperfect, force of 9, 14; 12, 15;

INDEX TO THE NOTES. 251

41, 19; 42, 11, 16; 43, 2; 48,
15; 49, 28; 54, 24; 55, 7; 64,
7; 65, 11; 66, 25; 67, 17, 21;
77, 16
ἵνα δή 40, 17; 52, 7
infinitive, dependent on an adjective
9, 9; present after expression of
promises 47, 26; in oratio obliqua 49, 31; for imperfect indic.
49, 30; 50, 15; aorist with ἄν
50, 21; for imperative 68, 9;
future 29, 27
ἱππάσιμος 37, 7
ἱπποβόται 46, 5
ἵππος χιλίη 37, 3
ἰρουργίαι 49, 24
ἰσηγορίη 46, 23
ἰσοπαλέες 29, 21
ἴσχειν ἀποκτεῖναι 57, 15; ἴσχειν
μή 57, 15
ἰσχυρόν, κατὰ τό 36, 8

Κάειρα 52, 10
καί 'actually' 50, 26; 58, 2
καί disjunctive 12, 1
καί...τε 7, 8
τῶν αὐτῶν καί 38, 10; τὠυτὸ καί
56, 18
καί...καί 71, 20
καὶ δὴ καί 11, 15; 40, 12; 49, 13;
72, 26
κακοῦν 15, 5
κακῶς ἀγορεύειν 49, 21
καλύβη 8, 14
καλῶς ἔχειν τινος 11, 4
κατά = κατὰ τά 5, 19; 12, 9; 52,
24; 55, 23; 72, 12: ἀνδραγαθίην
24, 26; αὐτὸ τοῦτο 22, 11; γένος
23, 10; γυναῖκα ἑκάστην 8, 11;
Λάϊον 35, 5; λόγον 4, 8; τὸ
ἰσχυρόν 36, 8; τοῦτο 19, 14; 50,
25; τὴν συμμαχίην 48, 1; τὠυτό
2, 15; στίβον 66, 10; χώρας 2,
19; τὰ κατ' ὑμέας 70, 22; repeated 48, 9
καταβαίνω 69, 18
κατάγειν 17, 28; 55, 14; 60, 23
καταγωγαί 31, 25
καταθύμιος 23, 12

κατακαίειν 60, 1
καταλέγω 21, 21
καταλεύειν 22, 26
κατάλυσις 31, 8
κατανέμειν 41, 10
καταπακτὴ θύρη 8, 15
καταπροΐξονται 68, 4
καταρτίζω 15, 22; 69, 14
καταστασις 56, 1
κατέδησαν τὴν ἐπὶ θανάτῳ 43, 10
κατειλεῖν 75, 12
κατελθεῖν 16, 26; κατελεύσεσθαι
77, 22
κατέργειν 37, 11; κατεργάζεσθαι
47, 2; 71, 16
κατέχειν 10, 14; 16, 18; -έχεσθαι
46, 28; 54, 13
κατηγεῖσθαι 25, 9
κατήκοντα, τά 28, 9
κατήμενοι 36, 20
κατιδέσθαι 21, 5
κάτοδος 16, 26; 36, 8
κατοίκισις 45, 13
κατυπέρτεροι 72, 24
κείραντες 37, 6
κέραμος 52, 18
κέρτομος 49, 20
κίβδηλος 54, 21
κιθῶνα ἐκδύεσθαι 69, 18
Kings of Sparta not to go out together 44, 25
κληδών 43, 8
κληροῦχοι 46, 4
κλώθειν 6, 9
κοινοῦ, ἀπὸ τοῦ 50, 8; κοινῷ στόλῳ
55, 3; κοινῇ γνώμῃ 37, 3; τὸ
κοινόν 70, 24
κομᾶν 42, 3
κόππα 34, 12
κουριδίαι 9, 20
κρησφύγετον 77, 13
κρίσις, 3, 6
κυρβασία 28, 18
κύριαι ἡμέραι 61, 1; cp. 30, 2

Lake dwellings 8, 4
λάσιος 4, 18
λέγων, ἔφη 21, 25; 29, 2; 30, 8
λευστήρ 39, 20

λέων 33, 18; 56, 20
λεώς, λεών 25, 6
ληϊστύς 3, 22
λῆμα 43, 12; 71, 14
λιπαρέειν 10, 16
λογοποιός 21, 19; 77, 17
λόγος 'a book' 22, 4; λόγον δοῦναι 40, 28; 44, 18; λόγον ἔχει 38, 25; λόγῳ 22, 17; ἀληθέϊ λόγῳ 24, 12; 52, 8; κατὰ λόγον μουνομαχίης 4, 8
λόγῳ argument 49, 28; 61, 21
λοχᾶν 76, 4

μαθόντες 54, 14; 73, 21
μάχη 'mode of fighting' 28, 17
μέγαρον 46, 13
μέλισσαι 5, 1
μέλλειν constr. of 10, 19; 58, 1; 44, 15 (meaning)
μεμετιμένος 69, 28
μέρεϊ, ἐν τῷ 41, 13
μετά adv. 8, 9; 9, 9; 11, 28; 13, 18; 15, 15; 18, 21; 24, 6; 33, 21; 37, 14; 38, 4; 39, 1; 42, 13; 44, 18; 66, 16; 71, 3
μέτα = μέτεστι 35, 21
μεταβάλλειν 52, 6
μέταλλον 9, 7; 13, 7
μετήσεσθαι 21, 10
μέχρι ἐμεῦ 73, 16
μὴ οὐ 47, 15
μηνίειν 49, 28
middle, force of 8, 11; 14, 13; 16, 5; 48, 23; 49, 4
μισθοῦσθαι 36, 12
μοῖρα 41, 8
moods, variation of 6, 27; 17, 24
μουναρχέων 35, 15
μουνομαχίη 4, 8

ναύκραροι 42, 7
ναυκρατέες τῆς θαλάσσης 21, 24
νεκυομαντήϊον 59, 26
νέμειν 16, 9; 42, 7; 56, 2
νέμεσθαι 28, 21; 62, 7
νεώτερα 10, 19; 68, 11; νεώτερον 61, 8
νῆσοι 18, 4; νῆσος μεγίστη 69, 18

νηυσιπέρητος 31, 24
νικᾶν 22, 5; 75, 1
νόθος 61, 15
νομίζειν 63, 4
νομιζόμενα 25, 9
νομός 55, 12; 66, 7
νοσέειν 15, 22
νόῳ σχών 59, 18
νυν 16, 14; 21, 13; 46, 23
νῦν δέ 37, 31; 55, 20

ξεῖνος 16, 23; 19, 17; 36, 27; 39, 7; 53, 22

οἷα τε 11, 14
οἰκηίῃ δαπάνῃ 27, 17
οἰκοφθορέεσθαι 16, 1
ὅκῃ 51, 28
ὅκως frequentative 16, 3; 36, 21; with future indic. 70, 22
ὅκως ἄν 64, 14
ὅκως = ὡς 53, 14; 69, 6
ὀλοφύρονται 2, 27
ὀνειροπόλοι 33, 21
ὀπέων 71, 19
ὁποδαπή 6, 24
optative, of modest statement 2, 1; 35, 5, 10; of indefinite frequency 22, 24: see ὅκως and ὡς
oracle, Delphian, consulted on leading a colony 25, 7
ὄργια 35, 23
ὅτε γε 55, 13
οὐ in comparative clause 61, 22; οὐκ ἐᾶν 62, 15
οὐρανὸς ἔνερθε τῆς γῆς 55, 10
οὗτος indefinite 50, 6; οὕτω 31, 14; 55, 19; 74, 26
οὕτω δή 22, 15; 51, 1
ὀφρυόεις 56, 23
ὄψις ἐνυπνίου 33, 9

πάθος 33, 10; 40, 12
παιωνίζειν 1, 14
πᾶν χρῆμα 62, 10
πανδαισίη 11, 12
παντὶ στόλῳ 27, 1
πάντως 71, 21
πάπρακαι 8, 24

πάρα 69, 1
παρὰ ποταμόν 25, 11; τὴν Ἰταλίην 25, 23; Κράθιν 26, 11; τὰ μεμαντευμένα 26, 14
παραδίδοσθαι 39, 21
παραθαλάσσιοι 14, 14
παραιτέεσθαι 19, 18
παρακαταθήκη 59, 16
παραλύεσθαι 45, 2
παρασκευάζεσθαι 18, 21; 20, 6
παραχρᾶσθαι 55, 22
παρεῖναι ἐς 42, 14; 70, 8
πάρεξ 3, 26
παρέχον 29, 24; -ει 64, 3
παρίστασθαι 38, 4
participle and indic. in coordinate sentences 22, 20; coordinate participles referring to different persons 34, 17—19; 78, 7
πᾶσα πολλή 11, 26
παχέες 16, 17; 46, 6
πείθεσθαί τινος 16, 12; 18, 23
πειρᾶσθαι with infinitive 22, 8; 42, 15; 55, 1; 70, 20; with participle 55, 1; τινος 47, 26
πέμπειν πομπήν 33, 22
πεπολισμένος 6, 30
πεπρηχέναι 69, 4
πέρι after its case 29, 17, 23
περιέπω 1, 4; 48, 2
περιέσχατα, τά 65, 21
περιλαβεῖν 13, 14
περίοδος γῆς ἁπάσης 28, 4
περιφλεύειν 46, 12
περόνη 51, 27; 52, 16
πεφραγμένοι 20, 8
πίναξ 28, 4
πλεόνως 10, 9; τοῦ πλεῦνος δέεσθαι 20, 12; ἐπὶ πλεῦν ἢ πρότερον 75, 24
πλὴν θανάτου 42, 8
πλήσσω 75, 26
πλοῖα μακρά 17, 7
πλοῖον 19, 26; 36, 29; 65, 5
plural verb with neuter substantive 72, 8, 23
ποιέεσθαι ἀσπαστόν 64, 6; μέγα 13, 16; ἐπέδρην 37, 28; συμφορήν 3, 12; 21, 7; 53, 21;

δεινόν τι 19, 11; 51, 24; δεινά 24, 15; δεινόν 25, 15; δίαιταν 29, 15; ἡγεμόνας 65, 7; πρεσβύτερα 36, 28; ποιέεσθαι 'to cause to be made' 49, 4
ποιῆσαι ἀναστάτους 5, 23
πολέμια, τά 46, 27
πολλὰ πρήσσειν 19, 24; τὰ πολλὰ πάντα 39, 13; πολλὰς ἐλπίδας 21, 7; 22, 1
πολλόν adv. 2, 3; 45, 26
πολυαργυρώτατος 28, 27
πολυπροβατώτατος 29, 4
πολύφημος 47, 6
πόσις [πίνω] 10, 16
πρεσβύτερα 36, 28
present, vivid, for future 25, 20; historical 49, 15; 78, 6
πρῆγμα 50, 4; 53, 12
πρήγματα 19, 28
πρήσσειν 75, 18
πρίν 16, 23; πρὶν ἤ 74, 26
προάστειον 6, 5
προδιδόναι 72, 19
προέστατε 28, 12
προκατίζεσθαι 6, 5
προπύλαια 46, 17
προσφέρεσθαι 70, 15
πρόφαντος 36, 24
πρόφασιν 19, 5
πρὸς βορέω 4, 11; θαλάσσης 7, 15; ταῦτα 77, 11
πρός adv. 11, 13; 12, 12; 40, 12; 77, 10
προσαναισιμόω 20, 11
προσεστήκεε 30, 19
προσεταιρίζεσθαι 39, 1
προσμιγνύναι 37, 20
προσουδίζειν 57, 12
προσπταίειν 36, 8
προσοφείλειν 48, 13
προσσχεῖν ἐς 36, 30
προστάτης 13, 9
προστίθημι 17, 15; -τιθέσθαι 41, 8
προσφέρειν 23, 24; -φέρεσθαι 70, 15
πρόσχημα 15, 21
πρόφαντον 36, 24
πρόφασιν 19, 5
προφέρειν 36, 22

προχωρέειν 26, 5; 36, 8
πρυτανήϊον 39, 27
πρυτάνιες 42, 6
πύλαι 31, 13; διξαί 31, 19
πωλέειν τέκνα 3, 15
πώρινος λίθος 36, 17

ῥαψῳδοί 39, 11
ῥήξας φωνήν 61, 6
ῥητοῖσι, ἐπί 34, 6
ῥυθμός 34, 15

σάν 34, 12
σάττω 20, 5
σβέννυμι 46, 21
σιγᾶσθαι 12, 6
σιγύνναι 4, 26
σιμός 4, 19
σινάμωρος 59, 16
σίνεσθαι 44, 12; 48, 12
σκηπτόμενος 66, 5
σκοπιή 6, 23
σπέρχεσθαι 19, 21
σπυρίς 8, 21
σταθμός 31, 10; καταγωγέων 31, 25
στέλλειν, 77, 19
στεφανηφόροι ἀγῶνες 66, 15
στίβον, κατά 66, 10
στίζειν 3, 19; 21, 1
στόλος 26, 27; 36, 22; 55, 3
στρατηγοί 23, 3
στρατόπεδον 'fleet' 22, 7; 72, 8
subject repeated 20, 27; 73, 11; 75, 22
subjunctive, deliberative 25, 7; 39, 18; 48, 20: after historical tense 48, 20; 52, 7
συγκειμένου 36, 17
συλλαμβάνειν 22, 8
συλλογή 68, 1
συμβαλέσθαι 55, 24
συμπίπτειν 20, 21; 21, 14
συμπράσσεσθαι 61, 23
συμφέρειν 48, 19; 73, 13
συνάπτειν στρατόπεδα 44, 17
συνεκπίπτειν 12, 19
συνελεῖν 25, 29
συνελευθεροῦν 27, 5
συνεξαγαγεῖν 44, 22

συνετετάρακτο 34, 4
συνηνείχθη 19, 9
σύνθημα 44, 10
συντάμνειν 24, 16
σύντομος 9, 5
συντυχίη 24, 12; 37, 31
σύρω 48, 10
σφάζειν ἐς 3, 10
σφέτερον αὐτῶν 22, 26
σφίσι=ἀλλήλοις 40, 28; 44, 18
σχὼν ἔρωτα 18, 28

τάδε for ταῦτα 51, 16; cp. 49, 10
ταμέσθαι 48, 23
ταῦτα ποιέων 39, 8
ταὐτὰ τά 63, 2
ταύτῃ 7, 15
ταφαί 4, 3; a tomb 37, 13
τεῖν 35, 9
τε...καί simultaneousness 20, 16; 24, 9; 51, 9; 59, 5
τε...οὐδέ 23, 22
τε...οὐ...τε 5, 17; 24, 25
τέμενος 53, 12
temples as banks 22, 3; destruction of 66, 5
τετράφυλοι 39, 2
τίλωνες 8, 24
τιμωρέειν 25, 27; 66, 22
τιμωρητήρ 47, 21
τις minatory 54, 29
τό=τί 44, 5; 47, 17
τόν 57, 14
τοῦ sc. χρήματος 55, 15
τοῦτο μέν...τοῦτο δέ 15, 17; 18, 1; 39, 11; τοῦτο δέ without τοῦτο μέν 26, 10
τραπέσθαι 5, 20; 7, 25; 34, 5; 35, 18; 50, 24
τρηχέως 1, 5; 48, 2
τρίμηνος ὁδός 33, 5
trireme, a private 27, 15
τρῶμα 76, 1
τυχεῖν δεηθέντας 25, 27
τὠυτό, κατά 2, 15

ὕβρις 46, 21
ὑπαρπάζειν 30, 9
ὑπάρχειν 66, 23

INDEX TO THE NOTES.

ὕπαρχος εἶναι 77, 13
ὕπαρχος Σαρδίων 14, 12; 43, 21; 77, 2
ὑπέγγυος 42, 8
ὑπεκτίθεσθαι 38, 1
ὑπεξέχειν 42, 13
ὑπερβάλλειν 30, 26
ὑπερθέωμαι 13, 24
ὑπό...ἀπιστίης 24, 16; ὑπὸ τούτων (*neut.*) 50, 14; ὑπ' ἀξιόχρεω 71, 27
ὑποβαλέσθαι 24, 15
ὑποθέμενος ἔπος 59, 10
ὑποκινέειν 69, 13
ὑποταμέσθαι 51, 13

φάμενοι 10, 3
φανερός 33, 20; ἐκ τοῦ φανεροῦ 62, 19
φατίζειν 34, 20
φερέγγυος 17, 4
φέρειν 34, 20: φέρειν ἐς 56, 17: ἡ γνώμη ἔφερε 74, 24; 77, 19
φεύγειν 16, 16
φεύγων ἐκφεύγει 61, 28
φήμη 42, 25
φίλα ποιέειν 22, 22
Φοινικήϊα 34, 21
φοιτᾶν 9, 9
φορέειν 52, 21
φόρος ἐπέτεος 29, 9
φρενήρης 24, 24
φρονέειν τὰ αὐτά 42, 22
φυγεῖν '*to be banished*' 16, 16; *cp.* 36, 6
φύειν 54, 28

φυλαί 41, 11
φυλακτήριον 31, 14
φύλαρχοι 41, 10
φυλάσσειν 6, 4; 24, 17; 55, 21; 71, 18
φύσις 74, 28
φωνὴν ῥήξας 61, 6

τὴν Ἀθηναίων χάριν 64, 21
χεῖρες 43, 11
χέω 4, 7
χοροὶ γυναικήϊοι 49, 19
χράω 1, 6
χρηΐζειν τινος 10, 26
χρησάμενος 24, 12; χρεόμενοι τῷ νόμῳ 25, 3; οὐδὲν χρεώμενος 43, 8; ἀγνωμοσύνῃ χρησάμενος 49, 11; χρησόμενοι (*oracle*) 36, 22
χρηστήριον 47, 15
χρηστός 70, 28
χυτρίς 52, 18
χωρέειν 28, 15; 53, 7
χῶρος 44, 12

ψῆγμα χρυσοῦ 65, 23

ὠνεῖσθαι γυναῖκας 3, 18
ὥρη 70, 17
ὡς *with fut.* 17, 1
ὡς=οὕτω 17, 20; 22, 27
ὡς ἄν *with opt.* 22, 18
ὡς εἶχον 37, 22
ὥστε=ὡς or ἅτε 20, 26; 25, 1; 49, 13; 54, 29
ὥστε *epexegetic* 55, 17; 68, 1

Cambridge:
PRINTED BY C. J. CLAY, M.A. AND SONS,
AT THE UNIVERSITY PRESS.

CAMBRIDGE UNIVERSITY PRESS.

THE PITT PRESS SERIES.

∗ Many of the books in this list can be had in two volumes, Text and Notes separately.

I. GREEK.

Aristophanes. Aves—Plutus—Ranæ. By W. C. GREEN, M.A., late Assistant Master at Rugby School. 3s. 6d. each.

Aristotle. Outlines of the Philosophy of. Compiled by EDWIN WALLACE, M.A., LL.D. Third Edition, Enlarged. 4s. 6d.

Euripides. Heracleidae. With Introduction and Explanatory Notes. By E. A. BECK, M.A., Fellow of Trinity Hall. 3s. 6d.

—— **Hercules Furens.** With Introduction, Notes and Analysis. By A. GRAY, M.A., and J. T. HUTCHINSON, M.A. New Ed. 2s.

—— **Hippolytus.** With Introduction and Notes. By W. S. HADLEY, M.A., Fellow of Pembroke College. 2s.

—— **Iphigeneia in Aulis.** By C. E. S. HEADLAM, B.A. 2s. 6d.

Herodotus, Book V. Edited with Notes and Introduction by E. S. SHUCKBURGH, M.A. 3s.

—— **Book VI.** By the same Editor. 4s.

—— **Book VIII., Chaps. 1—90.** By the same Editor. 3s. 6d.

—— **Book IX., Chaps. 1—89.** By the same Editor. 3s. 6d.

Homer. Odyssey, Books IX., X. With Introduction, Notes and Appendices by G. M. EDWARDS, M.A. 2s. 6d. each.

—— —— **Book XXI.** By the same Editor. 2s.

Luciani Somnium Charon Piscator et De Luctu. By W. E. HEITLAND, M.A., Fellow of St John's College, Cambridge. 3s. 6d.

Platonis Apologia Socratis. With Introduction, Notes and Appendices. By J. ADAM, M.A. 3s. 6d.

—— **Crito.** By the same Editor. 2s. 6d.

—— **Euthyphro.** By the same Editor. [In the Press.

Plutarch. Lives of the Gracchi. With Introduction, Notes and Lexicon by Rev. H. A. HOLDEN, M.A., LL.D. 6s.

—— **Life of Nicias.** By the same Editor. 5s.

—— **Life of Sulla.** By the same Editor. 6s.

—— **Life of Timoleon.** By the same Editor. 6s.

Sophocles. Oedipus Tyrannus. School Edition, with Introduction and Commentary by R. C. JEBB, Litt.D., LL.D. 4s. 6d.

Xenophon. Agesilaus. By H. HAILSTONE, M.A. 2s. 6d.

—— **Anabasis.** With Introduction, Map and English Notes, by A. PRETOR, M.A. Two vols. 7s. 6d.

—— **Books I. III. IV. and V.** By the same. 2s. each.

—— **Books II. VI. and VII.** By the same. 2s. 6d. each.

Xenophon. Cyropaedeia. Books I. II. With Introduction and Notes by Rev. H. A. HOLDEN, M.A., LL.D. 2 vols. 6s.

—— —— **Books III. IV. and V.** By the same Editor. 5s.

London: Cambridge Warehouse, Ave Maria Lane.

II. LATIN.

Beda's Ecclesiastical History, Books III., IV. Edited with a life, Notes, Glossary, Onomasticon and Index, by J. E. B. MAYOR, M.A., and J. R. LUMBY, D.D. Revised Edition. 7s. 6d.

—— **Books I. II.** By the same Editors. *[In the Press.*

Caesar. De Bello Gallico, Comment. I. With Maps and Notes by A. G. PESKETT, M.A., Fellow of Magdalene College, Cambridge. 1s. 6d. COMMENT. II. III. 2s. COMMENT. I. II. III. 3s. COMMENT. IV. V., and COMMENT. VII. 2s. each. COMMENT. VI. and COMMENT. VIII. 1s. 6d. each.

Cicero. De Amicitia.—De Senectute. Edited by J. S. REID, Litt.D., Fellow of Gonville and Caius College. 3s. 6d. each.

—— **In Gaium Verrem Actio Prima.** With Notes, by H. COWIE, M.A. 1s. 6d.

—— **In Q. Caecilium Divinatio et in C. Verrem Actio.** With Notes by W. E. HEITLAND, M.A., and H. COWIE, M.A. 3s.

—— **Philippica Secunda.** By A. G. PESKETT, M.A. 3s. 6d.

—— **Oratio pro Archia Poeta.** By J. S. REID, Litt.D. 2s.

—— **Pro L. Cornelio Balbo Oratio.** By the same. 1s. 6d.

—— **Oratio pro Tito Annio Milone,** with English Notes, &c., by JOHN SMYTH PURTON, B.D. 2s. 6d.

—— **Oratio pro L. Murena,** with English Introduction and Notes. By W. E. HEITLAND, M.A. 3s.

—— **Pro Cn. Plancio Oratio,** by H. A. HOLDEN, LL.D. 4s. 6d.

—— **Pro P. Cornelio Sulla.** By J. S. REID, Litt.D. 3s. 6d.

—— **Somnium Scipionis.** With Introduction and Notes. Edited by W. D. PEARMAN, M.A. 2s.

Horace. Epistles, Book I. With Notes and Introduction by E. S. SHUCKBURGH, M.A., late Fellow of Emmanuel College. 2s. 6d.

Livy. Book IV. With Introduction and Notes. By H. M. STEPHENSON, M.A. 2s. 6d.

—— **Book V.** With Introduction and Notes by L. WHIBLEY, M.A. 2s. 6d.

—— **Books XXI., XXII.** With Notes, Introduction and Maps. By M. S. DIMSDALE, M.A., Fellow of King's College. 2s. 6d. each.

Lucan. Pharsaliae Liber Primus, with English Introduction and Notes by W. E. HEITLAND, M.A., and C. E. HASKINS, M.A. 1s. 6d.

Lucretius, Book V. With Notes and Introduction by J. D. DUFF, M.A., Fellow of Trinity College. 2s.

Ovidii Nasonis Fastorum Liber VI. With Notes by A. SIDGWICK, M.A., Tutor of Corpus Christi College, Oxford. 1s. 6d.

Quintus Curtius. A Portion of the History (Alexander in India). By W. E. HEITLAND, M.A., and T. E. RAVEN, B.A. With Two Maps. 3s. 6d.

Vergili Maronis Aeneidos Libri I.—XII. Edited with Notes by A. SIDGWICK, M.A. 1s. 6d. each.

—— **Bucolica.** By the same Editor. 1s. 6d.

—— **Georgicon Libri I. II.** By the same Editor. 2s.

—— —— **Libri III. IV.** By the same Editor. 2s.

—— **The Complete Works.** By the same Editor. Two vols. Vol. I. containing the Text. Vol. II. The Notes. *[Preparing.*

London: Cambridge Warehouse, Ave Maria Lane.

III. FRENCH.

Corneille. La Suite du Menteur. A Comedy in Five Acts. With Notes Philological and Historical, by the late G. MASSON, B.A. 2s.

De Bonnechose. Lazare Hoche. With four Maps, Introduction and Commentary, by C. COLBECK, M.A. Revised Edition. 2s.

D'Harleville. Le Vieux Célibataire. A Comedy, Grammatical and Historical Notes, by G. MASSON, B.A. 2s.

De Lamartine. Jeanne D'Arc. Edited with a Map and Notes Historical and Philological, and a Vocabulary, by Rev. A. C. CLAPIN, M.A., St John's College, Cambridge. 2s.

De Vigny. La Canne de Jonc. Edited with Notes by Rev. H. A. BULL, M.A., late Master at Wellington College. 2s.

Erckmann-Chatrian. La Guerre. With Map, Introduction and Commentary by Rev. A. C. CLAPIN, M.A. 3s.

La Baronne de Staël-Holstein. Le Directoire. (Considérations sur la Révolution Française. Troisième et quatrième parties.) Revised and enlarged. With Notes by G. MASSON, B.A., and G. W. PROTHERO, M.A. 2s.

—— —— **Dix Années d'Exil. Livre II. Chapitres 1—8.** By the same Editors. New Edition, enlarged. 2s.

Lemercier. Fredegonde et Brunehaut. A Tragedy in Five Acts. By GUSTAVE MASSON, B.A. 2s.

Molière. Le Bourgeois Gentilhomme, Comédie-Ballet en Cinq Actes. (1670.) By Rev. A. C. CLAPIN, M.A. Revised Edition. 1s. 6d.

—— **L'École des Femmes.** With Introduction and Notes by G. SAINTSBURY, M.A. 2s. 6d.

—— **Les Précieuses Ridicules.** With Introduction and Notes by E. G. W. BRAUNHOLTZ, M.A., Ph.D. 2s.

Piron. La Métromanie. A Comedy, with Notes, by G. MASSON, B.A. 2s.

Racine. Les Plaideurs. With Introduction and Notes, by E. G. W. BRAUNHOLTZ, M.A., Ph.D. 2s.

Sainte-Beuve. M. Daru (Causeries du Lundi, Vol. IX.). By G. MASSON, B.A. 2s.

Saintine. Picciola. With Introduction, Notes and Map. By Rev. A. C. CLAPIN, M.A. 2s.

Scribe and Legouvé. Bataille de Dames. Edited by Rev. H. A. BULL, M.A. 2s.

Scribe. Le Verre d'Eau. A Comedy; with Memoir, Grammatical and Historical Notes. Edited by C. COLBECK, M.A. 2s.

Sédaine. Le Philosophe sans le savoir. Edited with Notes by Rev. H. A. BULL, M.A., late Master at Wellington College. 2s.

Thierry. Lettres sur l'histoire de France (XIII.—XXIV.). By G. MASSON, B.A., and G. W. PROTHERO, M.A. 2s. 6d.

—— **Récits des Temps Mérovingiens I.—III.** Edited by GUSTAVE MASSON, B.A. Univ. Gallic., and A. R. ROPES, M.A. With Map. 3s.

Villemain. Lascaris ou Les Grecs du XVe Siècle, Nouvelle Historique. By G. MASSON, B.A. 2s.

London: Cambridge Warehouse, Ave Maria Lane.

Voltaire. Histoire du Siècle de Louis XIV. Chaps. I.—XIII. Edited by G. MASSON, B.A., and G. W. PROTHERO, M.A. 2s. 6d. PART II. CHAPS. XIV.—XXIV. By the same Editors. With Three Maps. 2s. 6d. PART III. CHAPS. XXV. to end. By the same Editors. 2s. 6d.

Xavier de Maistre. La Jeune Sibérienne. Le Lépreux de la Cité D'Aoste. By G. MASSON, B.A. 1s. 6d.

IV. GERMAN.

Ballads on German History. Arranged and annotated by WILHELM WAGNER, Ph.D. 2s.

Benedix. Doctor Wespe. Lustspiel in fünf Aufzügen. Edited with Notes by KARL HERMANN BREUL, M.A. 3s.

Freytag. Der Staat Friedrichs des Grossen. With Notes. By WILHELM WAGNER, Ph.D. 2s.

German Dactylic Poetry. Arranged and annotated by WILHELM WAGNER, Ph.D. 3s.

Goethe's Knabenjahre. (1749—1759.) Arranged and annotated by WILHELM WAGNER, Ph.D. 2s.

——— **Hermann und Dorothea.** By WILHELM WAGNER, Ph.D. Revised edition by J. W. CARTMELL, M.A. 3s. 6d.

Gutzkow. Zopf und Schwert. Lustspiel in fünf Aufzügen. By H J. WOLSTENHOLME, B.A. (Lond.). 3s. 6d.

Hauff. Das Bild des Kaisers. By KARL HERMANN BREUL, M.A., Ph.D., University Lecturer in German. 3s.

——— **Das Wirthshaus im Spessart.** By A. SCHLOTTMANN, Ph.D. 3s. 6d.

——— **Die Karavane.** Edited with Notes by A. SCHLOTTMANN, Ph.D. 3s. 6d.

Immermann. Der Oberhof. A Tale of Westphalian Life, by WILHELM WAGNER, Ph.D. 3s.

Kohlrausch. Das Jahr 1813. With English Notes by WILHELM WAGNER, Ph.D. 2s.

Lessing and Gellert. Selected Fables. Edited with Notes by KARL HERMANN BREUL, M.A. 3s.

Mendelssohn's Letters. Selections from. Edited by JAMES SIME, M.A. 3s.

Raumer. Der erste Kreuzzug (1095—1099). By WILHELM WAGNER, Ph.D. 2s.

Riehl. Culturgeschichtliche Novellen. Edited by H. J. WOLSTENHOLME, B.A. (Lond.). 3s. 6d.

Schiller. Wilhelm Tell. Edited with Introduction and Notes by KARL HERMANN BREUL, M.A. 2s. 6d.

Uhland. Ernst, Herzog von Schwaben. With Introduction and Notes. By H. J. WOLSTENHOLME, B.A. 3s. 6d.

London: Cambridge Warehouse, Ave Maria Lane.

V. ENGLISH.

Ancient Philosophy from Thales to Cicero, A Sketch of. By JOSEPH B. MAYOR, M.A. 3s. 6d.

Bacon's History of the Reign of King Henry VII. With Notes by the Rev. Professor LUMBY, D.D. 3s.

Cowley's Essays. With Introduction and Notes, by the Rev. Professor LUMBY, D.D. 4s.

More's History of King Richard III. Edited with Notes, Glossary, Index of Names. By J. RAWSON LUMBY, D.D. 3s. 6d.

More's Utopia. With Notes, by Rev. Prof. LUMBY, D.D. 3s. 6d.

The Two Noble Kinsmen, edited with Introduction and Notes, by the Rev. Professor SKEAT, Litt.D. 3s. 6d.

VI. EDUCATIONAL SCIENCE.

Comenius, John Amos, Bishop of the Moravians. His Life and Educational Works, by S. S. LAURIE, A.M., F.R.S.E. 3s. 6d.

Education, Three Lectures on the Practice of. I. On Marking, by H. W. EVE, M.A. II. On Stimulus, by A. SIDGWICK, M.A. III. On the Teaching of Latin Verse Composition, by E. A. ABBOTT, D.D. 2s.

Stimulus. A Lecture delivered for the Teachers' Training Syndicate, May, 1882, by A. SIDGWICK, M.A. 1s.

Locke on Education. With Introduction and Notes by the Rev. R. H. QUICK, M.A. 3s. 6d.

Milton's Tractate on Education. A facsimile reprint from the Edition of 1673. Edited with Notes, by O. BROWNING, M.A. 2s.

Modern Languages, Lectures on the Teaching of. By C. COLBECK, M.A. 2s.

Teacher, General Aims of the, and Form Management. Two Lectures delivered in the University of Cambridge in the Lent Term, 1883, by F. W. FARRAR, D.D., and R. B. POOLE, B.D. 1s. 6d.

Teaching, Theory and Practice of. By the Rev. E. THRING, M.A., late Head Master of Uppingham School. New Edition. 4s. 6d.

British India, a Short History of. By E. S. CARLOS, M.A., late Head Master of Exeter Grammar School. 1s.

Geography, Elementary Commercial. A Sketch of the Commodities and the Countries of the World. By H. R. MILL, D.Sc., F.R.S.E. 1s.

Geography, an Atlas of Commercial. (A Companion to the above.) By J. G. BARTHOLOMEW, F.R.G.S. With an Introduction by HUGH ROBERT MILL, D.Sc. 3s.

VII. MATHEMATICS.

Euclid's Elements of Geometry. Books I and II. By H. M. TAYLOR, M.A., Fellow and late Tutor of Trinity College, Cambridge. 1s. 6d.

Other Volumes are in preparation.

London: Cambridge Warehouse, Ave Maria Lane.

The Cambridge Bible for Schools and Colleges.

GENERAL EDITOR: J. J. S. PEROWNE, D.D.,
DEAN OF PETERBOROUGH.

"*It is difficult to commend too highly this excellent series.*—Guardian.

"*The modesty of the general title of this series has, we believe, led many to misunderstand its character and underrate its value. The books are well suited for study in the upper forms of our best schools, but not the less are they adapted to the wants of all Bible students who are not specialists. We doubt, indeed, whether any of the numerous popular commentaries recently issued in this country will be found more serviceable for general use.*"—Academy.

Now Ready. Cloth, Extra Fcap. 8vo. With Maps.

Book of Joshua. By Rev. G. F. MACLEAR, D.D. 2s. 6d.
Book of Judges. By Rev. J. J. LIAS, M.A.. 3s. 6d.
First Book of Samuel. By Rev. Prof. KIRKPATRICK, B.D. 3s. 6d.
Second Book of Samuel. By Rev. Prof. KIRKPATRICK, B.D. 3s. 6d.
First Book of Kings. By Rev. Prof. LUMBY, D.D. 3s. 6d.
Second Book of Kings. By Rev. Prof. LUMBY, D.D. 3s. 6d.
Book of Job. By Rev. A. B. DAVIDSON, D.D. 5s.
Book of Ecclesiastes. By Very Rev. E. H. PLUMPTRE, D.D. 5s.
Book of Jeremiah. By Rev. A. W. STREANE, M.A. 4s. 6d.
Book of Hosea. By Rev. T. K. CHEYNE, M.A., D.D. 3s.
Books of Obadiah & Jonah. By Archdeacon PEROWNE. 2s. 6d.
Book of Micah. By Rev. T. K. CHEYNE, M.A., D.D. 1s. 6d.
Books of Haggai & Zechariah. By Archdeacon PEROWNE. 3s.
Gospel according to St Matthew. By Rev. A. CARR, M.A. 2s. 6d.
Gospel according to St Mark. By Rev. G. F. MACLEAR, D.D. 2s. 6d.
Gospel according to St Luke. By Arch. FARRAR, D.D. 4s. 6d.
Gospel according to St John. By Rev. A. PLUMMER, D.D. 4s. 6d.
Acts of the Apostles. By Rev. Prof. LUMBY, D.D. 4s. 6d.
Epistle to the Romans. By Rev. H. C. G. MOULE, M.A. 3s. 6d.
First Corinthians. By Rev. J. J. LIAS, M.A. With Map. 2s.
Second Corinthians. By Rev. J. J. LIAS, M.A. With Map. 2s.

London: Cambridge Warehouse, Ave Maria Lane.

Epistle to the Ephesians. By Rev. H. C. G. MOULE, M.A. 2s. 6d.
Epistle to the Philippians. By Rev. H. C. G. MOULE, M.A. 2s. 6d.
Epistle to the Hebrews. By Arch. FARRAR, D.D. 3s. 6d.
General Epistle of St James. By Very Rev. E. H. PLUMPTRE, D.D. 1s. 6d.
Epistles of St Peter and St Jude. By Very Rev. E. H. PLUMPTRE, D.D. 2s. 6d.
Epistles of St John. By Rev. A. PLUMMER, M.A., D.D. 3s. 6d.

Preparing.

Book of Genesis. By Very Rev. the Dean of Peterborough.
Books of Exodus, Numbers and Deuteronomy. By Rev. C. D. GINSBURG, LL.D.
Books of Ezra and Nehemiah. By Rev. Prof. RYLE, M.A.
Book of Psalms. By Rev. Prof. KIRKPATRICK, B.D.
Book of Isaiah. By Prof. W. ROBERTSON SMITH, M.A.
Book of Ezekiel. By Rev. A. B. DAVIDSON, D.D.
Book of Malachi. By Archdeacon PEROWNE.
Epistle to the Galatians. By Rev. E. H. PEROWNE, D.D.
Epistles to the Colossians and Philemon. By Rev. H. C. G. MOULE, M.A.
Epistles to Timothy & Titus. By Rev. A. E. HUMPHREYS, M.A.
Book of Revelation. By Rev. W. H. SIMCOX, M.A.

The Smaller Cambridge Bible for Schools.

The Smaller Cambridge Bible for Schools *will form an entirely new series of commentaries on some selected books of the Bible. It is expected that they will be prepared for the most part by the Editors of the larger series (The Cambridge Bible for Schools and Colleges). The volumes will be issued at a low price, and will be suitable to the requirements of preparatory and elementary schools.*

Now ready.

First and Second Books of Samuel. By Rev. Prof. KIRKPATRICK, B.D. 1s. each.
Gospel according to St Matthew. By Rev. A. CARR, M.A. 1s.
Gospel according to St Mark. By Rev. G. F. MACLEAR, D.D. 1s.

Nearly ready.

Gospel according to St Luke. By Archdeacon FARRAR.

London: Cambridge Warehouse, Ave Maria Lane.

The Cambridge Greek Testament for Schools and Colleges,

with a Revised Text, based on the most recent critical authorities, and English Notes, prepared under the direction of the General Editor,

The Very Reverend J. J. S. PEROWNE, D.D.,
DEAN OF PETERBOROUGH.

Gospel according to St Matthew. By Rev. A. CARR, M.A. With 4 Maps. 4s. 6d.

Gospel according to St Mark. By Rev. G. F. MACLEAR, D.D. With 3 Maps. 4s. 6d.

Gospel according to St Luke. By Archdeacon FARRAR. With 4 Maps. 6s.

Gospel according to St John. By Rev. A. PLUMMER, D.D. With 4 Maps. 6s.

Acts of the Apostles. By Rev. Professor LUMBY, D.D. With 4 Maps. 6s.

First Epistle to the Corinthians. By Rev. J. J. LIAS, M.A. 3s.

Second Epistle to the Corinthians. By Rev. J. J. LIAS, M.A. [*In the Press.*

Epistle to the Hebrews. By Archdeacon FARRAR, D.D. 3s. 6d.

Epistle of St James. By Very Rev. E. H. PLUMPTRE, D.D. [*Preparing.*

Epistles of St John. By Rev. A. PLUMMER, M.A., D.D. 4s.

London: C. J. CLAY AND SONS,
CAMBRIDGE WAREHOUSE, AVE MARIA LANE.
Glasgow: 263, ARGYLE STREET.
Cambridge: DEIGHTON, BELL AND CO.
Leipzig: F. A. BROCKHAUS.

www.ingramcontent.com/pod-product-compliance
Lightning Source LLC
Chambersburg PA
CBHW032046230426
43672CB00009B/1487